The RED Wall

A Woman in the RCMP

By Jane Hall

Published by

499 O'Brien Rd., Box 415
Renfrew, Ontario, Canada K7V 4A6
Telephone (613) 432-7697 or 1-800-465-6072
www.gsph.com

ISBN 978-1-897113-68-4
Printed and Bound in Canada

Cover art by Morgan Hall
Formatting by Robyn Hader
Printing by Custom Printers of Renfrew Ltd.

Library and Archives Canada Cataloguing in Publication

Hall, Jane, 1954-
The red wall : a woman in the RCMP / Jane Hall.

ISBN 978-1-897113-68-4

1. Hall, Jane, 1954-. 2. Royal Canadian Mounted Police--Biography.
3. Policewomen--Canada--Biography. I. Title.

HV7911.H34A3 2007 363.2082'092 C2007-902451-3

Second Printing 2008

Dedication

I wrote this book with the next generation in mind, but I dedicate it to the past, and to the memory of my parents, D.J. and Carmel Greenwood, whose parenting instilled in me the values of family, community, and the belief that if we all work together we can "maintain the right."[1]

D.J. and Carmel would be the first to acknowledge they were just one layer in the family wall whose foundation was laid by pioneers beginning with my French Canadian ancestors in the early 1600s: the Boisverts (the name changed to Greenwood in the mid-1800s), the Aubuchons, the Pepins, the Renauds (the parents of Quebec),[2] and the Yotts. They were joined by the Irish in the early 1800s: the Koens (though probably German Jews who married Irish brides and immigrated to Canada as Catholics), the Hursts, the Donaghues, the Cashmans, the Morans, and the McGlynns.

I would also like to dedicate this book to the members of my extended family, the RCMP: to those who have already passed into history; and to those who continue the traditions of honour and service and symbolize the ideals of Canada.

1 RCMP motto; *"Maintiens le Droit"* in French.

2 One of the original 400 elite soldiers sent by the King of France to protect his interests in New France and enticed to stay by grants of land.

Table of Contents

Acknowledgements

I would like to acknowledge my husband of twenty-five years, Len Hall, who never questioned why I needed to write this book even when I laboured for years at what must have looked like an obsession. During all that time, his only suggestion was that if I was going to tell the story, I "tell the *whole* story." I may not have told the whole story, but I have certainly told more of it than I would have without his support. I would also like to thank Robert Knuckle and Gillian Shaw for their valuable feedback on what I was doing right and where I needed to improve in my writing technique; and for reassuring me that the story was worth telling.

I would also like to thank Candy Smith for allowing me to glimpse behind her red wall to one of the most painful and tragic experiences a member can have: a fatal shooting. She will always be my friend and a personal hero to me. I would also like to thank another personal hero, Nancy Fehr, who was at India's consul general's house prior to and during the riot, and for providing me with an eyewitness account from its beginning until its end. I would also like to thank Ron MacKay, a friend and mentor, for his first-hand account of a murder confession and for his encouragement and suggestions regarding two important footnotes.

I am deeply grateful to Paul Palango for allowing me to cite and quote some of his revelations in his book The Last Guardians. I was so impressed with his intelligent, analytical, and brave insight into social, economic, and political influences on the RCMP he recorded as a civilian looking into the Force from the outside, that I was motivated to try and depict the view from the inside looking out.

I would like to thank Tim Gordon and his talented staff at General Store Publishing House for the support, faith, and patience extended to me. I hope this book lives up to all of our expectations.

Finally, I would like to thank my editor, Jane Karchmar, whose encouragement and patience helped guide me through the process of further refining the book; for her professionalism, support, and guidance. She didn't have a lot to say, but when I needed her opinion most, she wasn't afraid to tell me. She is true and honest, and those are the two qualities I admire most in heroes.

I also owe a debt of gratitude to my many friends both inside and outside the Force who encouraged me to publish the book without ever having read it. I hope I have lived up to their expectations and have succeeded in conveying what it was like to live through a social revolution.

Preface

I have always been fascinated by the rich stories of Canadians that exist in verbal history; the stories told by my parents' generation of past generations of heroes and villains; stories I felt needed to be recorded in writing but weren't. So much was lost. The dry facts of our past are recorded in history books, but the true flavour of the events and the background stresses and intrigues seemed missing. I pleaded with the storytellers I knew from that generation to write, but they did not. It would be hypocritical of me now if I did not at least try to do what I asked of them.

I regret I had to write this book in the first person. The story is not about me, and if it reads that way, then I have failed in my intent. It is an eyewitness account written by an average person living in an extraordinary time of social change. I hope this book is of value to the next generation as a record of the strides, steps, and stumbles made by someone from my generation.

I do not believe I am unique in finding that at this time in my life I have more questions than answers. Despite all of the advances in technology, science, and communications of the past thirty years, life may not have improved; we might just be too busy or too tired to notice it hasn't. It might be time for a renascence of the debates from the sixties on social responsibility, women's roles, and justice.

My purpose in writing the book was to represent my recollection of the events and societal trends I have noticed. Most of the names in the book are real, but not all. Some of the people I have written about are still in sensitive areas within the Force, and for that reason I have changed their names. I have done my best to protect the identities of the handful of members who caused me distress by changing their names and being intentionally vague. I have even changed the names of other members who worked close to them to further obscure their identity. I included the incidents because I believe other people have found themselves in similar situations and they might find some tools I learned from these encounters helpful. I have no wish to cause anyone, friend or foe, any distress. This book is about bigger issues than the individual failings we are all guilty of at different times in our lives. I am no saint and I do not intend to cast stones.

Introduction

Timing is important, but when it combines with the correct demographics, it can create some great possibilities. At no other point in history had information been so instantaneously available, the middle class so affluent, and advanced education so accessible to Canadians. Never before had such a disproportionately large number of youth been in a position to challenge and tear down the social and religious traditions of the past.

All things seemed possible for my generation. There was no mistaking the energy for change that was building. The base of power was shifting from money to information. Status quo was questioned and often rejected. Much has been written about the opportunities demographics created for the male baby boomers, but largely undocumented are the effects on women, which were slightly delayed but disproportionately greater.

Technology was the catalyst for an awakening global consciousness. Television facilitated an immediate and less-edited source of information. The traditional filtering of information through church and state was undermined by this new technology. A new global awareness expanded our view of the world and illuminated problems in a new light.

Television allowed the world collectively to hold its breath during the Cuban missile crisis. We grew up listening to tone alerts on CBS, ever aware that the "Cold War" could become WW III at any time. Some Americans dug bomb shelters in their backyards, while TV showed their children hiding under school desks as protection against a nuclear attack by Russia. It was almost amusing how naïve we still were.

Even so, we still felt safe until the assassination of John F. Kennedy. The boldness of the crime caused a paradigm shift, forever altering our perception of the world, stealing the innocence of a generation. The magnitude of the shock remained unequalled until Sept. 11, 2001.

Television also gave us cause to dream and celebrate. We watched Neil Armstrong take his first step on the moon on our black-and-white TV. Parents couldn't appreciate that we found watching the Beatles for the first time performing in North America on the Ed Sullivan show equally as exciting!

Civil disobedience was the order of the day for the youth of the sixties. We baby boomers protested in our music, dress, hairstyles, free love, and drugs, with the intention of upsetting the status quo; everything "establishment" was questioned and rejected.

While the Americans rioted in the streets against racial prejudice, the "quiet revolution" of the French Canadians had begun. One common point of social change that appeared to be a North American concern was the issue of women's rights.

Scientific advances in birth control provided the catalyst for the resurrection of the suffragette movement fifty years earlier, raising issues that were much more socially complex than most people realized.

Changing the status quo of women would also change the role of men, sending society into new, exciting, but also dangerous waters. The world was changing everywhere except on Wolfe Island, near Kingston, Ontario, Canada, and I couldn't wait to jump into a rising tide of change and be carried out with it, away from the safety and monotony of my childhood.

Canada, a young country, could be viewed as the personification of the "baby boom" generation. The 1960s were Canada's teenage years; Expo '67 announced to the world that Canada was coming of age, a world leader in science and communications, two of the driving forces for the new generation. It seemed that the entire country was in love with itself and ready to change the world for the better. It still seems like yesterday . . . we were so innocent, so energetic, so secure. We had such great expectations!

Much has changed during the social revolution of the past thirty years. Maturity on a national and individual level has come with great gifts and at great cost. Through this book, I hope to recreate snapshots of what I observed during this time. It is healthy individually and nationally to step back from day-to-day existence to try to see the evolution of our identity. If we can see clearly where we have come from, it may help guide the path to the future.

I believe Paul Palango was correct when he used the evolution of the RCMP as a barometer for the health of Canadian society in his book *The Last Guardians*,[3] and if I am right, the RCMP may also be a vehicle to better understand feelings of Western alienation as well as to chart the progress of the past thirty years of the women's movement.

If this book appeals to the average person and gives cause for nostalgic contemplation and fuel for debate, I will have succeeded in my purpose. The

[3] Paul Palango, *The Last Guardians: The Crisis in the RCMP and Canada* (Toronto: McClelland & Stewart Inc, 1998).

filter through which I processed events will have a bias, but I hope that my awareness of this, and my training as an investigator, will compensate and provide a balanced perspective that a wider audience can appreciate.

Chapter 1

Once Upon an Island

There is something very unambiguous about being from an island. Nature defines the boundaries of an island. You are either an Islander or not. I grew up with that simple clarity of identity. Though many people, like my mother, moved to the Island by choice, they were never really considered "Islanders." People would refer to them as "so-and-so from Sydenham," or Kingston, etc. To be an Islander you had to be born on the Island. It was my mother who told me this.

Wolfe Island, the largest of the Thousand Islands, enjoys a strategic location at the convergence of the four major waterways of the new world: the St. Lawrence, Rideau, and Cataraqui rivers, and the Great Lakes. All the major settlements of Upper and Lower Canada and most of the U.S. were easily accessible from this transportation hub of the New World.

Despite the Island's privileged location, Islanders rarely wander far from its familiar shores because they, more than anyone else, understand that just because you can doesn't mean you should. It has always been a dangerous business to leave the Island. The surrounding waters provide relief from the summer's stifling heat--fishing, swimming, and transportation to and from the island--but the cost for all the water provides is often tragic. Far too many islanders, mostly young, reckless ones, have died beneath the waves of misadventure. A terrible, non-refundable, toll for island life has been exacted from nearly all island families in one generation or another.

We islanders had a unique relationship with the endless, restless, unchanging waters that shaped and defined our existence. We knew where the best fishing holes and sandiest beach bottoms were, or when a summer gale was about strike; but only some islanders possessed the depth of knowledge to chart a course over the lake when it looked its safest but was at its deadliest. Islanders who could master the ice were rare, and my father was one of the best. He was never fooled by the surface of the water, frozen many feet thick, which looked stable but concealed swift, powerful currents running over shallow shoals

—Herrington

CROSS LAKE IN OPEN CAR—D. J. Greenwood and William Jeronimus of Wolfe Island came to Kingston today in a most unusual manner -- by driving here from Wolfe Island across Lake Ontario in an open 1928 Ford. For the first time this winter the Wolfe Islander did not make a crossing. While practically every other car in the city would not start, because of the cold, Mr. Greenwood's car started with one turn of the crank.

Blazing a trail on the ice.

that, in combination with the winds above, were constantly shifting the ice and undercutting it. The trails he marked from Wolfe Island to Kingston were trusted by the islanders.

After the First Nations people left for reservations, the Island was settled by a staggered series of immigrations. First, the French Canadians; then the Irish displaced by the potato famine; then United Empire Loyalists fleeing the U.S.; and finally, the Dutch Protestants displaced after World War II. All were looking for peace, freedom, and a place to plant deep roots for their generation and the next.

Time is much slower on an island where religion and traditions pass from one generation to the next. The surrounding waters insulated the islanders from the pace of progress on the mainland. Modern advancements are slow to come to island life. Although by the fifties most Island houses had electricity, the majority, including ours, did not have hot and cold running water. The Island still does not have a police detachment or a traffic light.

My father's side of the family immigrated to the Island from Quebec in the early 1800s. The next generation chose Irish brides during the second immigration.

Ferry in "Deepfreeze":

First Car Crossing on Ice Is Made from Wolfe Island

A-choppin' and a-driven' across frozen Lake Ontario in 30 below temperatures, D. J. Greenwood and William Jeronimus of Wolfe Island made the first car crossing to the mainland of the season this morning.

(For Picture See Page 17)

The trip across took three-quarters of an hour. "We came half way across last night," said Mr. Greenwood, "chopping through the ice every so often to see how thick it was."

* * *

The pair finished the testing this morning, cutting through the ice, sometimes, every few yards, to see if it would be safe.

"We weren't taking any chances," said Mr. Jeronimus.

Today was the first morning of the winter the Wolfe Islander didn't make a crossing. In the 1955-56 season it stopped on Dec. 23.

They came across in a 1928 model car. While practically every other car in the city wouldn't start because of the cold, Mr. Greenwood's car started with one turn of the cranking handle.

"It brought us across every day for twelve and a half weeks last year," he said.

"It shows that the ferry can keep going until it is safe enough to cross on the ice," said Mr. Jeronimus. "The reeve and the council have done a wonderful job in keeping the ferry going this year. We have had wonderful service."

Mr. Greenwood is going to claim another first at the weekend. His wife presented him with a seven-pound-two-ounce baby girl on Saturday; "Her first trip to the island will have to be across the ice," he said.

Mr. Jeronimus, who came from Holland, skated across for a week last year to get to his work on the mainland. "It will be impossible this year, the ice is so rough," he said.

Everyone on the Island was Caucasian and either Catholic or Protestant. The dominant religion was Catholic.

While other countries separated their population by race, Canada separated along religious lines between Protestant and Catholic. Catholics went to Catholic schools and socialized with other Catholics. You don't have to scratch religious surfaces too deeply to expose that old French/English division that Canada still occasionally struggles with.

My Irish grandmother on my father's side could think of no greater scandal than for a Catholic to marry a Protestant. That was the Island's version of a mixed marriage. I was certain that this would never become an issue for me; I had decided very early that I wanted no part of the subordinate status of "wife." I wanted power, adventure, and respect--and I wanted it for me. I certainly would not be happy to experience it vicariously through a successful husband. Thank God for youthful arrogance and ambition!

The workforce was divided along gender lines. "Women's jobs," such as secretaries and waitresses, were low-paying and dead-ended. "Men's jobs," even the ones that required minimum education and responsibility, such as truck driving, garbage collecting, etc., paid more than "women's jobs." Dual-gender roles like education and finance employed invisible barriers that maintained the social status quo. Teachers were females but principals and school administrators were men. Tellers were female and bank presidents were male.

Economic discrimination was accepted, even "justified," because working women were mostly single, just marking time before getting married and raising a family. The men, the breadwinners, required higher wages to support a family. Why then, I wondered, were single men not paid less than married men as well?

Those were unwelcome questions--the kinds of questions not asked in small rural communities. I was careful not to voice them too loudly for fear of being labelled a "Women's Libber."

Being a wife and mother was what society expected females to grow up and do. Motherhood was considered a full-time job. It was the order of things. It was going to take a lot of effort to change that. The first women in any non-traditional role would need to not simply meet, but exceed, male qualifications. Even then, there would be no guarantee of success. This threshold test was accurately articulated by John Glenn to a congressional subcommittee in July 1962. He was speaking in support of the newly drafted policy for recruiting and training only men as astronauts.

> "I think this gets back to the way our social order is organized, really. It is just a fact. The men go off and fight the wars and fly the airplanes and come back and help design and build and test them. The fact that women are not in this field is a fact of our social order," he said. "If we could find any women that demonstrate they have better qualifications [than men], we would welcome them with open arms."

I like to think that John Glenn and the subcommittee were unaware of Dr. Randolph Lovelace's physical and psychological tests on female pilots such as Geraldyn Cobb. His tests proved that women not only met the criteria, they surpassed NASA's endurance and psychological testing standards for astronauts.

A dozen of these women were halfway through the training regimen when NASA changed the rules. Astronauts were required to be recruited from the ranks of pilots--effectively excluding women.[4] This decision drew no publicity, public outcry, or legal redress. It was just the way things were.

The social order was very comfortable and it was not going to be easy to change. Thank God for pioneers and heroes. The choices I had were part of the legacy of opportunities created by people like Geraldyn Cobb and Dr. Randolph Lovelace.

The Island community was not large enough to support a high school. Students from the Island were bused to the ferry and across to Kingston. I entered Grade 9 at Regiopolis Notre Dame High School the first year females

[4] *National Post* (Nov. 7, 1998), page A13.

were allowed to attend the century-old school for boys run by Jesuits. The female students and the teacher-nuns who accompanied them felt the privilege and the responsibility of being members of the first group of interlopers. Nine years later, I recalled the same feelings as I began basic training at Depot.

There were a lot of conflicting opinions on the social changes occurring during the late sixties. Some saw them as progress, some as anarchy (or worse, as communism); others mourned the destruction of traditions. Male and female groups were divided over the positive or negative implications of these changes and the impact they would have on both their groups and society as a whole.

Children were never part of the debate.

Personally, I never gave the bigger picture a thought in those days. All I knew was, the doors of opportunity were beginning to crack open, and the few of us who stepped through did so quietly; even so, we felt the pressure to outperform expectations. The initial scrutiny was intense. No one wanted to do anything that could be used as an example of why these changes were not for the best.

I was a quiet, obedient teenager whose only act of social defiance was committed at my Catholic church. The dress code in those days was very rigid. Women wore dresses and covered their heads with hats or scarves; men wore suits, and hats that they removed when they entered the church. My younger sister Judy, ever the rebel, brought to my attention the reasoning behind this custom. "A man," she said, "takes off his hat in church because at the head of the man is God. Conversely, women wear hats in church because at the head of the woman is the man."

I still feel a bit of a flush remembering the following Sunday, walking down the aisle to my family pew and hearing the roar of disapproving whispers as I passed bare-headed--not exactly like burning your bra in a public demonstration but defiance enough in a small, close-knit island community. It may seem trivial by today's societal standards, but it was the first brave thing I recall doing; for me it was huge.

Grade 11 was the year I changed high schools to Protestant Kingston Collegiate and Vocational Institute, which bordered on Queen's University. The country kids from the Island seemed a little out of step with the student body of doctors' and lawyers' children. I really didn't care; high school was something you just had to get through.

I was torn between two future occupations: journalism and police work. Unfortunately, French was a prerequisite for Carleton's journalism program, and my second language was Latin. The closest I got to journalism was two summers as creator and co-editor of the Wolfe Island summer paper. My career choice was made for me. Things seem to have a way of working out.

Looking back now, I am a little embarrassed at the naïve arrogance and optimism I displayed in deciding I could be a peace officer. I had never even met a peace officer. I knew even less about the RCMP, which then had no uniformed presence in Ontario, outside of Ottawa. My guidance counsellor was shocked. I was the first female who had ever expressed such a career choice to him. He didn't try to hide his disapproval. Under duress, he supplied the research I needed.

I hate to date myself, but the RCMP was not accepting females at that time. The Ontario Provincial Police had begun to accept applications from females; however, I was not tall enough to meet their minimum height standard. At a whole five feet five inches (almost) and 115 pounds, I was a little short and light. The city of Kingston did have one female officer, but the prospect of policing so small a geographic area really did not appeal to me.

"You've been accepted to Queen's University. Why not go and think this through?" advised Mr. Stevens.

"I am only going to mark time. After I graduate, I will be a Mountie."

He nodded patronizingly. (Mr. Stevens, I hope you're reading this book.)

I do not regret my time at Queen's. I had a lot of maturing to do, and it began there. I studied art in Italy one summer with Queen's. By now, bare heads and pants were accepted female attire in North American churches, but you wouldn't get past the front door dressed like that in Europe.

It was an eventful summer. A U.S. president resigned; the students were invited to a formal dinner with the officers of an English warship on a military mission to Cypress. The world was an exciting and dangerous place outside of Wolfe Island. I couldn't wait to be a part of it.

University, my first step off the Island, was fun and full of interesting people, such as a girl from one of my Grade 13 classes, Christy Mayer. Christy, the daughter of a Kingston physician, was a beautiful person from the inside out. She had been part of the "in" crowd at high school--the ones with money and social influence. I was surprised she even knew who I was; but, as I discovered, there was a lot more to her than met the eye.

Christy's faculty choice, engineering, was both academically impressive and socially radical. At that time, it was accepted practice for universities to restrict female enrollment in fields like medicine and engineering. Female applicants required much higher academic grade point averages to compete for a very limited number of "female spaces" in those faculties. Just the sort of thing John Glenn had spoken about.

Christy was as happy to see me at Queen's as she was disappointed that her female friends from our graduation class were not there as well.

"What is wrong with them?" she asked me; as if I could shed any light. "They are all getting married and having kids. We are the first generation of women who can do or be anything. Why are they settling down so easily and quickly?"

Christy had a far more developed social conscience than I at the time. A social conscience was a luxury I could not afford. I had enough to think of in budgeting for my tuition and planning my future without worrying about anyone else's. Neither she nor I realized she had planted the seed of feminist social responsibility within me that day.

What a great role model for the modern woman she was: she had brains, beauty, personality, and social standing. I didn't know her well but I believe I understood her. As long as young women like her were around, I wouldn't need to worry about the bigger picture. It was a brief, chance encounter and our last. That summer, while visiting relatives in Europe, Christy was killed in a motor vehicle accident.

It was perplexing. Why did such a tragedy happen? Would she still be alive if she, too, had "settled"? Perhaps, but she would not have been content, and neither would I.

In 1974, the RCMP began to accept women as regular members.

After writing my final exams for my B.A. in the spring of '76, I knocked on the Johnston Street door of the Kingston RCMP detachment to make my application. A pleasant, good-looking, dark-haired, mustachioed, six-foot-two, twenty-something Mountie, one of about 16,000 in the Force at that time, greeted me at the door. He was very happy to answer my questions and provide the application. The Force may have been new to the idea of female peace officers, but their unbiased approach to the issue catapulted the women's movement decades into the future: "In the absence of any empirical evidence to the contrary, the assumption had to be that females would be capable of performing all the diversified duties in the Force equal to the males."

Had NASA made a similar assumption, women would have already walked on the moon.

The Force's decision to assume equality unless proven otherwise was unprecedented at the time. The theory that women could perform "male" roles was put to a true test, providing the experimental data the women's movement required. The RCMP became a world leader in the women's movement.

Other police forces may have accepted female officers before the RCMP, but these forces channelled female officers into non-operational functions such as communications or police/public relations.

The RCMP chose to maintain the same standards, training, postings, and duties for all recruits. The only exception was the height requirement. The minimum height for male applicants was five feet, eight inches. The minimum for a female was five feet, four inches. At that time, those were the average heights of males and females in Canada; it was only fair to alter that one standard.

National standard averages had traditionally been used as a baseline for the Force. Below average in any respect was not what they were looking for. A standard was a standard in those days. Being short, even a fraction of an inch off the minimum requirement, meant rejection. There were stories of recruits that stretched for months to gain 1/8th of an inch to squeak by the original Force doctor's examination, only to be re-measured partway through Depot and dismissed. Eyesight and height eliminated the majority of applicants.

Eyesight was such an integral part of policing that 20/20 vision was required to join. Linda Moulton, my first cousin, had been eliminated a year earlier because of the eye standard. Other recruitment standards included: age nineteen or older, Grade 11 education, Canadian citizenship, and fluency in either English or French. Potential recruits who met these standards were given a general knowledge exam and an in-depth interview. The next hurdle was a security clearance screening involving a financial check and a criminal check of both the applicant and his or her family and friends. Finally, neighbours and employers for the previous ten years were interviewed. The Force was looking for people of exemplary character and leadership abilities.

There were no extra points allotted for *exceeding* the height and eye requirements. To the contrary; if a male was taller than six feet, four inches, he might be denied employment because of the cost factor to make special-issue uniforms for oversized members. There were no similar restrictions for females. Our uniforms had to be tailor-made anyway because the small initial group made mass production economically infeasible.

An applicant could, however, accumulate extra points for advanced education or by scoring well on the general knowledge exam. As I said, standards were standards in those days. No wiggle room for special cases. Black and white but fair to all.

The process took time. The application process itself could take up to a year. Once an applicant was successfully screened, he or she was placed on a "waiting list." The lists were ranked based on the points accumulated during the screening process. Depending on the points and the employment needs of the Force, the process could take from eight months to three years. The Force took only the number of members from the top of the list that it needed.

I applied for the postgraduate Bachelor of Education at Queen's while I marked time waiting for the Force to call me. I was a bit surprised when Mr. Terry and Mr. Smith, my high school art and English teachers, provided such strong letters of recommendation supporting my application to the teaching program, because I certainly didn't see myself as a teacher.

I was equally surprised by how much I enjoyed my two months of practice teaching later that year. How did Mr. Terry and Mr. Smith see in me what I could not? I was only just beginning to realize I didn't know myself very well. I was flattered when one of the schools where I did my practice teaching expressed an interest in hiring me. It seemed that by accident I had found my second career. When I was younger I did not believe in fate--only accidents.

In the fall of 1976, I was invited to write the RCMP's entrance exam.

What would be asked in the general knowledge exam, I wondered? I thought I was preparing the evening before, as I reviewed various dry facts--the highest mountain, the longest river, the capitals of various countries--when in a fit of boredom I took a break, joining my mother watching a hockey game on TV.

At the risk of sounding un-Canadian, I had hated hockey since I was a child. The 1972 Canada-Russia final game was the only game I had ever watched start to finish, and only then as a matter of national pride. On Saturday nights, the TV was always tuned into *Hockey Night in Canada* and the three-way fight between Montreal, Toronto, and my mother's favourite--Boston.

We had a relative, Wayne Cashman, on the Boston team and a more distant relative, Dave Keon, on the Toronto team. I knew so little about the game (both my brothers, Joe and David, played) that I thought "icing" meant the Zamboni had to come out and fix the ice surface. I was in the room for only a few minutes that night, just long enough for Stan Mikita to receive a five-minute misconduct penalty for high sticking.

"Stan Mikita," the TV mediator interjected, "has twice won the Lady Bing trophy for being the most gentlemanly player."

I never gave hockey another thought until the next day, when, I read in disbelief one of the exam questions: "Which trophy is awarded to the most gentlemanly player?"

I wish I had dropped in on a baseball game so I could have answered correctly who broke Babe Ruth's hitting record. The general knowledge exam was quite gender/culture biased, but in those days, no one thought in those terms. It couldn't have been totally unfair, since I passed. That exam has long since been abandoned in favour of an aptitude-based test that has its own shortcomings.

Early in 1977, I was called to an interview with the staffing officer, a large, stern member[5] in a suit. He was extremely thorough as he reviewed the information

[5] "Member" is RCMP jargon, an in-house term used only by Mounties when referring to other Mounties. It is not a generic term for a police officer.

on my application. I had the distinct impression that he was suspicious of my motives for attending the Queen's University Bachelor of Education program. He confronted me in his heavy French accent.

"You have a Bachelor of Arts; that is good. Why are you now training to be a teacher? Do you want to be a teacher?" he asked, focusing intense, unblinking eyes on me; studying my reaction. I had a distinct and correct impression that he was more focused on my body language than on my words.

"I want to be a peace officer," I insisted.

"Then why are you training to be a teacher? It does not make you any more attractive to us," he countered.

"I suspect waiting on tables would not make me any more attractive, but that is what I am unqualified to do with a B.A. I find education an interesting way to spend my time waiting to be accepted by the RCMP."

I wasn't sure if he believed me. I hadn't yet perfected the art of reading people's body language.

"You have been driving for five years; no tickets. That is good," he said, refocused on the application form.

"Actually, I have been driving for closer to ten years," I corrected cautiously.

"You said in your application five years." The tone was accusatory, as if I had been caught in a lie.

"The question was how long had I had my licence. Wolfe Island is a farming community where driving is a function of ability and not age. I have driven tractors, snowmobiles, motorcycles, boats, trucks, and cars, both standard and automatic. But I didn't get my licence until I needed to drive in Kingston to get to Queen's."

He wrote silently for a long time. I wondered what he was writing. I hoped the honesty of the answer would overshadow the lawlessness of driving without a licence. His face remained unreadable--no hints to convey any information on opinions he was forming of me.

"Have you ever been involved in a public demonstration?" he inquired in an ominous tone. It sounded like he already knew the answer. However, by his reaction, he did not.

"Just once," I replied.

The campuses of the sixties and early seventies had been hot spots of civil demonstrations and civil disobedience. His grim face hardened further. He picked up his pen and prepared to write verbatim.

"Last spring, I joined some art majors to protest a bank's decision to tear down an architecturally significant heritage building in Kingston."

The protest, consisting of a few idealistic students handing out information at the bank's door, was a pretty tame event compared to other Canadian campuses, which had seen an influx of Americans avoiding, then protesting, the war in Vietnam.

After a brief notation of my account, his face softened slightly. I suspected he had expected to hear something a little spicier, though it should not have taken him by surprise; after all, I was attending Queen's, not Simon Fraser.

"What groups or organizations have you been or are you currently a member of?"

"I was a Brownie once."

"Did you join any groups at Queen's?"

University campuses in the seventies tolerated small, disconnected, fringe social and political groups. It was almost in vogue to protest the "establishment" by joining a group like the Communist Party of Canada. Fortunately, I was never interested in politics, but I did find a group to support--one whose radical social views promised to be unpopular with both the majority of the public and big business. Sensing my distress at the question, again any softness in the staffing officer's expression vanished. My eyes met his glare as he placed his cigarette in the ashtray and grasped his pen, poised again to record every word of my response.

"Yes," I said apologetically, "I joined the Non-Smokers' Rights Association."

Small wonder he looked confused; no one as yet had heard of our group. I was marginally relieved to see the pen exchanged for the cigarette, which he promptly extinguished. I had a sinking feeling that my response had offended him. The next question had the potential to be every bit as touchy, considering his heavy French accent.

"What has been in the papers recently?" he asked. It was a routine question to ensure applicants are well read and aware of societal issues.

The Quebec Separatist Party (the P.Q.) had stunned the nation when it swept to power in 1976. Separation and the ongoing political cat-and-mouse game between René Lévesque and Pierre Elliott Trudeau had become a passionate national obsession for the past year. I struggled to diplomatically phrase my response. I even managed to slip in the fact that my ancestors were French Canadian, looking for anything to combat the alienation I was feeling.

This interview was beginning to feel like an endurance test. Perhaps that is what it was intended to be. The first indication that I was still in the game came at the end of the interview. The officer informed me my parents would be contacted for an interview. It was standard procedure for female applicants of that time. The RCMP wanted to ensure that the parents did not object to their daughter's application. I was grateful for the "heads-up."

My mother was aware of my application and understood the appeal the Force held for me. A generation earlier, she had rocked the family tradition by choosing not to become a teacher. Intending to join the Second World War effort, she enrolled in nursing. How frustrating it must have been for her to be educated enough, but not old enough, to enroll in the three-year nursing program. The year's delay caused her to miss the greatest adventure of her generation. She graduated in nursing in 1945.

Still ready to break traditions and find adventure, she applied to a post-war industry in its infancy: passenger airlines. A California company was recruiting registered nurses as stewardesses, but again she was disappointed--rejected because she was too tall.

Marriage brought her to Wolfe Island, where she settled in as a working wife and mother. It was uncommon for married women to continue to work outside the home, a situation my father tolerated but was never happy with.

Each generation owes a debt of gratitude to the previous one as well as a responsibility to lay an even stronger foundation for the next. It is appropriate to pause at this point and acknowledge the seeds sown by the WW II post-war generation that created the baby boom and sowed the seeds for the renascence of the suffragette movement in the sixties.

It was impossible to predict what my father's reaction would be. Like crows, police on the Island were an ill omen. Ontario Provincial Police (the OPP) on the Island usually meant someone had died in either a car or boating accident. A police presence was an annoyance for the locals, interrupting the normal traffic of unlicenced vehicles and drivers. And it's not as if the OPP could sneak up on the Island; before the ferry landed, 95% of the Islanders were alerted to their arrival. Unfortunately, occasionally the 5% were surprised and "got pinched" for no licence or insurance.

I broke the news of my application to my father the night before the staffing officer called to arrange the interview. To my surprise, my father was proud of what I had accomplished so far in my life and of my plans for the future. (It seems it wasn't just *myself* I didn't really understand that well.) Fortunately, my father never understood the time frame of my application.

The neighbourhood enquiries were conducted in the village the same week as my parents were interviewed. One of the things I liked least about life on the Island was it was impossible to keep a secret in so tightly knit a community. It would be equally impossible to predict the reaction of this conservative community to such a radical career choice. It was a pretty bizarre idea back then--a female in police work.

My neighbour, Marg Woodman, let me know with a twinkle in her eye that she had received a visit from a Mountie. She was an excellent reference, a town council woman with whom I had worked for two summers to create student jobs through the federal government's Opportunities for Youth program.

Now that the news was out, I thought it wise to tell the rest of my relatives myself, rather than leave it to the grapevine. I had the perfect opportunity to do so the following weekend at my cousin Linda's wedding. This was the same cousin who had first applied to the Kingston RCMP and had just completed the Kingston city police force training, only to be faced with a life-altering choice. Her fiancé was accepting a mining job in Africa. There was no room for two careers in a marriage in those days.

The wedding was very much a family affair. I had six aunts and one uncle on my father's side at the wedding, but I only had to tell one for everyone to know. The perfect opportunity presented itself when Aunt Kay asked, "Have you gotten a teaching position?"

"No, Aunt Kay, I have decided not to be a teacher at this time," I replied.

As I paused to find the right words to continue, my aunt jumped in.

"I knew it," she said with an air of self-satisfaction. "I always thought you would be a nun."

My escort, Dave, nearly choked.

"Close," I said with great irony. "I am going to be a Mountie."

The anticipated shock spread collectively throughout my extended family. It was a toss-up as to whom they were more worried about: my cousin Linda heading off to the wilds of Africa, or me heading off to basic training in Regina.

Things progressed quickly from that point on. I received my engagement date, June 7th, 1977. The entire application process had taken only one year. The system that allowed extra points for education had moved me up the applicant list and into the first available troop of females.

Ontario is made up of three divisions within the RCMP. Technically, I should have travelled to Ottawa to be sworn in, but at my request it was changed to Toronto. My younger sister, Judy, who was living and working in Toronto, drove me to the RCMP headquarters building slightly ahead of time.

I was somewhat relieved when two other women about my size, Linda and Elsie, arrived for the same purpose. The male Mountie physique was well defined and impressed on the Canadian and world psyche, but there was no corresponding, acceptable model for females. We would become the point of reference on which that model would be shaped. We were all a little nervous and a little quiet.

In short order, we were summoned by the officer in charge. We swore an oath to God, and to Queen and Country; in doing so, we were enlisted for five years. I entered his office a civilian and exited a peace officer. I was more than a little concerned that I technically had a lot of authority and responsibility but no training. Depot would soon remedy that.

Plane ticket to Regina in hand, there was just enough time for my younger sister, Judy, to take me to lunch in the CN Tower's revolving restaurant. The 360-degree view was spectacular, the horizon clear and bright in all directions--the perfect setting for beginning an adventure.

Chapter 2

Depot

Linda, Elsie, and I sat quietly in the front of the plane listening to several young women at the rear giggling and singing "Farewell to Nova Scotia." It was a bit early in the day, and perhaps not the appropriate place for a party, but that did not seem to dampen their mood.

Regina's small airport looked like a small bus terminal. I wasn't surprised when we were joined by the singers from the plane as we gathered by a very military-looking young Depot driver. His stoic demeanour seemed to quiet down the East Coast girls.

I couldn't help but notice that the laid-back amusement was still being communicated between the Maritime girls through understated facial expressions. There was something repressively good natured, unmistakably intelligent, and slightly insubordinate about these girls. I knew we would become good friends.

The airport backed onto the base at Depot. It was a short, silent, drive, but for me a powerful one. Passing through the gates of the base felt important. Some words from Robert Frost's "The Road Less Traveled" popped into my head. Actually the road had been well travelled for over one hundred years--by men. It was the travellers, not the road, that were "green and wanted wear."

Depot seemed to fit with the bleak, flat landscape of the region. Square, boxy, military-style brick and stone buildings stood beside parking lots and empty parade squares. Modest military housing lined the far side of the main parade square. There were flagstaffs and plaques in some areas, open fields in others. Depot itself seemed very still, almost deserted. It had a strange surreal feel, like a scene from *The Twilight Zone*.

Suddenly, as if some silent military command had been issued, uniformed men began hustling out of the various buildings. Each group had exactly the same configuration: thirty-one members forming two horizontal lines, plus one person--the "right marker"--who stood apart and commanded the group to "form up." Some groups were dressed in brown pants and runners and stood, then later ran, on the roadways. Other groups were dressed in police blues with yellow stripes and shiny black shoes, well-pressed short-sleeved shirts with shoulder flashes, and military forage caps with a yellow hat band. These groups marched on the sidewalks.

There were more similarities than differences between the two types of groups. The members all appeared to be nineteen to twenty years old, six-foot-something, in great shape, hair shaved very short, often exposing "whitewall" tan marks bordering the hairline around the ears and on the top of the neck. The lack of head hair was often compensated for by thick, neatly trimmed mustaches. Regardless of whether they ran or marched, they were all in step and moved as a unit. Within two or three minutes, the streets were empty again.

Our van stopped, and we were directed to the duty office, which was in the basement of the mess hall. The duty hut was occupied by a duty corporal who professionally and pleasantly gave us a brief orientation as he began signing us in. We were shown the various ranks and symbols and the titles they commanded: NCOs (non-commissioned officers), i.e. corporals, sergeants, staff sergeants, and the corps sergeant major, were to be addressed by their rank as displayed on their uniform. Officers could be identified by their white shirts: inspectors, superintendents, etc., and were to be addressed as "Sir." As we began to relax, we began to chat among ourselves. Then the door behind the corporal opened.

"There will be no speaking unless spoken to in this office. Line up and shape up!"

Corps Sergeant Major Pomfret, the chief disciplinarian at Depot, was a large, gruff man with a deep, raspy voice that telegraphed his authority, experience, and disposition. If he were an animal he would be a grizzly bear. The power of his gaze made all of us feel uncomfortable as he studied us each briefly and then returned to his office--probably to make notes, I thought.

Pomfret's intrusion was more than sufficient to cure us of our nervous giggles and chatter, and we settled down, lined up, and signed in. Our troop number was nine. We were each given a time in/out card and told that when we earned the privilege to go off base during our time off we would have to use the time clock. Much like life on the Island, where being one minute late meant missing the boat, being late at Depot also resulted in dire consequences. Whether it was one minute or one hour, the punishment was the same: the offender would be paraded before the corps sergeant major, who had complete, autonomous authority to sentence the offending recruit to whatever disciplinary consequences he felt were warranted.

We were then directed to "C" block, the building that would be our home for the six months of basic training. There were two cadet guards posted just inside the entrance to the building. The office of the drill NCOs was located in the basement. "Stores," which issued all the uniforms, was run by a civilian tailor and was on the other side of the basement. The "sticky bun" (vending machines for candy and pop, etc.) and the canteen, a small retail outlet open during restricted hours, were located on one-half of the first floor of the building. The rest of the three-storey stone building was broken up into five half-floor troop quarters areas.

Our troop, the only female troop in Depot at the time, would occupy one-half of the second floor. The rest of the building's dorm areas were left unoccupied, except for one female member recalled to Depot to help with the first few weeks of our orientation.

To the left of the second floor stairs were large, opaque, double glass and steel-framed doors. The hallway on the other side was wide and short, then it elbowed in a ninety-degree turn to run the width of the building. To the left of the first hall was a large common room with a TV at one end and some couches. Large windows in this room overlooked the mess hall and part of the parade square; the drill hall was around the corner. To the right of the longest section of the hall was a large common washroom with lots of individual stalls and sinks and a large common shower area. On either side of the rest of the hallway were identical bedrooms.

Female troops were never given the option of the normal thirty-two-person military-style dorms that male troops were organized into. We were left to rumours and suppositions as to why. Perhaps the Force thought we needed more privacy. Males, particularly RCMP recruits, had had childhood experiences such as Boy Scout camps that we lacked.

Earlier female troops had been given larger half-dorms once or twice, but it was unclear why the practice had been discontinued. We suspected females were being isolated from the buildings housing the larger dorms and male recruits. Fraternization between male and female recruits would be actively discouraged in many unspoken ways.

Whatever the reasoning, as luxurious as a two-person room may have seemed to the male recruits, there were three major disadvantages that I could see. The two-person room slowed the rate at which we got to know other members of the troop. It also meant there was much more to clean and polish. Perhaps most important, we were sensitive to any special accommodations that might provide ammunition for small minds to say females were given different treatment. Fortunately, there was very little other ammunition.

The federal government's fiscal year begins on April 1st. Troops are numbered sequentially, starting at one, from April 1st till March 30th of the following year.

The process is repeated every year. Each troop contained thirty-two members from across the country.

Many mental, physical, and emotionally challenging tests lay ahead. Depending on the strengths and dispositions we brought to Depot, some tasks were easier for some than others. Members were expected not to gloat over individual successes, but to help more challenged members improve for the good and the ranking of the troop as a whole. We were striving for perfection as a unit rather than as individuals. Each troop's identity was moulded out of the total blend of individual dispositions, giving rise to a new collective personality--a personality distinct from any other troop before or after. As we would be reminded countless times, we would learn to be "a troop of one," only as strong as our weakest member.

There was an implied responsibility to maintain the highest traditions of the century-old Force. Members were trained to be the living link in the continuity of the RCMP's commitment to the Canadian public and the justice system.

The Force needs captains, not foot soldiers; warriors capable of exercising independent decision-making under extreme duress, but still able to act as a military unit when a larger task is at hand. Depot was the first part in our training to teach us the skills to develop the leadership abilities for which we had been recruited.

The Force was ending a period of aggressive expansion. A provincial contract to assume policing duties in British Columbia, followed by the manpower requirements for security duties post-October Crisis and for the Canadian summer Olympics of 1976 had caused the constable ranks to swell, creating the Force's own baby boom, a demographic anomaly destined to transform the Force.

There were so many surplus recruits following the Olympics that Depot was shut down for months. When it reopened, troops arrived at one-week intervals, beginning with 1 Troop. By the time our troop, the only female troop, arrived, there were already over 300 recruits and staff at Depot. Within a few more weeks, the population of Depot would be over 400.

Members of Troop 9 differed from the males at Depot in a number of ways--not just by our sex. Most male recruits were fresh out of high school. We were older by an average of five years and better educated. Collectively we held twenty-four university/college degrees. Perhaps the most important distinction was that not one of us had a father or even a brother in the Force. At that time, the family tradition of proud fathers followed by sons and brothers into the Force did not extend to daughters. A respected NCO confided to me years later what I had already guessed: no non-commissioned or commissioned officer would have allowed their daughters to face what we so naïvely did.

The lack of military lineage was one of the reasons female members had such a profound impact on the RCMP. The Force would have to adjust to us as much as we had to adjust to it. There was a touch of anarchy in our souls, which made us more likely to test the rules than follow them. Males joined to maintain traditions. We joined to challenge them. The results of the challenge would either expand the traditional role of women in society or validate the status quo. No one expected it to be a smooth road, nor were we sure where it would lead.

Once our belongings were put away, Linda, Elsie, and I reported to Stores in the basement of "C" block to get our kit. Up until this point, I had been relieved to note that most of the members of my troop were only slightly taller and a bit heavier than me. That relief was short lived when on route to Stores we passed Vivienne Stewart, Carolyn Jones, and Sherry Stearns carrying their kit to their rooms. The height of these three ranged from five-foot-eight to six-foot-two. These were statuesque women. I felt a little smaller when they glanced down and smiled as we passed.

The older male civilian behind the counter at Stores called us up one by one and matched our names to our regimental numbers. "Don't forget this number. It will be one of the most important numbers in your life," he said, trying to convey the significance of our new designation.

Each member of the Force is assigned a regimental number in sequential order, dating back to the origins of the Force in 1873. It signifies the unbroken line of service. It also indicates the member's rank in service to the Force. "Time in" dictated respect and acknowledgement of authority from junior members. One of the first questions an unfamiliar member will often ask of another is, "What is your regimental number?" Our troop's regimental numbers began in the 33990's.

At Stores we were loaded down with boots, coats, pants, etc. The entire "kit" covered bras to hats. It took several trips to and from our rooms to collect it all. Male kit was mass produced, but the female kit was tailor made. It cost the Force $5,000 to outfit a female and $1,500 for a male.

There was limited production of female uniforms. While the working uniform was scaled down in size and modified to accommodate the female form, our dress uniform was reinvented. A woollen red blazer, black skirt, white turtleneck, black patent-leather pumps, and a pillbox hat were substituted for the trademark red serge, Stetson, boots, and breeches. We looked like airline stewardesses. Perhaps my mother would have settled for that thirty years earlier, but I would not. Instead of the cross strap and Sam Browne (gun belt) to house service revolvers and handcuffs, they issued a purse!

We were disappointed, but as bad as it was, it could have been worse. Initially the Force had intended for female members to carry the purse on active duty. We owed the first female troop in September 1974 a debt of gratitude for fighting the issue, winning a partial victory by allowing the Sam Brownes into working order for female members. The matter of a different uniform was a symbolic principle that irritated and embarrassed female members for years. The Force was not ready to understand it for over a decade. The Force, overly sensitive to potential rumours regarding the sexual orientation of female members, viewed the boots, breeches, and Stetsons as too masculine in design for females.

I was in the process of stowing my kit when my "pit partner," Katie, arrived. "Pit" really was a term defining the dual responsibility we held for the cleanliness and order of the room. Katie, a native of Ottawa, was a blonde, five-foot-seven, slightly plump, sometimes uncoordinated, twenty-year-old with an endearing and sometimes irritating "little sister" quality about her. Although Katie was larger and stronger than me, she never mastered the ability to handle the floor polisher, a large industrial machine with a spinning polishing disc at the bottom that created the glass-like finish on the dorm tile floors. Trying to out-power the machine resulted in the user's being quickly exhausted and then tossed around. I intuitively knew technique would be more important than brute strength. A bit of balance and leverage were all that was required. I polished, she dusted.

Over the next three days, as the remainder of the troop arrived, it became apparent the uniformity of size and appearance the male troops shared did not apply to females.

With the exception of three French Canadians, our troop was white and English Canadian. Some had been teachers, some students, some clerks, and one had been a dental hygienist. Carol Ann Rose, the only married member, had been a psychologist prior to taking a fifty-percent pay decrease to join the Force. She wasn't unique--about half of us had turned down or quit equal or better paying jobs to enlist.

Monetary compensation has never been a valid reason to join the Force. The original members of the Northwest Mounted Police were paid seventy-five cents a day from 1873–79, and after fighting successfully to maintain Ottawa's authority in the Riel rebellion, the pay was reduced to forty cents a day and the land grant of 160 acres that had been promised members was reneged upon by the Canadian Parliament. Our first commissioner, George A. French, resigned over the shabby treatment of the members by its politicians, in a grand and futile gesture. Members have always been long on principle but short on political power. Members of the Force would not see seventy-five cents a day again until 1904.

Female recruits shared an intangible motivation with current and past Mounties, an appreciation for grand and sometimes futile gestures to "maintain the right." It wasn't financial reward that excited us but the opportunity to be allowed to step into Canadian and social history in our own modest way.

Troop 9, in alphabetical order (thirty-one members; one dropped out):

Elsie Arnold	Kincardine, Ont.
Judy Best	P.E.I.
Anne Brown	Peterborough, Ont.
Terry Buchanan	Regina, Sask.
Linda Butler	Toronto, Ont.
Louise Fansher	Govan, Sask.
Joyce Graham	P.E.I.
Jane Greenwood	Wolfe Island, Ont.
Carolyn Jones	Victoria, B.C.
Janet Kerr	Indian Head, Sask.
Renie Lague	West Brome, Que.
Kathy Long	Kentville, N.S.
Colleen MacDonald	Shubenacadie, N.S.
Brenda MacFarlane	Antigonish, N.S.
Valerie MacLean	Montreal, Que.
Joan Merk	Saskatoon, Sask.
Shirley Miller	Annapolis Royal, N.S.
Janet Olive	Fort Qu'Appelle, Sask.
Jacqueline Olsen	Sherwood Park, Alta.
Maureen Oracheski	Wainwright, Alta.
Candy Palmer	London, Ont.
Pat Roach	Amherst, N.S.
Lorraine Rochon	Hull, Que.
Carol Anne Rose	Milford, N.S.
Candy Smith	Sault Ste. Marie, Ont.
Doreen Smith	Vermilion, Alta.
Thelma Spinney	Yarmouth, N.S.
Sherry Stearns	P.E.I.
Vivienne Stewart	Victoria, B.C.
Marie Van Veld	New Glasgow, N.S.
Katie Weigert	Ottawa, Ont.

Troop 9 Photo

Initially, we naturally tended to group with others from our own region, but there appeared to be more to the groupings than geography. The girls from the Maritime and Prairie provinces, along with those from British Columbia and Quebec, had individual strong regional identities. The only unifying sentiment they shared was a pronounced dislike for Ontario, which they viewed as arrogant, rich, politically powerful, and condescending to outside regions. This attitude was quite a surprise to me.

The loyalties of the people from Ontario were reversed, identifying in national terms first and to a lesser extent provincially. I could not understand the root cause of this fracture in our national identity, and it distressed me to think Canada was not the happy, homogeneous whole I had grown up believing it was.

Several lively evening debates were generated focusing on the future of the country. I could not understand the disenfranchisement and disdain the people of other provinces felt for "the East." Strangely, "the East" referred to Ontario, which is geographically closer to the centre of Canada than some of the other provinces.

To be fair, it wasn't the people of Ontario with which the rest of Canada had a problem, it was the centralist view of Canada the federal politicians in Ottawa took, choosing, in order to remain in power, to cater to Ontario and Quebec as the provinces with the most political seats. How Canadian of us to allow self-serving politicians to focus on two provinces and treat and occasionally exploit the rest of the country like colonies!

Other countries might have descended into civil war over the imbalance in political representation and feeling of alienation, but as Canadians we wrote letters of complaint and held peaceful, noisy rallies. In the interest of troop unity, I decided to avoid conversations involving politics and concentrate on things more relevant to our new reality.

The dormitory rooms were Spartan in decor. Along the wall were a large wooden closet, and a credenza for writing and storing clothes. Each bedroom had a mirror image of itself on the other side. The white sheets were ironed in place and covered by a grey "horse blanket" with angular corners precisely matching the overhang of the bed against the other wall. Not a speck of dust was on the sill or the Venetian blinds, which hung in a large, single window. The walls were plain and beige. The polished tile floor reflected the objects in the room like a hazy mirror.

This was the only acceptable state that a recruit's room was allowed to be in. Rooms and the dorm were open to inspection every morning before breakfast on weekdays and subject at other times to any surprise inspections drill staff wished to spring.

As a female troop, we had one advantage over the surprise inspections the male recruits endured. NCOs could not burst in unannounced. A five-minute warning was required to ensure no one was caught in her underwear. It was remarkable how much could be done, or hidden, in five minutes! To compensate for this advantage, drill staff occasionally inspected the dorm while we were in class, often tearing it apart for no discernible reason.

Lou Gjos, a female graduate from an earlier troop, had been recalled for a few weeks to help orient our troop into the routine of Depot. She had been carefully chosen by Depot staff because she embodied what they expected a female member needed to be to succeed in the Force. I recall one of the male NCOs predicting in glowing terms that she would be the first female officer in the RCMP.

Lou was tall, competitive, and closer in age and disposition to the male recruits than most of Troop 9; no wonder the men thought she would be successful. She was quite helpful in showing us how to make and iron our beds, polish our kit, explaining some of the protocols of a military organization, and warning us of some of the pitfalls that earlier members had fallen into; but the most important piece of wisdom I gleaned from her occurred at a party we had been invited to by 1 Troop.

One Troop was the senior troop, even though they were really only nine weeks senior to us. The previous shutdown of Depot after the Olympics caused Troop 1, a junior troop, to occupy status of "senior troop," prematurely inflating some of their egos. A suite off base had been rented for a party only Troop 9 was invited to.

At the party, the right marker of 1 Troop, the nineteen-year-old son of a superintendent, got into a disagreement with our mentor over the physical inferiority of female peace officers to males, particularly as it might effect the "backup" situation.

The centre of the room was quickly cleared, and the two antagonists sat back to back in Depot ground fighting form. Lou was not afraid to compete head-to-head with the males; she already had lots of experience to draw on from her six months at Depot the year before, where she had been a member of a rare mixed troop composed of eight women and twenty-four men. Lou may not have been as strong, but she was faster, and knew Depot moves and techniques her opponent had not yet been taught. Youthful arrogance combined with alcohol led to a near draw as the battle of the sexes was played out before our eyes.

It struck me as I watched that she could not win the match because the confrontational model being used would not allow it. Either outcome would be a loss. If the male recruit won as expected, his concerns over the physical competence of females as backup would have been supported. If she won the fight, she would have humiliated and alienated a member of the group she wanted to be included in.

No, this was not a healthy way to foster good working relations. I learned a lot that night as I watched the male recruit's expression change from smug overconfidence, to fear, then anger as he entertained defeat. There were more lessons to learn from the faces of his troop mates empathetically cheering him on.

We females would need as many men as possible cheering for us if we were to succeed. We needed to *build alliances* if we were to achieve professional, equal, relationships with men. Men and women were in uncharted territory at the time, but I was pretty sure open confrontations would not help us achieve our goals.

Three friends from 1 Troop struck up friendships with Katie, Linda, and Elsie at the party and talked them into joining them in the Depot marching band. It seemed like a non-threatening way to integrate into a coeducational unit.

There were advantages and disadvantages to belonging to Depot's band. There would be no "extra duties" like Depot security and roving patrols, etc., in the off-hours. Band members also did not have to endure the morning inspections by senior troops of their rooms and uniform. The downside was that band practice was at 6:30 a.m. every weekday. They also were required to participate in the weekday noon-hour parades. Several more of my troop mates decided to join the band; some played bugle, some drums, blending into the ranks of the males according to their height.

Three of our troop decided to play glockenspiel, a portable xylophone-type instrument. It was a welcome addition to the band with its high, clear notes balancing the thunder of the drums and the roar of the bugles. Unfortunately, it took five recruits to make a line in the band and no alpha male recruit would be caught dead playing the band equivalent to a flute. Two more members of my troop needed to "volunteer."

The trio convinced another member to be the fourth, then turned their sights on me, someone with no music training and no great desire to be in a band. Unencumbering my off-hours in evenings and on weekends didn't motivate me, as I had already decided Depot was a poor place to get distracted by romantic attachments. I can't recall why I acquiesced to their wishes but the decision added an extra dimension to my Depot experience.

All of our troop had arrived by June 10, the first official day of our training. We all dressed in fatigues (uniforms consisting of running shoes, brown work pants, perfectly pressed short-sleeved uniform shirts, and that ridiculous pillbox hat). There was nothing to polish in this order of dress. The peak and hat band were patent leather. This order of dress, fatigues, was only one notch up from issue overalls.

We carried our books and gym strip in matching gym bags purchased locally. We had picked yellow bags to coordinate with the yellow stripe we hoped to wear when we earned our marching orders. Until then, we had to run on the road from place to place.

Our first right marker, Sherry Stearns, was six foot two, the tallest of us all by a good four inches, making her a natural choice to stand apart from our ranks in her new role.

The right marker role was that of a coordinator--someone who shouted commands to facilitate the troop's moving as a unit from class to class.

Classes at Depot were a mixture of physical training and academics. The weighting of classes changed as we progressed through our six months of training. The first two months of Depot were dominated by physical training. After we had attained peak physical condition, hours spent in swimming and physical training (PT) were replaced by more academic subjects such as law.

Drill was the one class that seemed constant throughout the six months.

Cpl. Roulx was our drill corporal. He was in his late twenties, six-foot-one, in perfect physical condition, with piercing blue eyes, a large, reddish, handlebar mustache (a must for all drill staff), and a stern, guarded expression that never changed. His voice projected authority, mock disdain, and a light French accent. He played his role as disciplinarian and instructor for our troop flawlessly. He was a man the troop grew to respect and admire for his professionalism and fairness.

Years later, when Robert Knuckle tracked me down doing research on his book *Beyond Reason*,[6] he asked if I had found Cpl. Roulx attractive. Obviously some of my troop mates had said he was, but I had never thought of him in those terms. At first, the concept felt uncomfortable to me, like some kind of sacrilege--like thinking a priest was attractive. Twenty-some years later, after giving the matter fresh thought, I have to admit I did.

We assembled as best we could for the first drill class and awaited Cpl. Roulx's arrival. We were nervous with anticipation, recalling all the horror stories the more seasoned recruits had told us. The empty drill building echoed with the sound of Cpl. Roulx's perfectly shined high browns and spurs as he made his entrance. His march forward, swagger stick neatly tucked under his right armpit, was punctuated with a loud crack as he slammed his boot down. He pivoted ninety degrees to a halt facing our troop and stood in silence, a model of physical and sartorial perfection.

He seemed aware of, yet totally indifferent to, the wide-eyed stares of my troop as we summed up the man who, for the next six months, would alternate between devil and guardian angel for our troop; an enigma whose personal thoughts were always hidden behind an impenetrable wall of professionalism. If Pomfret was a bear, Cpl. Roulx was a cougar--lean, quick, and dangerous, but beautiful to watch.

The right marker yelled "Troop!" and we all snapped to attention. Standing at attention is much more demanding than civilians might think. It is common for members to faint if they hold the position too long. It's a bit like an internal game of Russian roulette to know when to break ranks before someone has to pick you up off the ground.

The visual power of Mounties standing at attention in ranks is undeniable. Standing at attention in ranks means every joint is locked, every muscle is tight, head up, eyes front and focused to form a wall of bodies in which members blend with each other like bricks. Of course, like bricks, each of us may have minor differences in size, shape, or colouring, but standing shoulder to shoulder

[6] Robert Knuckle, *Beyond Reason: Murder of a Mountie* (Dundas, Ont.: Kayson Publishing, 1997).

in formation, the overall impression of the whole is what is noticed--not the individuals that make it up. Even this early in our service, we understood that at an unspoken emotional level, the "red wall" was a show of strength and solidarity unique to the RCMP.

Cpl. Roulx walked slowly along the rank, staring at each of us individually top to bottom; up the front rank and then down the back. The silence amplified the sound of his boots and spurs. He finally reached the end, slammed his right boot down, marched to the front, turned, and faced us dead centre. If he wanted to intimidate us, he had succeeded.

His exact words are lost by now, but the message was clear: we were a mess and in the wrong order of dress. Even though we did not have our marching orders, we were required to attend drill in oxfords and blues. He gave us an unreasonable amount of time (five minutes comes to mind) to get to our dorms, dress appropriately, and return--or the troop would be paraded.

It was a disgrace to be paraded either individually or as a troop. "Paraded" meant being sent into the corps sergeant major's office for punishment, which could be confinement to barracks or extra duties. Avoiding the disgrace, either individually or as a group, was powerful motivation. It's amazing how fast you can move when you have to.

Upon our return, Cpl. Roulx inspected us a second time, and again we were told our turnout was lacking but not so much that we would be paraded. That was our first indication that he was not unreasonable. There wasn't much left of the class at that point, but he left us with one insulting decree.

"This troop is fat. There is nothing worse than a fat woman in uniform. If I catch any members of Troop 9 eating dessert at the mess hall, in the 'Sticky Bun,' or having pizza delivered to the dorm, I will parade the whole troop. Is that clear?" he shouted.

"Yes, Corporal!" came our unified response.

"Bullshit!" several of us thought.

The message was less sexist than it sounded. The RCMP did not want any of its members, male or female, to be overweight. Male recruits who were packing extra weight were singled out and put on notice to slim down. Recruits who remained overweight had that noted on their files and it had a negative impact on their evaluations.

Desserts in the mess and the Sticky Bun were easily monitored by drill staff. Pizza was entirely different. Of course we could have simply indulged at one of the local restaurants when we were out on a pass, but where would have been the fun in that? It was easy enough to smuggle in the occasional pizza and to smuggle the empty cartons out to the large green garbage bins behind the male dorms to prevent detection. Even when the unmistakable smell of pizza drifted down to the Drill Office in the basement of our dorm building, the drill staff were never able to find the evidence to prove the offence. Troop 9 played cat and mouse with the drill staff for the remainder of our Depot stay.

On the surface, drill might have appeared to be a subject that should have been cut out of the training program when the horses were eliminated from the training in 1967. The marching drills were identical to the movements of the mounted drills the Force had been executing for over one hundred years. These historic equestrian movements still dictated the number of recruits in a troop as thirty-two. Drill, however, was much more than that. We soon came to understand that drill was an integral part of Depot's psychology of discipline, tradition, respect, control, and pride, individually and as a group.

Drill was conducted in a large arena-sized brick building with polished hardwood floors. On the walls were the flags of every province, the Canadian flag, and the Union Jack, as well as the RCMP obligatory stuffed buffalo head that adorns every detachment across Canada. The building was empty except for bleachers on either side of the front door and the "training aids" immediately in front of the bleachers.

In the beginning we were not sure why Cpl. Roulx referred to the incredibly shiny galvanized steel garbage cans as "training aids." We weren't even sure why the bleachers were there. The building was able to accommodate only one drill class's manoeuvres at a time.

We didn't have to wonder for long. During our second drill class, a group of summer tourists on a guided tour were escorted to the bleachers to watch. They were no sooner seated than Cpl. Roulx ordered an out-of-step troop mate to stand inside the "training aid" and polish it. When another troop mate joined in with the muted chuckles of the tourists, we learned why there were two "training aids."

It was standard for drill corporals to punish a troop for substandard manoeuvres by demanding twenty-five to fifty push-ups. This was apparently Cpl. Roulx's first female troop, because he didn't realize women lack the upper body strength to do male push-ups in great numbers. Unfortunately for both Cpl. Roulx and the troop, he chose a time with a civilian audience of tourists to discover this.

"Give me twenty-five!" he barked.

As hard as we all tried, we began to shake and collapse at around the eight count. It was terribly embarrassing for all concerned.

Cpl. Roulx found more creative ways to show us when we had disappointed him. One day, he marched us to the rear of the drill hall but didn't give us the order to stop. As embarrassing as it was, we continued to pretend to march, bodies up against the rear wall like some kind of over-wound toy soldiers. We were better off than the three girls for whom an open back door lay in their path. They were nearly to the gun range by the time Cpl. Roulx finally gave the order to stop--not that they could hear him. One of the troop was sent to retrieve them.

At times it was difficult to believe female members outperformed the male troops in certain classes, but drill was one of them. Marksmanship was another subject that women tended to excel at--though in first two months, you would not have known it from Troop 9's performance. The unlikely advantage was rooted in our initial lack of experience with firearms. There were no bad habits to unlearn; we only had to master the correct trigger control method. Though female troops had lower initial scores compared to the male troops, the trend often reversed itself in the later stages of Depot.

Shooting was one of three core subjects where a failure at Depot meant back-trooping for remedial training or dismissal, depending on the recruit's abilities. Law and driving were the other two. The standard required to carry a gun was like other standards of the time: completely uniform for all members, tough but fair. Having the authority to use deadly force was never taken lightly.

Perhaps in the States police officers could shoot a "fleeing felon," but in Canada this was not a justification for use of force--members were expected to give chase, not shoot, in those circumstances. The use of "deadly force" would only be justified if there were an imminent threat of death or severe bodily harm to a member of the public or to the Mountie. The RCMP does not fire warning shots. Members only pull a service revolver if they intend to use it, aiming for the greatest mass; unfortunately, all but one of the vital organs are in the area of greatest mass.

Firearms training was done at the range building located in the back property of Depot, approximately a quarter mile from the rest of the buildings. The range building housed two indoor small arms ranges, a rifle range, a room for tear gas training, and several classrooms. During one of our first lectures on safely handling firearms, a picture was removed from the centre rear wall to reveal a bullet hole through the wall into an admin office caused by an instructor demonstrating "dry" (empty gun) firing techniques. He was the first, but not the last, member I heard of mistaking a loaded gun for an empty one.

A minimum score was required to pass Depot. If during the timed qualification shoot a member scored higher than average (240/300 for hand guns and 120/150 for rifles), members displayed crossed revolvers or rifles on the right sleeve of their jackets. In the event that the member shot a perfect score, a gold

Crown was added above the crossed firearms. As a female troop, we hadn't quite grasped the connection between being a good shot and being "macho," but I do vaguely recall some Freudian theories brought forth to explain it.

The stationary paper targets were poor preparation for the real thing. It is quite possible to be an expert marksman in competition shooting and perform terribly in a real police shooting incident. Unfortunately, the technology didn't exist for that level of relevant training for twenty years. When it did become available, the RCMP was one of the first police forces to embrace it.

Physical training (PT), swimming, and self-defence made up the physical courses. Fortunately we had a runner as a PT instructor. We spent our fair share of time doing male push-ups, challenge circuits, and lifting weights, but the emphasis was on running and cardiovascular conditioning.

"Lucky us," I thought on our first outside run, "no hills to run up."

Unfortunately, our two PT instructors were a little more creative than anticipated, and they ran us up and down the four flights of stairs at "C" block until we were ready to collapse. Nothing was going to be easy at Depot--except running, which becomes easier the more you do.

We all joined the extra running club that all recruits were encouraged to join. Everyone was expected to complete 200 extra miles of running on our own time, and there were 500- and 1,000-mile clubs for really fanatical runners.

No female members had ever completed even 500 miles when Judy Best, an ex-phys-ed teacher, set her sights on the 1,000-mile mark. Running was Judy's passion, and her lanky, five-foot-nine build was perfect for it. She was the only one in the troop who could pace the male instructors in a sprint. If anyone could run 1,000 miles, she could. As serious as she was about running, I was not.

Running was a lot more interesting with a little chit-chat, a good way to visit and get to know different troop mates. I had ridden a bike since Grade 1 and had strong legs but I needed to build up different leg muscles for running. I started at the end of the group and slowly visited my way forward during the first four weeks of training. No one but Judy seemed to notice how much I was improving.

I was never as good as Judy in her prime because I had only one speed, and Judy could always turn it up a notch at the end and sprint. I was just fine with that; it helped maintain my low profile as I watched the PT instructors pushing Judy to run faster in class.

For safety, recruits were advised to run in pairs and never to run if it was raining. Regina had some beautifully violent thunderstorms, and a runner might be the tallest object on the horizon.

The physical training inside the gym was gruelling. Double squat thrust and stances in timed, challenged circuits were set on military standards. The only task I could never really get the "hang" of (excuse the pun) was chin-ups--again, because of upper body strength.

Our gym clothes consisted of issue blue shorts, runners, white socks, and a white t-shirt with our names across the front. There was a little more of my name, "Greenwood," than there was of me. A month into training, the staff sergeant in charge of PT returned from a back operation. Backs and knees are the most common work-related injuries in the Force. From the look on his face, he was probably still in considerable pain, but it did not deter him from inspecting our troop on his first day back. As usual, I was trying to blend into the rank when he stopped in front of me and asked, "Greenwood, where are you from?"

No one really knows where Wolfe Island is unless you are from it, so I replied in general terms.

"Ontario, Staff."

Rejecting my answer, he pressed, "Ontario is a big place; where in Ontario?"

"Near Kingston," I replied, wishing very much that he would just move on.

"Does the place you are from have a name?" he asked again.

"Wolfe Island, Staff."

"Wolfe Island!" he snorted. "I bet you think you're something because you're from Wolfe Island," he said as he finally moved down the rank.

My expression was blank, but inside I was thinking: "What a shit! First he badgers it out of me then he ridicules the information."

It was months later before I found out that the staff sergeant was from Gananoque, twenty miles outside of Kingston, and he had recognized my family name. Members of the Force were a much more intimate group than I had expected.

We had been at Depot only a few weeks when a track and field meet occurred. The only co-ed event of the day was a traditional tug-of-war, a popular event among men--particularly the military, police, and firefighters. Most of us had watched but never participated in one but we were determined to try. We were given a crash course in pulling together.

Although there is some technique to the event, in the end it often comes down to weight and strength, and we were badly outmatched in both. Troop 9 picked up our portion of the rope opposite a junior troop determined to put up a good fight; but with each successive pull, our troop lost ground as, foot by foot, we were slowly dragged toward our inevitable defeat. We were just one pull away from being dragged across the line when all of a sudden we began to hold our ground, and even though our male opponents dug in, still we did not lose ground, and as we pulled back, slowly we started to gain some. We were so intent on the battle we had not noticed the unsolicited extra male hands at the end of our rope evening up the match! In retrospect, that day's event became a personal metaphor of occasional future conflicts I would later find myself in within the Force.

While the track meet provided an opportunity to build my confidence in some of the physical events, I knew our first swim class would keep my head from getting too far into the clouds.

The waters surrounding Wolfe Island were home to large, black, water snakes, which had provided more than enough motivation for me to never venture more than a stroke or two from shore. My lack of swimming ability was something I was about to regret.

The troop was lined up alphabetically at the six-foot mark on one side of the Olympic-size pool. The other side was lined with very nasty swim corporals ready to assess and group our individual swimming ability level. As with any troop, the skill ranged from lifeguard level to self-taught to non-swimmers. Unfortunately "G" meant I was ninth in line.

The pool was very wide, certainly farther than I had ever swum; farther than I thought I could.

"State your name, province or town of origin, jump in, and swim over here," demanded a well-built instructor in a Speedo.

I hoped in vain that at least one of the first eight would be a non-swimmer as each of the eight shouted the required information and then dove in, using the crawl to quickly get to the other side. All too soon it was my turn to face potential drowning.

I stepped forward and shouted, "Greenwood, Wolfe Island." Then I added, "I can't swim!"

"Get in the pool," was the angry response.

"But I can't swim," I repeated.

"Get in the pool!" commanded the swim instructor.

I was feeling very centre stage, uncomfortable, and a little frightened as I contemplated my next move. Surely I would not drown with so many people now focusing their attention on me, so I jumped. It was not a pretty sight. I swallowed a lot of chlorinated water. It wasn't graceful, either, as I repeatedly bounced off the bottom amidst the occasional dog paddle, awkwardly making my way to the side, where the corporal stood. I reached desperately for the pool deck, only to be pushed off by an amused corporal.

"Greenwood, you can't swim!" he remarked.

"Yes, Sir. That was what I was trying to say," I said weakly.

"Don't call me 'Sir.' I work for a living," he said, pushing me off the side again.

I apologized for addressing him as if he were an officer and he finally let me grasp the side.

"We will put you in with the swimmers," he advised.

"But I thought we both agreed I can't swim, Corporal," I protested.

"Yes, but most non-swimmers don't even get in the pool. You are already beyond that. If you really have trouble, we will move you down."

Wait a minute! I thought, *they are changing the rules. No one said getting in the pool was optional.* They were right on both counts. Four non-swimmers further down the alphabet did not jump in over their heads. One of that group was a weak swimmer, but still a better swimmer than I, who hid her ability successfully for several weeks until she was caught swimming.

I hated being the weakest member of the swimmers but had to admit it would have hindered my learning to be in the non-swimming group. That is not to say I did not cast envious eyes to the shallow end as I struggled every class not to drown.

The pool had one fatality (an electrocution) in its past, and I was determined not to make it two. There was a list to which my name was permanently attached. The official title of the list escapes me but we just called it the "shit swimmers" list. People whose names appeared on the list were required to practise after hours in the pool twice a week, but I attended six times a week. Everyone except Vivienne Stewart seemed to have a weak subject at Depot. Mine was swimming. I learned to count down the week by the number of swim classes I'd had.

Swimming was part drill, part physical training, and part discipline. The instructors played the role of antagonists to perfection. Some seemed to enjoy it more than others.

Many times we marched into the pool to find that they had dropped the water level by several feet. No water ladders were ever used in Depot, unless you count the ladder to the high diving board. Instead of push-ups for punishments, we would be tasked with fifty in-outs of the pool. Unlike male push-ups, females could master as many in-outs as the male recruits, because our legs helped propel us up, proving excellent conditioning; part aerobics and part muscle toning.

At the end of swimming class we were given a nearly impossible length of time to shower, dry, and travel as a troop to the next class without one minute to spare. On several occasions, persons unknown entered our change room while we were in class, and tossed our kit together into one unorganized pile--or, worse yet, the showers. We could never be sure if it was one of the swim staff or the self-defence staff that shared the other half of the building. It really didn't matter who was doing it, there wasn't anything we could do about it except move even faster. The next class's instructors didn't want to hear excuses. Mounties don't complain.

The final physical class was self-defence. The first month was weighted heavier with swimming and PT as we got into shape; then in the second month self-defence became more common on the schedule. The sergeant in charge was certainly a capable instructor for our introduction to karate, but he did little to hide his disdain for our troop, often beginning his instruction of a karate technique by saying his job was to show us the technique, even though it would not be effective for females because we lacked the upper body strength to execute the move effectively. "We are teaching you this because we teach the males this."

The atmosphere of self-defence was softened by the presence of two corporals who were quite pleasant when the sergeant wasn't around. Fortunately, karate was a relatively small initial component to the overall self-defence training.

Ground fighting, the main event, involved arm bars, come-along holds, hair pulling, lateral neck restraints and "horse bites," which consisted of grabbing a handful of the inside thigh of an opponent and twisting. These techniques required mastery of leverage and knowledge of anatomy for pressure points and pain receptors. Speed and finesse minimized the importance of strength and size. Now that was something females could use.

Ground fighting was not about style but about winning and doing it quickly. Recruits sat back to back until the sound of the whistle. We would then use every trick we had been taught to either immobilize or cause the other to "tap out"--when a recruit slapped the mat with a hand in admission of defeat, not something any of us wanted to do, but it was better to tap out than to pass out.

There were no rules in ground fighting. The only objective was to cause the opponent to give up, with minimum damage to either party. It was very useful, practical, job-related training. I do not know how many calories each class burned; I only know that we were very quickly getting into the best physical shape of our lives.

Physical classes were alternated with academic ones. It seemed like going from 100 miles per hour to full stop. We would push our bodies to their limits and beyond in PT, swimming, or self-defence, then shower, change, and get to the next class in ten minutes.

Very soon after sitting at my desk, I would notice how warm the room was--more than likely the result of the troop's collective body heat. Soon my eyes would lose focus. That is what happens when you begin to fall asleep with your eyes still open. A quick glance around the room would confirm we were all in the same dilemma, rosy-faced troop mates, eyes glazed, swaying slightly as we fought our own bodies to stay awake.

Falling asleep in class would be punished by parading individually; or collectively, if too many troop mates did it. Recruits were allowed to stand at the back of the class if they felt fatigued, because it is difficult, but not impossible, to fall asleep standing up. Others of us had personal strategies we employed to combat sleep, like Jacqui Olsen who would give herself a charley horse at the first sign of sleepiness. I personally would rather be paraded than go to that extreme.

The academics ranged from typing, CPIC (Canadian Police Information Centre), human relations, history, and law. It seemed to us that most of the instructors at Depot were angry with our troop with only a couple of exceptions: our admin instructor, Cpl. Allard, and our history/human relations instructor, Cpl. Alexander.

Cpl. Allard, a French Canadian, taught us the boring but necessary typing, report writing, and communication skills. Since any recruit who could type sixty words a minute was exempt from the class, half our class met that requirement the first day.

I struggled, with the remainder of the class, at forty words a minute for almost the entire eight-week course. Typing was necessary because all forms and reports were typed and secretaries were a luxury the Force preferred not to pay for.

Typing was also necessary for CPIC. Information on vehicles, arrest warrants, criminal records, etc. could be accessed or imported immediately from any part of Canada. This was cutting edge use of a very new technology for any police agency.

It was easier to learn how to use CPIC than to master the portable and vehicle radios. Dealing with a police radio while driving is a lot more demanding than listening to music. Radio codes and the international phonetic alphabet were taught to minimize air time and maximize clarity of information.

Cpl. Allard's limited skill in the English language sometimes led to hilarious instructions. One day he advised us with a straight face: ". . . and you don't fuck on the air."

Of course he meant you don't *say* "fuck."

It was nice to have a corporal we could feel comfortable enough to laugh with. His big brown eyes could not disguise his empathy for our troop, and as the months passed, Cpl. Allard became a combination of brother/soul mate to our troop. Perhaps because he was one of the few French Canadian instructors, he could empathize with our troop's occasional feeling of ostracism.

Cpl. Alexander, who taught human relations and history, was a widower. A female member from the first troop had married him and left the Force to help raise his two young daughters. Although we had been assigned a troop counsellor, our relationship with him was quite distant and strained. Cpl. Alexander and his wife, Barb, filled that unofficial role. His sensitivity to underlying issues, particularly involving youth crime, was about fifteen years ahead of the shift to community police theories. His insights on the history of the Force were equally enlightened.

The history of the Force is so intertwined with the history of Canada it is really inseparable from it. The country was only five years old when the first Canadian prime minister, Sir John A. Macdonald, created the North West Mounted Police by an act of Parliament. The evolution of the Force since 1873 mirrored the evolution of Canada, from its simple origin based on a military model, to the complex, multifaceted organization it is today.

The RCMP has always been more than a national police force, more than a national symbol; it is the soul of Canada. Its ideals of justice, honour, and peace are in total harmony with the country and its citizens and remain a source of pride that forms our national identity.

Canada was a nation created by a legal, thoughtful act, not in revolution and violence--the same kind of act that created the Force to protect the citizens of the country through the administration of justice.

Canada would be a much different and smaller place without the Force. It was because of the friendship born out of fairness and trust between the leader of the Blackfeet, Chief Crowfoot, and ranking officers of the RCMP, that the RCMP was able to negotiate treaties that allowed Western Canada to avoid the bloody wars south of the 49th parallel.

The ability of the Force in the early days to maintain order was rooted in the respect the First Nations had for the fairness and courage of national heroes like George French, Sam Steele, James MacLeod, James Walsh, and Jerry Potts.[7]

When Chief Sitting Bull entered Canada in the Cypress Hills area with over 6,000 Sioux fresh from their famous encounter with Custer and the Seventh Cavalry, the peace was kept by Supt. Walsh and a handful of members. This was accomplished through respect for bravery, justice, and leadership on both sides. Canada is not short on heroes. (Unfortunately, it is a little short on *political* heroes.) The power base of the Force has always been in the West where its

[7] Nora and William Kelly, *The Royal Canadian Mounted Police: A Century of History* (Edmonton: Hurtig Publishers, 1973), p. 45. The friendship established in 1874 between the RCMP (at that time the NWMP) and Chief Crowfoot of the Blackfeet Nation opened the door to similar cooperation with other Western tribes, the Bloods and the Peigans.

members lived, worked, and died with their fellow Canadians. Unfortunately, the insights the leaders of the Force offered Ottawa on realities in the West were mostly ignored.

The federal government also turned a deaf ear to the advice of the empathetic Northwest Mounted Police, which saw some legitimacy to the Metis position in Manitoba. The Force was ordered to subdue the Metis, contributing to the war with Louis Riel.

While the leadership within the Force may not have always agreed with the government of Canada, the RCMP never lost sight of its military duty to execute its orders. To do otherwise would result in a coup, and that is just so un-Canadian!

Despite the friction that often marred the relationship, the success of the RCMP in its original task resulted in the federal government's continuous expansion of the Force's mandate to include new geographical and legal areas, from protecting Canadian claims of sovereignty in the West by protecting the natives and early settlers from whisky traders and marauders, to keeping the peace in the North for the miners during the gold rush at the turn of the last century.

In times of peace and of war, the RCMP became the most efficient and dependable instrument for the Canadian government to defend its sovereignty at home and abroad when necessary. The task of keeping the peace by the administration of justice was accomplished by an undermanned and under-funded Force that established a Canadian pattern based on respect for the rule of law, forming the foundation of a distinctly different attitude towards law enforcement. The strength of the system lay in the support of the public, not the might of the Force.

During the past 130 years, the Force has expanded to provide a presence in every province and territory of Canada, in addition to postings in many countries around the world. Achieving a balance between the RCMP's dual responsibilities of representing the interests of the average Canadian to the federal government and representing the federal government to the Canadian public has vexed the Force for over one hundred years. In times of good government, the RCMP and Canadian society flourished. As Paul Palango in his book *The Last Guardians* so astutely observed, the RCMP is "a touchstone for the larger political and economic picture in Canada. . . . It is the last national institution--other than the federal government--linking the country together."[8]

The members of the RCMP represent the personification of Canadian society as a whole. As more than one world leader has observed, no other nation in the

[8] Paul Palango, *The Last Guardians: The Crisis in the RCMP and Canada* (Toronto: McClelland & Stewart Inc., 1998).

world holds its police force in such high regard that it is a national symbol.

Our history class taught recruits the past to help them understand their responsibilities in the present, which required a member of the Force to maintain the right without fear or favour and to protect the public good and Canadian interests. Depot was the common training ground used to maintain the national standards of justice. Law dominated the academic class time after the first couple of months. The Canadian Criminal Code, rooted in English Common Law, reflected the continuous evolution of Canadian societal standards.

By the end of six months at Depot, a recruit received more criminal law training than law students from the best universities. In some isolated postings, members still served as the Crown counsel when the travelling judges came to town. The police, lawyers, and judges were expected to use the law to protect society by exercising independent wisdom and discretion.

Judges were expected to consider many things when deciding a case, such as the nature of the offence, the conduct of the police, and the intent of the accused, as well as the crime's impact on the victim and the community at large. The rights of the individual were protected but never at the expense of the rights of the community. The concept of a "reasonable man" was referred to many times in the Criminal Code. The concept empowered police to execute the law in a timely, impartial, and effective manner. Police actions were not expected to be always absolutely correct, only reasonable in their assumptions and actions at the time they made their decisions.

The *Canadian Bill of Rights* was the balance that ensured the powers granted to police were exercised wisely and fairly. The courts and the police operated as a unit to shield, protect, and uphold the public and its right to a safe and free society, free of corruption and political interference, and above all to never allow the administration of justice to fall into disrepute[9] in the eyes of the public.

Guardians of one of Canada's fundamental cornerstones of society, the justice system had been entrusted to the RCMP for over one hundred years. Canada in turn demanded the highest standards of moral, intellectual, and physical abilities from its guardians. Small wonder that the Canadian identity became intertwined with the persons tasked to maintain the right.

Depot remains one of the things the RCMP does best: a common experience uniting all regular members of the Force, forming the foundation of the acceptable standard of police professionalism for which Canada is famous.

[9] Protecting this principle was a key and powerful yardstick a judge could use in exercising his discretion on a case. The entire justice system was tasked with insuring the public would never lose faith in the justice system. For example, if a clearly guilty person were acquitted on a technicality, the public would be outraged, which could lead to the undermining of the public's perception of, and support for, the justice system.

The training at Depot helped form the foundation layer of each member's professional wall.

As Neil Armstrong predicted thirteen years earlier, females who wanted to break new social ground would not just have to meet existing standards, they would have to *exceed* them.

The RCMP had levelled the field and handed us the ball. It was up to us to run with it.

December 7, 1977 Troop 9 Graduation

Chapter 3

Walking on the Moon

Halfway! Three months into training was something to celebrate. By this point, everyone who was still at Depot was prepared to go the distance. We had lost only one member: one of the young French Canadians, too homesick to continue.

The official celebration was an afternoon barbeque at a local park. Our troop was joined by a few instructors and their wives for an afternoon of hamburgers and a casual game of baseball. It was a pleasant, muted affair.

The real party was an unofficial gathering the next day in our "C" block common room that began well but nearly ended in disaster. "Mom" had just returned from the one visit home married members were allowed during training. She smuggled in a six-pack of Schooner beer to treat Brenda and Kathy and to educate Vivienne and me about the superiority of East Coast brew. Candy, who did not drink, would have to rely on our assessment.

We had no sooner cracked the contraband (alcoholic beverages were strictly forbidden in residence) when our very strict right marker walked in, voiced her dissatisfaction with our rule breach, and left. Her disapproval did not dampen our mood because the five-minute advance warning NCOs were required to give before entering our dorm had given us a false sense of security. I made a teasing comment concerning the quality of the beer that sparked a "tickle attack," leaving me on the floor yelling "help!"

Those calls for help landed us all in a delicate situation. Our mood sobered instantly at the sound of high browns on the stairs. My friends sprang into action and, after grabbing all the evidence, they hid in the first bedroom's closet. I was beginning to recover motor control on the floor of the common room when the duty NCO came bounding in. In a glance he assessed my room, then turned to continue his sweep through the dorm. "Parading" was a doorknob away when I shouted, "Stop! You can't go any further--there are girls in underwear in there."

He paused. It felt like forever as he reconsidered his next move before he returned to me.

"I heard someone screaming," he said.

"Oh . . . that was the TV," I said. We both looked at the TV, which stared back blankly.

"I just turned it off."

I knew he didn't believe me. Surely he could smell the beer.

"Are you sure no one is in trouble up here?" he asked.

"Yes," I responded, thinking to myself: *not yet, anyway.*

He looked down the hall in the direction of the other rooms. There was a faint, repressed smile on his lips as he withdrew, leaving me with a parting piece of good advice: "I'd keep the noise down if I were you," he suggested as he disappeared through the door.

It wasn't what he said, but the way he said it--he wasn't fooled; he was giving us a break. Through the Force grapevine, within a year, I confirmed my suspicions: we had been informed on--and it wasn't by our right marker. Few secrets are ever successfully kept within a Force filled with professional questioners constantly seeking the truth. I laughed to myself as I realized it would be harder to keep a secret in the Force than on the Island.

By halfway, recruits who had decided to leave the Force were gone; anyone remaining was planning to go the distance. In the first three months, recruits were constantly pushed to their limits physically and emotionally. Recruits were athletic, arriving at Depot in good shape by civilian standards. The RCMP, however, has military standards. Our training is longer and tougher than any others, including the U.S. Marines.

Recruits were very military in appearance. The shaved male heads at Depot stood out in contrast to the shaggy hair style of the 1970s. Mustaches, the only form of facial hair allowed by the RCMP, were grown almost in protest and everyone who could grow one, did. The size and shape of the mustaches were strictly enforced by drill corporals proudly flaunting non-regimental handlebar mustaches.

Female recruits could not be dealt with so uniformly. The only guideline for female members' hair was a loosely worded directive that indicated it should not be so short as to be considered unfeminine, and long hair was to be styled off the collar.

I was the only one in the troop who had long hair. After one week of training, it was obvious that any hair that hadn't been pulled out in ground fighting would be in very poor shape from being in a wet bun between showers after physicals--so I cut it. I was surprised that several of the male recruits took the time to sit beside me at the mess hall and mention the change sadly. I suppose since there were only thirty-one female recruits and around 400 males, we were probably all individually noticed.

I had no intention of taking any notice of the male recruits. I even lectured my troop mates who did, pointing out the pitfalls of marriage and of romantic relationships while at Depot. I could quite correctly have been labelled anti-marriage, a sentiment of which the Force would have approved.

Several of our troop were engaged when they arrived at Depot, and one was married. When the Force decided to accept women back in 1974, they also for the first time allowed married persons to join. For the previous 101 years, recruits had been required to be single. In the distant past, junior members were not allowed to marry for seven years; after the 1940s the time was reduced to five years (three for certain municipal contract locations) for a relatively short period, then reduced to two years before it was abandoned altogether in the early seventies.

The Force's anti-marriage attitude was rooted in economics. Single members could be transferred from barracks to barracks on short notice and at little cost. I worked with staff sergeants who recounted being informed on a Friday afternoon that they had been transferred effective the coming Monday to a detachment hundreds of miles away.

It was also part of the nature of the Force to expect undivided loyalty and dedication from its members--something similar to what the Catholic Church appears to ask of its priests. As a matter of fact, it was not unheard of for men to leave the seminary to become Mounties or vice versa. The personality types are similar.

Learning to show the public a proud façade began on parade at Depot. As a member of the band, I got a taste of noon parade in advance of the majority of my troop.

The parade square is the domain of the highest of all non-commissioned ranks, the corps sergeant major. On the parade square, he is supreme even over the commissioned officers. Ours was a large man who fit his authority well. He stood like a statue, his swagger stick neatly tucked under his right arm, in flawless uniform, boots, breeches, and Stetson. The leather of his uniform was so polished from years of "spit shines" that it looked like wet plastic. He modelled a perfection all members strove for. We all awaited and dreaded his inspection. As he passed each recruit, beginning with the band ranks, his unflinching gaze on member and kit missed nothing. It seemed to take a long time for him to reach our glockenspiel rank. Once he got there, he really slowed his inspection. Out of the corner of my eye I watched as he paused to inspect the first three women of the glockenspiel rank, without a word. Then it was my turn. I don't recall when I began to hold my breath. I really wasn't even aware I had done so until I released it as he stepped by towards the last one in the rank. I'd only halfway exhaled when he stopped and returned to stand directly in front of me. Searching out my name tag, he asked in a disapproving tone: "Greenwood, how tall are you?"

This inquisition was worse than the PT staff sergeant's badgering, because it was in front of practically all of Depot as well as onlooking tourists.

"Five foot five, Corps Sergeant Major," I replied firmly.

He almost snorted as he turned as if to resume his inspection; then he paused and turned back for a further challenge: "How tall does a woman have to be to join the RCMP?' he asked in a very annoyed tone of voice.

Fortunately, the flush of red is the same for anger as it is for embarrassment, as one emotion over took the other.

"Five foot *four*," I replied again firmly but devoid of any hint of my emotional state.

Once more, he turned as if to go, only to turn back on me one last time. Peering down with disapproving eyes of steel he snarled, "I don't think you are five foot five. I don't think you are even five foot four. Tomorrow I am going to bring out a measuring stick and measure you."

With that, he turned and finally did continue his inspection as I pictured the humiliating vision in my mind. Silently I railed against his arrogance, his unfairness. Although I had just squeaked by the height requirement, I was a fraction of an inch taller than the first two, whom he had passed by. Why was he picking on me?

I really didn't know why, but I did know I wouldn't give him the satisfaction of revealing he had bothered me in the least. At any rate, I didn't have long to brood on it. The band leader commanded the band and troop movements to begin. The drums established the beat, followed by the blare of bugles in their first song. Then it was our turn. The big day we had practised for so many hours was upon us.

We had sounded so good when we had practised playing the music, and we were very capable of marching in drill class with the rest of the troop. It was a shame we hadn't practised doing both simultaneously, thereby avoiding having to learn in front of everyone that day that it is difficult to do both well--or even at all. We were halfway through the first verse and wandering very badly in our ranks when we shifted the focus to our marching. That resulted in our notes becoming very scattered until they finally just faded away mid-song.

Later that evening, as I relived the humiliation of the noon parade in my mind, I wondered why we were in such a race to get out on parade. Now we were committed to the next day. We practised most of the night marching and playing, playing and marching. We did it in our dreams, went through it the next morning, and even skipped lunch to get that last five minutes of practice before the parade.

Finally it was time, and out we marched again and halted in front of the corps sergeant. I was quite relieved to see only a swagger stick under his arm and not a yardstick. When he inspected our rank, moments later, he paused as if he suddenly remembered something. "Greenwood, I was supposed to measure you, wasn't I? Tomorrow I'll bring my stick."

By now I suspected--correctly--that he had no intention of measuring me; he was just testing my emotional control. I must have passed, because the matter was dropped. But not before he fired an even broader insult to the rest of the glockenspiel rank. "Well, girls, are you all going to play the same song today?"

Looking back today, I can appreciate the humour of his statement, which escaped me that day. I am happy to say the second day's performance was a huge improvement over the previous one's. And it wasn't just our musical ability that was improving.

The physical metamorphosis was obvious. Body fat was reduced to minimum standards, and muscles were increased. The shift in emphasis from heavy weights to aerobic conditioning had transformed us into lean fighting machines, capable of running down a fleeing criminal while retaining the stamina to complete the arrest.

The personality changes were far more subtle. You need to believe in miracles before they can happen. Depot was teaching us to believe. We were becoming confident in our own strengths and our ability to overcome all challenges. The uniform and our deportment projected professionalism. Policing situations tend to be highly charged and explosive, with emotions ranging from rage to grief. We learned to control our own emotions, projecting calm no matter what we felt; how else could we make order from chaos? Depot instructors provided role play to help us develop these skills.

The insults and taunts we endured from NCOs on the parade square and in class meant to season us for the field were successful--to a point. While one male standing nose to nose insulting everything from boots to lineage may produce a fear or anger response in male recruits, the drill staff soon learned such a tactic had different effects on both female and native troops. By nature, females seemed to possess a more developed emotional intelligence. It was an advantage at Depot that we never interpreted a verbal rant by a frothing corporal on the parade square as a threat. We would stand firm stoically, avoiding any hint of emotion, playing our part in the charade. However, if the verbal onslaught went on too long or conjured some humorous vision in our minds, Joyce Graham would begin a muffled giggle so infectious it would ripple through the troop. We strained physically to control the corners of our mouths and to stop our shoulders from shaking in repressed laughter. There was something unintentionally emasculating in our response.

More than one NCO on parade crossed that invisible line, which Cpl. Roulx so intuitively learned to avoid. Sometimes, as the muffled hum began, an NCO would mistakenly believe he could stop us through further intimidation. He soon learned that course of action only amplified the problem. His only honorable course of action was to swallow his pride and discontinue his abuse before the infection cascaded to the male members on parade and the situation really got out of hand.

The only other troop that appeared impervious to insults and intimidations was a First Nations troop of special constables at Depot that summer. This troop was all male, and if they cared what was said to them or about them by any member in authority, they never gave any hint of it.

The special constable rank was limited to specific duties such as airport security, surveillance units, or reserves. Being a "special" had its own advantages. Training was shorter and less intensive, and specials had the luxury of knowing where they would be assigned to work and had no threat of transfer. These advantages were measured against the disadvantages of lower rank and less pay. The special rank was a dead end. Specials served a purpose for both the Force and the Canadian public. They did not cost as much to train or employ. Special constables did not need to meet the standard recruitment requirements demanded of regular members. They could be shorter than the height requirement, academically less competitive, need glasses, or, prior to 1974, they could be married. Occasionally, a special constable would use the rank as an entry point. It was uncommon but not unheard of for a special to return to Depot for a couple of months' further training to achieve the rank of constable. In our Depot stay, only one special returned for that purpose.

The summer tourist audiences at Depot were our first indication that the Canadian public may have been surprised by, but approved of, the new female presence in the Force. Public support remains a cornerstone on which the RCMP is based. The RCMP carries out its duties with the lowest ratio of police to population in the Canadian policing community. Members were often responsible for order in a large geographic area with little or no backup. Without public support, the RCMP would not be able to maintain order.

By the end of the summer, our band and the rest of the troops had been marching together as a unit for nearly three months. We had become very skilled and performed many complicated marching patterns for appreciative crowds. Our band--even our glockenspiels--had achieved a level of competence seldom seen in the rotating population of Depot. It seemed like a lifetime since we had made our humble debut, unable to play the simplest of tunes. Our favourite tune to end the parade, "The Maple Leaf Forever," often elicited smiles and cheers from the crowds. Noon parades were actually getting to be fun until one day the corps sergeant major decided to bring our heads out of the clouds and fail us during his inspection.

"Did you polish the welts in your boots?" he thundered at the first female glockenspiel player in our rank.

"No, Corps Sergeant," she replied.

What are boot welts? I was thinking as I heard him demand the same of the next two. Apparently they didn't know either, since they had the same deficiency. It was my turn. I almost blurted out, "NO, Corps Sergeant!"

But he didn't ask. He silently passed by the fifth and last glockenspiel player as well.

"You three report to my office after parade," he ordered the three he had challenged.

When we found out what "welts" were,[10] we looked hard at the shines on all our boots but we couldn't see any reason why three failed and two passed inspection. As punishment, they lost their weekend privileges. It was very unfortunate, because, like most of us at that point in training, we often booked weekends in hotels to change the scenery. The guilty parties had planned to explore one of the surrounding cities (Saskatoon, I believe) with three members of Troop 1. That had to be postponed.

The mystery intensified the following week when those three, boots gleaming, failed inspection once more for another invisible infraction--wrinkles, I think. Again they were restricted to base for that weekend. They became almost paranoid, studying us two to see what we were doing that was so much more acceptable than them. Although I could not be sure, I suspected that it was their inter-troop friendships after hours and not the condition of their kit that was the cause of the punishments.

The oppressive mood that had dominated our first few months at Depot lightened noticeably after the halfway point. Some attributed the change as a sign of recognition by the upper management that Troop 9 was trying as hard as possible to be the best troop at Depot. Others suggested the improved mood

[10] The welt is a strip of leather sewn around the boot upper portion to attach it to the sole.

was based on our growing seniority at Depot. Seniority in the Force always commanded respect.

None of us realized that changes in an organization as large and complex as the Force are seldom influenced, or obvious, at the constable's level. In retrospect, I now see the major reason for the change was the arrival of our new officer in charge (OIC), Supt. Mills. The officer he replaced had been completely unknown to us; he may have been absent on leave prior to retirement, commonly referred to as "retirement mode." Once the new camp commander arrived, we quickly learned an energetic, kind, pleasant hand was now at the helm of Depot.

The new officer was a small man, by the standards of the day. He always had a smile on his face and seemed genuinely interested and proud of each of his many recruits, females included. Mills loved to run. He often joined the Wednesday evening four-and-one-half-mile summer run from Depot to the airport and back. The last Depot run of the season was scheduled for the end of September. Mills decided to make a race of it. He purchased three trophies for the males and three for the females--first, second, and third place.

The race was the talk of Depot. Morale soared because members are naturally competitive. Depot was abuzz with a burning question as to who among the 400-plus men would be the fastest recruit.

Two outstanding athletes had spent the summer runs alternating first and second place on Wednesday nights. The physical training staff were betting on one, the self-defence staff on the other. The sense of competition and excitement reminded me of the Canada-Russia '72 series.

No one outside of our troop gave the female runners a thought. Our troop assumed Judy Best would take first place within our rank of thirty-one. She had already set a Depot record by being the first female to log 500 miles, and that was accomplished before halfway. The gruelling commitment she made to running, however, was taking its toll. Her knee was beginning to swell when she ran. She never complained, and no one outside of our troop seemed to notice she had begun to limp after running.

When the fateful evening came, all of Depot turned out to participate. The weather was perfect for running; excitement was in the air. The two heavily favoured recruits finished a distant second and third behind a rookie from 14 Troop. No one could believe it when this gaunt, weathered old man (all of twenty-eight) was called to the podium to take the first-place trophy. No one knew before the race that he was a competitive marathon runner. It was a good lesson, demonstrating to all of us never to underestimate an opponent on the basis of size or age.

That wasn't the only upset that day. Judy and I didn't expect to win the race, but we knew we were determined to make a respectable showing for our troop. At about three miles, Judy's knee really began to cause her trouble, and her pace began to slow.

"Go on!" she said.

This wasn't the way it was supposed to be. Judy deserved to win, not me. In my mind winning carries too much responsibility--you are too much in the spotlight. Once you win, you are expected to keep winning. I preferred to keep expectations low, then pleasantly surprise people when necessary.

At that moment, however, the honour of the troop was at stake, and I had to make a good showing. Reluctantly, I left Judy behind and ran my young heart out. In the final stretch, I could tell by the cheers of the recruits who had already finished the race and now stood at the finishing line that someone was close behind me. I never saw him, because he didn't pass me. I guess I can be competitive under the right circumstances.

Several days after the race, I was eating dinner when a male recruit I had never met sat down and struck up a strange conversation.

"I was hoping to go home this weekend but I can't now."

"I'm sorry," I replied, thinking he needed a shoulder to cry on.

"It's because of you I can't go," he said mournfully.

I was very curious now. Was this some kind of roundabout pickup line? "Because of me?" I inquired.

"I was the one behind you in the race. How can I go home and tell my father I was beaten by a girl?" he explained.

I still believed this was some kind of clumsy pickup line--a reason to start a conversation. "Surely you are not serious," I played along.

To my amazement, it became apparent he was. He looked and sounded depressed, and somewhere in his mind I had caused it. Trying to cheer him up, I pointed out that he had finished in the top ten percent of Depot; but he would not be consoled. The fact that a female had run some silly race slightly faster than him had shaken his opinion of himself, and in his mind was going to create a potential rift with his father. I urged him to go home, promising to say nothing about the race and suggesting he do the same. He seemed so young, so wounded. I felt guilty but how could I have known it was that important to him? I decided to try to avoid direct competitions with male members in the future.

At the halfway point, we received assessments from all of our course instructors. It was a good time to get feedback on our performance. I had been in school for seventeen years without a break and was used to studying and writing exams. No challenge there. Actually our whole troop was very academic. Vivienne Stewart and Candy Smith set the academic pace, closely followed by the rest of us.

The standard of driving a vehicle that a recruit was required to attain was nothing less than professional. Many long hours were spent driving the streets of Regina using a very defensive, efficient driving system, designed to keep both members and public safe.

The ability to drive well was necessary and respected; however, traffic sections were not: "Better to have a sister in the whorehouse than a brother on traffic." This is a universal adage within the Force that everyone learns at Depot. The driver training corporals, all of them career traffic men, didn't seem to be bothered that other sections of the Force felt that way. Traffic members were stereotyped as simple-minded dolts who would give their own mother a ticket, but that perception did not do the instructors justice. Most were accident analysts who could reconstruct traffic events using complicated math formulas and plan drawings. They gave us a glimpse of their knowledge when they taught us accident investigations.

My driving mark was good--not great, just good. I scored much higher in troop ranking in marksmanship and academics. The only surprises in my marks came in my three physical courses: swimming, PT, and self-defence.

I braced myself for the swimming assessment and nodded in agreement as the swim instructor informed me of my "D" for performance, an accurate rating of my aquatic ability.

"But," he added, "we have given you an 'A' for attitude. We have never seen anyone that hated swimming as much as you put in so many extra hours trying to improve."

I hadn't realized attitude could count nearly as much as performance in non-core subjects.

I expected to do well in physical training but I felt quite overrated when they recorded A's for both performance and attitude. Perhaps placing first female in the race was a good thing. I was on a roll; or so I hoped, as I left to collect my self-defence marks.

I had enjoyed self-defence once we got into the practical ground fighting and compliance holds. I liked the two corporals who assisted instructing but I never cared for the sergeant. (It was not just *my* observation that the only time he smiled was when one of us got hurt.) I was completely unprepared for the "D" he gave me for performance. I was so shocked I don't even recall what he ranked my attitude at but I am sure it wasn't much better. I had expected a "B" because, although I was lighter than most of the girls in my troop, I was fast and flexible.

"D!" I said in disbelief. "How can you justify that?"

I was confused and a little angry. I had just come from PT, where they had rated me in the top two percent of the troop. I certainly didn't expect to get a "D."

"You are too light," he said. "The average weight in your troop is 155 lbs. A fight comes down to weight, and you haven't got it."

I was in perfect condition for my height and frame. If I gained the forty pounds he felt I needed, I would be fat. We clearly had what the Force refers to as, a "personality conflict"--a great big personality conflict. He thought I was useless and I thought he was a jerk, but I had the bigger problem, because personality conflicts in the Force are always resolved in favour of the higher-ranked member. That is the nature of military organizations: sergeant vs. constable--checkmate.

Because I took his assessment personally, it wounded me emotionally. I struggled to keep the tears from beginning to well in my eyes. If I continued to challenge him, he would never change his mind and I might lose control and cry. This was one man to whom I would never show a sign he would interpret as female weakness.

We glared briefly at each other and I left. Later that night I brooded on the exchange. I was as angry at myself as I was at the sergeant. I should not have been taken by surprise, especially by him. I was equally dissatisfied by my response to the situation. Any male in my situation would have turned that anger back on the sergeant and confronted him. But what did I do? In an all-too-female reaction, I turned my anger inward and was in danger of imploding.

Perhaps I did deserve the "D"--not for my physical self-defence abilities, but for my lack of emotional control. It was an enigma to me how I had easily learned to remain emotionally detached from the taunts and insults of other instructors, yet could be so wounded by a sergeant I didn't even like. I resolved to learn to do what males did instinctively: to react with an offense rather than a defence, to always keep my guard up, never back down, and never let them see you cry.

As the months progressed, the range of our scores began to spread. I was one of the more competent shots.

Shooting is really not rocket science. It is simply a matter of concentration, trigger control, and lots of repetition--"muscle memory."

We wore earmuffs to protect our eardrums from the echo that amplified the volleys of shots inside the indoor range and had safety glasses to protect our eyes. Everyone on the "line" had to be equipped with safety equipment, safety glasses, and earmuffs before the corporal could give the order to fire. You could taste the lead in the air by the end of the first round of shots. The health hazards of inhaling lead were just starting to be monitored by the instructors.

The importance of mental concentration and performance was painfully illustrated one day on the range when one of my troop mates, Lorraine Rochon, failed to hit the paper target with even one shot at very close range. None of us knew until later that night that Lorraine's mother, who had been terminally ill with cancer, had passed away that day. The entire troop mourned with her. Her experience was a painful reminder that our lives outside Depot were continually changing. My older brother, the first of my siblings, got married two weeks after I began Depot, and I missed the wedding. Some members of our troop were engaged to be married when they arrived at Depot. All but one of those engagements had been broken by now.

Life was changing and so were we, as we became more confident and assertive. As we relaxed our emotional defences within the troop, more of our own unique personalities began to show. The earlier habit of calling everyone by his or her last name, as the NCOs did, was discontinued in favour of nicknames. These nicknames often evolved out of humorous incidents we encountered during Depot.

Sherry Stearns was "Bigfoot." Oddly enough the nickname had nothing to do with the size of her feet. She earned the name one history class when I noticed she had lost the battle with sleep. There she sat, head propped in hand, eyes glazed over, when Cpl. Alexander asked for the name of an Indian tribe. I whispered the answer, "Blackfoot," as I nudged her foot. She slowly became aware that the class and Cpl. Alexander had focused their attention on her.

"Blackfoot," I whispered again.

"Bigfoot," she responded, and it stuck.

Carol Ann Rose, a former psychologist and an old lady of twenty-eight, was "Mom." Katie Weigert was "Chomper." Her name referred to an unfortunate tendency she had to resort to biting when losing a ground fighting match. This made her an unpopular ground fighting partner but not the worst opponent our troop had to face. We started ground fighting against the males in the second semester. The smallest of the male recruits was at least as heavy as Sherry Stearns. For our troop, it was a great way to test our self-defence skills on men. The vast majority of criminal offenders are male. It was equally beneficial for the male recruits, who would occasionally be called on to physically restrain women. The goal was to control the opponent without using excessive force. "Excessive force" is a legal threshold police must always be mindful of. The law a uthorizes peace officers to use only as much force as is necessary to enforce the law or protect the lives of citizens or themselves. Recruits were expected to assess the threat level, then move to one level higher in force than the opponent to gain control of him or her. For example if the suspect were trying to escape, we would grab him. If he pulled away, we used come-along techniques; if he pulled a knife, we pulled a gun. "You don't bring a knife to a gunfight," was a bit of black humour we learned at Depot.

The fights against the male recruits did not involve simulated weapons. Their size advantage was enough. There was one move we might find necessary to use against a male opponent in the field that we would not use against recruits at Depot. It was always wise to put their minds at ease right up front that we would not be hitting (more like a punch, followed by a grab and a twist) below the belt.

There was some truth in the sergeant's assertion that a fight comes down to size. I needed every advantage to hold my own. I found two techniques that could level the field. If there were less than six inches and fifty pounds' difference in my opponent's size, the leverage an arm bar gave me could be quite effective, providing I was fast enough to take the opponent by surprise and get it on. If the recruit was bigger, and so many of them were, my only hope was a carotid artery restraint commonly but incorrectly referred to as a "choke." Even if I was lifted off my feet, they couldn't get it off quickly enough. The "choke" really is a great police move. In under a minute the fight is over, with minimum damage to either party because the hold disrupts the blood flow to the brain, not the oxygen to the lungs.

I was fast and flexible and the males always underestimated me. As strange as it may seem, my lack of stature was a great advantage to me. I gained a lot of confidence in those matches. Most of the time I was able to hold my own, but there was one match when I lost badly.

Matches always began with opponents sitting back to back on the mats. The recruit I was paired with (my sergeant's choice) was known for breaking the noses of his own troop mates. His first match, against Katie, had sent her straight to the Depot hospital with a neck injury. The recruit was eight inches taller and more than 100 pounds heavier than me. My only hope was to try and stay out of his grip for the two minutes of the match. Most people turn to the right, I decided to turn the opposite way, but my first and only strategy was flawed. I turned into a wall of muscle. I felt him pick me up and my feet never touched the floor again. He tossed me up and slammed me down like a rag doll and then continued to repeat the process. I lost track of what direction was up or down. It was excessive. So brutal, I later learned, one of his troop mates had to be physically restrained from coming on the mat to my rescue. I think the sergeant was his only fan. In the end, I survived--no broken bones, just a little battered and bruised.

We began our rifle training around this time. The indoor rifle range was very long, measuring 100 yards. The rifles were .308 calibre, with scopes. If your face was too close to the scope, the recoil would cut you between the eyebrows ("scope bite" in Depot jargon). We had been wondering, but didn't dare ask, what had caused the telltale injures on some of the senior male recruits.

The first position the instructors had us fire from was kneeling. Even though I did my best to brace for the impact, it blew me backward, out of my stance, against the rear wall. As my self-defence instructor would have pointed out, I could have used a little more weight in this situation as well! Mastering this weapon was going to require all the technique and physical strength I could muster. There is a fine line between getting your eye close enough to focus on the distant target but not so close as to get hit with the recoil. The rifle had to be buried tight in the shoulder and the whole body braced to absorb and defuse the recoil. Holding the heavy rifle horizontal and absolutely steady to complete the shooting cycle required upper body strength. The task required physical endurance and mental discipline.

One day at the range, I was unfocused and I didn't realize I had not put my earmuffs on as the line was called to order, and this went unnoticed by the instructor, who gave the order to fire. When I shot simultaneously with the other thirty rifles, the sound in the indoor range was deafening. I was so stunned that several others fired a second shot before the instructor halted the line.

"You won't do that again," he said.

He was right. My ears rang for many days after that. *Well, at least I never got a "scope bite,"* I thought. Little did I know then that the damage to my hearing was much worse.

As our life at Depot settled, people got comfortable with routines. One of the routines on a Friday or Saturday night included the constables' mess. The mess was located at the bottom of the mess hall directly across the street from our dorm. It was a safe place to relax, have a drink, and hear a song on the jukebox.

Troop 8 had noticed our pattern fairly early in our stay and always seemed to be there ahead of us. The men's collective troop personality was very pleasant and playful, almost a mirror of our own. They always seemed to rise above the stress of recruit training and have a good time. We would no sooner have taken our seats than one of their group would play the current hit song, "You Picked a Fine Time to Leave Me, Lucille." They didn't just play it on the jukebox; they would circle our table and serenade us in a very humorous, melodramatic fashion.

It begged for, and received, a response from our troop. There were a number of songs popular at the time you might think would appeal to our troop: "I am Woman/ Hear me Roar," "Hit the Road, Jack," "I'm Just as Bad as You," to name a few, but you would be wrong. The song we played and sang in kind was Tom Jones's, "Say You'll Stay until Tomorrow." It became a good-spirited ritual each time our troop arrived at the constables' mess.

Depot staff hoped the constables' mess would keep recruits from local watering holes in Regina, where the short-haired members were easy to pick out. Regina could be a very rough town. There was a large First Nations population on the streets, the descendants of warrior tribes.

Male recruits were unwelcome competition for the descendants of the settlers as well, at local bars, the hunting grounds of some local females. It was hard to outshine a man in uniform: an alpha male, a secure future, and a ticket out of town. Several bars were placed strictly out of bounds because of bar brawls.

Male Mounties may have been viewed as a good "catch" by the opposite sex, but female Mounties were not. If our occupation was divulged it, tended to dominate the conversation from that point on. Civilian males viewed us as curiosities or conquests.

Our troop had one advantage: no one suspected who we were and we didn't tell them. We became masters of evading the question or changing the topic as soon as someone asked, ". . . and what do you do?"

If someone pressed further, we often said we were government employees. That response always stopped further questioning, as they assumed we were clerks or secretaries.

Depot was the first place we noticed that our career choice might hinder our social calendar. The situation had no immediate impact on several of us, who were quite content to remain detached at Depot. The girls who did want to date were limited to recruits. Dating recruits posed its own set of problems, as my three romantic glockenspiel troop mates had already found out in the "unpolished welts affair," but they weren't the only ones.

One of our members who had been in what seemed to be an open, respectful relationship was forced to deal with the conflicting emotions of betrayal and sympathy, after learning her boyfriend's fiancée had been killed in a motor vehicle accident back home. Another, who was involved with a senior recruit, learned he got married the weekend after his graduation.

The worst betrayal by male recruits occurred in public, during an "interview and interrogation techniques" class. The instructor, after delivering the lecture portion of the class, asked for a volunteer to demonstrate interrogation techniques. I was amazed so many hands went up. I suppose the challenge of matching wits was intriguing. The "volunteer" never suspected it was a tasteless trap.

"How did you spend your weekend?" he began unexpectedly.

We watched in shock as the instructor, who clearly knew every detail of her romantic escapade with a recruit boyfriend, reduced her to tears. Every detail of the weekend was exposed in what seemed like an endless and sadistic performance.

It wasn't as though she was a sixteen-year-old caught in the back of her father's car. This was a twenty-four-year-old young woman whose reputation was being attacked. There was no justification for the shameful conduct of the instructor. It was exactly the type of situation our troop counsellor had cautioned us about, but that didn't make it right.

All the rest of us could do was to learn at the expense of my troop mate. We would have to be very careful whom we dated. The speed with which a vicious rumour could spread through the ranks was incredible. The males seemed completely oblivious to the double standard that allowed them to brag, with macho pride, about the same behaviour that destroyed a female's reputation. The young woman's conduct may have crossed Depot's sexual tolerances, but the instructor's conduct had crossed ours.

Very shortly after this occurrence, perhaps in a related incident, our dorm failed inspection. For the first and only time, we *all* lost our marching orders. It seemed the entire troop was under attack. Relegated to wearing fatigues and running shoes, we were feeling quite embattled when Shirley Miller, who always managed to put Depot crises in perspective, asked with her usual East Coast clarity, "What's the big deal? You don't have to polish running shoes." She was one of the younger, quieter members of the troop but old beyond her years. She didn't say much, but she was usually bang-on when she did. We survived the humiliation of fatigues and running shoes for one week before our status was restored.

The weather had turned so cold by mid-October that pencils were required when writing outside because the ink froze in our pens. Our troop was getting restless and began spending weekends off base. That Thanksgiving weekend, almost everyone left. My group of pranksters, Vivienne, Kathy, Mom, Joyce, Brenda, Candy, and myself, remained. Our group had been responsible for the majority of the practical jokes to date. Most of them were uncomplicated, like jumping out unexpectedly from a closet or grabbing an unsuspecting ankle from under a troop mate's bed. There was even an unsolved hanging of "Preacher Mo's" cookie monster in our common room.

This time, we wanted to do something a little more challenging, engaging the whole troop--a devious, hilarious prank to greet them as they returned from the weekend away. The first stop everyone always made was the washroom. We created a life-sized dummy from green garbage bags stuffed with crumpled newspaper in a pair of our issue overalls and propped it up in the third toilet stall. The finishing touches of orange rubber gloves, boots, a hat, and a false face perfected our illusion. The first two empty stalls were locked. All night and through the next morning, we listened: first came the steps of a returning member, then the sound of one then two thuds as she encountered the locked stalls, and finally a blood-curdling scream. The startled recruits weren't annoyed for long. They quickly joined our conspiracy and delighted at scream after scream. One of the victims even took it upon herself to improve upon the design by adding a male appendage to the dummy. The set-up was so good, the next morning, half-awake, I forgot our mischief of the night before and even gave myself a start! Everyone enjoyed the joke.

Humour is one of the safest and most effective ways to deal with stress. Members could find humour even in the subtlest of circumstances through their intuitive understanding of the unspoken emotional language. Members read people the way people read books. The hardest people to read were other members. Only members knew how to read through another member's wall. It was one of the natural abilities recruiters looked for, one in which studies have suggested females may have a genetic advantage, an ability that was being honed as well at Depot. By the halfway point, it was almost as though at times we could read the minds of our instructors--all except for Cpl. Roulx. Only once was he taken off-guard enough for our troop to see the man behind the wall.

Cpl. Roulx had spent the first three months of Depot badgering Sherry Stearns to stand up straight. Posture is very important in conveying authority in uniform. Sherry, who had been over six feet since the age of twelve and now stood close to six feet two, had spent most of her life slouching. It was understandable that Sherry was self-conscious about her height. If a man were tall, there was an implied genetic, macho, superiority announcing someone whom you had to look up to. An exceptionally tall woman, on the other hand, could make men feel inadequate.

I am not sure if the reason Sherry finally began to straighten up was entirely the result of Cpl. Roulx's badgering, or the six-foot-five recruit my friends and I noticed her walking with down the streets of Regina one Saturday afternoon. They seemed completely oblivious to the stolen glances of those who passed; such a regal, handsome couple of young giants.

The amazing thing was that the next day in drill class when Sherry stood taller, the whole troop felt taller. Cpl. Roulx didn't notice the metamorphosis until he finished, as he always did, the individual troop inspection with Sherry. Out of the corners of our eyes we watched Cpl. Roulx's gaze begin at her shoes, slowly, routinely, systematically moving up as he searched for poor polishing or wrinkles, until it ended with Sherry's looking slightly down to meet Cpl. Roulx's cool blue eyes. Even in his high browns, he was the one looking up, quite possibly for the first time, to a woman. The exchange cracked his stoic, stony expression enough to reveal a twitch under his mustache as he contemplated the bittersweet results of his success. It was a fleeting yet defining moment for everyone present before the wall returned and troop nine's Pygmalion disappeared behind it once more.

Cpl. Roulx became very proud of our personal and professional development and the attention it garnered. Sometimes newly arrived recruits were directed to attend and watch "Roulx's Angels." One of the other drill corporals, who had a sleazy disposition, viewed our troop through very different eyes. This tall, arrogant instructor, "Cpl. Highbrowns," had a very uncomfortable way of leering at female members. Given any opportunity, he loved to "bug" us. "Bug" in today's jargon translates into harassment. He was even bold enough, while marching on parade, to lewdly whisper to female members he fancied, "Do you want to hold hands?" We did our best to ignore and avoid him. Through rumours, we were aware that he seemed incapable of maintaining a stable relationship with females in his private life. This behavioural indicator was the first piece I collected in trying to solve the puzzle of harassment.

When Cpl. Roulx took leave during our pass-out (preparation for graduation) exercises, Cpl. Highbrowns volunteered to take his place. It was a minor challenge of our professionalism to remain emotionally neutral as he strutted about; one we easily met.

On his final day, we were practising receiving our badges to a junior troop audience. Cpl. Highbrowns relished his role as the OIC. We took turns marching forward and halting face to face with him for a quick salute, after which he presented our badges; then we marched back to our troop ranks. The exercise was going flawlessly, and the drill hall echoed with the sound of our firm, precise, footsteps, until it was my turn. I marched forward, halted, saluted, and received my badge, when to my surprise, the corporal bent down low, to a point where he was literally face to face with me, and returned my salute. He intended a cheap joke at my expense, but I had the last laugh. My expression remained unchanged as I finished my salute, turned, and raised my left foot high, then, brought it down, *aiming for his boots.* If he had not jumped back at the last moment, I would have scraped my heel the length of his gleaming high browns, destroying years of "spit polish." The audience laughed as he regained composure.

I couldn't resist a quick glance back and a flashed Mona Lisa smile at the corporal as he looked up, just to let him know my actions had been deliberate. I didn't care and fully expected to be called into the corps sergeant major's office for my behaviour; but I wasn't. Completely by accident, I had stumbled upon an effective defence strategy within the Force--although it would take me years to recognize when I had enough ammunition to fight back within the system.

Cpl. Highbrowns was worried that I would go on the record to his superiors with the truth. Truth and justice were held in even higher esteem than rank in the Force. I had more to complain about than him, and he had more to lose than me. If I went on the record and made a case for a "conduct unbecoming an officer" charge in service court, the next promotion Cpl. Highbrowns was already coveting could be delayed for five years. Promotion boards rely on the last five years of performance evaluations or A26s in making their decisions.

Corporal Highbrowns had to "tap out." It didn't take much weight to make Cpl. Highbrowns back up. Too bad the self-defence staff sergeant wasn't watching to see me beginning to learn how to use the little weight I had effectively.

Our days as Troop 9 were coming to an end. Groupings within the RCMP are transitory in nature. They all follow the same three-step pattern: storming (establishing position in the group), forming (becoming a unit with common purpose and identity), and mourning (grieving for the inevitable breakup of the team). "Storming" better describes the jockeying for position that the alpha males engage in. In true female form, we "jelled." We had arrived nearly six months earlier, strangers from coast to coast, with little more than a common goal to unite us. Depot gave us a sense of community, pride, and identity that would survive a lifetime.

The news of our division posting marked the beginning of the third stage. For some of us, it wasn't just the loss of the troop that gave reason to mourn. Nadeau, the commissioner we had engaged back in June, had retired that summer, and Commissioner Simmons had taken over. Simmons reinstituted the old policy of not posting recruits to their home divisions for the first five years of service. The reintroduction of the old policy caused a major change in the expectations of many of my troop mates. We may all have signed an engagement agreement to serve anywhere in Canada, but clearly some of us had hoped to return home.

We had a staffing interview a month prior to the postings. One of the first things we heard about Staffing was not to trust them.

"If you tell them where you *don't* want to go, they will send you there," was a well-circulated rumour at Depot.

"Where would you like to be posted?" asked the staffing NCO.

"I agreed to go anywhere in Canada when I joined," I said cautiously.

"So you wouldn't mind a Prairie posting?" he asked coyly. Apparently my dislike of the flat, waterless landscape of Saskatchewan was more commonly known than I had realized.

"I am sure there are some nice places in Saskatchewan; I just haven't found them yet," I said. My attempt at diplomacy caused the staffing NCO to smile before he laid his cards on the table.

"Three of your troop are going to remain on the Prairies. If you don't want to be one of them, tell me now and forget that old rumour about Staffing. You can trust me." I decided to follow my instincts and pleaded: "For God's sake, don't leave me on the Prairies. I have never felt so landlocked in my life. I know I can't go back to the Great Lakes, but please put me where I can see some real water. Either coast is fine by me."

"You'll be glad you trusted me," he said. Then he left me with a parting piece of wisdom, years ahead of my service level or understanding: "Never think you are indispensable to the Force. Stick your hand in a bucket of water, then pull it out and see what kind of hole you leave behind. That is the hole you'll make the day you leave the Force."

A man who understood water! I knew I was right to trust him, and he did his best to accommodate my wishes and those of most of the troop. The transfer list was posted the following week, and British Columbia, the province with the largest coastline in Canada, was next to my name. Most of the girls were equally satisfied, but one of my troop mates, transferred to Newfoundland, was not. Apparently people from Nova Scotia did not consider "The Rock" as part of the Maritimes.

As unhappy as she was with her posting to Newfoundland, Brenda MacFarlane was happy to be that close to her desired posting in Labrador. Unfortunately, the new bilingual policies of the federal government were not initially beneficial to the francophones, and the two remaining troop mates from Quebec had not scored well enough on the language exam to serve in a bilingual province like Quebec.

Ironically, Vivienne Stewart, a French major and the only "tested" bilingual member of Troop 9, was sent to Quebec, even though she had wanted to remain in the West. That was another unofficial Depot lesson; make sure it's to your advantage before you volunteer to be tested.

Within a couple of weeks, I received my specific detachment posting, to North Vancouver, from within my new division, and I confess I was a little worried. Vancouver was the third largest city in Canada, and I was anything but a city girl. Linda, on the other hand, was getting her mind around Duncan Detachment, a small town on Vancouver Island. We both thought we would have been happier with each other's postings.

I sent a CPIC message (similar to today's e-mail) to my new detachment to say hi. A radio dispatcher answered immediately with a very warm, "Welcome aboard, get out your gumboots. We are entering rainy season."

Everyone in the troop seemed quite happy with the responses they received from their new postings. We were aware that detachment commanders had been put on notice after a female recruit from an earlier troop had been sent a rude response to her initial CPIC. We were aware, even expected, that we could encounter negative attitudes. It was hardly a secret. One NCO's letter in *Pony Express* (an RCMP national newsletter) complained that he had been forced to take a female member, and now she was pregnant. He demanded the member be taken to "service court" and charged under the RCMP Act (a disciplinary act for members of the RCMP) for either the charge of "conduct unbecoming," or under the section dealing with self-inflicted wounds.

"How could pregnancy be self-inflicted?" I joked; but it didn't defuse the tension. Some of us would face tougher postings than others. The reality of getting ready to move kept us from thinking too long or hard about negative possibilities.

While most of us were wondering about our new homes, trainers, and detachments, a few of the troop members were already fantasizing about their move into specialized sections. Specialized sections were highly competitive. I thought they were getting a little too far ahead of themselves. All recruits were expected to serve at least two years, more reasonably five, in General Duty, before specializing. The first female to be selected for specialized postings would be groundbreaking within the Force.

Jacqui Olsen, a young athletic member, wanted to be on dog section. Joan Merk, a teacher from a farming background, wanted to be on the Musical Ride. Joyce Graham wanted to be on drug squad. Two out of the three achieved their career goals.

I even had a secret goal of my own. As much as I disliked the Prairies, I thought it would be important to have female instructors at Depot. However, that would be at least ten years in the future, and I didn't want to get too far ahead of myself.

The last month was a bit of a blur. Our final assessments were given. I scored well in all the subjects except, of course, for a marginal pass in self-defence. The second time around, I expected nothing more. No one should ever be able to surprise someone twice. It wasn't my highest ratings that gave me the greatest satisfaction, but my "B" in swimming. It was not a gift that I actually achieved a Bronze Medallion level at the end. I had pushed myself harder both physically and emotionally in that class than any other; at the end, I had mastered the course and grown as an individual because of it. That was really what Depot was all about--a personal endurance test that united and bound the Force together as a powerful, proud, efficient unit, capable of things far greater than any of us could achieve as individuals.

Finally, Troop number 9 was added to the plaque in the drill hall to denote our status as senior troop. We held that honour for the week prior to graduation. During that time, a new female troop (Troop 20) arrived. We were proud to know that our troop had helped pave the way for acceptance. We had done our part; now it was up to them to carry the ball.

Our families arrived in Regina for the pass-out ceremonies in the first week of December 1977. The day of our graduation was so cold even block heaters couldn't get most of the cars going. Those of us not from the Prairies were happy with our postings out. The families were treated to demonstrations of each of our physical classes. Sunday morning, we hosted a mass in the Depot church, the oldest building in Regina. Later, there was a formal dinner and dance in the drill hall. During Superintendent Mills's final speech, he spoke very positively about our abilities and training and his confidence that we would meet the challenges that lay ahead with skill and dignity. It was a comforting standard message that he tempered with the reality of our unique situation. He openly admitted he did not know what lay ahead of our troop. Females in the RCMP were simply too new a phenomenon. Troop 9 was only the fifth all-female troop to graduate.

"We can't tell you what your daughters will face. We don't know. They will be charting new ground. All we can say is they are well-trained, and we trust they will succeed."

We all were prepared to take a leap of faith to chart virgin social territory. It was exciting and frightening at the same time. We had no way of knowing who among us would be welcomed, who would be merely tolerated, and who would be shot within the next few weeks.

Chapter 4

Constance Who?

Graduation from Depot allowed me to escape the landlocked, monotonous prairie landscape. I was destined for my first posting, North Vancouver, which would take me to the farthest western reaches of mainland Canada; but not before I returned to Wolfe Island for a quick visit.

December in Ontario seemed remarkably warm after Regina. The Island hadn't changed--only my perception of it. Now that I was no longer threatened by the day-to-day peace and stability of the Island, I was beginning to appreciate it; not enough to give rise to any reassessment of my future, only enough to spark a vague understanding of why some could be content to "settle" on the Island.

My decision to join Linda Butler in a drive to the West Coast in the dead of winter was unknowingly reckless because I hadn't yet begun to understand how big or different Canada really was.

Linda's 1968 Polaris, weighted down with everything she owned, handled so badly I wondered if we had exceeded the weight recommendations for the vehicle; although it would have been hard to tell with any certainty, considering the icy road conditions.

I had no idea Ontario was so wide. It took three days just to get to Kenora. The prairies meant another three days of driving in blowing snow before we reached Calgary, where we got our first view of the Rockies. I wondered how many more Eastern Canadians were as unaware as I of the breathtaking splendour of the untamed, untainted West, which rose before us. The Appalachian "Mountains" in the East, worn down and rounded by the ravages of time, hardly deserved to share the geological classification as mountains.

The mountain roads were the most dangerous part of our trek, providing two more days of treacherous winter driving through the most beautiful landscape in the world, leaving me both relieved and saddened when we finally reached the horizontal landscape of the Fraser Valley. The lush, green fields took me completely by surprise. Why didn't I know part of Canada could remain green all year round? My troop mates had been right about my limited, centralist view of Canada. I didn't understand how fresh and different the West was, but that was about to change.

It felt surreal, after battling the harsh Canadian winter, to reach so unexpected an oasis. I felt like Dorothy when she emerged from the woods to see the Emerald City.

Later that afternoon, I reported to North Vancouver Detachment, two days ahead of my posting date. A pleasant civilian front desk receptionist informed me that my watch was working as she ushered me into the NCO's office to meet my new sergeant.

The NCO's office was strategically located a stride away from both the front desk and the radio room. The office walls were glass to facilitate the visual monitoring of the interior movements in the detachment. A radio scanner and dispatch microphone sat on the NCO's desk. Nothing happened on the watch without the watch commander's knowledge and, if warranted, direction; nothing of importance, anyway.

My sergeant was a large man who managed a cheery grin even with a pipe clenched in the corner of his mouth. He had a genuine chuckle in his voice as he welcomed me to the watch. It sounds strange, but he reminded me of Santa Claus. Sergeant Santa could see we were tired from the drive and directed the corporal to show us to the motel on Capilano Road.

The next day, Linda continued on to Vancouver Island to become the first female member at Duncan Detachment. That afternoon, the most senior female member stationed at North Vancouver, Cathy Robertson, arrived at my door to help me get oriented to the city and introduced to the detachment.

Cathy, a member of the third female troop in the Force, was the first female member posted to North Vancouver. She was only twenty-one, an obvious extravert, and very happy to show me around and share her experiences and insights.

North Vancouver was a very positive, progressive detachment that had more female members--six, counting me--than even some divisions. There were fewer than 150 female members coast to coast at the time.

The officer in charge of the detachment was very open to new ideas in policing and obviously felt it would be beneficial, or at least worth an experiment, to have one female member in each of the six zones into which North Vancouver was broken up.

The lower mainland detachments, the only big city policing responsibility of the RCMP, needed to be creative to modify the policing model used in small towns to fit big city issues. Zone policing was used as a tool to break up a large city into smaller quadrants.

North Vancouver's six zones each had their own distinct characteristics.

Deep Cove was a sleepy, established bedroom community just northwest of the Second Narrows Bridge stretching along the Burrard Inlet, containing both Mount Seymour, an active ski mountain in the winter and hiking paradise in the other months, and the Dollarton Native Reserve.

The reserve was quiet most of the time, except for the occasional cougar call, or when the residents decided to exercise their land rights by blocking the Dollarton highway in a passive, symbolic protest. During those times, the public used the alternate route of the Mount Seymour Parkway.

Lynne Valley Zone, a newer bedroom community, was anything but sleepy. It was a busy zone on the cusp of an emerging and growing social order of two working parents. The double income meant the houses were fancier, but the youth problems were proportionately larger as well. Break and enters (B&E's in police jargon), car thefts, wilful damage, and large, sometimes riotous, parties on weekends were the order of the day in Lynne Valley.

City North and *City South* Zones were geographically smaller but had the highest call volume because they were more densely populated and contained the majority of the businesses and bars.

The busiest of the two zones was City South, which had a rough "white man's" bar one block east of Lonsdale Avenue on 3rd Street, and the First Nations equivalent one block west. Of the two, the white man's bar was the roughest, often erupting with bar fights spilling into the parking lot.

City South was the location of a second native reserve, whose primary problems appeared to be poverty and alcoholism. It seemed contradictory to see these social problems surrounded by some of the most expensive land in the country. The natives on this reserve were not violent by nature; they were very respectful of authority and had a deep sense of community.

The most affluent zone in North Vancouver was *Capilano* ("Cap"), a large bedroom community of upper middle income families north of the Trans-Canada highway. The parents who lived in Capilano could afford nannies or private schools to fill the void of reduced parenting. Most of the time the zone was quiet, but occasionally a riotous party would occur when Mom and Dad were out of the country. Normally, the most exciting thing that happened in this zone was the occasional bear or cougar that wandered down the ravine corridors that followed the many mountain streams down to the inlet. The most common crime was B&E.

It was possible to get a little lost in the twisty streets on the mountainside north of the Number 1 Highway, which sliced through the city, but nature had built in some hints for newcomers like me to help avoid the embarrassing position of admitting being lost to the dispatcher. "Just point your car downhill and find a street with a yellow line. Only through streets have yellow lines, and downhill will lead you out," Cathy advised.

Pemberton, my zone, was the best of all the zones in North Vancouver. Pemberton was responsible for the sulphur wharves in the south, the business community of car dealerships and Capilano Mall that lined the four-lane Marine Drive, as well as the small bedroom community of Pemberton Heights. We even had a slightly problematic bar. Pemberton had a little of everything, providing a great variety of work without being overwhelming.

Pemberton provided backup for the three neighbouring zones of City South, City North, and Capilano. As a "backup" you got to attend exciting calls without being responsible for the follow-up or paperwork.

Pemberton zone also had the strong, complementary, management team of a pleasant sergeant and a no-nonsense staff sergeant. I felt truly lucky to have been assigned to Pemberton, even if it was by default.

Adrienne Moncrief, the fifth female member to arrive at North Vancouver, had been slated to go to Pemberton Zone; however, since Pemberton's corporal had so strongly opposed a female addition to the zone, she was reassigned to Capilano. Their corporal, Bush Halpenny, had no qualms about female members. He often joked that in his last posting, the only member he couldn't beat in a fight, he married--resulting in one of the first marriages between members still serving in the Force. (Anyone who knew Gladys was never sure if it was a joke or reality.) The marriage resulted in a transfer to LMD (lower mainland) because in Staffing's mind, LMD was better equipped to handle the new reality of members married to other members. There, husbands and wives could work in separate city detachments but still share a common household.

My corporal's dislike for female members was such an open secret that my colleagues went out of their way to assure me the chain of command would not tolerate unfair treatment. I correctly deduced there wasn't any reason for this corporal's attitude to worry me, with so many members already "watching my back."

North Vancouver was an extraordinary workplace: happy, busy, and creative. It is hard to overstate the role of detachment commander in setting this tone of empowerment, particularly when dealing with a rapidly changing social and political climate.

The pace of social change at the most fundamental level of society, the family, was nothing short of revolutionary. North Vancouver adapted to accommodate rapidly changing policing demands without compromising the principles and highest standards expected by the Force for service delivery. Other large LMD detachments, such as Burnaby and Surrey, were struggling with the task while North Vancouver Detachment learned to dance.

The stage had been set by the previous superintendent, whose laid-back policing approach began the groundwork for the transition of the traditional military disposition of the RCMP to the empowerment of the constable and NCO ranks.

An example of the contrast in management styles at other LMD detachments arose one legendary occasion when the superintendent of Burnaby called North Vancouver to complain that he had witnessed one of North Vancouver's members not wearing the uniform hat in Burnaby Detachment's parking lot. He was shocked when instead of being assured that the member would be disciplined, North Vancouver's superintendent responded by saying, "I don't think half my members know where their hats are!"

To a civilian, the matter of wearing hats may seem trivial, but in a national organization so authoritative in nature and centralized in its command structure that it would not allow its members to change from summer to winter uniform until the commissioner in Ottawa decided it was cold enough, this was huge.

When Superintendent D.K. Wilson arrived in North Vancouver, he continued on with the relaxed, supportive atmosphere that fostered the creation of new and highly effective policing techniques. While Burnaby struggled with low morale, member breakdowns, and the occasional suicide, North Vancouver achieved the highest "clearance rate" of any detachment in the lower mainland.

"Clearance rate" was a term denoting the ratio of reported crimes to solved crimes. It was a simple mathematical way of keeping score on who was winning, the police or the criminals. Every crime was reported back then, and all were investigated. The Canadian public and the Force not only expected its members to fight all crime without fear of favour, they expected us to win the battle against lawbreakers. North Vancouver Detachment inspired winners.

The average service level in North Vancouver Detachment was a mere three years, and the majority of constables were in their early twenties. As junior constables, we created our own community of young, energetic workers. We needed that energy and peer support because working in large cosmopolitan areas was like an immersion course in policing. Within three years, members in LMD Detachment would encounter a greater variety and faster pace of police work than anywhere else in the country.

It was soon obvious that the stigma Depot had attached to LMD had been created by instructors with only small-town policing experience and no appreciation for city policing. Rather than being the "armpit of the Force," LMD policing was exciting, varied, and innovative. The hectic pace of work left no time for petty politics and was the perfect setting to take a chance on new policing concepts such as female members.

The detachment was strategically located on the northwest corner of 13th and St. Georges Streets, directly across from the fire department and the Lions Gate Hospital. The courthouse was on the second floor of the detachment.

The large apartment complexes that lined St. Georges were often occupied by members who preferred to walk to work. One of these apartment buildings, aptly nicknamed "Stetson Heights," became my first home in North Vancouver. The landlady was a huge fan of the RCMP and spent evenings monitoring police frequencies on her scanner. It surprised me that so many people, just ordinary citizens, monitored our work.

Each member had a distinctive style when responding to and later summing up the essence of the call. This often led to entertaining exchanges between members peppered with dry, often brilliant, flashes of humour. In an unexpected way, members became something like radio personalities to this group of civilian fans.

However, they weren't the only ones listening in. We were constantly cognizant of the necessity to guard our conversations from media looking for breaking news to rush to, criminals listening for their cue to exit, and the station NCO if we began to sound unprofessional. Fortunately, station NCOs are operational and less likely to "sweat the small stuff."

Luckily, North Vancouver Detachment was too small to support a non-operational radio room corporal. Non-operational or administrative positions within the RCMP were the equivalent of being benched on a football team. Burnaby had a rather notorious nitpicker in that position, the type of person who seized every opportunity to pounce on any member he could to compensate for his own feelings of inadequacy. One evening, at the end of a high-speed chase, a member caught in the adrenalin rush said the "F" word on the radio. The air was pregnant with an immediate silence as everyone cringed in anticipation of the radio room's "little man" response.

"The member who made the last transmission, identify himself."

The only answer was deafening silence.

"The member who made the transmission, identify himself immediately!" The command was repeated.

Perhaps the "little man" was getting excited but the operational members were beginning to relax, realizing the uniformity of their voices had camouflaged the identity of the offending member. The final response was a perfect illustration of how quick wits could snatch a decisive victory from an impending defeat. In an act of defiance, punctuated with humour, the radio silence was shattered by the question, "Are you fucking crazy?"

Despite the radio room corporal's best efforts, he remained the only person on the air that night who never discovered the identity of the offender.

Fortunately, that exchange occurred prior to the implementation of a radio computer system called Computer Aided Dispatch, or CAD for short. The new system automatically identified the police car when the member keyed the microphone. CAD did more than track a member's status on a computer printout; it replaced the complaint form, minimizing police time required for paperwork and maximizing policing. North Vancouver was policing paradise!

The Ten Code, the old-fashioned police radio abbreviation system that assigned numerical values to various common police situations such as unauthorized listeners or coffee break, was still used to communicate with other members when on portable. The code that got everyone's attention and adrenalin rushing was a call of 10-33: "Member in danger--help me, quick!"

Adrenalin rushes are a way of life for emergency workers. The hormonal response to danger produces extra energy and power for the famous "flight or fight" response. Members instinctively react with the "fight" response; fortunately, the majority of the offenders react the opposite way.

Adrenalin fuelled a lot of foot chases and allowed the suspect to run a little faster and farther than normal. Chases almost always came down to an endurance test. No wonder they had us run that ten-mile route at the end of training. If, however, the "fight" response were triggered, the suspect could be expected to have greater strength and endurance and a reduced pain response.

However, it was not adrenalin's effect on the suspect that posed the greatest danger to peace officers. The amount of adrenalin experienced in the role plays at Depot was just a warm-up for recruit field training, because only in the field, when your life is truly at risk, would the rush of the hormone unload in sufficient quantities to paralyze or energize muscles and brain functions. How a recruit responded to the first life-or-death situation in the field would be the most accurate measure of his or her suitability for the Force. If a recruit were "lucky," he or she would experience that situation at least once while on recruit field training and in the company of seasoned members.

Recruit field training (RFT) consisted of a mandatory six months' on-the-job experience immediately following Depot. RFT was an internship under the supervision of an experienced member where the skills learned at Depot were practised in the field. It was also a time to teach recruits the law specific to the province and town to which the recruit had been transferred.

Law classes at Depot focused on the "Criminal Code," the common legal denominator throughout Canada. Individual provinces had the authority and responsibility to draft laws and provincial statutes in areas such as the Motor Vehicle Act or the Government Liquor Act. Municipalities had the power to enact minor by-laws such as parking restrictions and noise by-laws.

The RCMP was in a position to offer contracts to provinces to provide access to well-trained and well-equipped peace officers at a financially attractive rate because the federal government bore the cost of the infrastructure for recruitment and basic training. It was an offer eight out of the ten provinces could not refuse. Through these provincial contracts, municipalities and townships had the opportunity to choose to strike smaller contracts to provide city or town policing rather than creating their own city or town police. Even British Columbia and Newfoundland, which joined Canada after 1900 and already had provincial police forces, saw the economic and professional benefits in contracting with the RCMP for day-to-day policing and allowed their provincial forces to be absorbed into the RCMP.

In the contract provinces, the RCMP's GD (general duty) members, the GPs (general practitioners) of the policing world, answered the public's call for help, whether it was a barking dog or a murder. The RCMP was responsible for maintaining the security and peace of their communities. Through this relationship, the Canadian public developed an intimate understanding and trust for the RCMP. This relationship was true in all but the two richest and most populous provinces, Ontario and Quebec; these provinces retained their own provincial police forces.

General duty, the most difficult police role to do well, seldom gets the respect it deserves, even within the Force. General duty members are dispatched to rapidly changing and unknown situations with little information and no opportunity to obtain more and are tasked to assess, defuse, contain, and survive. High call volume twenty-four hours per day, during every eight-hour shift, is the backdrop against which GD members make life-altering decisions on a daily basis--the perfect environment to train a recruit.

RFT was the most important experimental phase in the integration of females into policing, the success of which did not solely rest on the members, but with the public and criminals as well.

Trainers often have a profound effect on a recruit's developing policing style, an effect which was enhanced when the recruit and trainer shared similar dispositions and size. The system had worked well for the men for over one hundred years.

We female recruits presented several challenges to the Recruit Field Training concept because we were too different in size and disposition to simply copy what the men did, nor did we want to; many of us felt if we abandoned our nature in order to succeed by simply copying men, it would have been a betrayal, even a defeat, on the most fundamental level of the women's movement.

The greatest challenge for early female members was the lack of female role models. Developing a successful female policing style was virgin territory and a critical test in which the social evolutionary stakes were much broader than simply female competency in policing. If we females could do one of the toughest traditionally male jobs, on our own terms, then we could do any job. This was a high-profile experiment with very fundamental social consequences.

My trainer, Stew Mcleod, was a very senior constable with ten years' experience, a little over the preferred service level, but he already had experience training a female. He was a large man, six feet two and about 220 pounds, a weightlifter and marathon runner. An injury--a broken arm--that he had suffered while arm wrestling spoke volumes about his character as well as his physical conditioning. The bone had broken, unable to take the strain of his muscles locked in a prolonged stalemate position, in a competition with another member in which neither would yield. He had pale grey eyes and a voice so low it seemed to come out of his toes. He reminded me of the actor Jack Palance--physically, and by his laid-back, confident demeanour.

We had only one shift together before he left for a three-week vacation with his family. It was just time enough to discover what he liked and disliked in recruits. He did not like excitable members who could escalate confrontations; or who took unnecessary chances in driving or entered into avoidable confrontations. Both of these actions, in his opinion, reflected bad planning and personal shortcomings. Like most big members who had nothing to prove, my trainer saw no glory in fighting.

"I have only been in one fight in my entire service," he told me, "and that was a little guy. The worst thing was, I couldn't really hit him because it would have looked excessive, but he didn't mind hitting me. I couldn't even charge him with assaulting a peace officer or resisting arrest because a judge would have looked at the size difference and shook his head."

Neither of those charges were common back then because a certain amount of "street justice" kept the courts unburdened with incidents better dealt with immediately and informally. This policy all but eliminated the likelihood of the offences in the first place.

Stew believed most persons being arrested would comply if the member took the time to explain why it was happening and what would happen next. "If they don't look like they are going to comply, keep talking till the backup arrives. Just the sight of another police car will probably gain their co-operation. If they still want to fight, at least they have been given every opportunity to avoid a little pain."

I knew I was going to like my trainer.

Fellow zone members Billy Thorardson and Chris Bomford were assigned to take turns riding with me until my trainer returned from the Caribbean. Billy was the senior of the two, with almost three years' service.

Starting work three thousand miles from home, one week before Christmas, was a bit of a bummer, but everyone in the Detachment went out of their way to keep my spirits up. On our first evening shift, during a lull in the complaints, Billy drove down and parked our police car under the Lions Gate Bridge at the mouth of the Burrard Inlet.

The view was breathtakingly beautiful: the water looked like glass, mirroring the sparkling lights of one of the world's most beautiful skylines. There I was, as far west as I could be on the mainland of Canada from Wolfe Island, but still I was never far from Burrard Inlet, which emptied into an even larger body of water than the Great Lakes, the Pacific Ocean. Superficially so much had changed, and yet on a fundamental level, very little.

The landscape may have been more developed and more visually spectacular, but the water's tides and currents continued on unaffected and unaware, in an ebb and flow that settled my mind and comforted the very essence of my soul. How did Billy know that this spot would be so familiar and comforting to me?

Actually, he didn't, as I soon realized when the reason we had parked announced itself within minutes of our arrival.

The sound of Christmas Carols intruded into my thoughts. I was amazed to see a flotilla of private boats decorated with Christmas lights travelling up the river in formation and projecting out Christmas music over the water as they went along. This wonderful, non-traditional way to celebrate the season was my first clue that life in Western Canada was a little more laid-back, a little more creative, and a lot different than anyone in the East seemed to understand. There seemed to be a certain playful irreverence for the strict traditions and institutions of the past in which the East had remained mired.

Billy and Chris enjoyed the job and each other as they focused on the "shit rats" (criminal element), or just "rats" for short. In the lull between assigned files, the police had the discretion and the responsibility to be proactive by creating self-generated files. Relying on the sixth sense, often referred to as police intuition or gut instinct, routine vehicle checks almost always netted outstanding warrants, drugs, and stolen property.

Self-generated files were a source of pride and competition within the detachment. This intuition should never be confused with the later American invention of "profiling." There were far more variables taken into account. It had nothing to do with stereotypes and everything to do with highly developed almost unconscious observational skills, along with an understanding of human nature in combination with the confidence and mandate to trust and act on instinct.

Not every stop reaped an arrest, but nearly every stop involved a person with a criminal record. The information from these stops was recorded, including the vehicle used and associates present, and forwarded to our plainclothes section and division headquarters, where the information could prove useful and occasionally critical to solving major crimes at a future time.

The checks were also an effective deterrent to potential criminal activity. There was an unspoken dialogue between the "FPSers" (referring to someone with a fingerprint/criminal record) and the peace officer sharp enough to check him. (Note that I am not being politically incorrect. It was very unusual to deal with a woman in a conflict with the law in those days. The past twenty-five years of equality seem to have earned females a greater percentage in criminal activity--not exactly one of the initial goals in the women's movement.)

The criminal element does not like being watched; they left the area for less patrolled streets. If the message wasn't clear enough in the first check to move them on, after the second or third check in as many blocks, by different members, they usually got the picture. Harassment? Perhaps; but selectively so, with the sole purpose of keeping our area safe for the public. The criminals rarely complained, because those were the rules of the game back then, a game in which everyone knew his or her role.

The public expected the police to maintain the peace and keep the streets safe. The communities and the courts had confidence in the police to use their discretionary powers wisely to protect them without bringing "the administration of justice into disrepute."

I was amazed at the accuracy of the members in identifying a "good check" but found they were unable to articulate what they had observed that tipped them off. They often said "it just didn't look right" or "it didn't feel right." Police intuition was critical to good policing. The safety of members on the road seemed to me to be a skill based in part on continuous observation that flagged the smallest change in surroundings while on patrol--part emotional intelligence and part information retrieval.

Two primary sources of information were the briefings that began each shift in the constable's room, where the incoming shift was told what had occurred on the previous shift. The second source of information was the monitoring of all the calls dispatched throughout the city. The information was stored in memory until something in the routine patrol was matched. It was a little intimidating to watch seasoned members achieve this complex multi-tasking with seemingly little effort, but I hoped I could develop the skill--after all, females were supposed to be natural multi-taskers.

There was, however, another basic police skill of equal importance I needed to develop that would be more of a challenge because it was a skill that the male brain was usually better at. General duty members had to quickly assess exploding situations and formulate an effective course of action to resolve them. This task was more suited to the male mind, rooted in their single-minded hunter ancestors. Initially, I was distracted by all the visual details of the situation while I watched the male members effortlessly "cut to the chase." It seemed I would have to learn to think like a man. If they could learn to multi-task, which was easier for me than for them, I was sure I could master their screening process.

The calls I participated in were primarily routine calls those first few weeks, and I stayed comfortably in the background of my male partners. Complainants were comfortable talking to men--after all, when they called the police they expected a male officer to arrive. There were a few puzzled glances cast my way, but on the whole I remained quite invisible.

I was not even close to the public's perception of a Mountie. I was small and female, and though I was twenty-three, I looked like a teenager. I didn't mind watching and learning during those first few days, but by the second week, it was clear Billy and Chris had decided it was my turn to handle a few routine enquiries.

Chris, the larger member, dwarfed my size. He was the personification of the public's expectation of what a Mountie should look like. He proved so distracting to most people they seemed to barely notice me.

"Your turn to do the talking," he said, after we were assigned a routine call.

He parked in front of the modest bungalow and then stood out of sight at the very corner of the steps as I knocked on the front door. In short order, the door was cracked open by a well-dressed woman in her mid-seventies. I was just about to speak when she called to her husband, sitting on the couch behind her, "Dear, the Girl Guides are here."

The situation only went from bad to worse as Chris added to the confusion by bursting into laughter, bringing himself to the woman's attention for the first time and causing her to look at Chris, then at the police car parked at the curb, then back at me. "You're not from the Girl Guides?"

Trying to salvage my dignity, I had just introduced myself as "Constable Greenwood" when her husband arrived at the door, two dollars in hand, for the purchase of cookies. Chris fell off the step into the flower bed at this point. The poor old couple was very apologetic when the matter was finally cleared up. Like the majority of the general public, they had never heard of female peace officers.

I implored Chris to remain silent on the incident, but there are few secrets ever kept in the Force; over a three a.m. coffee break the following night, Chris recounted the embarrassing incident to Billy Thorardson. Now it was Billy's turn to pipe up and recount an earlier incident he had remained silent on in which an elderly female complainant under similar circumstances had patted me on the head and called me "a cute little thing."

I knew that if the public had a hard time understanding I was a peace officer when I was standing in front of them in uniform, it would be much harder if I was just a female voice on the phone; so I tried to conduct all my inquiries in person. But it wasn't always possible.

The constable's room was always full at the end of a shift as the watch members diary-dated or concluded the files. No one had been home at one of the neighbours of a daytime break and enter earlier in the day. A simple phone call was all that was required. A man answered the phone.

"Good afternoon, sir, I am Constable Greenwood of the North Vancouver RCMP, and I would--"

"Constance *who*?" he interrupted, trying to place my voice.

In a slightly louder, deeper voice, but still under the room's buzz: "Constable Greenwood of the North--"

"Constance *who*?" he repeated, still completely confused. "Do I know you?"

"No, I am a *peace officer*, sir, investigating your neighbour's break-in. Constable Greenwood."

Finally the man understood his mistake. Unfortunately, everyone else in the constable's room did as well. I hadn't noticed that as my voice had risen theirs had quieted. At least they were polite enough to wait until I hung up before they had a laugh! The public had some pretty entrenched assumptions based on sex and status back then, and it would take some time before they adjusted.

The majority of complaint-taker/dispatchers were female. Occasionally, after assigning a call they would mention that the complainant had been rude. The information appeared unreliable because in almost every instance the complainant would behave very respectfully to the members, myself included.

During the investigation, the complainant would often complain about the dispatcher's manners, causing the members to suspect it was the *dispatcher* who was having an off-day.

As you can imagine, any excuses about "that time of the month" did not receive any support from me. Still, I must admit even I was unclear who had fired the first volley until one day when a young dispatcher enlisted my aid as I dropped off my paperwork at the office.

"Could you call this man back? He refused to give me enough information to complete the complaint form." She added apologetically, "It is in your zone and would have been your call anyway."

I took the unfinished form and grabbed a phone in an unused interview room.

"Mr. Smith, this is the North Vancouver RCMP calling. I just need--"

He burst into my conversation. "I don't care what you need, little girl, I told you I want to speak to a peace officer, not--"

I had heard enough; my turn to cut him off. "I *am* the peace officer, and if you want to continue speaking to me, you had better change that tone."

There was shocked silence for a moment on the other end of the line before a much more civil voice resumed the conversation and answered the initial inquiries. I couldn't wait to meet him face to face. He obviously didn't feel so big or powerful when a woman held more authority than him. When I arrived at his house, his demeanour was overly polite and submissive as he tried unsuccessfully to convince me the complaint taker had instigated the confrontation.

This incident vindicated the civilian staffs' complaints with the members and endeared me to them. I had great respect for the complex multi-tasking of their job, which at times could be more emotionally and intellectually challenging than police duties. They may not have had to deal with the threat of physical danger but they had the verbal abuse of the public, and occasionally a member, to cope with.

Underrated and underpaid, dispatchers were pivotal players in keeping members and the public safe. Experienced dispatchers could make even a rookie look good. It wasn't just fair, it was wise, to give them the respect they deserved.

Now that I had endeared myself to the civilian staff, I decided to see what I could do to make similar inroads with the male members. I made several discreet enquiries to find out who, among the female members already posted to the detachment, was held in highest esteem, and why. The overwhelming opinion was that Adrienne Moncrief held that position.

She wasn't the most senior, or bigger, noticeably smarter, or prettier than the other four. What separated her from the rest in the males' eyes appeared to be her willingness to just get in there and do the work--even if she might occasionally be in over her head. I thought back to swim class at Depot and knew I could do that, too. She was constantly checking cars, quick to volunteer for extra calls, and thoroughly investigated all calls she was assigned to without any hesitation. She carried her weight, and the men respected that.

During those first few weeks, I spent extra shifts and a few days off riding with Adrienne to see if I could learn anything else from her. What I noticed apart from the qualities I have already mentioned was that Adrienne did the job in a low-profile manner without sacrificing her femininity. She wore make-up, had long hair neatly tucked in a bun, and was unmistakably, unapologetically feminine in her mannerisms and speech. The men seemed to have far less problem with that than with females who tried to be one of the boys.

It became clear to me that females would be far more acceptable as peace officers, both to the Force and the public, if they remained true to their feminine nature. How fortunate I was to have the luxury of learning from and being able to socialize with other female members. I received letters on a regular basis from Linda, Candy Smith, and Vivienne Stewart describing very different environments.

Vivienne Stewart had been posted to Three Rivers, Quebec, where the "highlight" of her shift was raising the flag and shovelling the ice off the steps. She didn't know if it was the fact that she was female or that she spoke Parisian French rather than Québécois that no one was very helpful or welcoming. Perhaps it was a little of both.

Candy had been posted to Virden, Manitoba, where she was the second female member in the small prairie town stop on the Trans-Canada Highway. Not much went on there except stolen vehicles taken by bored youths for joyrides.

Linda, the first female in Duncan Detachment in the centre of Vancouver Island, was feeling rather out of place as a city girl in a rural detachment. Duncan could be a rough town on a Saturday night, and it wasn't long before someone took a swing at her and she quickly broke his nose--not surprising, considering her martial arts background, but certainly humiliating for the man.

As rumours tend to, the fight got bigger and more violent with each telling, characterizing Linda as a quick-fisted Amazon. I believe that was the only fight she had while stationed at Duncan. Being beaten by a woman was and perhaps still is one of those ego-shattering situations a man does not want to encounter.

About two weeks after I had arrived at North Van, half an hour before shift change at 4:00 p.m., Billy Thorardson and I arrived at a garage on Marine Drive to pick up a repaired police car. This would be the first time I would be alone in a police cruiser (P.C.). Of course, I was only supposed to drive it the eight blocks back to the detachment.

I was taking the long route when "Delta 8" asked over the radio for the assistance of a marked police car in City South Zone. I wasn't sure what kind of a section operated the "Delta" cars. General duty cars were "Bravo," and traffic section operated the "Charlie" cars; that was the limited extent of my indoctrination to that date.

"Bravo nine is clear," I quickly advised.

There was a long, pregnant pause before the Delta car asked the dispatcher: "Is there anyone else?"

"It's shift change; she's the only car on the road."

I was far too naïve and eager to be offended.

After another pause, a reluctant voice advised, "There is a blue pick-up truck north on Chesterfield from 3rd Street which may be an impaired driver."

I was excited. This would be my first real file. I had just positioned myself at 11th Street and Chesterfield Avenue when a pick-up matching the description drove slowly north through the intersection.

"Driving evidence," I thought to myself as I pulled behind to follow, to observe for reasonable and probable grounds to support an impaired charge and justification for the breath test demand. I was shocked to see the pick-up proceed through a red light at 13th Street and Chesterfield, up onto the sidewalk, and stop just inches from the light standard. I turned on my dome lights and parked in the intersection and was just exiting my police car when I saw his reverse lights come on. I leapt into my police car and threw it into reverse so as not to be hit by the pick-up. I turned on my siren, and he slowly pulled over, half-way down the block on Chesterfield.

Mentally I reviewed my training on impaired drivers. The adrenalin had heightened all my senses. I radioed my location and the licence number of the pick-up, then approached the driver, who had remained in his vehicle. With some difficulty, he rolled down the window to speak with me. The driver was about thirty years old, very rough and dirty in appearance, and very intoxicated. His broken nose, facial and hand cuts, and dried blood on his face and clothing gave mute evidence to his recent brawling. There was little doubt from his appearance that he had lost the fight.

"Have you been drinking?" I asked.

"Just a couple," was his textbook response.

From the beginning of the stop, I had split my attention between the suspect and the driver of a grey older car that had pulled over several car lengths behind my vehicle. A friend of the suspect? I wondered. The driver of the suspicious vehicle, having exited his vehicle, was leaning against his front fender pretending to read a newspaper. This unknown male was also about thirty, much bigger than the suspect, and dressed in similar clothes without the dirt and blood. They were definitely connected, so I decided to finish up as quickly as possible before he decided to get involved. The suspect was extremely intoxicated and failed the roadside tests badly.

"You need to listen to this," I said politely, trying to soften the effect of reading the breath demand. "You are under arrest and have to come back to the Detachment for a breath test." I opened the back door of my car.

The familiar sight of the back seat of a police car caused him to tense up in a posture that always precedes a fight, but fortunately he didn't appear very bright (even when sober, I suspected) and he just couldn't seem to think on his feet quickly enough to adapt to the fact that I wasn't a big, mustachioed Mountie but a young woman. Even the bad guys in those days had a code of conduct about hitting a woman or a child. I used that momentary confusion to slip the cuffs on and get him into the back seat.

The unknown man from the grey car remained motionless, still pretending to read his paper as I got back into my P.C. "Home free!" I thought. As I keyed the radio microphone to run the impaired's name and date of birth through the CPIC system, he suddenly realized he didn't want to be in custody. His "complaints" were broadcast in the background of my radio transmission and I finished my transmission by asking if, "perhaps an extra member could meet me at cells."

It was a noisy but short two-block drive to the detachment, which became very quiet as I pulled into the cellblock bay where all of the members of both day shift and afternoon shift in various states of half dress lined the prisoner bay. The suspect's attitude improved immediately when he thought he was going to get a beating. When I opened the car door and ordered him into the cellblock, he was barely audible, responding, "Yes, Ma'am," as he followed me like a whipped puppy.

I didn't know for some time what happened in the prisoner bay after I left the members, who were wondering how I had arrested and apparently beaten one of the nastiest criminals of the North Shore. They didn't have long to wonder because the grey car, which was actually Delta eight, and the suspicious man, who was Cst. Rick Winslow, arrived and jumped in with a humorous fabrication of the events leading up to the arrest.

"It was brutal," he couldn't resist. "She must be a black belt or something; he never got a chance to even touch her."

It was too delicious a rumour to suppress; a small female member inflicting that kind of street justice on that calibre of criminal. The rumour spread like wildfire.

The real story was far less entertaining. The drug section had been watching the suspect around the clock for days and they wanted him picked up and locked up for the night so they could get some rest and not have to go hunting for him in the morning.

Funny stories, true or not, travel a lot faster and further than truth, both inside and outside the Force. You can't really fault the members for looking for a laugh to balance out the tragedies police work routinely exposed its members to.

Six weeks after we graduated, the unthinkable happened: a shooting involving several RCMP members, an ambush followed by one of the longest and bloodiest police shootouts in Canadian history. One member, Dennis Onofrey, was dead, one had lost an eye, and Candy Smith was in critical condition in a Brandon, Manitoba, hospital.

Candy had been one of the top members of our troop. Everyone in Troop 9 knew that by disposition and skill, she would have performed better than most of us under fire.

When I flew to Manitoba to offer emotional support, I found Candy in intensive care at the rural Hospital in Brandon. Candy's transport, the night of the shooting, had been destined for a larger trauma centre in Winnipeg, but en route her caregivers realized Candy wouldn't survive the longer trip. It was already a miracle she had survived being shot at such close range *first by a 20-gauge shotgun and then by a .308 rifle.* The extensive physical damage preoccupied the medical professionals, but the psychological wounds were ignored. I listened as she began the "Would have, should have, could have . . ." second-guessing now known to the police community as post-traumatic stress disorder. The greatest damage Candy suffered in the shooting did not come from a firearm.

The medical facilities in Brandon's small hospital were so stretched with the task of treating two shooting victims it chose to house them together. Like a scene scripted for a macabre horror movie, Candy and the female suspect lay in hospital beds with only a curtain separating them, prolonging the psychological siege which had begun days earlier.

It was a situation that would never have occurred if anyone in authority had been trained to understand or appreciate the emotional damage that occurs in shootings. But post-traumatic stress disorder was unknown--or at least unspoken of--in the Force at that time, and the medical community seemed to prefer to heal the body and ignore the mind.

Candy needed help, and three days later I unsuccessfully tried to convey that to the officer in charge of the investigation during our drive back to Winnipeg Airport.

"I spoke to her, and I think she is handling it very well. She earned her spurs," was his assessment.

"Respectfully, Sir, I disagree," I said. There was little more I could do for her than that at the time.

The officer wasn't malicious; he simply didn't understand the need. Mounties were trained to help everyone except themselves. We had all bought into the image that we were part of the red wall that formed the foundation on which Canada had been built. Mounties were the ones to whom everyone turned to for help, so how could we ask for help for ourselves?

The officer may also have been trying to shield Candy from any negative criticism that might occur in that misguided macho culture if she received counselling. There was a huge stigma attached to asking for such help within society and especially in the policing community--a stigma that has not yet totally disappeared.

The criticism happened anyway. Although the members closest to the incident and the investigators who knew the truth supported Candy, it didn't stop some small minds within the Force from seizing the opportunity to begin a cowardly whisper campaign, using the incident to spread their anti-female views. Behind closed doors in the locker rooms, an ill-informed, malicious, rumour mill distorted the incident, blaming the female recruit for the outcome.

The day after the tragedy, Nancy McKerry, a member of 20 Troop, the only female troop at Depot at the time, recalls that an instructor burst into her class and accusingly announced: "Anyone in this troop who doesn't feel they can shoot someone can leave now!"No male troop was given that ultimatum.

The hypocrisy of the armchair quarterbacks was not lost on the female members. Over ninety-nine percent of the Force retire without ever have to fire their guns in the line of duty. Yearly qualifications firing at paper silhouettes are completely different than combat situations. None of them had been in the situation they felt qualified to judge.

This rush to judge and condemn a member shot in the line of duty, by even a handful of its own members, was unprecedented within the Force. Immediately, and for years after, every female member on the Prairies felt the unfair suspicions and resentment the misinformation caused. In the past few months, however, I have spoken to two male members who were in Manitoba on the night of the shooting, and they made me realize not all Prairies members deserve to be tainted with the broad brush I used in classifying the vocal minority and the silent majority who left them unchallenged.

The only good that came from the tragedy was that since the unofficial volunteer ERT (Emergency Response Team) proved so valuable at the hostage-taking situation that developed after the shooting, the Force decided to develop the unit based on the Prairie model.

It wasn't just some small minds within the RCMP that twisted the tragedy to accommodate gender-biased issues. Candy was thrust into the limelight of a very public trial outside the Force as well.

Sensational headlines clouded the brutal crime. Hours of testimony on the stand were briefly covered as the media instead focused on Candy's one moment when she paused to shed a tear. It was a social taboo for a man to publicly cry at the time. Crying was something women and children would do, but something the public would not expect of a peace officer. Public crying was viewed as a sign of weakness. The harsh, unsympathetic media planted a lingering doubt that female peace officers might not be strong enough to do the toughest part of a man's job after all. Ironically, the only truth exposed in the paper's coverage was about the media.

We female members now knew what we had suspected: the media couldn't be trusted.

The tragic irony of the incident is this: That night during the first gunfight in which any female Mountie had ever been involved, Candy's performance was outstanding. The details of the terrible night are still not common knowledge, even though Robert Knuckle's book[11] meticulously documented the shooting fifteen years later.

Candy, her trainer, and two other senior members attended to a motel room around midnight to investigate an overdue rental car. They were taken by surprise by the man and woman who waited inside ready to open fire with a rifle and a shotgun. Badly outgunned, the members ran for cover, unaware that the first shot had mortally wounded one of their own. The members at scene were pinned down and unable to see each other. In the prolonged gunfight, one of the three remaining members was shot in the eye by pellets from the shotgun. Candy had taken her closest cover, the doorway a neighbouring unit, where she stood her ground under fire.

After the scene had grown quiet, the suspect, apparently thinking all the members had left, stepped out from his motel doorway with his back partially turned to Candy. She watched as he looked down behind a van where, unknown to Candy, Dennis Onofrie's body lay. Candy was also unaware

[11] Robert Knuckle, *Beyond Reason*.

that the two male members had been forced to withdraw from the scene and she was now alone. She didn't understand why the senior members did not challenge the suspect, seemingly leaving the task to a recruit. After a moment that seemed like an eternity, Candy commanded the suspect to drop his gun. Instead, he dove into the room, and her only clear shot narrowly missed him. The exchange had turned from dire to deadly now that the two suspects knew exactly where Candy was pinned down and that she was all that stood between them and escape.

With only partial cover, badly outgunned and outnumbered, Candy kept the suspects pinned in the room until one of the shotgun blasts struck her in the hip, knocking her to the ground in the open. From that position, she continued the fight, covering the doorway, hoping to hold the scene for backup--a backup that came too late. The second shot caused massive internal damage as a three-inch shell from a .308 rifle travelled from the top of her leg through her torso. The suspects left her for dead as they made their getaway.

Canada is not short of heroes. We just don't acknowledge them.

I arrived back in North Vancouver at the same time Stew, my trainer, returned from holidays. As a trainer, he would have to return to working a full midnight shift instead of the late afternoon shift he was accustomed to. The older you get, the harder it is to stay awake past three a.m.

The majority of RCMP detachments are rural, and calls after two a.m. are handled on an on-call basis. The big cities, however, require twenty-four hour protection covered by eight-hour shifts. A stretch of seven-day shifts (8:00 a.m.–4:00 p.m.) was followed by an equal number of afternoon shifts (4:00 p.m.–midnight) and then midnight or "graveyard" shifts (midnight–8:00 a.m.). The graveyard shift was aptly named, wreaking such havoc on internal body clocks that scientific study predicted a shift worker could lose as much as ten years' life expectancy. By the third midnight shift, everyone on our watch felt ill and looked grey, often taking all of the three days off after the shift just to recover.

After two a.m., when the calls started to die off, Stew would start to nod off. After he drove through a couple of red lights in the wee hours of the morning, he decided to turn over the wheel of the car to me when he began to tire. He added one caveat before he entrusted me with the driving while he "rested": "Don't drive over any bridges."

There had to be a good story behind that one. I knew just the person to ask: Stew's first female recruit, who was now posted in Burnaby and lived in Stetson Heights with Jimmy, a member of North Vancouver Detachment.

"Well, it's kind of a funny story . . . now, I guess," she said uncomfortably. (I felt a little bad; I thought she would know the story, but I didn't realize she would be part of it.)

"Well, it was midnight shift. Stew was resting his eyes while I drove. The last thing I remember, before being woken up by the sound of my PC scraping against the guide rail of a bridge, was driving onto it. There really wasn't much damage to the PC, but the rocker panel did have to be replaced. It was terribly embarrassing for both of us, but at least I learned how to write an A10 [police car accident report] without getting the damages assessed against my pay."

Jimmy spoke up, punctuating the story with the typical North Vancouver humorous twist I was beginning to expect: "Stew wasn't too upset. He had the rocker panel mounted and he presented it at our wedding in honour of the night my wife and he 'slept together.'"

I might not have run into any problems playing chauffeur, but Stew had a bigger--or perhaps I should say a smaller--problem with me.

Police cars had bench seats, and I was shorter than Stew's first female recruit. Both seats moved when adjusted for the driver, which meant Stew's knees were almost touching his nose when I drove. On more than one occasion, Stew moved to the back seat, where he could stretch his legs out; but when he did, I wasn't allowed to drive on any well-lit, two-lane streets, for fear someone would notice. I didn't dare try overtly to wake him up, but I had my methods, choosing bumpy or winding streets on my property checks in attempts to rouse him from his slumber. I tried to take a different route each time to mask my intention. Any delusion on my part that he had not figured out what was going on was shattered one early morning as I drove through the pothole-filled path beneath the Lion's Gate Bridge. He opened his eyes, looked mildly amused, and grumbled, "You must have stayed awake all day to think of this one!"

"You said I couldn't drive on bridges--you didn't say anything about not driving under them," I countered.

On one of our first midnight shifts together, my trainer pulled up beside a First Nations man who had passed out in the doorway of a business.

"That's Joe. It's too cold to let him spend the night there. Arrest him for 'drunk in a public place,'" he instructed me.

"No problem," I said as I exited the police car to wake Joe up.

"Joe, Joe," I said, gently shaking his shoulder to rouse him from his intoxicated slumber. As he started to get his wits about him I continued. "Joe, you are under arrest for being drunk in public. We'll give you a warm, dry place to sleep, and you can be on your way in the morning."

"Aw, you cops are all alike. You're just picking on me because I'm an Indian," Joe muttered without looking past the yellow stripe of my lower trousers.

"That's not true, Joe," I corrected. "I have no preconceived stereotypes of natives; there are none on the island I come from. You're the first I've ever met."

Looking up with an expression of surprise and curiosity, he seemed to realize I was not the typical size or sex of a normal peace officer. "No kidding?" he said with a touch of wonder.

"No kidding, Joe. You'll be the first. You will be like a kind of ambassador to introduce me to your group," I said.

Using the wall to steady him as he stood up, he adjusted his clothing and pulled his long black hair into a pony tail before he said, "We are a good group. Just some of us don't know enough not to drink."

"That's a problem some of my Irish ancestors had as well," I said.

After booking him into cells, my trainer, who had not overheard our conversation, couldn't get over how remarkably gentlemanly Joe had behaved in the car and at the station.

The whole incident was slightly ironic because one of the original tasks of the Force was to protect the natives from the problems alcohol had created for them. The times may have changed, but the original mandate had not.

One of the first calls Stew and I attended together was a school alarm one night in Capilano Zone. We got lost, but it didn't seem to bother my trainer, because most alarms are unfounded, and the few real break and enters were historical because of the built-in delay in the system of alarm company reporting.

When we finally reached the school, the smashed front door attested to the fact this had been the scene of a crime, causing another delay as we waited for the dog master to arrive to help search the large building. Finally, all three of us--four, if you count the dog--wandered into the building to begin the low-key search. The criminal was most certainly long gone, but almost as an afterthought, the senior members asked me keep a lookout in the backyard, "just in case someone comes flying out a window."

I could scarcely believe my eyes when the first thing I saw as I emerged into the backyard of the school was exactly that.

"Stop, police!" I shouted, then quickly used my portable to radio a brief message of the foot chase I was beginning.

"You might take me in the sprint," I thought to myself, "but I will get you in the distance."

The yard was large and dark, but all I had to do was keep him in sight and wear him down. He was hemmed in by a six-foot chain link fence. The soles of his running shoes were just in sight as I paced him along it. Suddenly the fence rattled and shook as he apparently scaled it, then I heard a blood-curdling scream and a splash, followed by silence. I strained, trying to pierce the dark of the other side with my flashlight, when I was quickly joined by my trainer and the dog master, both panting harder than the dog.

The darkness had hidden the fact that the fence bordered a deep ravine created by one of our many mountain streams. The suspect was lying on his back, after falling into a freezing stream twenty feet below the top of the fence.

The call for an ambulance precipitated a series of radio transmissions from a number of curious watch members offering to help, wishing to know "the story." But they would have to wait.

It was almost an hour before the hypothermic seventeen-year-old could be transported by backboard to the hospital. Later that night, I happened into the constable's room just as my trainer was wrapping up an embellished version of the events.

"All I heard was, 'and take that!'" he said, intentionally adding to the rumour of my already exaggerated reputation for injuring the bad guys. I was beginning to understand that these silly distortions were just part of being accepted into the group.

I was so honoured to be accepted into the group that I was at first perhaps a little too sensitive, too proud, to accept any advantages my gender occasionally elicited from members, the public, and even offenders.

One of my impaired drivers, a man with a long record including several previous convictions for impaired, erupted into a string of profanity in the breathalyzer room after he received the results of his first breath sample.

"Just a minute," the senior male member who was the breathalyzer technician said, "there is a lady present."

The accused immediately stopped and in an apologetic tone said, "I'm very sorry, Ma'am. I forgot myself."

I accepted his apology and bit my tongue until he was booked into cells.

"You didn't need to say that. I am sure I will hear worse before my career is finished," I said politely but firmly to the member as he finished cleaning the machine.

"I didn't do it only for you--I didn't like his language, and I'm glad he stopped."

It was a lesson that gave me one of my first "aha!" moments, in which I caught myself losing a bit of the self-centredness, and perhaps a little of the insecurity, of youth.

Pemberton Zone had a problematic bar that occasionally hosted a large, early morning outdoor brawl in the parking lot. It was the scene of the first violent call my trainer and I had been dispatched to.

We arrived as backup to see that the first two members at the scene had more than their hands full separating and arresting the two combatants before the hundred or so intoxicated onlookers found an excuse to join in.

The situation was very close to getting out of hand as we rolled to a stop, because a drunken female had grabbed one of the constables from behind as he struggled with a prisoner. The female obviously felt untouchable because she knew if a male member grabbed her, the drunk onlookers from the bar could use the excuse of coming to the rescue of a female as a catalyst for a potential bar brawl. How unfortunate for her I was there, because the same social code that applied to her also applied to me.

The come-along hold worked as quickly and effectively in the field as it did in Depot. Actually it worked far better, because civilians don't know the moves. The fight dispersed quickly after that, and all of the members were happy a potential riot had been avoided.

Although much of our time at Depot was spent learning how to subdue individuals, members by nature don't like to fight and consider fighting a last resort--a failure, of a sort. It wasn't long before the male members began to realize female members had a calming, defusing effect on most situations, something they learned to appreciate and use.

The victims, who quite often were women or children, also appreciated the lighter, empathetic presence of female members. As the public perception of female members rose, victims often specifically requested female members be assigned.

Even the majority of suspects, which were almost exclusively men, seemed relieved when it was a female peace officer who was arresting them because they could surrender to a female without the kind of male posturing that men engage in with other men. Apparently, gender outweighed police status in the criminal subculture, a culture where it was a social taboo for a man to hit a woman, letting the offenders off the social hook for at least putting up a token resistance at the time of arrest. For some suspects, there were a few more self-serving motives than chivalry crossing their minds when they were being arrested by a female.

To fight with a female would risk an open invitation for any man witnessing it to champion the woman's cause physically. At bar patrols, it became routine for one or two of the patrons to follow me around, usually really large tattooed men with criminal records, just hoping to come to my rescue if someone gave me trouble; but no one ever did.

Criminals guilty of crimes against women or children were "skinners" and at the bottom of the criminal social order, fair game for violence perpetrated by other criminals. I was fortunate to police in an old-fashioned, polite, traditional world--one with manners and respect for authority.

Occasionally a man of the sort who based their macho reputation on fighting with male peace officers really didn't want to go without a fight. That was when the most compelling reason to not fight a female surfaced: the fear he might lose. The humiliation involved, especially if a female as small as myself won, seemed to be just too much to risk.

The ease with which I arrested men was a source of mixed amazement and amusement to the rest of the watch. I found it rather ironic that the three qualities my old self-defence instructor had believed worked against me the most--my small frame, lack of weight, and gender--were my greatest assets on the street.

Once every six months, the entire zone would have an all-day meeting to cover training, plan tactics, and socialize. My first meeting happened about three months after my posting.

The members of Pemberton Zone were all big, even by Mountie standards, except for the corporal and myself. I noticed that big guys naturally related well to other big guys, not because of size but because of disposition. Smaller men seemed so much more intense and too often tried to compensate for their lack of size through unnecessary aggressive tendencies, creating what was commonly referred to in the Force as the "little man" syndrome.

Little guys didn't understand that big guys don't like to fight because they have nothing to prove--they know they are big. Much in the same way that men secure in their masculinity do not feel threatened by women.

Although my corporal was a "little man," the staff sergeant in charge of the zone, George Monk, was more than big--he was larger than life, and this zone meeting provided my first glimpse into a local legend.

George was a very solid, weathered NCO, who looked like he could have been one of the original participants in the "march west" over one hundred years ago. He was a no-nonsense type of guy who *expected* his members to get complaints. That's how he knew they were doing their job. Of course he meant complaints from the bad guys, not the citizens. Citizens did not complain so long as the "administration of justice was not brought into disrepute." There was no reason to complain so as long as their families and property were actively protected; and remarkably few criminals complained, because they were treated fairly.

At the meeting it was George who had a complaint. He complained about the loss of an effective police tool when the Liquor Control and Licencing Act replaced the old Government Liquor Act. Under the old Act, the police had the discretion to seize and auction off any vehicle used in contravention of the Act. That meant an underaged drinker found in possession of liquor or an open case of beer in the car could put Mom or Dad in the position of having to buy back the family car at the next auction. It was a tool members seldom had to use. The first offence was normally dealt with by an informal chat on the front steps of the family home with the parents of an offender, and ended with the standard parental promise: "Thank you very much, Officer. I can handle this from here. Junior will not come to the attention of the police again."

It was a promise rarely broken. That was how the system worked best. Swift legal consequence held young offenders accountable if the parents failed in their responsibility to raise their children to respect the law.

"No one wants to be accountable anymore, and the law is starting to accommodate that way of thinking. If you take the teeth out of the Act, offences will increase," he complained; and he was right. George didn't stifle his complaints even if it was the Force he took issue with.

George was a man with a huge vocabulary that he unleashed in memos to superiors on midnight shifts. As I passed the NCO's office at four a.m. one morning, I was drawn by the rapid, hammering sounds of a manual typewriter ringing out like bullets hitting a paper target. George, chain-smoking unfiltered cigarettes while sipping black coffee strong enough to turn even the strongest stomach, paused from his furiously two-fingered typing and asked: "Greenwood, you're educated [referring to my degrees, I assume]. How do you spell----?" I don't recall the word because I had never heard it before nor, I believe, since.

"Sorry, Staff, I don't even know what that means."

"Hum," he murmured with muted amusement, "neither will the staffing officer."

He looked like a rather large, mischievous Irish leprechaun, up to mischief just for the delight of it. George appeared to limit his extensive verbiage to written submissions. When he spoke to people he was quite direct and, if frustrated, quite blunt--as a concerned citizen who called seeking assistance for a cat that had been stranded on top of a telephone pole for several days could attest to. George, the day shift station NCO at the time, assured the complainant that the cat would come down when it was hungry, but she disagreed, and after several unsuccessful but polite minutes of debate, George ended the conversation by saying, "Madam, could you tell me how many skeletons of cats you have seen atop telephone poles?"

Apparently it was a rhetorical question, because he promptly slammed the receiver down after asking it.

George was a man's man in what was still a man's world. By his own admission, the only person he answered to was his wife. It was quite cute to hear Staff Sergeant Monk after several beers at the legion, as was the customary round-off to a zone meeting, refer to himself as "Mrs. Monk's little boy." It was this stable, loving relationship that was the correct indicator that Staff Sergeant Monk would be a fair and positive supervisor to any female member under his command.

It was during that zone meeting that a plan was hatched by the corporal to tackle the growing problem of underage drinkers at the bar in Pemberton Zone. I was paired with another young member, and we were to go undercover into the bar to check IDs. It appeared the corporal might not have liked the idea of having a female member, but that would not get in his way of getting the job done. The plan worked very well because I looked like an underage drinker myself.

Friday afternoon and Saturday night, paired with a young male member named Chris, I made the surreptitious rounds dressed in jeans. Multiple charges were laid, and the Liquor Control and Licencing Branch was given a copy of our report, resulting in a week's suspension of the bar's licence. The following month, we repeated the operation, imposing a much longer time period.

As Billy Thorardson took the liquor licence off the wall the second time to shut down the bar, an enraged bar manager vocally blamed me and suggested I would be happy with the suspension. It wasn't just me--the whole zone was. The bar manager left his job shortly after, and the bar raised its standards and lowered our complaints in the area.

The success of the sting seemed to thaw my relations with the corporal, and he explained that the reason he did not like females in the Force was rooted in a betrayal at his old detachment. Investigating a rumour of an extramarital affair, he confronted a friend who was also the trainer of a female recruit. He had believed both of them when they denied the truth of it. I was left to wonder if the first few females could have that much impact on the reputation of all female members; or if the incident was only an excuse to justify the corporal's bias. Perhaps a little of both, I suspected.

My arrival in North Vancouver was part of an influx of new recruits arriving on an almost weekly basis at that time. A group of us who liked to work hard and have fun became very good friends on the job. Not all females nor all French

Canadians were welcomed, but then again, neither were all male members from traditional backgrounds.

A young French Canadian male affectionately nicknamed "Chuckie" was also accepted into our ranks. Chuckie had been caught in the language bind that the bilingual policy had created for Quebecers who spoke only French. Until he became fluent in English, he couldn't be posted to a bilingual province like Quebec. Chuckie was quite smart and was already verbally functional in English, which he spoke with a noticeable but charming French accent.

The members understood that as difficult as it was for recruits to perfect a second language as well as learn a new profession, it could be much more difficult for young brides dropped into a foreign culture and language without family or friends. More than one leave was approved in those times by our superintendent to allow for a member to return to Quebec and try to coax his young wife back to North Vancouver.

The federal government under Pierre Trudeau's mandate had begun aggressively recruiting French Canadians, resulting in some of the English applicants having to remain a little longer on the waiting list. Chuckie was very sensitive to the strain the policy was causing in the work environment and he stopped me in the parking lot one day and offered an arrangement: "They don't like the French or the females very much. You and I should stick together and look out for each other."

He was probably right. The few who did not like the French also disliked the females, viewing the French as queue jumpers and the females as interlopers. The hostility he perceived had its origins ten years earlier behind the closed doors of Ottawa. We couldn't change politics, but through hard work perhaps we could overcome the damage created by it.

As I looked into his large, brown, unblinking eyes, I was touched that he was willing to form an alliance. I thanked him for his suggestion but said I was sure we could win even the most skeptical member over through hard work and intelligence in the field.

The Force had not gone untouched by the quiet revolution in Quebec. Fortunately, a political "trial balloon" suggestion that the Royal Canadian Mounted Police be completely renamed to the bilingual "Police Canada" was given a frosty reception not just by the Force but by the Canadian public as well.

The Force had a history of fair treatment on language issues. Since 1873, applicants have been equally qualified if they were fluent in either official language. Members suspected that these new policies would allow special interest groups within the government, as well as the politicians themselves, to later interfere with and undermine the structural integrity and independence of the Force. Time would prove them right.

The relationship of the RCMP with the government in Ottawa and its prime ministers had been strained since its original task of settling the West had been accomplished.[12] During the 1970s, the Force appeared to have a love-hate relationship with Trudeau.[13] The members of the Force respected Trudeau's courage and decisiveness in handling the October Crisis, but they didn't like his focus on bilingualism and his attempt to preserve a historic, almost romantic vision of Canada that benefited the East and, at best, ignored the West and the North. The Force had never lost sight of its original mandate to maintain national unity west of Ontario; at times it seemed the federal government had.

By disposition, Trudeau appeared to have more things in common with the Mounties than the politicians and bureaucrats in Ottawa. He was athletic and adventuresome, liked to party, and liked pretty ladies. There was no direct political interference in the duties of the RCMP when Trudeau was prime minister.

Through VIP security duties, members of the Force got to know Canadian politicians on an almost intimate level. In the performance of these duties, members observed all the sides of VIP personalities--not just the image marketed to the public. Unlike the majority of politicians, who are quite often arrogant, slippery characters, Trudeau was the same no matter where he was or whom he was talking to. On a personal level, the members of the Force liked and respected him, as a man and a father. Members also knew he respected them as well. It was some of his policies, not the man, that they distrusted.

The last recruit to join our watch before the end of my recruit field training was "The Cat." You could always tell who would fit into our group by how quickly he or she was assigned a nickname. The Cat looked vaguely familiar to me but I didn't realize why until several weeks later at a three a.m. breakfast, when through the usual small talk I realized he had been a member of the troop we had fought in self-defence. It was his troop mate who had so thoroughly

[12] Nora and William Kelley, *The Royal Canadian Mounted Police/A Century of History* (Edmonton: Hurtig Publishers, 1973). The book documents the strain the early commissioners felt when dealing with Ottawa, and their resistance to political interference in the operations and promotion selection of members. The friction between the federal government and the RCMP led to the resignation of the Force's first commissioner, George Arthur French (p. 55).

[13] William Beahen and Stan Horrall, *Red Coats on the Prairies/North-West Mounted Police 1886–1900* (Regina: Centax Books Print West Publishing Services, 1998). Page 5 of this book backs up the same complaints, beginning with the first commissioner of Ottawa's alienation from the people in the West and its often antagonistic relationship with the NWMP, which had become the voice of the settlers, Metis, and First Nations people--a voice they did not want to hear.

thrashed me. I was grateful he let the conversation end before any of the details of the event were revealed to the others at the table.

Several days later, through the grapevine, I heard his impressions of the fight and took some comfort in them. The troop mate was viewed as an unpopular rogue, a black belt who often beat up even his own troop mates during class.

My reputation was still intact. Apparently it's more worthy of respect to lose a fight against overwhelming odds than to win an easier one. The important thing is to stand your ground. Male values are curious, but I was beginning to understand them.

Another thing male members valued was marksmanship, and the annual shoot, conducted at our outdoor range in the protected watershed of Seymour Mountain, provided a chance for some friendly competition.

Members qualified on revolvers and shotguns, but only the score on revolvers was important, because all you really need to do with a shotgun is load it and point it in more or less the right direction. Everyone was required to attend and achieve a standard of accuracy for revolvers. It wasn't just embarrassing not to make the standard--the standard was a licence to carry the weapon. A poor score would result in remedial shooting and removal from active duty until the score improved.

Not surprisingly, there was always an unspoken competition to achieve a high score each year at the detachment. Many side bets were placed between partners over the shoot.

I suggested to my trainer that we make a wager, and he accepted, requesting a "forty-pounder" of whisky as a prize if he won. The prize I wanted was much more creative and humorous. Every midnight shift at four a.m., my trainer and I had no choice but to go to breakfast at Denny's Restaurant, the only twenty-four-hour restaurant on the North Shore, because if we didn't attend for breakfast, we would be attending to a brawl as hungry drunks congregated at the diner. There was choice on the menu, however; in fact, there were *three pages* of choices, yet every night my trainer would perform the ritual of reading all of the menu, placing it in the pile on the table, saying: "I think I will have a knackwurst Reuben."

The waiter would come over and every time take an order for bacon, eggs, and hash browns. My trainer would no more eat sauerkraut then wear a pink shirt.

If my score was higher than his, I wanted him *to order and eat the knackwurst Reuben.*

I didn't know that I had challenged one of the best shots at the Detachment when we made the bet, not that it would have changed my attitude. I was just having fun. My trainer, on the other hand, was in a slightly different position because our private bet became common knowledge. It became a good-natured battle of the sexes, because if I won the bet, it would mean that I probably could outshoot most of the Detachment.

Like the "Mighty Casey Jones," the hometown favourite lost--probably because he had psyched himself out. As we headed down for breakfast the next midnight shift, every member on the watch took turns asking on the air what my trainer was hungry for. In stoic noble defeat, he never flinched as he ordered and ate the Reuben. He even commented that it was much better than he had anticipated and might even order it again in the future--but he never did.

Capilano Mall was part of Pemberton Zone. One day, my trainer and I were called to a grocery store for a complaint of shoplifting--one more check mark in my Recruit Field Training Book. We were taken to the security office, where two seniors sat. They had concealed an amount of cheese in the husband's inside coat pockets. I was embarrassed for them to be so humiliated at their age and to have to continue the ordeal by returning them to the office for fingerprinting and photographing. I asked if that was really necessary in this case. "Yes," was the answer. The store had a blanket policy on theft, and senior theft was not uncommon. At the office, as I asked the required questions on the form, they both froze when I asked for their next of kin. It was their son.

"You are not going to tell him, are you?" they pleaded, breaking down once more.

My heart was aching for their pain as I assured them I would not--the question was only a formality. After I drove them back to their car in the mall, I regretted my promise. Shouldn't their son know that his parents were in such dire economic straits they were forced to steal food? I was locked into my promise and did not call, but always regretted I could not. Several months later, the prints I had taken were returned from Ottawa because they were not clear enough to process, and I was requested to retake them. I was no longer a recruit at that time, free to exercise my own discretion, and I used it by diverting the charges from the courts and declining the fingerprint request.

Six months had flown by, and in June I was off "the book"--the Recruit Field Training book that had to be completed by the trainer and submitted with my exam scores. The final exam was an open-book research assignment. I answered all the questions except the last one, on the Customs Act. If North Vancouver Detachment had such an act, I hadn't found it, so I left the question unanswered--much to the chagrin of my trainer. I had written a perfect paper except for the omission. I hadn't realized he was trying to break Chris's RFT high score. I believe there was another bet riding on it. If I had known about the bet, I would have looked a little harder.

I knew how my trainer saw me, but I was curious to see how my sergeant would rank me on my first annual assessment. Yearly assessments within the Force were extremely important documentation for future promotions, even though that was a long way off. Sergeant Santa had always been kind and pleasant, but he was a big man who valued size. He had even joked at a zone meeting that he was getting complaints of a driverless police car and suggested humorously that I sit on my briefcase to help me see over the dash. I volleyed back if the heavier members wouldn't squash down the springs in the seats, I would have no problem.

It is one thing to make a joke; it is sometimes a different thing to have it turned on you. Weight was a sensitive issue in the Force those days. Overweight members would be removed from operational duties and not recommended for promotion. But the sergeant was not fat, just big, and apparently he could take a joke. He liked my "cheekiness." His comments on the assessment read: "Although this member is small in stature, she is very aggressive and capable."

High praise indeed from a respected NCO, and more relevant than remarks by a Depot self-defence NCO. I had passed the second hurdle on my journey.

I was excited and honoured to be viewed as an equal among the other junior constables on the watch. The training wheels were now off. This was the end of my official training and the beginning of my real education.

Chapter 5

Policing in the Fast Lane

Police work in North Vancouver was interesting, exciting, and often entertaining. The shifts flew by. Filling in off-hours was much more difficult. At work I was part of a tightly knit team with a common purpose. It seemed the Detachment had accepted the concept of female peace officers much more quickly than the remainder of society, and fortunately North Vancouver was a large enough city to blend into anonymously.

Female members like Linda, posted to small rural detachments, were not as lucky. She might as well have remained in uniform 24–7. Everyone in town knew who she was, what she did or didn't do, at work and off duty. She didn't have to do anything to be the talk of the town. Her experience seemed common to the females in small-town postings. Perhaps I wouldn't have traded her postings after all.

Every couple of months when Linda's and my shifts would align, she would make the escape to North Vancouver to join Joyce Graham and me for a girls' night out on the town. These escapes quickly grew into "girls' night out" for any available female member in North Vancouver. The men seemed intrigued that we were setting up our own social circle, mirroring--yet in a slightly more refined way--some of their off-duty antics. I am proud to say, unlike our male peers, no internal investigations into "conduct unbecoming" were ever generated because of one of our gatherings. The gatherings began to grow in membership as word of them spread, and other female members from various detachments started to attend what soon became an unofficial support group.

Through our gatherings, we female members were able to distinguish between general social issues we would have to bear with and personal adjustments that could help us improve, by sharing strategies and experiences others had found successful. Sometimes the only help we could offer those overwhelmed by the loneliness was a shoulder to cry on in the company of peers who understood the cathartic value of tears.

"I haven't had a date in a year," a member from Burnaby confided, in a tearful burst of emotional honesty during one of the first inter-detachment gatherings.

"I haven't had a date since I joined," another volunteered.

The rest of us quietly exchanged looks of acknowledgment and relief. All of our social lives had been dramatically curtailed since joining, but now we could take some comfort as we realized the problem was external and not internal as many of us were beginning to fear. Our shattered social lives were an unexpected, unwelcome, but not unique side effect of the social adjustment phase for women stepping off the pedestal in pursuit of equality.

Despite the social revolution of the sixties, which the science of birth control made possible, societal expectation hadn't changed much. The conflicting goals of the women's movement and the romantic ideals of the time had created a dysfunctional environment in which female members found themselves ensnared. Our career choice had broken one or more of three unwritten social taboos that could undermine a romantic relationship.

Women were not supposed to be taller, smarter, or more successful/powerful professionally. Men didn't date threatening women--or if they did, often they were looking for a conquest, not a partner.

A frustrating "Catch 22" developed for many female members. Those that didn't date were "lesbians" and those that did were "easy." Either way, we could easily become the subject of locker room rumours. The stories I heard from female members in other detachments made me very appreciative of the support I enjoyed at North Vancouver Detachment.

Compounding the problem of social isolation was the lack of role models for female members. By disposition and position, we were not like the other females in the police social group. We had more in common with the male members than the clerks, dispatchers, or wives. We were striving for legal and professional equality, but we were not men--nor did we want to be.

Women in policing became the subject of intense social and intellectual curiosity, spawning multiple psychological surveys. We began to feel like overworked lab rats. We lost our motivation to participate in these questionnaires when we realized the studies were simply cataloguing information, not being used as a diagnostic tool. Any solutions to facilitate female integration would have to be developed by the rats.

Female members shared a professional/social twilight zone with female pioneers in other traditionally male occupations such as doctors or engineers, but it was the lawyers and judges we got to know the best.

Dierdre Pothecary was one of three Crowns assigned to North Vancouver. Female lawyers were as uncommon as female members. The first time we met at a Crown counsel pre-trial interview, we were both pleasantly surprised to see a female face connected to the name. Dierdre was young and small, but professionally she was a giant, demonstrating remarkable skills at trial and great empathy for the victims of crimes. She was tireless in her efforts on their behalf and unaffected by the macho grandstanding and intimidation attempts of the male defence lawyers when a magistrate or judge wasn't watching.

North Vancouver had three magistrates, each with their own quirks. The youngest judge, Judge Paradis, was a very quiet, well-respected professional. He felt a kinship to the police and our efforts to maintain the peace and order in the community he called home. He was one of the fairest, smartest, and nicest judges I encountered.

The oldest judge, Judge Layton, was a weathered man, who always seemed unengaged with the matters at hand in the courtroom. I can still picture him, head propped on one hand, elbow anchored on his desk, his gaze focused somewhere outside the window of the courthouse as he mindlessly doodled on paper with the other. It seemed the case was half over before he would show any sign of interest in it--until his "guilty" verdict at the end, when it became apparent he had not missed anything that had been presented.

He remained a bit of an enigma to me until one day when, during my testimony, I glanced at his blotter and realized he wasn't doodling; he was drawing the participants of the trial, usually the accused. He was actually quite a talented caricature artist. He continued drawing until I had covered all the elements of the charge in my testimony necessary to sustain a conviction, then he would stop and put the pen down. Armed with that knowledge, I made it a point to keep giving evidence until I saw him put his pen down.

The third judge, Nancy Morrison, was uncommonly female. Many of the male members felt she was too kind to the young offenders. Some members sarcastically referred to the offenders as her "children." It was the beginning of a judicial trend of a softer approach to young offenders. Some of the "children" may have squandered her mercy but others quietly disappeared from the judicial system.

There was an unspoken kinship shared by Dierdre, Judge Morrison, and the female members. There was a professional empathy for the hurdles we faced both on and off the job, but it wasn't just the female members of the legal profession who extended an unspoken aura of acceptance and support for me. The male judges and even the male Crown seemed protectively paternal during our encounters. Male members noticed and even envied the pleasant relationship that developed between officers of the court and myself, which stood in stark contrast to some of their experiences.

The head Crown didn't seem to care if the members were insulted when he disagreed with the recommended charges. Unlike the American system of justice, Canadian police recommend the charges to be laid and are prepared to confront Crown counsel if they disagree. The police tended to choose the charges that best fit the crime rather than a lesser offence that might be easier to win in court. At times, the relationship could be almost hostile between the head Crown and members.

One charge that was nearly impossible to get by the North Vancouver head Crown counsel was "assaulting a peace officer." Minor assaults were expected to be quickly and effectively dealt with through "street justice." The balance in the system meant that minor complaints of "excessive force" were equally rarely approved.

Police, criminals, lawyers, and judges knew the rules of the game: if you hit a peace officer, he or she will hit you back--just once, but hard enough to discourage a second swing. It wasn't therefore surprising that very few chose to take a swing or even to resist arrest. This system worked extremely well for everyone, including the taxpayers, who did not have to foot the unnecessary bill for court and legal aid lawyers trying to deal down their offences by processing unfounded charges.

I was therefore surprised during a pre-trial interview, after mentioning there had been a brief struggle before the accused had been cuffed, when the head Crown offered: "Do you want to add 'resisting arrest or assaulting a peace officer'?"

It had been a brief, half-hearted attempted to escape and was certainly not worthy of the court's attention. Even if it had been more, I was mindful of the double standard I would establish if I agreed, so I thanked him but declined the offer.

"Are you sure?" he again asked.

Here was the author of many members' court frustrations, offering to champion me. Chivalry in unexpected places is always a delight.

Court could be a nerve-wracking experience. Defence lawyers were an unpredictable bunch. No one liked surprises on the stand. While waiting for a court appearance one day, I noticed Rick Winslow pacing up and down the hall. He seemed uncharacteristically pensive.

"When do I get to talk to the judge?" he asked.

I pointed out on the court list that his case followed mine.

"Yeah, I know that, but when do I get to talk to the judge . . . tell him what was *really* going on?"

The stress in his voice awakening a vague memory of something I heard at

Depot helped me to realize why Rick was so concerned. Travelling circuit judges still existed in remote detachment areas, like the one Rick had transferred in from. The first few years of his service had been formed in an echo from the past roots of the North West Mounted Police over a hundred years earlier. Rick was used to picking up the judge from the airport the night before court, and, over a beer and pizza, the members would brief the judge on the case, the impact on the community, and the disposition of the suspect. The next day, a member acting as Crown would repeat the story officially secure in the knowledge the judge already knew the score. Even in small detachments, that simpler, more intimate system of justice was disappearing, becoming only a distant memory of how justice used to be.

No wonder Rick was concerned; even though he'd had several years of service, this would be the first time he would be presenting evidence in such a formal setting.

"Sorry, Rick. The only conversations we have with judges are on the stand in the big city," I informed him.

"No kidding." He looked a bit like a deer caught in the headlights as he shook his head slightly back and forth and muttered "Damn!" It was surprising how much unexpected humour occurred in the courthouse and even on the stand.

One of the more tenacious and sometimes flamboyant defence lawyers was known within the member's ranks as "Slippery Sam." Sam employed an arsenal of well-planned, aggressive defence tactics, and one of his favourites was to probe young members' ability to handle themselves on the stand by seeing how far he could push them during cross-examination. The magistrates of the local court seemed to tolerate these courtroom theatrics, but he would never have attempted them in the higher courts. I was not exempt from his "testing," as I found out on our first encounter when he challenged the construction of a photo lineup used to identify his client.

"Constable Greenwood, when you assembled this photo lineup, you placed my client's photograph as number seven, did you not?"

"That is correct your honour," I said, directing my answer to the judge, not the lawyer, as I had been trained.

"And does our society not place special significance on the number seven?" he asked in an accusatory tone worthy of Perry Mason. I really didn't have a clue where he was going with that line of cross-examination.

"Not that I am aware of, your honour." Sam seemed as displeased with my answer as my refusal to focus on him. Stepping closer to the stand I occupied, but careful not to encroach on the judge's space, he scoffed at my answer and began what turned into a verbal banter.

"Is not Sunday known as the *seventh* day?"

"I guess Monday is the first." I studied the judge's expression to see how he would interpret my response. I was relieved to see a look of amusement and perhaps a little surprise at my combative response. It appeared his judicial tolerance for courtroom theatrics extended to both sides of the case, within limits.

"Do you not buy your milk from the 7-11?" Sam shot back.

"No, it's too expensive." The judge really should have shut us down at this point, but he seemed to be enjoying the verbal sidestepping.

"Do you not play a game of chance in which seven is very lucky?"

"No, I don't."

"Do you play no games of chance?" We were so far afield at this point, everyone in the court was smiling.

"I play bridge."

"Your honour, that is a game of skill, not a game of chance," Sam "complained" to the judge, who could not hide the fact he was enjoying the whole exercise.

"I agree, your honour," I chipped in.

"So do I," said the judge, finally ending the debate. "I think you have gone as far as you can with this line of questioning and I see no problem with the accused's being number seven in the lineup."

I found police work was a remarkably funny profession outside of court as well.

Marine Drive, the main road in my zone, was a four-lane urban street full of stop and go traffic from six a.m. till midnight. It seemed I spent most of my day and afternoon shifts stopped at red lights in heavy traffic, where an awkward but humorous ritual began to repeat itself. When a driver's peripheral vision catches a police car stopped in traffic beside his or her vehicle, few can resist a casual, quick, side glance. Clearly a female peace officer was not what they expected to see, causing the quick, casual glance to pause halfway, as people continued to stare with a confused look of disbelief. I guess they were trying to figure out why a Girl Guide was driving a cruiser!

Since my peripheral vision worked as well as theirs, I was painfully aware of the situation and a bit embarrassed, so initially I chose to pretend I was unaware of their stares and to look blankly forward. As this ritual played out over and over again, I began to get comfortable enough with it to have a little fun by making eye contact, smiling, and politely waving at the drivers, who were frozen in their stare, mouth open. Sometimes I even had to point to indicate the light had changed and they were holding up traffic. The poor people would snap back to reality and drive off as quickly as legally possible, trying to regain their composure.

Now that I was "off the book," I was enjoying the freedom of choosing my own patrols and tasks to busy myself when not answering calls. I checked a lot of cars, did a lot of property patrols and bar walks. One night around three a.m. when I pulled over a suspicious car, I noticed a second vehicle pull over about a block behind me. It caused a little "déjà vu," reminding me of my first impaired. The second vehicle remained parked as I conducted the check of the suspicious car. After I finished with the first driver, I walked back to see why the second driver had stopped. I found a middle-aged man, an average citizen, who had been on his way home from work. "Just wanted to make sure you didn't need help," was the reply.

He was surprised to see I was female. When he had stopped, it had everything to do with his civic responsibility and nothing to do with my gender. This was the first but not the last time I observed this unsolicited support from the public at large. One midnight shift six months later, the same scenario was played out again, only this time the Good Samaritan was Judge Paradis. What a great society we had then! In today's reality, if a car stops, it's more likely to contain a person with a video camera trying to capture the next "Rodney King" incident to sell to the media. Things had changed, and one of the biggest changes in the police culture in the seventies was the female face of the RCMP.

Both complainants and accused seemed a lot more relaxed when dealing with a female peace officer back them. I found it a tremendous advantage to look so young, naïve, female, and small. I took a lot of statements. Any accused statements were accepted unchallenged by the defence lawyers. After all, the only issue at that time relating to a statement's acceptance involved the voluntariness of the utterance. "Were you threatened or intimidated by Cst. Greenwood?" was the required question.

Before the accused could answer the question, most defence lawyers would rush to their feet and accept the statement. I never had a statement challenged in court. Once a fifteen-year-old accused was given the opportunity to answer the question and the response was: "By Cst. *Greenwood*?"

The inference in his voice elicited smiles from the judge as well as the lawyers as they conceded the absurdity of the question.

Everyone, including myself, was surprised at my success in obtaining confessions and criminal intelligence from offenders.

It was a good thing that people found it easy to confess to me, because I really didn't have a clue how I would handle an interrogation. The only interrogation my trainer had demonstrated during my recruit field training had not been successful, and the only lesson I took from Depot's class on interrogation was that members kiss and tell.

I took a lot of the statements from victims of sexual assaults; mainly rapes. Female victims and children preferred to give their statements to females. I was asked to take a statement for any sexual offence reported when I was on duty. It was a brutal immersion course in sexual predators and their behaviour.

Like most "good" girls of the day, I knew less about sex, let alone deviant sexual behaviour, than the average thirteen-year-old today. I was so naïve, the male members found it funnier that I didn't understand the subtle sexual innuendoes of some off-colour jokes than the joke itself. There I was, recording details of behaviour I never even suspected could occur, while trying not to look shocked to the victim or naïve to the other members.

Due to the prevailing social obsession with female virginity, only a portion of the most clear-cut sexual assault cases were reported. Female virginity was revered and respected, something directly connected to their dignity and worth as a person. Once it was lost, no matter what the circumstances, the chaste, pure status of the woman could never be reinstated. In many parts of the world, this culture of oppression is still in place.

The societal obsession with female virginity was often responsible for a second victimization. Rape victims needed to prove they were in no way responsible for misleading the accused into thinking the sex was consensual. Defence lawyers were quite often brutal in their character attacks on the victim. The psychological damage this dual victimization caused was enough to last a lifetime. Street workers, estranged wives, and sexually active single women felt abandoned by the justice system at the time.

At least there was some justice in the sentencing back then. Rape, an indictable offence, usually ended in the Supreme Court, and a conviction resulted in serious jail time. On the other hand, an acquittal meant what was left of the victim's reputation in the community was destroyed. It was a high-stakes game many victims chose not to play. It seemed only the courageous or naïve reported the crime.

Although I never considered myself a "women's libber," I could get passionate about blatant inequalities based on sex. Nowhere was the status of a woman more subservient and dependant than that of wife. Canadian society was still adjusting to the legal recognition of women as "persons" with equal rights and not the property of fathers or husbands. Mainstream society still tolerated the social trap wives brutalized by their husbands found themselves in at domestic disputes. Only extreme cases of battering were reported. Charges were seldom filed.

Wives were the perfect victims, held hostage often either by economics or social expectations. The husbands were perfect bullies, terrorizing their families in an effort to mask their feelings of insecurity and inadequacy.

I raged internally to hear the wives forgive their attackers, sacrificing their safety and dignity for the economic and social stability of the family, often for the sake of the children. In extreme cases, we would lock the husband up, but by morning the wife would drop the charges and the pattern was set to repeat.

Members were frustrated at the cyclical nature of the abuse they were helpless to stop. The children, frightened and enraged, seemed destined to repeat the dysfunction in their own futures. It was little wonder members hated "domestics," the most dangerous call to attend. More members have been injured or killed investigating domestics than any other crime. Fortunately, almost all other crimes were easier to deal with.

While on patrol, members were expected to be proactive in their policing. "Self-generated" files indicated more than a good work ethic. It was often apparent which specialized section a uniformed peace officer aspired to by the nature of these files. Members interested in traffic wrote a lot of tickets, those interested in drugs looked for seizures at every opportunity, those interested in crime prevention volunteered for school talks. I felt I was far too junior to have any immediate aspiration to pursue specialized sections. The choice to focus on impaired driving was made for me by fate.

The first impaired motor vehicle accident I attended was so tragic it hardened my perception of the crime. A sad series of events caused me to become the catalyst for the accident. Just before midnight, Lions Gate Bridge patrol had asked for assistance with an impaired driver in the parking lot of the Plaza Hotel. Nobody liked doing impaired at the end of a long shift, and the afternoon member, my corporal, was no exception, opting for the quick fix, a twenty-four-hour suspension. Though the driver and passenger promised on everything they held holy that they would book themselves into the hotel and sleep it off, they did not. A half hour later, they were driving eastbound on Marine Drive when they spotted my police car about ten blocks away on what they tragically mistook for an intercept course. I was just beginning my midnight shift and was unaware of the earlier file and twenty-four-hour suspension. Thinking only of escape, they turned directly into the path of a motorcycle.

The victim, a young photography student, on his way to capture the moonlight on the inlet, never had a chance. The driver was genuinely remorseful, but that didn't mend a shattered body and future.

Impaired driving was almost socially acceptable in those days--well, maybe not "acceptable," but at least tolerated. This was a second impaired offence for the driver, and I chose to risk alienating the local judge by serving a notice to "seek greater punishment." Judges as a rule did not like notices forcing them to sentences on the higher end of the scale of punishment, because it took away some of their discretion, but in this case the presence of the victim in a wheelchair flanked by his supportive family made the notice easier to accept. After the case, I promised myself never to give an impaired a break by issuing a twenty-four-hour suspension.

Impaired drivers were easy to find and a good way to fill in the tail end of a midnight shift, because it would take approximately three hours to process them. Roughly a third of the drivers on the road after eleven p.m. were impaired. By two a.m., when the bars emptied out, the ratio was closer to half.

There was a lot more drinking back then, even within the ranks of the RCMP, but when we partied, we either walked or were driven home in a police car, commonly referred to by members as a "Buffalo Cab." The term was a reference to the trademark buffalo crest on the side doors of the car.

Our after-shift parties were at the oddest hours. On the morning of the last of seven midnight shifts (midnight till eight a.m.), we would all gather at the home of one of the watch members and have breakfast and a beer.

There, we discussed the successes and tragedies of the shift with the only people who could truly relate: other members. It was more unofficial debriefing than party. The real parties were a lot more fun.

The two biggest parties of the year celebrated Veteran's Day and Christmas. On Remembrance Day, everyone who wasn't working got into red serge and joined the parade of veterans up Lonsdale to the Legion.

The year 1978 was the first time there were sufficient female members off shift to form a rank. It seemed to have a symbolic value, not just to the four of us in the rank, but to the WW II veterans, both male and female. The audience lining the street broke into spontaneous, unexpected applause as the female rank marched past. Although it had sometimes happened at Depot, the feeling in the parade that Remembrance Day was much more powerful. These were veterans applauding, no doubt remembering the uncelebrated service and sacrifice so many women contributed to the war effort. We were so overwhelmed we lost our step briefly. We smiled as we regained our stride, only to hear a voice from the rank behind teasing, "They don't look as good out of step."

That is what I remember when I think of those days in North Vancouver: quick wits and good-natured fun. At the Legion, a day shift member collected all the Sam Brownes (gun belts) and secured them at the Detachment while we partied with the veterans.

Our military training, rank structure, and protocols made it easy to participate in wars and peacekeeping duties in times of need. Our ranks have officer equivalency not just in the Canadian Armed Forces but in the American as well. An unspoken bond of mutual respect defines the relationship between the RCMP and the military. Legion parties were uniformed members affairs only, but the Christmas parties were open to spouses and dates.

The Detachment ran a skeleton shift to allow maximum attendance at the Detachment Canyon Garden's Christmas party. Attendance and intensity of parties remains a far more accurate barometer of the morale of the RCMP than any survey, no matter how statistically accurate it might claim to be. Morale was high in North Vancouver.

The dance floor, full of couples rocking to the music, occasionally transformed with a single loud stomp of Constable Gary Proulx's foot and a quick exchange of a smile, signalling an unspoken, almost subconscious command to "attention" answered by all the members on the dance floor. In an instant we all fell in step, rocking the floor with our combined weight as we moved as a unit. The Red Wall could not only dance, it was surprisingly good at it, adapting and interpreting the music through a single, intuitive consciousness. Our ability to become an efficient military force at a moment's notice, with a common, uncompromising purpose, was a source of pride within the Force, a comfort to Canadians, and a threat to some politicians.

Once a member finishes Recruit Field Training, he or she is separated from the trainer to assist in the transition to the next stage, that of junior constable. My new partner, Cst. Sleepy, was a very senior constable with a long commute. His thirteen years' service was extremely uncommon in those days.

Cst. Sleepy was a laid-back type of guy who always seemed overly sleep deprived. At the end of one shift, we couldn't find him. Assuming he had parked to take a nap and had overslept, we "tested" the tone alert.

The tone alert is a high-frequency alarm that is dispatched to all cars to alert them to an extremely dangerous crime in progress. The surge of adrenaline members feel at the tone would please Pavlov's theorists. When there was no response from Cst. Sleepy, we were beginning to worry as we headed back to our cars to look for him. Then someone noticed his police car in the parking lot. Back inside, in response to the second call on the office P.A. system, he came down the stairs from the court section of the Detachment with the design of the leather bench firmly imprinted on one side of his face!

Perhaps someone was trying to re-energize him when they gave him a recruit to train, but being a trainer is a lot of work, and senior constables have a lot of leave. With Cst. Sleepy away, I had his recruit Mikey to ride with me for the first few months. This was very strange situation, as I was barely off recruit field training myself. No female had yet trained a male recruit, because we were too junior. Although everyone knew that day would eventually come, even the men who were getting comfortable with equality between the sexes did not appear to be too comfortable with reversing the social order in a situation where a male would hold less power than a female--a concept few males would be comfortable with, but Mike wasn't one of them. On one occasion, I walked into a conversation in the Constables' room just as Mikey was asked: "Is Jane your trainer?"

"Yes, she is," Mikey proudly answered. Although I corrected him, it soon became clear that more than one had asked the question when I wasn't around. If Mikey didn't care, I guess I didn't need to, either. It gave the locker room gossipers something else to banter about. A female training a male, and a junior one at that!

Mikey and I had some very interesting files to gather.

One of the first calls we got involved a stolen credit card at a car rental company. In 1978, credit cards like VISA and American Express were just beginning to become common. The credit card companies involved quickly realized the police would not get involved if the owner of the card had simply gone past the limit. That was a civil matter. If, however, it was reported as a theft, they knew we would seize the card. We arrived with an open mind at the scene.

The rental car clerk and the suspect met Mike and me at the door, each eager to tell his side. I spoke to the suspect, who co-operated by producing ID from Atlanta, Georgia. The card was in his last name but a different initial, a nickname he went by--a clerical mistake, he insisted.

"Perhaps because of my travelling I was over the card limit. The card is definitely not stolen," he lied convincingly.

He was well spoken and well dressed. I should have taken special note of the expensive running shoes he was wearing. All the clerk knew was that the credit card company had told him the card was stolen. Mike had just disappeared into the back office to check the story directly with the credit company by phone when the suspect grabbed a customer entering the store and threw him into me as he quickly fled out the door.

The foot chase was on, through the car lot, across Marine Drive. I left a trail of police equipment for Mikey to follow: first my hat, then the complaint form, followed by my flashlight. After dodging four lanes of noonday traffic across Marine Drive, we were again bounding through another car lot. The suspect, who had taken a few more chances crossing Marine Drive, had a quarter block lead on me when he vaulted a small white picket fence on the eastern border of the lot. How unfortunate for him he was looking back at me rather than down at the six-foot drop to the pavement on the other side. He landed hard and was still at the spot where he fell when I reached the fence. As I climbed over, he got up and ran through the lane continuing east, and I lost sight of him. He was nowhere to be seen up or down the deserted residential street I emerged onto. I reached for my portable radio only to find it had been lost along the way. He couldn't be far. I soon discovered him hiding in a bush on a front lawn. His head was bruised and scraped, and one of the knees of his pants gaped open. Assuming he had given up just like those I had pursued in my other foot chases, I ordered: "Turn around and put your hands against the house."

He stood up and faced me like a cornered animal. He stared at me and through me with a look of primeval savageness I had never encountered before or since. At a subconscious level, I knew I was in mortal danger. The surge of adrenalin almost overpowered my fine motor control. I had to fight to maintain my composure and mask my fear. I could feel my body trying to shake. Two competing emotions were struggling for control, fear and aggression. Time slowed.

This was long before batons, pepper spray, or stun guns were part of police force options. The suspect *outweighed* me by one hundred pounds. He glanced down at my holster, and I knew exactly what he was planning.

In an unconscious act of self-preservation, acting purely on instinct--police instinct--I pulled my revolver. *Better in my hands than his*, I reasoned silently as I repeated my initial order.

"Turn around and put your hands against the wall."

Again he ignored me, glaring back through me with cold, reptilian eyes.

The gun had been a bluff--a bluff that wasn't working. I had been trained not to draw my revolver unless I was prepared to use it, and at this point I wasn't. Once you have pulled your gun, you can't fight with it in your hand. My choice had limited my next move. I wondered if I had been premature in pulling my weapon based on an instinct. I didn't have time to second guess myself. I had to get the suspect restrained quickly because I knew he was planning his next move, still calculating the odds of getting my gun, looking for an opportunity or hoping to create one.

I repeated my command, and still he ignored it and challenged back, "Wait a minute, you haven't read me my rights yet!"

We were now in a psychological struggle for dominance, one he lost as I lowered my voice and stepped forward just out of his reach. Meeting his glare, I snarled: "This is Canada and you don't have any! Now turn and put your hands against the wall."

What a thing to say! I still can't believe that just popped out of my mouth. Anger had won. I was angry, much more angry than scared, and the angrier I got, the less scared I was.

My unexpected response had thrown off his plan. Mikey, who had followed the trail of uniform and equipment to locate us, rounded the corner of the house as I snapped the second cuff on. As we walked the prisoner back to the police car I glanced at my shaking hands. I thought of Candy and the shootout. How did she do it? What a nightmare it truly must have been.

Mikey drove back to the Detachment prisoner bay as I silently interrogated myself. Why had I pulled a gun on an unarmed man contrary to the police training I had at the time? Did I overreact? Did I panic? How would I have justified my actions if things had not de-escalated?

This was the career-defining situation members hoped to encounter while still on recruit field training with backup close by--the moment of truth, in a trial by fire, to see if the member had the right stuff for the job. I wasn't sure I had passed the test. I had lots of questions I needed to answer, even if I didn't like the answers. It didn't matter to me that everyone on the watch, including the NCOs, was very happy with the outcome and felt I had done an outstanding job. I was always my toughest judge and my jury was still out.

After the suspect was booked into cells, I began the investigation into the theft. The credit card had been stolen and used in the U.S. for goods and to book the flight to Vancouver from Atlanta. I finally made phone contact with the man who reported the credit card stolen. It was the brother of the accused. With great concern he asked, "Did he hurt anyone?"

The suspect had an American record for grand theft and robbery. He knew he would face a lengthy term in prison as a third-time offender. It was the American equivalent to a similar guide in sentencing habitual offenders in Canada. The suspect had told his brother: "I will never go back to jail again. I will kill the next police officer who tries to arrest me."

His words provided the vindication I was demanding of myself. I now understood the value of police instincts and was comforted to know I had developed a reliable set of them.

In the prisoner's effects, Mikey and I found a key to a room at the Park Royal Hotel. Neither of us had ever done a search warrant, but we pulled out the code and had just begun the forms when S/Sgt. George Monk tapped Mike on the shoulder and asked in his throaty, mischievous voice, "That American is complaining that he was injured in the arrest. Did you bend him a little?"

Mikey took delight in advising Monk, "I didn't arrest him, Jane did."

This surprised and amused George. He was chortling to himself when he asked if I could take the suspect to the hospital to be checked out. There was no doubt the American was still hoping for an escape opportunity. When I pulled out my cuffs for the transport he quickly informed me he thought his wrist had been broken in the fall. Too bad he hadn't anticipated leg irons.

In the rented hotel room, we recovered many stolen items from the U.S. They were parcelled up with him, and he was deported to the U.S. authorities for incarceration. We could have prosecuted him as well in Canada, but that would have been a needless expense for the public when the Americans were ready to toss the book. I confess I was a little relieved that I wouldn't have to explain to a judge my cryptic, and somewhat misleading, comment about his not having any rights in Canada.

Unlike the American courts obsessing with the lengthy "Miranda" warning, Canadian courts required only that an arrested or detained person be informed "as soon as is practical" of the reason for the detention and his right to remain silent. I read him his Canadian rights in the back seat of the police car when it was safe to do so. Canadian law made policing simple and easy.

Nowhere was it easier than in North Vancouver, where even the geography was on our side. The city could be effectively closed off by monitoring three strategic traffic exchanges, the first narrows (Lion's Gate Bridge), the second narrows (The Iron Workers Memorial Bridge), and the Number One Highway at Capilano Road. For that reason, our criminals tended to be local, causing North Vancouver's crime pattern to mimic that of a small town, or even an island. This made it much simpler to eventually identify the offender and solve the crime. Typically, ninety-five percent of the crimes are committed by five percent of the population. It is a huge advantage to know that five percent lives locally.

Clearance rates were a source of pride and competition beginning at the zone level and continuing on up to the detachment level. The true measure of how effective a police agency is rests not in the number of offences but in their *outcome*. North Vancouver proudly held the bar for other detachments, with the highest "solve rate" in the lower mainland. That efficiency didn't happen without clever strategies.

The GIS (General Investigation Section) monitored crime trends to determine if patterns could be detected to identify serial offenders. The constable in charge of monitoring B&E (break and enter) statistics was a Don Rinn. Break and enter was a serious crime back then, an indictable offence punishable by five years to life in prison. The severity of the law reflected the public's expectation to feel safe and secure in their own homes.

Every uniformed member who attended a B&E completed a form that had been developed to assist the GIS section to identify the MO (*modus operandi*): point and method of entry and exit, items taken, type of house/business, time, date, and location of the offence. From this information, educated assumptions could be made about the suspect(s). There was a huge spike in B&Es in the summer and fall of 1978. Through confidential information, Rinn was confident he knew of at least three active "targets" that were responsible for the majority of the crimes.

North Vancouver's GIS Section was staffed by a small but effective group of senior constables responsible for major investigations such as murder, serial rapes, arson, armed robberies, and organized crime activity. They were an elite group to which most uniformed members aspired. However, this group lacked the manpower to staff the bold plan Don Rinn had created to tackle the B&E problem.

When the rumour began to emerge that a surveillance unit was going to be formed using uniformed members rotating from each of the zones, everyone began an unofficial competition for the spots. Everyone except me. I needed allies, not enemies.

I had already learned at Depot that members, both male and female, don't like to lose--especially to a junior member or a female. If I were selected, I would be offending on both counts.

Realistically, it was far too early in my service to make the leap to plainclothes, even if it was only a six-month rotation. I was only just beginning the learning curve a good general-duty member needs. I felt quite overrated. I had been lucky so far and I knew it.

My sergeant took me by surprise when he asked me into his office one night at the end of an afternoon shift. "How would you like to take the first rotation to the new squad?"

I responded, "Thank you for considering me. I am flattered but I think I need more uniform experience."

I could tell he was surprised that I would not jump at the opportunity. "I think you are ready for it. Why don't you just think about it?" was his reply.

I was still thinking about it when several days later the list for the new squad was out and my name was on it. My name was also still on the shift schedule for the zone. I just kept coming to work in uniform for the next week. Toward the end of the week, as I entered the hall to the Constable's Room, I saw a lanky, thirty-year-old, dark-haired man dressed in a plaid shirt and jeans leaning against the wall. It was Rinn. Before I could enter the safety of the Constable's Room, he spoke. "I think you are supposed to be on my squad," he said in a quiet, almost shy way.

The jig was up.

"I was a bit confused because they still have me on the zone schedule," I hedged.

A uniformed member not lining up to get into GIS was a little odd, but then again I never really tried to be "Monty Mountie."

The following morning, I reported, in plain clothes, to the upstairs GIS section as instructed. I didn't know any of the GIS members, and they didn't know me, because I had not done my GIS rotation while on recruit field training. Introductions and orientation were the order of the day. I was in good company. Adrienne Moncrief had been selected for a coinciding GIS rotation.

Adrienne's partner and mentor in GIS was Cpl. Gerry Tilley. Tilley was a large, red-haired, freckled man with an irrepressible sense of fun. He had been Don Rinn's partner prior to the formation of the new B&E squad. The two had been a powerful investigational team that delighted as much in solving difficult cases as they did creating complex practical jokes to spring on each other.

The sergeant, Ron MacKay, had been newly promoted from crime prevention. He had beaten out Tilley, the GIS home favourite, for the position, which caused a bit of unspoken tension and resentment in the small section.

The staff sergeant in charge of the plainclothes unit, Tom Hill, was pleasant, but not one to be taken lightly. He was so well connected within the Force he had a reputation for having unsatisfactory people transferred overnight by one strategically placed phone call. Members and even civilian staff would show up for work only to find their desk was literally no longer where they had left it. He had been the one who backed Rinn's groundbreaking pitch to form a surveillance/investigational unit to target criminals.

Headquarters had a surveillance unit, Special O, which could be assigned to major cases such as serial armed robberies, gang/organized crime, or drug investigations. Special O was staffed with special constables who tailed the suspects but did not get involved in investigations or court. It took a lot of paperwork and a bit of politics to get Special O to assist in a detachment file, rendering the unit unsuitable for Rinn's plan.

Rinn's squad was much more flexible and practical for detachment purposes. Three of the six rotating members supplied by each of the watches were assigned to one of two shifts. Rinn was my team leader. The second team was headed by the second full-time GIS member, Herb Wilburg.

The structure of the B&E squad was noncompliant with the command structure of the Force. To be in charge of seven subordinates, Don Rinn should have been a sergeant, not a senior constable. It was no small feat when S/Sgt.

Hill convinced the OIC to allow the infraction solely because Rinn was the best person for the job.

This new squad required its own office in the already cramped Detachment. Our second-floor office was small, but all we needed was a phone, two desks, and a filing cabinet; almost all of our time would be spent on the road. Several rental cars and a truck had been leased for the unit. We had no special equipment, just large portable radios that we concealed in our winter clothes and standard issue shoulder holsters. We also had no surveillance training for either driving or on foot. I had the impression this was going to be police training in the fast lane.

Every day in GIS began with a coffee flip. Without exception, every member would flip. Then, depending on odds or evens, people were eliminated, in groups at first, then down to the remaining two. It was never about the money--it was always about not losing. Once eliminated, everyone would delight in teasing the more animated members like Rinn, Tilley, and Hill, who never wanted to lose at anything. Rank meant nothing in this ritual. I think "the coffee flip" deserves a place in management books as a morale builder. It was also a great way to gain some insight into the characters with whom I would be working.

It appeared to me the only thing that Rinn or Tilley liked better than winning was beating each other. The fact that they no longer worked directly with each other actually made it easier for them to continue their practical joke battles.

The other two members of my four-person team were Gordy Oak and Dave Zack. Gordy was a quiet, slightly built senior constable who had recently worked on drug section. He brought to the team a lot of job knowledge in an unassuming manner.

Dave Zack, the only other really junior member on either team, had worked very hard to earn his spot among the senior members of GIS. I recognized the mischief I saw in his eyes and we quickly but quietly formed an alliance. We realized the perfect set-up we had to anonymously execute practical jokes.

We alternated targets between Rinn and Tilley, comforted by the knowledge they would blame each other. It was a little like "Spy vs. Spy"[14] with a twist, once Zack and I entered the picture. The quality of the practical jokes appeared to be directly proportional to the morale of the section as well as the quantity and quality of the police work being done. That was no doubt the reason S/Sgt. Hill did nothing to interfere with them.

After a while, Rinn and Tilley began to realize someone else was at work, but it never seemed to cross their minds that the two most junior members in GIS would dare tweak their noses. Zack and I even offered to help with the investigation. The corporal in charge of drug section was a likely suspect.

[14] As in *Mad* Magazine.

Sometimes there was even a clue left behind to implicate his section.

It wasn't surprising that drug section was staffed by the roughest and wildest of the members, considering the violent, disgusting criminals they targeted. It was an open secret that no female members would be welcome on the rough-and-tumble drug corporal's section. That made setting him up an even better joke.

Late nights spent in smoky bars on drug work had no appeal for me. I was not sure why Joyce Graham had set her career sights on it, but I did know she would have her work cut out for her if she wanted to crack that "old boys" culture of the drug section.

B&E squad's first target was based on Rinn's "confidential information." Informants are the most efficient way to do police work in the remarkably connected subculture of criminals, a community like most others in which rumours of who did what got around with speed and accuracy. Being able to handle and cultivate informants was a necessary skill for the majority of the plainclothes sections.

It was not an easy skill to learn, requiring a practical understanding of motivation in criminal minds. The theories I had learned in psychology were of little practical use in this reality of shadow and dysfunction. Nothing was straightforward. Motives for informants varied from reducing their charges, to money, to taking out the competition. Members' interpersonal skills were taxed as they formed uneasy relationships with criminals in the quest to fight crime. The courts understood and protected the police need to handle informants.

I was impressed at the easy way Rinn handled himself in this snake pit. Rinn joined the Force from Snowflake, Manitoba, armed with a Grade 12 education, and became the most effective peace officer I ever worked with.

It soon became obvious why I had been selected for the squad. If people were having a hard time understanding I was a Mountie in uniform, they would never figure it out when I was in jeans and sneakers. I was like a secret weapon. Not only could I get very close to the unsuspecting target, but, when partnered with a male member, the cloak of psychological invisibility was extended to him as well as we were subconsciously written off as a couple.

One B&E criminal can commit up to twenty crimes in a day. We would watch as they happened and would then follow them to the "fences." It was so easy in the first few months. A unit like this was unheard of back then. We were careful not to disclose our tactics. There were guilty pleas and sketchy Crown briefs and a near-perfect clearance rate.

Rinn and Gordy handled the confessions, rolling over new informants and new information to move up the crime chain, like a local coin and stamp dealer who was fencing stolen jewellery and coins. It takes a lot of documentation to obtain a warrant for a wire tap, but Gordy knew how. Zack and I monitored the calls, which gave insight into the lower levels of organized crime.

The majority of the B&E's were conducted by juvenile males, but the fences were adults, with small businesses as fronts, preying on them like pimps. These were men active in the local small business community and chamber of commerce, the kind of people who would cry "innocent" and "harassed" when the heat was stepped up. It was like a play. They would try to act the role of wrongly accused for the media and the public. There was so much trust in the justice system at that time, people intuitively knew the police would have good reason if they were charging someone.

Most members go all their service without working on a wire tap. Letters from troop mates like Linda, talking about stolen bicycle investigations, helped me appreciate how lucky I had been to end up at North Van Detachment.

A couple of months into the rotation, Adrienne and I were asked to assist Headquarters Drug Section with an undercover operation. We would be nothing more than window dressing in a major trafficking file, but it proved to be valuable insight into a very secretive arm of the Force.

An undercover operator, a.k.a. the UC, would be closing a large deal for the purchase of cocaine at one of the local high-end strip bars in Vancouver. The UC needed a girlfriend (Adrienne), and the inside cover person needed one, too (me). It was a dangerous assignment. The large sum of money involved raised the possibility the drug dealers might simply shoot the UC and take the money. There is no honour among thieves and even less in organized crime.

Adrienne and I got dressed up and wired up. The strip club, the most upscale in Vancouver, almost looked legitimate. We were seated at a large booth with the target and his associate. North Vancouver's drug squad and the rest of GIS were outside in a van monitoring every word said at our table both for evidence and our safety.

Several "reserved" tables in front of the stage remained empty as the female entertainment strutted their stuff. Halfway through the night, a group of twenty women arrived and occupied the tables. "How odd," I thought. They looked like intoxicated secretaries. The enigma was solved when during the half-time show, a large, off-white male took the stage. I am sure the younger readers are thinking, "so?" but in 1977 this was shocking. The women were having the equivalent of a bachelor party. If any of them had inhibitions about screaming, catcalling, or participating on stage with the performer, they didn't show it. Adrienne and I were embarrassed as we watched the mostly naked dancer stick lollipops in progressively more intimate spots on his costume only to see the secretaries remove the candy by mouth.

When the half-time show was over, the women left and we were back to business, but the deal did not go down that night. I can't recall what glitched the plan, but such is the fluid nature of drug operations. Later at the debriefing in the Detachment, the members who had been monitoring in the van wanted to know what all the female screaming had been about. Neither Adrienne nor I would tell, but the Vancouver members did. What a joke the members thought it was to have such a role reversal as female members watching a male stripper! They didn't yet fully comprehend that just because we wanted to work in a male-dominated field, it didn't mean we wanted to copy their behaviour.

Adrienne and I put in a second guest appearance one Grey Cup Sunday to assist the combined RCMP/VCP task force named Coordinated Law Enforcement Unit, or CLUE for short. CLUE had been monitoring several "common gaming houses," one of which was in North Vancouver. Since gamblers, too, are a remarkably connected subculture, the multiple takedowns of the numerous offending homes had to be precisely coordinated, not just with the teams simultaneously entering all entrances and exits from the house but also with all other units throughout the lower mainland.

Adrienne and the member with whom she was teamed stealthily positioned themselves at the front door to the home as a rather large VCP member and I took up a position at the rear door. Suddenly, the VCP member raced to the unmarked police car and returned carrying a sledge hammer.

"Almost forgot my key," he said in answer to my unspoken questioning look.

"GO!" commanded a voice on the radio a second later.

The VCP member swung back the sledge hammer then slammed it into the side of the house making a large hole in the stucco.

"Damn!" he said, and then he hit his mark. The back door fell into the house, landing squarely on the hall floor with a loud thud, hinges and frame still attached. Our entrance froze everyone in the house--which by this time included Adrienne and the other member--into a shocked silence. The CLUE member was the first to recover, directing Adrienne and me to take control of the female bookie, sitting at a desk beside the phone, a well-used ashtray, and a half-spent notepad and pen. I still remember the feeling of disappointment as I realized the reason Adrienne and I had been requested to assist: it was only because of the atypical gender of the suspect. We were expected to be nothing more than matrons for the investigators! However, we were about to demonstrate that female peace officers could be much more than that.

Just then, the phone rang, and Adrienne quickly took charge of the suspect to ensure she did not answer the phone send out an alert.

On the second ring I answered.

"Barb, it's Roy. I would like to place a bet on the Lions," a male voice said.

"Go ahead," I said, lowering my voice in an effort to sound more mature and more like a smoker. Either my voice was off or my word choice was different because the caller became immediately suspicious and asked, "You don't sound right. Is everything okay there?"

I cleared my throat and coughed a bit and then said in a gravelly voice, "Yeah, just got a bit of a cold. How much is your bet?"

He paused, still suspicious, deciding if he should continue; so I turned up the pressure.

"I can't tie up the line, Roy. Do you want to bet or not?"

Like any true gambler he threw better judgment to the winds and placed his wager. I took several more before we left--the perfect evidence to ensure a guilty plea. As we walked over the back door with the accused to leave the residence, she shook her head and, speaking directly to the VCP member who had wheeled the "key," said: "The door wasn't locked. You just had to turn the handle."

Adrienne and I found it hard to suppress a smile at the information at the time, but in hindsight I think the VCP member really didn't care, because he liked using the key.

These occasional guest appearances with non-North Vancouver squads only made me appreciate the progressive work atmosphere female members enjoyed in North Vancouver Detachment and throughout most of the RCMP. Adrienne and I were more than happy to return to our normal GIS duties after our little adventures.

B&E squad had been so hastily created that none of us had the benefit of surveillance training; consequently we often lost our target before our shift was finished. The squad had its skeptics, and the last thing any of us wanted was to return to the office empty-handed. In the event we lost the target, the remainder of the shift became a competition between B&E partners to see who could uncover the best criminal code "bust." Like most of our competitions, the losers had to buy the winners beer at the Legion after shift. This created an invaluable opportunity for junior members like myself and Zack to learn how to further develop our natural emotional intelligence by focusing on reading body language. It was a race against time and each other as we scoured the streets of North Vancouver from our unmarked cars looking for the unconscious nuances in movements of criminals; nuances that speak more clearly and loudly than words in a language peace officers must become fluent in.

With remarkable ease, we caught theft of and from vehicles on a regular basis; but Zack held the record for detecting and thwarting the most serious crime, an attempted armed robbery of a Mac store. Perhaps competition had its purposes after all.

Herb Wilburg was team leader of the other squad, or "Herbie from the B team," as Zack and I were cheeky enough to call him. Through years of hard work, Herbie had made it to the GIS section, only to share an office with Zack and me, barely off recruit field training. We had jumped pretty far pretty fast. Of course, we could have been a little more respectful but where would have been the fun in that? It was all good-natured razzing; Zack and I were just a little better at it.

It was fortunate Rinn understood I was an apprentice, not competition. I felt like a recruit again when Rinn invited me along to check out some vague information regarding a career criminal now working for a moving company. Rinn and I attended the suspect's apartment to "heat him up." As we knocked on the door, Rinn informed me that he wanted me to get the serial numbers and model numbers of anything in the apartment that could be run on CPIC.

How was I supposed to do that with him looking on? I thought as the door opened. I was at loss as to how to accomplish the task Rinn had given me. The interview was just a formality, Rinn assured him; his name had come up and we were just checking it out. At the end of the interview, Rinn asked if I had anything to ask. I think they were both caught off guard by the simple direct approach I took.

"Do you mind if I record some serial numbers?" I asked.

Of course, he could have refused but that would have raised our suspicions, and he had just told us how honest he now was. If he had known how efficient our computer system was, he would probably have been more stressed. Rinn was even surprised when the system identified the TV as stolen, providing grounds for the subsequent search warrant and arrest. Apparently I had passed the first test, because Rinn presented me with another after the suspect was booked into cells. "You will take his statement."

My stress level jumped. We had one charge of possession of stolen property but that was only the tip of this crime spree. We could place him near and around crimes, but we lacked direct evidence or the overwhelming circumstantial evidence we needed to sustain a conviction. We needed a confession. I did not feel competent as an interrogator, but, as usual, Rinn had a plan.

"I want you to take a written, warned statement from this guy. Make sure you cover these questions on his activities and locations in relation to these offences. Don't challenge him on anything. Just get the statement and then call me in."

I didn't see how that was going to be a great help but if that was what he wanted, I would try. The suspect appeared relieved to see that he was so unimportant that an obviously junior member like myself was handling the interrogation.

I took my time explaining in the simplest of terms the police warnings. He, of course, had memorized these warnings long before I was born. He had years of criminal activities to comfort him as he looked across the table at so unmatched an adversary. It was of course in his best interest to provide a plausible lie as to how he came into the possession of the TV: "I bought it in a bar. Didn't know the guy who sold it."

It was a good lie, one which could potentially defeat a charge of "possession of stolen property." Unfortunately for him, CPIC identified the victim of the theft as one of the moving company's clients. One of the most useful skills from Depot was masking all emotional response. I never batted an eyelash as I recorded his answer.

He began to relax, thinking he really was as smart as he believed. As instructed, I continued asking the questions and recording the answers. Some of the questions I already knew the answer to, some I didn't. With each successive lie, he grew more and more at ease. He answered each and every question. Why wouldn't he? I would believe anything, apparently. My hand was aching when I finally finished, and he read over and signed the statement.

"I just have to show this to my boss and I will be right back," I stated as I left the interview room.

Rinn was delighted to read the incriminating responses the suspect had committed himself to. I wasn't sure what his plan was, but apparently it was unfolding exactly as he had wanted.

"This is perfect. Let's go. This time let me do all the talking."

I had the feeling I was about to watch a master at work, and I was right. The suspect was still seated at the interview table when we returned. Rinn took my old seat opposite him while I quietly sat in the chair by the door.

"I see you have given Cst. Greenwood a statement," Rinn said in quiet, almost soft, voice; the kind of voice that makes you unconsciously strain a little to make sure you catch every word.

"Yes, I have co-operated fully," the suspect responded, still confident that he was going to win the game. He smiled at me and I smiled back. There was a brief moment of silence, which was probably quite reassuring to him, then Rinn began to switch gears.

"I don't think you have been completely honest." Again Rinn spoke in his quiet, soft voice. The suspect looked confused as Rinn went in for the kill.

"I don't think you have been honest at all. As a matter of fact, this statement is full of lies and I can prove it. You have been lying to this peace officer."

At that point, they both paused and looked at me. In a moment of revelation

I could see myself through their eyes. To the suspect, I was a young, naïve, non-threatening female, someone he had let his guard down to. To Rinn, I was someone he hoped would be smart enough to learn how to use that perception to good advantage.

The suspect could not mentally adjust quickly enough to the turn of events his statement had caused. Keeping him emotionally off balance, Rinn moved in. As he spoke, Rinn's voice had gradually become stronger and louder. Even though he was only speaking at a normal level as he delivered the brilliant, climactic question, it sounded as though he were shouting: "Do you know what the penalty is for lying to a peace officer?"

There is of course no penalty for lying to a peace officer. It happens all too frequently; however, in Rinn's dramatic presentation it sounded like a serious crime.

"Give me the statement back and I will tell you the truth," the suspect pleaded.

Rinn refused. The suspect immediately confessed in a written warned statement anyway. He confessed to everything we suspected and much more.

The confession was iron-clad, completely voluntary, and with no threat or coercion. Even if the suspect had not confessed, he would have been convicted because of the first incriminating statement committing him on paper to events we could prove were lies. Rinn's intellectual shell game in interrogations was a clever strategy, something I could adopt once I returned to uniform--just one of many effective policing strategies I would learn from him.

After the B&E Squad's first takedown, I was tasked with delivering a thick prosecutor's sheet containing over a dozen charges against the B&E Squad's first target. I respectfully knocked on his office door and, after handing him the prosecutor's sheet, I sat down to await his response.

"It might take some time to review these charges--you may not wish to wait," he said.

"I have been instructed by Rinn to wait until you approve them all," I said, noticing a faint smile eroding the corners of the Crown's mouth at my response. There seemed to be some professional history mixed with respect in his expression. In an almost amused tone he asked, "And what have you been instructed to do if I don't approve them all?"

"I have been instructed to stand upon your desk until you do," I said dryly.

"You have?" he asked a little shocked at my stoic response.

"He did, and I will," I said with a twinkle in my eye, which elicited a smile. He took a second longer look at me, a bit surprised and pleased that Rinn finally had an apprentice.

"Well, we can't have that. Tell Rinn I won't deal them down."

It wasn't long before another detachment lured Tilley away with a promotion. Tilley's transfer party was attended by the entire GIS section. After a warm-up party at the Legion, we took over a large room in a Chinese restaurant on Lonsdale. The tables had been set up along the wall in a "U" formation. No one was feeling any pain as we awaited our food orders. Zack and I were seated at one of the inside ends of the shoe. He leaned over and asked, "Do you think it would be funny if Rinn got a pie in the face?"

"What?" I couldn't believe he would suggest it. It was a little over the top even for us.

"I bet if I paid a waiter $5.00, he would 'pie' Rinn," Zack said matter-of-factly.

"I think that's going too far," I whispered.

"I'll be right back," Zack said recklessly, as he disappeared from the room.

Quickly I searched the faces of the members seated near us to see if anyone had overheard the plot. Three seats up and across the table, my gaze was met by Tilley. By the wink of his eye and the smile on his face it was clear he not only had heard, but now knew who had been behind the recent mischief in GIS.

Oblivious to the new turn of events, Zack returned alone. I had just finished telling him we had been found out when a waiter, cream pie at his back, entered the room saying, "Fone ca' fo' Winn."

Rinn, who had his back to the waiter, spun around in his seat and said, "I'm Rinn."

A perfect pie in the face was delivered, one he never saw coming. The whole room was stunned, except of course for Zack, Tilley, and myself--we broke into hilarious laughter. Rinn took off his glasses to expose the only part of his face not covered in cream--his eyes. I have never seen people laugh as hard as they did at that moment. Even Rinn had to suppress a smile as he pointed accusingly across the room to Tilley. "Tilley, you asshole!"

Tilley never let on he was not the author of it. He was probably sorry he hadn't thought of it himself.

Being "pied" instantly became a tradition at every subsequent GIS party, creating a bonanza in tips for the waiters and waitresses. It was almost like a badge of popularity to be "pied." That didn't stop nervous members from instinctively diving for cover under the table whenever someone new entered the room. Not all sections had as much fun working and playing together as GIS.

Adrienne and I had been pleasantly surprised at the acceptance we had found as the first two female members on the tightly knit GIS section, but apparently not everyone in the detachment was happy.

A rumour was beginning to circulate suggesting there was more than a professional relationship going on between Tilley and Adrienne and Rinn and myself. The men were outraged, unaccustomed to betrayal from within the Force. Adrienne and I took it less personally, knowing the attack fit the pattern of harassment other female members had occasionally encountered at other detachments. The only thing surprising to us was not that we had enemies in our ranks but that we had so few, and, more important, that we had many more friends and supporters watching our backs.

Tilley's imminent transfer allowed Adrienne to finish the last month of her rotation. To protect both Rinn's and my reputations, I returned to the watch the next shift. It wasn't the blow to me that the character assassin might have wished for. As much fun as I was having on the squad, I was always cognizant that teams formed in the RCMP were transitory in nature. I was secretly looking forward to my return to uniform to demonstrate some of the skills I had gleaned on the squad. I felt privileged to have been exposed to such experienced members and exciting crimes so early in my career.

I was returning to the watch a much more effective, confident member than when I had left and I was eager to prove it.

Chapter 6

Back in Harness

I returned to general duty with a newfound respect for the harness bulls of police forces, the first line of response to the public's cry for help. These were the unsung heroes who routinely made life-and-death decisions without the luxury of time, complete information, and immediate backup. Specialized plainclothes sections that came in after the scene was secured and settled by the uniformed members knew how tough uniform work was, especially for Mounties. The RCMP remains the only major police agency that uses single-person patrols in general duty work.

Unlike city police forces, partners in the RCMP share an area, not a car--a work environment union police forces have deemed unsafe. The understated, yet strong, nature of partnerships in the Force is defined by this policy. Like guardian angels, members continually monitor each other's calls and dispatches and decide if they should arrange their patrols to include a drive-by. Sometimes you see them, sometimes you don't, but you always know you are not alone.

The reality that in an instant everything could "go sideways," leaving someone's (most often the member's) life hanging in the balance is one of the many reasons police partnerships are intense, almost intimate relationships built on trust and professional respect that only police and soldiers can really understand. Small wonder partnerships sometimes sparked jealous reactions from spouses.

The future integration of female members into the police community would be founded on our ability to be accepted as equals in these partnerships. Senior female members were keenly aware of the price special consideration, career shortcuts, or modifications in work expectations, based on gender, would command if any of us accepted the occasional opportunity--a price that would be paid by the next generation of females.

I was determined to resist all temptations and achieve success the hard way. The only intergenerational debt I would entertain would be one owed to me if I could leave a legacy of acceptance for the female members who would follow. My past successes in foot chases, defusing fights, arrests, and shooting seemed more impressive to the male members and challenged their traditional concept of Mounties, not only because I was female but because I was so small and looked so young. It's not that difficult to turn disadvantage to advantage if you can accept who you are and not try to be who you think you should be.

My new partner, Cst. Daryl Little, who was anything but little, was content that I required no extra backup and was capable of providing him assistance if he required it. He was very friendly and confided over coffee that he was keenly interested in competing for the next B&E squad rotation. I was fairly oblivious to the enhanced power I wielded based on the friendships I had made in plainclothes.

The partnership unofficially extended to include the two junior members in the neighbouring Capilano Zone, Gary Proulx and Len Hall. Each of the four of us had unique strengths to bring to the group.

Gary's quiet, pleasant demeanour appeared at odds with his nickname, "cement hands," unless you knew he was a black belt. Len was fresh off recruit field training. What he lacked in experience he made up for in enthusiasm. Daryl, the most senior in service of our group, was only twenty-two. He had grown up in B.C. and had a good grasp of local problems and who was causing them. We became an effective, productive, and homogeneous team.

Like any team, we were only as good as our coaches; or, in our case, our corporals. My old corporal's replacement, Dick Smith, was one of the best. He was a bundle of knowledge and energy. We often had to race him to calls. If there was a "Monty Mountie," Dickie was it, right down to the spit shine of his boots--as I found out one time.

I was dispatched to the continuation of a file that had begun a week earlier. Unfortunately, the complainant, a mechanic, did not have the file number or the member's name. In an effort to identify him, I asked what the member looked like.

"He was six feet, six-feet-two, about twenty-five, with a mustache."

"That describes everyone on my watch except me," I laughed. "Was there anything else outstanding about him?"

He paused for a minute, then stated: "Yes, he had the best shine I have ever seen on a pair of shoes."

"Dickie Smith," I correctly stated without a doubt.

The irony of the situation was, the complainant was literally covered from head to foot in grease, yet it was well-polished shoes that made a lasting impression, not Dickie's strikingly strawberry blond hair or boyish freckled face.

I formed a hypothesis that memory was a very personal, subjective view into the witness's personality and values. I was learning much more about psychology outside of the classroom than I ever did in. The mechanic may not have had shiny shoes but it didn't stop him from admiring them, forming a lasting impression of Dick Smith and the Force by association. Depot's fixation on spit shines and body weight had some relevance on the job after all!

We all graduated lean and fit, and that was how the Force intended for us to stay. If a member picked up weight on detachment, he or she would be removed from public view to an administrative, non-operational position as punishment. The "fat" list didn't just affect work assignments; it also had a negative impact on yearly assessments and, ultimately, promotions. Although heavy-handed, it was an extremely effective method of maintaining both the image of the Force and the health of its members. Members were encouraged to stay active both off duty and on.

It wasn't difficult in those days to fill the empty last hours of midnight shifts by picking up impaired drivers; after all, one in three cars on the road after two a.m. was driven by an offender. I became so experienced at spotting them that when I pulled over a suspected drunk driver, I would radio the code as a "68"--"impaired"--rather than "69," designating a routine traffic stop.

One night, filled with the pounding rain unique to rainforests like the wet West Coast, I pulled over a Triumph sports car on 13th Street hill. The driver was drunk and unco-operative, refusing to get out of the car. In the moment it took for her to grind the gears in an attempt to escape, I reached through the open driver's window to take the keys. It was a stupid and dangerous thing to do, the type of action we had been cautioned about at Depot not to take. I soon found out why when, to my surprise, the keys were not on the steering column as I expected. Fortunately, I got my upper body out of the car just before she tore off east on 13th.

Between my haste to return to my car and the rain, I didn't notice that Len had just pulled in behind me as backup. I radioed in my first vehicle pursuit, and my surveillance experience from B&E squad took over as I broadcast our speed and direction of travel, east, toward the Detachment, where most of the night shift was waiting. Unbeknownst to me, Len followed in silence.

The members inside the Detachment raced to their cars parked in a row on the far side of a cement wall in the parking lot that faced south onto 13th Street. They didn't have to wait long before they saw the red sports car fly by, the driver nearly losing control as she rounded the corner south on St. Georges. Their feet were poised on their accelerators as I roared by.

As I rounded the corner at St. Georges, the suspect car hit the high sidewalk to its right, sending a long trail of sparks flying like a blowtorch from the rim. As the disabled vehicle slowly came to rest halfway down the next block, I was more than a little annoyed to see that I was alone with no backup.

I was in the process of placing the suspect in the back of my police car when the rest of the night shift caught up with me. It wasn't until coffee later that I heard about the potentially tragic accident my pursuit had caused.

The instant my police car passed the Detachment, the waiting members hit the gas, unaware that Len was also in pursuit immediately behind me. There were police cars braking and sliding all over the street and lawns at 13th and St. Georges. Poor Len nearly got himself killed trying to back me up.

Later, in the breathalyzer room, I learned the reason I couldn't locate the keys when I reached for them. The car was not a Triumph as I had thought. The impaired was quite insulted that I had made that mistake.

"It's an Alfa Romeo," she stated in a snooty but slurred manner. I had never heard of that brand of car, but it was obviously expensive.

"Well, it's toast now! Too bad ICBC [the provincial government insurance everyone had to carry] won't cover an impaired accident." ICBC could be even tougher than the courts, as I had learned on an earlier case.

That case began as a report of strange lights along the Capilano River. By the time emergency crews and I attended, two intoxicated lawyers had made their way up the bank to the road. The owner of the new Mercedes Coup knew exactly the lies to tell to ensure that a successful prosecution would be all but impossible.

They were returning from a late night at their Vancouver office when the infamous "black dog" caused him to lose control and drive down the river bank, where they had no clear idea how long they sat in shock. Without independent evidence to the contrary, it would be impossible to prove the time of the accident, and, by inference, the time of the offence of impaired driving--one of the elements of the charge.

The driver and his friend further muddied the waters by claiming to have been so shaken by the accident they drank a mickey of Vodka before throwing the bottle into the river. His friend backed up every word. Lawyers!

Still, I wasn't ready to toss in the towel so quickly. As I pulled out the breathalyzer demand card, he reached for his neck and requested an ambulance. I chose to accompany him back to the hospital, hoping at least to let him sweat a little.

At Lions Gate Hospital, the doctors and nurses weren't fooled by his transparent claims of neck injury, but it was an effective stall because it forced them to examine him for fear of a later civil suit. I was about to leave, abandoning any hope of justice for this pathetic excuse of a man, when his friend asked if the suspect wanted him to call his wife and let her know where he was.

"Oh, God yes. Poor Alice. She'll be worried sick."

His friend left for the pay phone but returned almost immediately, asking, "Do you have any change?"

The suspect reached into his pocket and held out a handful of change and his wedding band, no doubt removed for the night's activities. He flushed with embarrassment as he quickly put the ring back on his finger, too ashamed to look at either the nurse or myself as we watched in disgust. He remained silent until his friend returned.

"Alice shouldn't drive when she is upset. Can you phone her back and tell her to take a cab?"

"Actually, she said she'll see you when you get home."

It was obvious the suspect wasn't fooling anyone that night, least of all his wife. The nurse and I smiled as we left the room.

A week later, I was surprised when the accident report in which I had indicated I suspected alcohol as a contributing factor resulted in a phone call from an ICBC claims adjuster. I was pleased to discover that the civil threshold for burden of proof was much less than criminal. The Mercedes was a write-off, which ICBC would not cover. Even a high-priced lawyer would feel that financial pinch. Not that he would ever let on to any of his upper-middle-class neighbours in North Vancouver.

There were no "street people" then in North Vancouver, with one exception: a transient glue-sniffer from Surrey named Lyle. Lyle would occasionally show up in North Vancouver for several months at a time. He was quite a sight to see: long, uncut, unkempt hair with white, hardened glue streaking his long, dark beard, a harmless indigent who slept in Salvation Army drop boxes.

Lyle existed in his own little reality, one created by the glue fumes in the plastic bag secreted in his coat pocket. Members were quite empathetic towards Lyle and the occasional drunk they found on the street when the winter nights sometimes dipped below freezing. They would arrest them, book them in for a warm, dry bed, and release them in the morning without charge.

Unfortunately, it soon became apparent that Lyle was a walking lice habitat. Police cars and cells required disinfecting and fumigation every time we rescued him. Finally, word came down from the top ordering members not to arrest Lyle again unless he had committed a murder and had the smoking gun in his hand.

Poor Lyle, even the Salvation Army began to lock the hatches on the drop-off boxes at night. Eventually, he moved back to Surrey, where his family lived. It was rumoured he found a way out of the glue addiction and back into society.

The lack of people living on the street back then wasn't because there were fewer poor or mental patients; they were just better cared for, with a social net waiting to catch them if they fell. Canadian morality at that time expected families and government to protect individuals at risk with or without their consent, to provide order and protection for the individual and the accepted social order.

The occasional runaway who showed up on the street would be quickly scooped up under the authority of the "Juvenile Delinquents Act," which gave police and the courts ample powers to ensure that children were protected from predators and their own poor choices. They would either be returned home, if it was a suitable environment, or placed in foster care. The system wasn't perfect but it was better than the disease, exploitation, and addiction that awaited them on the street. Today's runaways and schizophrenics may have more individual rights, but they appear to have a poorer quality of life.

Before the eighties, "street people" were individuals living outside the law, choosing the street to make money. It was a subculture made up of prostitutes, pimps, and drug dealers who carved out their turf on Davie Street in downtown Vancouver. The first time I drove down Davie at night, I was shocked and a little embarrassed to know inner city problems were not just an American phenomenon. How depressing it must have been to "walk the beat" as a Vancouver City Police officer.

Perhaps it was this policing environment that caused the Vancouver City Police (VCP) to develop an aggressive law-enforcement persona. Even the criminal element seemed keenly aware of the difference in police cultures between the RCMP and VCP. On more than one occasion, a person with an outstanding Vancouver arrest warrant turned himself in to the North Vancouver RCMP rather than be arrested by the VCP.

The Vancouver City Police seemed to enjoy its rough-and-tumble reputation, oblivious of the fact that its macho subculture had prevented it from providing a leadership role for female police. VCP had had a few token female peace officers as early as the 1900s, but women continued to be frustrated into the 1970s with the limited roles of matron, public relations, and clerical jobs to which the "Women's Squad" were restricted.[15] The Force may have been late to hire women as peace officers, but when they did, there was no distinction in training or police roles based on gender lines. Female peace officers throughout

[15] Joanne Bearnish, "The Skirted Minority," *Thin Blue Line*, Vol. 3 No. 1 (a semi-biographical article in the official publication of the B.C. Federation of P.O.).

Canada used the RCMP's model to expand their roles.

Members of the RCMP enjoyed a kinship with all police forces within Canada, in an older sibling kind of way. Perhaps it was our size and the unfettered scope in enforcement duties; or maybe because Hollywood had created a romantic, noble image of the Force while it depicted American city police forces and federal enforcement agencies as corrupt or incompetent. Whatever the reason, it seemed other Canadian police forces and federal agencies chose the "red wall" against which to measure professionalism. But even the best of families don't get along all the time.

The sibling rivalry between members of Vancouver City Police and Mounties, fuelled by alcohol and male hormones, on one occasion erupted into a brawl at the private police club owned by the Vancouver Police Union. VCP may have had a reputation for being rough, but the fight between the two police departments seemed to end in a draw, even though both sides claimed victory.

In contrast to Vancouver City Police's rough-and-tumble culture, the city police in West Vancouver appeared overly polite and quite British. West Vancouver P.D. was tasked with policing the richest residential neighbourhood in Canada. Where there is money, politics is not far behind. Not much real crime went on except the occasional wild party hosted by the local bored rich children of lawyers, councillors, and celebrities. The small West Vancouver force often had to request North Vancouver RCMP to back them up at wild beach parties.

There was no shortage of volunteers in North Vancouver willing to show these offenders that the law was indeed impartial in Canada, and the RCMP didn't care if their parents were well connected. In an effort to limit the response, North Vancouver's NCOs were ordered by the operations officer to send only two police cars if West Vancouver called. In compliance with the order, the next time the call for help came from West Vancouver police, only two police cars were dispatched, but they were packed with more members then I thought could physically fit. The last person I saw squeeze into the car was my staff sergeant, George Monk.

It was an open secret that the small municipal city police force of West Vancouver liked the disregard the RCMP felt for local politics and demonstrated when it came to enforcing the law. The autonomous nature of the RCMP as a separate agency of the federal government meant that local political interference was not a factor in administering Canadian law in the RCMP, as a North Vancouver politician found out one night.

The call for help from a distraught woman fearing for her life sent every clear member racing to the mayor's house. I was first to arrive, followed closely by the Capilano Zone member. The suspect, the mayor's son, had fled in a vehicle after a minor assault on the mayor's fiancé, but not before he had uttered an earnest threat to return and finish the job.

I remained to take the victim's statement while the other members left the scene to make patrols for the suspect. I had just handed the woman the finished statement to read and sign when the suspect's car pulled into the driveway behind my police car.

"It's him! He's come back to kill me!" she shrieked in fear, as we both watched him storm past my vehicle toward the house. It had never crossed any of the members' minds that the suspect would dare return to the residence while the police were still there, because no one in his right mind would do so.

"Hide!" I whispered as I grabbed my portable radio. There was only time to call "10–33" before the suspect burst through the door in a rage.

"Where is she!" he demanded, as he attempted to pass by me in the living room in search of his prey. I stepped in front of him to halt his advance and lied, "She's at the hospital. You are under arrest for assault."

He didn't seem to care about the arrest part of my statement; he was intent only on locating the woman. He paused, trying to decide if I was telling the truth; whether he should continue searching the house or race off to the hospital. The moment of pause was followed by a sharp turn as he tried to retreat toward the door. As I grabbed his arm to complete the arrest, the headlights of my closest backup slid into the driveway in a four-wheel drift, boxing his vehicle in. In textbook RCMP fashion, a show of force was all that was required. The suspect gave in without further resistance.

At three a.m., I was just finishing the prosecutor's sheets when the station NCO forwarded down a phone call without comment or direction.

"I understand you have my son in custody, Constable," said the voice.

"That is correct," I said, not sure what kind of attitude to expect.

"That's good. He is not thinking straight. I am out of the country until Wednesday. I would like him held until I get back." The words were spoken by a person in authority used to having his requests complied with.

"That is not my decision or yours; I am afraid it will be a judge's," I said politely but firmly. There was silence on the other end of the line for a minute; then a more human voice, the voice of a concerned father, spoke: "Of course it is. I apologize if I sounded harsh, it's just that I am so far away and I am afraid of what could happen if my son is let out before I return, not just to my fiancé, but to my son as well." That was a voice I could work with.

"I am in the process of preparing the paperwork that will be used by Crown when your son is brought before the judge in the morning. I was recommending custody or, at the least, a restraining order. If you have relevant information on why you feel there is a continued real danger, I will include it in the notes to the prosecutor and he may raise it with the judge."

He did provide information, and I did what I could, but no more than I would have done for any father in a similar situation. Politics and police work do not mix.

Political corruption is not inevitable, but it is more of a danger when your boss or his/her friends or relatives are the subject of offences.

The autonomous military structure of the RCMP and federally negotiated contracts insulated members of the Force from local influences. The transfer policy resulting in out-of-province members' enforcing the law helped to ensure that the law was impartially enforced. Members had little chance of stopping their uncle for speeding, their old hockey coach for impaired driving, or their nephew for B&E. This type of unfettered response to crime is one of the reasons the RCMP was so trusted nationally and internationally. As respect for the Force grew, the Federal government trusted the RCMP with more and more responsibilities through new contracts. Through each new contract, the Force's size and responsibilities continued to expand into municipal, provincial, and federal enforcement areas.

The RCMP absorbed some provincial police forces and took over the enforcement responsibilities in other federal agencies such as Customs and Excise. The RCMP's one-agency, multi-task, multi-jurisdictional policing is a model admired and envied throughout the international community of law enforcement. The RCMP's responsibilities are handled by thirty-two different agencies in the United States and its one-stop investigational and enforcement structure means it is unencumbered by the territorial end fighting, petty jealousies, and breakdowns in communications that other countries' enforcement communities sometimes struggle with and the underworld thrives on.

Although the RCMP was shielded from external politics, it was not, as I once naïvely believed, above internal subterfuge. I stumbled upon, quite by accident, a powerful secret that unofficially controlled promotional opportunities within the Force.

The mystery began when I was attempting to locate the owners of the assortment of stolen property I had seized while executing a search warrant. It was a simple matter to match most of the recovered items to the theft reports, except for two items that I suspected had a common origin. One was a large, antique, leather-bound book, a guest or member registry with "Masonic Lodge" moulded onto the cover, and the other was a large, ceremonial-looking machete similar to the one in the crest on the book. Both items had never been reported stolen.

I was aware of a sign "Masonic Hall" on the second floor of a Lonsdale Street business building, so I went but never found anyone there. There had never been a call to or from the location, and there was no property reference registered with the Detachment. The number listed in the phone book was answered only by an answering machine. No one returned my calls.

I was getting frustrated. Without a lawful owner, I couldn't prove the items stolen and lay the appropriate charges. Even more disturbing, the items would have to be returned if the accused requested them.

I brought my dilemma to S/Sgt Hill, who seemed amused at my complete lack of knowledge concerning a group that predated the Crusades. I was openly frustrated at their apparent disinterest in their property. He laughed as he handed me a telephone number and a name.

"Once they know what you have, I am sure they will call," he correctly predicted.

The person I spoke to was evasive and unco-operative, refusing to admit even that the items were stolen. He wanted the property back without any further investigation. There was an undertone of condescension in his voice, but I was uncertain whether it was for my position as a peace officer or my gender. Either way, I didn't like it and quietly turned the table.

"You can have the book back as soon as I photocopy the contents for court." I had hit the nerve I was looking for, forcing him to co-operate; but he didn't like it.

My interest had been piqued by this mysterious group. I decided to do what all peace officers do best: ask a lot of questions. The Queen's Rule of Judges protected the peace officer's right to ask questions. Asking questions was more than our right: It was the key to basic police work, one we used to uncover the truth and expose secrets; it was one of the most powerful tools for a well-trained peace officer. That was why it was all but impossible to keep any secrets within the RCMP. Members hate secrets, and I asked my questions to uncover a closely guarded one. I soon discovered there was a powerful organization intertwined in the power structure of the Force.

The officer ranks of the Force were riddled with Masons. As a matter of fact, very few NCOs or commissioned officers were *not* part of this group. Although it was unclear how long the Masons had held this grip on the inner structure of the Force, it was an open secret that an invitation to join the Masons extended by a higher-ranking member was the first step in a long and successful, often rapid, series of promotions.

A very unflattering picture was emerging of a shadow structure not only within the RCMP, but also in most police agencies, as well as the halls of Parliament. Some of my youthful arrogance about being fairly well informed and educated was shaken, along with my naïve idealism. I wondered how I could have been so unaware of such a powerful organization.

Perhaps it was because there were no Masons back home on Catholic-dominated Wolfe Island. Apparently Masons didn't care for Catholics much; but for a group that didn't like Catholics, they seemed to share much of their organizational structure, as well as their sexist attitudes.

Masons were men. Their wives and daughters could be Daughters of Job, but the power lay with the Masons. It reminded me of the Knights of Columbus and the Catholic Women's League, but this group was much broader-based and politically powerful. I wondered how many glass ceilings have a large "M" etched in them. I didn't stop to realize that two of my strongest and most powerful supporters at the Detachment were Masons. In hindsight, most Masons seemed to have been adjusting to the new female reality in a rather enlightened way for the times.

The Masons were not that popular within the male junior constable ranks, either. It was an authoritarian power structure the baby boom constables, not just the female members of the Force, were not happy with. The change in demographics at the constable rank had caused a paradigm shift in the disposition within the Force, one which seemed to take Ottawa by surprise.

In 1979, Treasury Board's bilateral decision to renege on a pay raise ignited an unprecedented act of defiance by the constables of E Division. It wasn't the first time Ottawa had treated the membership of the Force as if they were conscripts in an army, but it was the first time the membership of the Force openly challenged the shoddy treatment. The outraged members called a hasty meeting at Deer Lake in Burnaby, where members were prepared to entertain all options, even unionizing.

Pressured by Ottawa, NCOs and officers, in an unsuccessful bid to intimidate members, strongly recommended that members who valued their career not attend. Internal Investigations Section snapped pictures side by side with journalists as members crammed into the hall. All eyes in Ottawa were abruptly turned from Ontario and Quebec to the West. It was a defining moment in the history of the Force.

The RCMP was teetering on the brink of a union. The members in Quebec had had union leanings prior to this, but they lacked the numbers and the influence within the Force to be viewed as anything but a radical fringe element.

One-third of the manpower of the RCMP was stationed in E Division. The RCMP's strength had always been in the West, and we were finally prepared to use it. Where we led, the rest of the Force would follow.

Treasury Board was forced to back down and a union was avoided. The Ottawa bureaucrats and politicians had been caught off-guard by the insubordination in E Division, a mistake they had no desire to repeat.

After Deer Lake, it was clear to the politicians there was a point beyond which members would not be pushed. So they turned their sights to an easier group's budget to raid, the Canadian military.

There remains an unspoken bond and empathy for the military within the ranks of the RCMP. It was more than the "brothers in arms" camaraderie that results when groups share the battlefield in war. Historically, we had also shared the meagre fiscal value the Canadian government allotted to the military. Pay levels within the Force began to rise only in the mid-1970s, in an effort to curb recruitment of trained peace officers from better-paid union police forces. It's a shame the military had no private sector equivalent.

Through conversations with career wives, I began to appreciate how shabbily treated members had been by the Force, and the devastating effect it had on their wives and children. Poverty level pay, no pay for overtime, and constant transfers ensured a fiscal dependency on the Force. Force housing, a double-bladed benefit, provided the illusion that a member could afford a family home, while ensuring their continued dependency on the government to provide it. Still, it was better than the basement suites constables could afford on the open market. No wonder the Force had prohibited marriage in the first few years of service. The members couldn't afford it.

The wives of the NCOs, often nurses and teachers, did not feel compelled to excuse the Force's actions in the same way their husbands might. Perhaps that was because the frequent transfers that benefited their husband's careers had exactly the opposite effect on theirs. A good friend of mine, Janet Hill, gave me some heartfelt advice early in my career: "Stay until you get a pension; that is your independence."

It was selfless wisdom she was gifting. She knew what it was like to restart a nursing career, losing seniority and pension benefits with each new town they were transferred to. Like so many wives, she had sacrificed her individual financial security, forever binding her to the good nature of her husband. She was one of the lucky ones who had a lifetime commitment with a member who was a devoted husband and father; yet still she regretted losing the financial independence her own pension would have given her, even if it was only psychological or symbolic.

The symbolic power of money, like so many things, means different things to different genders. For men, money is equated with power; to women, money represents freedom. Like my mother, Janet had been a female pioneer from the previous generation who had chosen a career determined to never be dependent on anyone and to be free to do what she wanted when she wanted. Although retiring was not part of my consciousness at that point, I gratefully filed her advice away in my memory before returning to my immediate concerns of developing my skills in enforcing the law.

An eighteen-year-old First Nations girl from the north of British Columbia was raped. She had been staying with her female cousin on the City South Reserve while she attended Capilano College. Unfortunately, the cousin had been befriended by a young white criminal, Gus. While the girl's cousin was away at bingo, Gus committed the rape.

Gus and I had already crossed paths while I was on B&E squad, when he was an under-parented teen. Although some of the members I worked with felt sorry for him and believed he could be "turned around," there was something about the way he looked at me that always made me wary and uncomfortable. There was never any doubt in my mind after hearing the victim's story that Gus was guilty or that he would be convicted for it--a sentiment that I was surprised to learn wasn't shared by the rest of the Detachment, as I found out shortly after his arrest at a social function. Rape was never a slam-dunk back then, but I had successfully charged enough sex offenders to feel confident this was a winning case. I was surprised to hear a senior member, whom I respected, predict that I would never convict Gus of the rape. Thinking he was only playing devil's advocate to tease me, I challenged his reasoning by asking: "What makes you so sure he'll walk?"

The answer shocked me, and it was becoming harder and harder to do that.

"Because she is native. They give it away."

I could not believe someone I respected so much had said something so flagrantly racist. He had never given any indication of racist views before or after that conversation. In hindsight, I know now he was not a racist; he was a realist, only stating the societal bias that held that perception in Western cities. Western white society had become desensitized to the young, disenfranchised native youth who flocked to the cities only to end up in cycles of addiction and prostitution. This biased perception was an extra hurdle the prosecution would have to overcome if the case were to be successful. Luckily, Deirdre Pothecary was Crown, and she and I were not beyond believing we could topple windmills.

But there was another thing working in Gus's favour: his lawyer. The court-appointed defence lawyer, Slippery Sam, apparently also believed that his client would not be convicted. He was so confident of a favourable outcome that he waived his client's right to a preliminary trial, electing to be tried by the local magistrate. Sam was an extremely capable and experienced defence attorney who suspended moral judgment on his clients and pursued acquittals with equal passion regardless of their guilt or the crime. He was a dangerous lawyer for any member to face in court. If there were any opportunity to get his client off, he could be counted on to aggressively pursue it. These professional characteristics had earned him the derogatory nickname of "Slippery Sam." It was a title of which he was secretly proud; he took it as a sign of validation that he was doing his job well if he made Mounties nervous when he was the courtroom adversary.

Sam's decision to elect the local magistrate for the trial was a bit of legal brinkmanship inferring that the Crown's case was so weak that a preliminary trial before a Supreme Court trial was unnecessary. Normally, an indictable offence (the American equivalent of a felony) would follow after the defence had had a chance to test the strengths and weaknesses of the Crown's case in the local Magistrate's Court. It was a legal power play that placed Gus's fate in the hands of the local magistrate.

Normally, the spectator seats for local trials remain empty except for immediate family. For this trial, however, the seats were filled with residents of the City South Native Reserve in a show of support for the victim. Slippery Sam was keenly aware of the inferred public pressure the audience might have on the magistrate; he seemed particularly concerned with the youngest member of the audience, a fourteen-year-old native boy. Fearful his presence might play on the judge's sympathies and suspecting Deirdre or I had planted him to that end, Sam raised the issue in court before he began his cross-examination of the victim.

"Your Honour, before I begin, I have noticed there is a young man of tender years in the court. The testimony will probably be quite graphic and I am concerned if it is appropriate that he is present for it."

"I appreciate your concern and I have already given this matter a great deal of thought; however, my foster son is very interested in this case and has convinced me he should remain."

The judge's statement stunned the officers of the court as the legal minds reassessed the social dynamics of the case, which had just been turned upside down. Deirdre and I exchanged smiles from everyone except Sam, who dropped his head in defeat, crushed by an invisible windmill as it fell. The victory was that much sweeter knowing the entire City South Reserve had just witnessed Canadian justice at its best. Victims will only remain victims until they know they can fight back. The conviction took Gus off the street for many years.

The Canadian system of justice, a cornerstone of society that moulded our distinct nature, was simple, flexible, and accountable to the citizens, not the lawyers. It was a system that served justice, not the law, by empowering police to do what a reasonable person would do to maintain order and public confidence in the system. It attracted young, idealistic Canadians to the ranks of the RCMP because the tools were there to "maintain the right."

The young men and women who made up the ranks all shared core values of truth and justice and duty to the public, but we fitted those core values into very diverse personalities. When members weren't occupied with out-thinking criminals, we often turned our sights on each other, creating and executing elaborate practical jokes. The complexities of the humour, which employed accomplices, twists, and double twists, reflected the intelligence of the members as well as their fun-loving nature. Everyone in the Detachment was fair game. Even the dispatchers weren't exempt. One night, the watch took turns radioing in an impromptu, fictitious, high-speed chase involving a stolen vehicle that eventually ended in a crash, totalling the car. The fun began when the member "at scene" asked the dispatcher to query CPIC for the registered owner of the new, expensive, sports car.

"That's my car!" screamed the alarmed dispatcher as she quickly ran to the parking lot behind the office. There she found her prized vehicle surrounded by the police cars from the entire night shift who had set her up. The dispatcher's emotions quickly changed from fear to relief to irritation, and finally to pride in having been chosen as a victim. Members had to really like you to go to that amount of work in executing a practical joke! But we didn't have a monopoly on practical jokes.

A minor investigation into a "gas no pay" turned into quite an adventure. It started when I attended the West Vancouver address of the registered owner of the "suspect" vehicle; definitely not the home of a person who fails to pay for gas. Apparently, the owner and his doctor had switched vehicles on the day in question. I left my card, and later that afternoon the doctor phoned me at the Detachment.

"This is a mistake. I have the receipt for the gas," the doctor protested.

"I have no doubt it is an internal theft at the gas station, but I would like to have the receipt in hand when I confront the thief," I assured him. "Is there some time tomorrow evening when I can pick it up?"

"I am going out to dinner and won't be home until late," he said with noticeable relief mixed in with a mild Irish accent.

"That isn't a problem for me if it isn't for you. I am working all night."

"All right, then. I will call you tomorrow night when I get home."

At 11:45 p.m. the following evening, the dispatcher called me on the air. "Bravo 9, Dr. Hyde called to say he is home and will be expecting you at midnight."

"10-4, I'll be 10-8 to West Vancouver for the next hour."

"You mean it's not a joke?" asked the dispatcher. "You know, Dr. Hyde . . . midnight meetings . . ."

"No, it's legitimate." I understood why she might think that, considering all the practical jokes that were constantly being sprung at the Detachment. Little did I know that before the night was out I would be wondering the same thing.

The address led me to an upscale, high-rise apartment close to the beach. I rang the apartment, one of four penthouses in the building. I was a bit surprised when the phone was picked up but no one said hello.

"Dr. Hyde, it's Cst. Greenwood."

Odder still, the only reply was the click of the release on the door lock. I stepped off the elevator to the unmistakable low mantra rumbling of the Gregorian chant, emanating from the door to Dr. Hyde's apartment, which was slightly ajar. Like any well-trained peace officer, I stood with my back to the wall as I opened the door to peer in, but to be truthful, it was only from curiosity, not caution. I had learned to trust my police instincts and I could sense nothing dangerous or malicious.

Slowly I opened the door, appreciating the effort that had gone into the staged event. The apartment was in total darkness except for the flickering of dozens of candles reflecting off the walls and ceiling. I peered down the hall to where it elbowed. At the elbow stood an antique chair with a large candle on the seat illuminating the distorted head of a Royal Dalton figurine perched on its back.

As I walked down the hall, the chanting became louder as I neared its source in the darkened living room. The robed figure who stood in front of the sound system was in shadow, backlit by the Vancouver skyline framed by the windows behind. He looked like a Druid priest, his arms folded in front of him, his hands neatly tucked up his floor-length robe sleeves, his face completely in shadow. Only his ragged salt and pepper beard was distinguishable from the robe. As bizarre as the scene was, I still did not feel threatened because I understood it. It was the type of joke I might have staged for someone else. I refused to be entrapped and I proceeded as though everything were normal.

"Dr. Hyde?" I enquired.

Remaining in character, the figure still did not speak, responding only with a slow, dignified bow of his head in acknowledgement.

If he could pretend to be a Druid priest, I could pretend not to notice, though I could hardly suppress a smile at the elaborate ruse that had been created for me.

"I don't wish to interrupt your privacy, so if I could just have the receipt we spoke about, I'll be on my way."

The din of the Gregorian chant was a fitting backdrop to our little standoff as we waited to see who would step out of character first.

"I give up!" conceded the doctor, tossing back his hood to reveal his face finally. "I thought this whole situation was so unthinkable I had to do something to make it memorable."

"Trust me, you have succeeded," I said with a smile before adding a caution: "But did you stop to consider it might not be wise to try to scare someone who carries a gun?"

"Oh, I did. If you had shown *that* kind of reaction, I would have turned the lights on right away!"

Several hours later, at four a.m. coffee, I shared my adventure with some members of my watch. They weren't sure if I was pulling their leg or not, the story was so bizarre, until one of the members proclaimed, "Just a minute. Dr. Hyde? That's my doctor, and it sounds just like what he would do!"

One of the biggest problems I occasionally had to contend with was over-protectionism by well-intentioned members. Protecting women and children was part of the culture males had been raised in. Male members had to get by the fact I was a woman if I was going to pull my own weight. Once, shortly after recruit field training, I caught a dispatcher trying to screen one of my calls. The call was a request to check on an elderly resident who hadn't been heard from for several days. No one liked sudden death calls, but it was my area and I asked for it to be reassigned to me. There is a smell to death, which, like a tornado sky, you never forget once you have experienced it. That day wasn't the first and certainly not the last time I encountered it.

Later at the office, I asked the dispatcher, a retired B.C. peace officer, why he had tried to avoid giving me the call.

"I just didn't want you to have to deal with it," he replied in a very fatherly way. I appreciated his paternal instincts but asked him to put them aside in the future. These new roles were going to be a learning experience for the men as well as for the women.

The learning process was not without a few challenges--like a male member who thought he could call me every time he needed a female arrested. I tactfully made my point by asking him what he would think if I called a male member every time I needed a male arrested.

By far my biggest challenge was my new partner, Cst. Intense. Intense, newly transferred in from Vancouver Island, was one of those larger-than-life personalities that peppered the ranks of the Force. He was young, handsome, good-natured, and quite red-necked on women's issues, in a charmingly New Brunswick sort of way. I could appreciate why he was so comfortable with society's status quo for men; it had worked well for him. He was popular among his peers, his career had been fast-tracked by his supervisors, and his wife, Suzy, an ex-beauty queen, adored him.

Intense was senior to me by several years. I had to constantly remind him it was his service, not his gender, to which I sometimes deferred. He was immediately given a recruit when he arrived: Cst. Mischief, also from the East Coast. Though they were culturally similar, by disposition they were quite different.

Mischief was laid-back and fun-loving, while Intense could be very intense. It didn't take Mischief long to figure out that the mention of either of two "hot button" topics, French or female members, would spark intense, passionate debate between Intense and myself.

Mischief would mischievously toss out the bait and then watch in amusement as the verbal sparks flew. There was really no point to the debate. We must have sounded like Gloria Steinem arguing with Archie Bunker. Neither of us would waver in our convictions, but that never stopped us from taking the bait every time Mischief tossed it out. It wasn't Intense's opinions I wanted to change--it was his actions.

It didn't take long to notice that even on routine stops, Intense felt compelled to follow me around. After several discussions on the point, I promised to keep him informed of my activities (after all, he was the senior member) if he would restrict his behaviour to acceptable backup.

It was in the scope of this arrangement that I advised him one day shift that I was trying to "turn" a local criminal and would be making a visit to his home. "Turning" is police slang for creating an informant. I had about four hundred dollars' worth of traffic tickets I could write for a motorcycle stop the previous night shift to use as leverage to try to "turn" some useful information on local criminal activity. Intense watched from the sidewalk as I knocked on the door.

The criminal had an extensive record and an identical twin. They had capitalized on their identical appearance in their earlier criminal career by making it impossible for witnesses to identify the accused in court. The strategy worked well until one of the twins received a scar running the length of his torso, in a near-fatal knife fight.

Intense watched from a distance as this six-foot-three, tattooed, scarred man with hair down to his waist politely responded to me as if I were his mother, not a peace officer. When I returned to my police car, where Intense had remained, he shook his head and said: "Only you could speak to that man like that and get away with it."

He was finally beginning to understand that it was often easier for a female peace officer to deal with really macho criminals back then. I had no qualms about exploiting a fading window of opportunity in the cultural twilight before society exchanged chivalry for "political correctness."

My little demonstration for Intense worked almost too well; one night shift months later, I could have used some backup and he was nowhere to be found.

I was parked south of Marine Drive at about two a.m. doing my paperwork, when a car shot by so fast all I caught in my peripheral vision was a blur of red. The brief flash of the brake lights indicated he had seen me, too. The car disappeared into a side street a quarter of a mile to my left before I even got my car into drive. Since I was so far behind and had only the vague description of a small red car, there was little point in broadcasting the incident.

There was no sign of the vehicle when I turned onto the residential street I had last seen him turn into. I pulled over and as I tried to guess which direction to look in next, the suspect, who surprisingly had been parked at the far end of the street, turned his lights on, did a U-turn, and parked in front of the residence across the street from me.

The driver and sole occupant of the car quickly got out of his car and proceeded onto the property. I only had time to dispatch my approximate location as I jumped out to stop him before he entered the residence. It always gets messy and dangerous when people are confronted in their homes. Bad luck on his part--or perhaps good luck on mine--had brought us face to face.

From the state of his face, it was obvious he had been on the losing end of a recent fight. It was also apparent he was impaired. Intense and Mischief still hadn't shown up, so I began to stall by enquiring about his injuries. He had stalked his girlfriend to a local bar only to discover her in the company of another man. To add insult to injury, he had started a fight, which he lost.

As he spoke, he began to get angry all over again, reliving how he had been betrayed and humiliated by a female. I could sense the transference in his eyes as his hands started to flex in a prelude to a vicarious revenge.

For once being a female was a big disadvantage, and the situation was deteriorating quickly. I could not wait any longer for Intense.

"You're under arrest for impaired driving. You will have to come back to the Detachment for a breathalyzer test."

I was hoping to derail the impending attack, but he stood defiantly motionless, in an alcohol-enhanced rage. The moment of truth came and passed as I put my hand on his upper arm to complete the arrest and felt the muscles in his arm tense then relax. I breathed a huge sigh of relief as I secured him in the back of my police car. As the door slammed shut, Intense and Mischief popped up from their hiding place behind a nearby parked car across the street.

"Thanks for all the backup!" I snapped, more than a little annoyed that they had secretly watched a potential fight without offering assistance.

They laughed as they recounted their plan to wait until the suspect took the first swing, one they were satisfied I could block, before they would come to my rescue--a situation I would have disliked, as much as Intense would have enjoyed it. But before the case was finished, I would have the last laugh.

Back at the Detachment, the suspect remained defiant and refused to take the breath test. Impaired driving had a number of defences, but refusing a breath sample is all but unjustifiable in the court's eyes. A charge of refusal is very difficult to defend unless there is a compelling, defendable reason to refuse the test. It became clear the accused had been less than candid with his own lawyer at trial when he asked Cst. Intense, the breathalyzer operator, who had recorded the refusal: "Isn't it true the reason my client refused was because he hadn't yet been able to contact a lawyer for legal advice?"

I found it more than a little ironic that even Intense seemed embarrassed as he contradicted the lawyer and recounted the accused's reason for his refusal.

"No, Your Honour. He told me he was refusing because he didn't believe women had the right to demand anything from men."

"Your Honour, I can assure you my client was not referring to any advice I gave him," the lawyer quickly said, trying to distance himself from the comment.

"I should hope not!" scolded the judge as he suppressed a smile.

Shortly after the conviction, Intense was transferred to GIS on the "officer candidate" fast track.

Despite all our heated arguments and our ideology differences, Intense and Suzy were part of a close-knit group of my friends. Intense and Suzy, Gary and Sandy Proulx, Brent and Jay Barber, and Len and I spent many enjoyable nights eating, drinking, and debating the social revolution in a monthly dinner group. Len and I were the only unmarried couple in the group.

I couldn't believe that someone as opposed as I'd been to long-term romantic attachments had become one-half of a couple. It was a good thing my troop mates whom I had lectured long and loudly on the virtues of remaining single modern women, role models for the next generation, were not around to see what was becoming of me.

Len and I had become a couple almost by accident. I was not in a rush to date another member, having learned a painful lesson on the price a career could demand on a female member's personal life. I had started dating a member just before I was transferred to B&E squad. The crazy hours and lack of a schedule a surveillance unit entails contributed to the premature ending of the relationship. Police work has never been conducive to domestic bliss for male members, and it appeared it would be an even greater barrier for female members.

Successful members are married to the Force, but if wives and girlfriends seemed willing to accept second billing, my experience had taught me male members were not. Hardly surprising, considering what hot commodities male Mounties were on the singles scene--they were not likely to sit and pine for anyone.

My hesitation allowed the time for our relationship to gradually develop from coworkers to friends before I allowed myself to acknowledge Len's desire to date me. He had been a hard guy to resist, considering his good-natured East Coast charm and good looks. There was one problem. As I remarked earlier, male members are seldom left wanting for female company.

Len was dating someone else, a tall, slender, ultra-feminine secretary at the Detachment--the one with every hair always in place. I wasn't comfortable with that. Once bitten, twice shy. If he wanted to date me, I had rules. I dated only one person at a time and I expected the same of whomever I dated. A cheeky attitude from someone wearing army boots, but one he quickly met. Throwing good judgment to the winds, I decided to date him, even though I knew dating a coworker was not the safest thing to do. But after all, if I hadn't been prepared to take risks, I wouldn't have left the Island.

Len and I were very well suited to each other. Each of us was from a Catholic family; he had two sisters and a brother, while I had two brothers and a sister. He had a degree in commerce from St. Mary's University. No one except our closest friends knew we were dating. It was a matter of professionalism as much as privacy that our work relationship didn't change.

At work, I was more likely to have coffee with my new partner, Cst. Mischief, than Len. Mischief was an excellent partner with no hang-ups about working with a female member and had little time for those who did. Mischief's career aspirations lay in Dog Section.

Mischief had done his homework on how to make it into the close-knit Dog Section. On his own time, he rode with dog masters and raised shepherd pups for the dog training facility at Penhold, Alberta. Mischief learned everything he could about this specialized section, including the discouraging piece of information that female members were not welcome. Apparently it was an open secret within the section that female members could apply but they would not pass the orientation.

I thought of my troop mate Jackie Olsen, who had set her sights on being the first female on Dog Section back in Depot. Apparently she also had heard the open secret and decided not to be invited to fail the dog orientation screening process. The only other section that I knew of with so blatant a ban was the Marine Section. Some doors were shut a little tighter than others.

Luckily for me, the doors at North Vancouver detachment were all ajar. As a matter of fact, once a female slipped through a door, you could almost get caught in the draft as one exited. That nearly happened to Adrienne and me when the first female member on traffic section had just finished her six-month rotation. The staff sergeant in charge of traffic seemed to feel he needed a female to replace a female.

Both Adrienne and I were wary of perpetuating the labelling of a position held by a female as a "female" position. This simple-minded tokenism is a close cousin to the old quota system that in the past offered limited female opportunities, providing motivation to sidestep the position.

With the support of her NCO, Adrienne avoided the rotation because of a "manpower shortage" on her watch. I used a more devious tactic to evade the rotation: "I am flattered by your offer. I was hoping I would get an opportunity to take the motorcycle course and join the motorcycle team, if I was lucky enough to get a traffic rotation," I said, feigning enthusiasm as I watched the staff sergeant's expression change from offence to defence.

Clearly the thought of 110 pounds of me on a 750 Hog (Honda) was enough to discourage this and any further attempts at recruitment.

"I think this rotation is filled; I just wanted to know if you'd be interested in the next one," he quickly countered.

I felt a little guilty at the scope of opportunities that were opening up. Corporal Gary Sexsmith, who was in charge of the CPU, or Crime Prevention Unit (school talks, etc.), made no secret that I could join his team any time. "CPU--we want you!" he would chant, reminiscent of the old World War I poster. It was a great section, but a little too similar to the dead-end female positions in the Vancouver Police Department.

I had something to prove to myself--and perhaps to the status quo--that I could only do by mastering the tougher policing roles. Even S/Sgt. Hill tempted my convictions by offering me a position on Fraud Section. It was almost where I thought I wanted to be: in GIS or NCIS (National Criminal Intelligence Section), but not quite. Paper chases didn't excite me.

"You only want me in fraud so you can borrow me to assist B&E, Drugs, or GIS when it's handy to have a female. I would really like to work for you, but not on Fraud."

"God damn it! You are the most insubordinate member I have ever met!"

He wasn't really upset. He must have liked my deductive reasoning and "in your face" attitude or he wouldn't have been offering me a position in the first place. He'd be back with something better, I hoped. If I was wrong, it didn't matter. I liked the unpredictable nature of street work much better than I would have liked Fraud Section. Still, even some frauds could be interesting, as I found out one day shift not long after my conversation with Hill.

I had won the race for the microphone to claim a call concerning people soliciting for an unfounded charity at a local lock manufacturing company. It was the type of file that members love to sink their teeth into. It was a chance to maintain the right against the lowest of the low--those who would prey on the good nature of Canadians for fraudulent purposes.

As I entered the lobby of the company, I took note of five people seated there: three businessmen and two nuns in full black and white Dominican habits. Constable Rick Gunn arrived as backup and joined me as I enquired at the front desk.

"Can you tell us what is going on?" I asked.

In a hushed voice the receptionist said, "My manager will explain in his office."

"Are the suspects still here?"

"Yes," she said, whispering now. "The two seated by the door."

"The nuns?" I said in quiet disbelief.

"My manager has Staff Sgt. Hill on the line; he can explain everything."

"Keep an eye on them, Rick, while I sort this out," I asked before disappearing into the manager's office.

The manager produced a letter requesting a donation of approximately twenty thousand dollars' worth of double-keyed, deadbolt locks. Enough to equip a small prison. The letterhead, the titles of the Order, and the signature heavily implied they were part of a Roman Catholic order based in Quebec. I picked up the phone and S/Sgt. Hill explained.

"They are a cult looking to establish a Western branch. There have been allegations of kidnappings, brainwashing, child molestations and other sex offences. We are watching them closely. Try to get as much information as you can but be careful--sometimes they stay in character and act like nuns, but they are unpredictable and dangerous."

The thought of shaking down a nun was not something I ever considered and it certainly went against my Catholic upbringing.

"Are you sure about this?" I asked Hill.

He laughed, knowing how awkward the whole situation would be, especially for me. Then he assured me, "They are no more Catholic than I am." Well, I certainly knew he wasn't a "bead clacker."

"All right, I'll do it, but if I go to hell because of this I am going to recommend you as my cellmate."

All eyes were on me back in the reception room as I squatted in front of them. Their well-practised angelic smiles changed to distress as I spoke.

"I am Cst. Greenwood, Sisters. Your request is rather large and unusual. I've been asked to make some enquiries. Do you have some picture ID I could see?"

With pathetic fluster meant to garner sympathy and emotional support, they located their papers. I watched uncomfortably out of the corner of my eye as the civilians shifted in their chairs, pretending not to notice but hanging on every word. The image was terrible: a peace officer hassling two nuns. Even my partner had slowly moved back towards the door, then out into the parking lot in an attempt to distance himself from the investigation.

The ID was printed in Chicago and listed only their adopted saint names and the address of the U.S. location where they had taken their "vows." Although the ID itself told me very little, it provided the grounds for the next enquiry and a slightly more solid legal footing if they decided to step out of character.

"Are you Americans or Canadians?"

"Canadian," they replied simultaneously as feigned compliance was replaced by a hint of defensiveness. The psychological tide had turned. Mounties wear the most official hats of any enforcement agency in Canada and probably in the world, providing an enforcement arsenal we can draw upon during any investigation. Among those hats is one for authority under the Immigration and Customs Act.

"Then I will need to see a birth or baptismal certificate."

They complied because they had to. The interview that followed was tense but restrained. The civilians didn't seem to see below the superficial level of the dialogue to the cat and mouse game that was afoot, which was what both the "nuns" and I wanted.

When it was all over, they seemed quite relieved to leave, even if it was empty-handed. In the parking lot, I scoffed at my partner for leaving me to be the bad guy.

He said, "You didn't need me. I would never have known that nuns have different names. How did you?"

"The advantage of being raised Catholic, I guess."

Back at the GIS office, my old partners and boss were pleased to received the new intelligence. They also took full advantage of more good-natured teasing about a good Catholic girl hassling nuns. I never knew what to expect when I worked G.D.

At the end of a day shift, I picked up a phone message from an unknown staff sergeant requesting I meet him, out of uniform, in his hotel room in Richmond. I might have been a small Island girl, but meeting a strange man in a hotel room didn't sound right to me.

"Something wrong?" Cpl. Dickie Smith asked, sensing my distress after I hung up. After telling him about the mysterious request, Dickie smiled and advised: "I think you should go."

I always trusted Dickie's advice. The next day, I was met at the hotel room door by a plainclothed staff sergeant, a member of Ottawa's Drug Section. Inside the room, he opened a file with my name on it and confirmed my service record to date.

"You know why you are here, so let's begin," he said as he closed the file.

"Actually, I haven't the faintest idea why I am here," I said.

It was his turn to look puzzled. "I am the undercover coordinator. You must have requested this interview to be considered as a UC operator."

"But I haven't."

This was clearly an unusual circumstance. Apparently it is very difficult to get this kind of opportunity in the Force, particularly if you are a junior member. Obviously someone with some influence and rank had recommended me. It was both flattering and a bit unsettling to know I had a secret friend in high places (at least higher than my level).

"Then you must have requested Drug Section," the coordinator suggested, trying to determine how I had ended up in the room.

"No, I haven't," I said.

It was fairly obvious to both of us that someone who looked as un-Mountie as I did might make a natural undercover officer. So I spent the next two hours learning all about the UC program. It sounded like it was straight out of a Hollywood movie: group infiltration into criminal organizations, living a lie for months at a time before arresting the criminals who had been duped. Very exciting, very challenging; but as with anything, there were some prices to pay for the choice. Undercover operators had to put their own lives on hold for the period of the operation, and after it was over, it was unlikely they would be reassigned to their old detachment. The emotional barriers UC operators developed to keep from getting too emotionally attached to the targets were often difficult to remove later when dealing with friends.

Still, the opportunity might have been tempting if I had not liked my life on and off the job at North Vancouver Detachment so much. I needed a better reason than professional ambition to request a transfer. If that weren't reason enough, I would have had a moral dilemma accepting an unsolicited shortcut to a specialized unit knowing that if I had been a male member I would not have been offered this opportunity.

If it is wrong to be excluded from a job based on gender, wouldn't it be equally wrong to accept one *because* of it? I believed it would be. I also believed that if the first wave of females didn't maintain a moral high ground, we would be handicapping the ones to follow. There is that old social conscience making things harder again.

Truthfully, there was one more reason I turned down the offer. I was arrogant enough to feel I could obtain more challenging career opportunities within the Detachment. As a UC operator, I would have been an investigational tool for serious cases, while as a GIS member or CIS member I would be the lead investigator. Tactfully I declined the UC course, saying it was too early in my career to specialize.

I was flattered when the interviewer offered to keep my file open but inactive in case I changed my mind. I didn't mind leaving professional doors ajar. For the moment, I found general duty work enjoyably unpredictable, where even the most routine call could become a matter of life and death.

Like the day I started a cold winter day shift with a humble "found property" complaint that turned into much more. Morning walkers had discovered a small antique-looking suitcase in the stream along the trail below Pemberton Heights; one they were sure was not present on their walk the previous evening.

I was thinking perhaps it had been discarded by a thief until I opened it. The suitcase was like a neatly packed time capsule, with turn-of-the century clothes, an antique straight razor, and a Japanese passport for a father and son dated in the early 1900s.

I had this sinking feeling there might be a confused old man wandering or dead in the densely forested bluff area surrounding the stream. We needed a dog, but that meant calling out an exhausted dog handler who had been off shift only a couple of hours.

North Vancouver had two dog handlers, a laid-back, polite East Coaster and a growly fellow whose moods seemed to range from angry to angrier. Members use to joke that the only thing meaner than the handler was his dog. I knew by the dispatcher's resistance to my request which one was on call. It wasn't long before the dog corporal was en route and on the air challenging my judgment.

I had made some pretty big assumptions in this file, I was not so politely told after the dog failed to find a track. The corporal did not hold back as he berated me for my mistake--which had cost the Force money (overtime) and him sleep--as he packed up his wagon.

"How in the hell did a junior member like you convince a station NCO to authorize a call out based on nothing more than female intuition. I'm going to--" He abruptly stopped his rant, mid-sentence, as he refocused his glare from me to the edge of the forest.

With great relief I turned to see an elderly Japanese man stumble out of the bushes following the sound of the corporal's raised voice. It was more than a bit ironic that it was his yelling, not the dog's tracking, which had helped locate the man.

"I couldn't have located him without you," I complimented the corporal, who seemed a bit disarmed by my off-beat sense of humour. The old man was transported to Lions Gate hospital for treatment of the confused state often caused by severe dehydration and mild hypothermia.

I hadn't taken offence at the corporal's wrath because I knew it was cocky junior members, *male or female*, that irritated him. Unfortunately, that wasn't true for a notoriously moody City South corporal who thought he would embarrass me over the air one midnight shift when I asked for a tow truck to change a slashed tire on my police car.

"If you want to be paid the same as a *man*, then you can change a tire like a *man*," Cpl. Anger-Management snapped.

"I'm paid to be a peace officer, not a mechanic," I shot back, in unapologetic defiance.

Unlike small rural detachments, lower mainland members did not have to change tires, a policy I was more than happy with. I had never changed a tire in my life and did not want to learn how to use a jack in uniform. If the corporal hadn't been so quick to pounce on me, or perhaps if I hadn't responded so abruptly, the dispatcher could have tactfully advised him my request wasn't out of line; but now that the verbal gloves were off, no one dared get in between us.

"Dispatch, cancel the request for a tow truck," ordered Cpl. Anger-Management, pulling rank. "Now what are you going to do?" he taunted.

"I'm going to wait for the tow-truck driver who is monitoring this frequency,"

I snapped.

Neither one of us was prepared to back down in so public a dispute. Of course, in a battle between members, the higher rank almost always wins; but it didn't have to come to that because Cst. Mischief beat the tow truck and came to my unsolicited rescue, shooting into the parking lot in a four-wheeled drift.

"I'll change the tire," he said as he waved off the tow truck.

"No, you won't!" I protested.

"You can't stop me," he laughed; and he was right, as he proceeded to provide a face-saving out for both the corporal and myself. "There is no point in getting into a pissing contest with a jerk NCO if you can avoid it."

He was right again.

It wasn't the only time Mischief had tried to come to my rescue. One afternoon shift, Mischief and I were bored--so bored that we both showed up at the same break-and-enter complaint in a neighbouring zone. We were standing inside the front hallway of the complainant when we heard the unmistakable sound of a vehicle collision in front of the residence. We rushed out just in time to see the offending vehicle speeding down a side street. Mischief broadcasted the incident as I jumped into my car in pursuit. I just caught the tail end of the vehicle turning onto another side street as I got my car in drive. Moments later, as I turned onto that street, the situation played out again and again on the short and boxed-in unfamiliar residential streets of the unfamiliar zone, until I lost sight of the suspect car completely. I think the suspect was as lost as I was.

Mischief and everyone else on shift were heading to my location, if I could just figure out exactly which street I was on. Just then, out of the corner of my eye, I caught the red glow of lights reflecting off a back fence halfway down an alley. Down I drove and discovered the suspect car parked in someone's backyard with the driver kicking at the badly damaged passenger's door in an attempt to escape.

From the damage I could see, it looked as though the driver had used his collision with parked vehicles to guide him down the road. Finally he emerged from the passenger's side just as Mischief drifted into a four-wheel stop in the lane behind my car. I was in the process of placing the suspect under arrest for impaired driving when Mischief reached over me and lifted the suspect off the ground, tossing him against the trunk of my police car. I couldn't believe Mischief, not Intense, was interfering with my investigation.

It was only after I booked him into cells that I learned the details of the suspect and the reason for Mischief's uncharacteristic interference. The previous shift's NCO had released the accused for impaired driving at the end of his shift against the investigating officer's recommendations. Not only had the accused fought with them, he had threatened to kill the next police officer he dealt with. Unlike the first suspect who had made a similar threat, this one was much too drunk to do anyone any damage except in a car. I must have been mellowing after working so long with overgrown Boy Scouts because I didn't take offence at Mischief's attempt at a "good deed."

The accused had been responsible for a total of thirteen hit-and-run charges in the space of only a few blocks. He was held in custody, and the next day the judge took his licence on the spot. The new operations officer/inspector made a point of introducing himself before he congratulated me in the constable's room on my next shift. It was a good start to a sometimes shaky relationship.

Operations officers, the detachment disciplinarians, were responsible for, among other things, ensuring that the military standards of conduct, dress, and deportment remained high. My resentment of the female hat placed me on a collision course with the new officer.

The female uniform was a touchy point with the majority of female members at the time, from the blazer and short shirt to the ridiculous pillbox hat (better suited to an organ grinder's monkey). We desired uniformity with our male peers. The hat in particular was detested, because it was the one part of the workday uniform that constantly reminded us of a gender distinction.

Constable Chris Wozney had made the issue of the hat a personal crusade, conducting a survey of female members to highlight its operational deficiencies. The commissioned officer to whom she submitted her report reprimanded her for wasting the Force's time and paper on the issue. A social conscience often comes at a professional cost.

It seemed to me that large organizations like the Force and the Catholic Church were using hats as a passive form of discrimination. If as a teenager I wasn't afraid to sin in church, it should not have been surprising that I was prepared to take some risks in the Force as a young adult.

I chose a practical as well as symbolic solution to the issue. Everyone on my watch was supportive; they even supplied the male uniform hat. It was a fashion statement the other female members began to follow until the inspector felt he had to put an end to the female insurrection.

Kit was a matter of policy, not choice, I was reminded in an informal reprimand. In an act of passive-aggressive insubordination, I decided that if I couldn't wear the male hat I wouldn't wear any hat, except when the inspector was on shift. That left my afternoon shifts and midnights safe--or so I thought.

For several months, the strategy worked; until one midnight shift when the off-duty inspector drove past my police car and discovered me dealing with some undesirables *sans chapeau*.[16] He ordered me "paraded" in front of Supt. Wilson for punishment. I am sure I was the last female member the superintendent expected to see in his office. It had been clear from his comments on my assessment and early transfer to plainclothes that he had high expectations for me. I feared I may have let him down by causing myself to be paraded before him.

It was the first and only time I was officially "in shit," although in hindsight it really wasn't a big deal. A uniform infraction was normally not even elevated to his level, but now that the matter had been officially raised by his second in command, the superintendent was forced to deal with the matter. I entered the corner office with trepidation, hat under my arm.

"Cst. Greenwood, you are here because the operations officer observed you in public without your hat on."

"Yes, sir, he did," I confessed.

"As a uniformed member, you are required to wear your hat any time you are in the public view."

"Yes sir," I again agreed. What else could I do?

From the expression on the superintendent's face, it was clear he was curious why a member like myself would risk a reprimand for so minor but basic a requirement.

"Why don't you like to wear the female hat?" he asked, allowing me an unexpected but welcome chance to voice my and other female members' objections.

"It's not simply a matter of aesthetics, although a strong case can be made on that issue. The female hat is poorly designed for operational duties. It simply won't stay on my head. Whether I am leaning forward to check a driver's licence, or chasing someone, it always falls off. It looks ridiculous and I feel ridiculous in it, which in my opinion defeats the purpose of the uniform. Female members don't understand why we need a different hat."

After pausing to consider my response, he asked me to put it on, and I did. He studied my hat for a moment, then said, "It must fit better than that. Try pushing it down a little."

I did and the hat sat tight on my head for only a fraction of a minute before it popped up, surprising both of us. I noticed the corners of his lips move ever so slightly, as if bitten from the inside. Then without saying a word, he turned his swivel chair to face the window and I saw the gentle yet unmistakable movement of his shoulders as he struggled to suppress his laughter. The whole

[16] *Sans chapeau* is French for "without hat." It was a frequent accusation made by drill staff back at Depot and would mean an immediate parading before the corps sergeant-major.

encounter was going much better than I had hoped. After a minute or two he turned back around. "Try not to let the inspector catch you again."

I smiled back, acknowledging the semantics of his precise instructions. He didn't say I had to wear the hat; he said *don't get caught.* Apparently I hadn't damaged my reputation with the superintendent too badly, because shortly after the hat reprimand, he selected me for two tasks.

The first was a draft back to the General Investigation Section for a one-year rotation, only this time I would have an opportunity to work on major crimes, such as murder, arson, and armed robberies. I couldn't believe the career opportunities that were being offered me. Maybe I didn't have to be a Mason after all. I hoped I was deserving of the professional breaks the superintendent was giving me. The second task was equally high-profile: an interview with a reporter as a representative of the female members in the Force.

A *Vancouver Sun* reporter, Renee Doruyter, was doing a series of articles on females in non-traditional roles and had focused on women in the police and the military. I would have preferred the Force's response to have been the standard "no comment." I didn't want to say or appear to say anything that might be used to cast female members or the Force in a poor public light. I soon discovered I had nothing to worry about.

Renee, who was only slightly older than I, was one of the pioneers of female rights. While I was secretly cheering the women marching in the streets back on Wolfe Island as a teenager, she was marching in them. I am sure she was a more suitable candidate for the article.

It was a humbling experience to speak to someone of her background. I felt a little like an opportunist, a "Janey-come-lately" cashing in on someone else's battles, unworthy to be in the presence of a real trailblazer. I really hadn't had to fight for much--not yet, anyway.

She reminded me of Christy Meyer, as passionate and proud of the successes of the women's movement as she was disappointed with the new counter-movement, "Total Women." She worried that the next generation of females would abandon the goals of the women's movement by returning to the traditional roles of wife and mother. Like Christy, she had caused me to take a look once more at the bigger social picture dealing with the role of women. Perhaps because I was from a slightly newer generation of feminists, I could be more dispassionate about the movement.

I felt a little insubordinate when I suggested perhaps the liberation movement was about "choice," not *which* choice to make. Perhaps modern women were a little guilty of dismissing the role of mother, and the next debate needed to be between women. My view of the Total Women's movement was also a little more optimistic.

"What if there were a pattern to social evolution for both individuals and society, a kind of natural law of social balance, defined by an equation dictating that for every social advance there will be a backlash, but when the pendulum of social change stopped, it would never retreat to its initial starting point? What if the distance between the starting and ending points were the true measure of social progress? Just as energy could never be lost, neither could social milestones." The social jury was still out on the matter. Only time would tell if the theory was well-grounded or just wishful thinking. However, the interview didn't end with such heavy theorizing.

Renee returned to the practicalities that had brought us together by asking if the photographer could take a photo, for the article, of me standing by my police car. In the parking lot, the photographer struggled without success to get a photogenic shot of me in my uniform hat. In frustration, he queried: "Can you take the hat off for the photo?"

"I would love to. No one hates this pillbox more than I do. I think one of the reasons I am headed back to plainclothes is to avoid getting into any more trouble with my operations officer because of it. But if my picture appears in the *Vancouver Sun* without my hat on, even my superintendent couldn't shield me from the trouble I'd be in."

They didn't understand what I was talking about, but took me at my word and snapped the unflattering shot.

Chapter 7

Arsons and Murders and Rapes, Oh My!

With three years under my belt and hundreds of successful investigations and interrogations, I rejoined the General Investigation Section for a one-year rotation feeling less of a pupil and more like an understudy. It didn't take long for my confidence to be rattled when I learned with whom I would be working.

My new plainclothes partner, Cst. Rick Wait, was a large-framed, six-foot-two fellow with a gruff demeanour, coarse features, and a very low, serious voice that he used sparingly. He had a reputation on the street for being quick and aggressive in a physical fight. What was S/Sgt. Hill thinking? We looked like an odd couple--polar opposites, in policing terms. Hill shared his thinking with me, behind closed doors, during my "welcome to the section" talk.

"The GIS section is small, almost too small to handle some of the major cases that come our way. My job is to draft and cultivate a team of investigators with many and varied talents to ensure all the legal bases are covered." He took a slow drink of his coffee.

"Don Rinn is a great team leader and extremely good at informants. He has the pulse of the street at his fingertips. Sgt. MacKay is an expert interviewer/ interrogator and the most articulate and clever member on the section when giving evidence in court and handling cross-examinations. Rick Wait is a good investigator who usually jumps to the right conclusions but may be tempted to skip a few steps while following his assumptions. Rick Jones is a well-documented A to B investigator well-suited to frauds and the administrative organization of major cases; he will make sure someone covers all the steps. Craig Gates is a workhorse and a gifted investigator. Constable Intense keeps everyone energized and enjoying themselves even when there is an overwhelming workload. You, also, have something unique to offer the section," he said, not specifying. "I need each of the members on my team but I don't need two of them."

Well, that might have explained why his section was such a collage of personalities, but I must have missed something because I still didn't understand why Rick was my partner. Revealing one of his own hidden skills, Hill answered my unspoken question.

"You and Rick are the most natural good cop/bad cop investigation combo I have ever seen."

Now that I understood, I didn't like being typecast into any policing role. Even one in plainclothes chafed against my insecurity. In my youthful self-absorption, I had not stopped to consider that Hill had typecast the male investigators as well, and none of them seemed offended.

But what was the "something unique" I had to offer the section? That well-crafted, ambiguous, hedged statement was worthy of a clever lawyer. I felt he had extended a compliment, but it could just as easily have been a veiled insult. That was the way Hill liked to keep his members on their toes in their professional relationship with him--supportive and encouraging on the surface, but with an underlying uncertainty that kept everyone from feeling complacent.

The good cop/bad cop strategy may have been effective, but it was predictable and a little boring. I waited for the right crime to demonstrate I had more potential. The first major crime of the year for Hill's team, a murder, would not be it.

The body of a naked female might have been washed out to the Burrard Inlet as intended, had it not been caught up on a rock in the shallow river bed. She had been sexually assaulted, beaten, and then dumped into the tributary of the Seymour River for dead, where she drowned. The two sets of footprints in the area indicated we were looking for two males; the prints and a partial tire impression were the only physical evidence left at the scene.

The first step in any murder investigation is to identify the victim. It was a sad social comment that in this case it took more than ten years to get beyond step one. Medical evidence was of limited use and conflicting concerning ethnic origin. The more experts we used, the more possibilities we got. Some experts believed she was First Nations, while others believed she was Asian, perhaps Japanese or Chinese. One felt she could have been of mixed Aboriginal/Asian origins. Age estimates ranged from eighteen to thirty. Scrapes on the pelvic bone indicated she had given birth at least once. The only certainty science could offer was that she was intoxicated at the time of the attack.

The seasoned GIS members were in agreement on the most plausible scenario for the assault/murder. They hypothesized she was one of the nameless group of disenfranchised natives who, after leaving the poverty and alcohol abuse of her reserve, had migrated to the downtown east end of Vancouver, only to become embroiled in a similar cycle.

Young native girls would appear on the Vancouver streets from the country looking slim and pretty, but within months they would age physically and spiritually a lifetime. By disposition, culture, and gender, they were the perfect victims for street predators. Society, politicians, and even the police accepted this sad cycle as status quo. The streets of Gastown were littered with cheap apartments and seedy bars where businessmen profited from this depressing lifestyle.

The origin of the crime no doubt was in one of these bars, where two men plied her with liquor, then conned her into accompanying them with a promise of money or more alcohol. Initial inquiries at one of the bars on East Hastings indicated she had been there on numerous occasions. No one could say if she was there the night of the murder. People like that are part of the "white noise" of Gastown. No one really notices if they are there or not. No one cared enough to remember her name or anything about her.

Her photo was published in the local papers with an appeal to anyone who knew anything about her to come forward. All of the native bands in B.C. and Western Canada were canvassed. Then the search was widened to all of Canada and down into the States. Still no one knew her. Missing persons reports were monitored for matches. Still nothing. How sad to think this daughter, sister, and mother would be so unimportant as not to be missed. The predators had selected their victim well.

We had a few false leads, including one that prompted a quick trip to Victoria for Rick and me. Someone in the First Nations band by Collwood thought he recognized her from the picture in the paper. The banks were closed because it was a weekend. S/Sgt Hill opened the safe to give us cash advances for the ferry, hotel rooms, and incidental expenses on the trip. This was long before the days of Interac, and few people carried credit cards.

"Would you like $100, $200, or $300?" Hill asked me.

"If it's all the same to you, I would like $300. We don't know how long we will be over there and I would hate to get caught short."

"No problem," he said with a quiet laugh of approval. "I wish I could convince my daughter to think like that."

"I am sure Patty would ask for the same if she were ever in my situation, once she becomes a member," I said. I had gotten to know Hill's, wife, their two sons, and three daughters well enough to know his youngest, adventuresome, daughter would be attracted to the Force.

"I would not allow any daughter of mine to join the Force," he said, using his menacingly authoritative voice--a tone that worked well on junior male members, but never on me. I am quite sure it would never have worked on Janet or his daughters, either. Perhaps that is why he was neither surprised nor irritated when I always spoke my mind regardless of the rank and experience differential between us.

"You might not allow it, but I am going to wager you you won't be able to stop her," I teased. His face winced at my prediction, but left it unchallenged as he handed me $300 with quiet resignation.

It was that paternal tone that defined S/Sgt. Hill's relationship with me. Before September of '74, supervisors in the Force had little difficulty relating to the members under their command. After all, they were very much cut from the same cloth: similar backgrounds, dispositions, and goals. Female members were a whole new breed of Mountie, presenting new challenges for male supervisors and peers. I couldn't help but notice that how my male peers and supervisors related to me revealed more about their personality than mine.

Whether or not a supervisor had daughters was not as predictive of a positive outlook for female members as you might think. I soon discovered the best predictor of a positive male mindset toward women as equals in the workplace could be found in his ability to maintain a healthy, happy, stable relationship with his wife or girlfriend, and his mother, off the job. Hill was a good father, but more important, he was a good husband.

The lead on Vancouver Island was a false one, and the investigation came to a standstill. Staff Sergeant Hill asked me to talk to a psychic who thought she could contribute to the case.

Contrary to movie plots, police do not consult psychics; however, psychics occasionally contact police. The trend was much more pronounced in the seventies when Hollywood gave legitimacy to the possibility that something more exciting than old-fashioned investigations could solve crimes and catch killers. The publicity inadvertently encouraged the frauds and crazies who also would step forward claiming to be psychics.

The psychic from Richmond, B.C., was neither of these. She had several documented successes locating and/or communicating with deceased persons, according to the Simon Fraser professor who was taking a one-year sabbatical to document her abilities.

Unfortunately, she was unable to provide useful information to further the investigation. Like so many legitimate psychics she seemed to have random flashes, sometimes relevant, sometimes not, to the subject at hand. After the investigation is completed, some of the visions may fit the facts. Unfortunately, the input is so confused I am not aware of any case that has been solved through this means. The only psychic assistance in solving crime I can attest to is the underrated and under-studied police instinct or intuition.

She wasn't the only creditable psychic who offered to assist with the case. Rick and I went to the second psychic's North Vancouver home with some of the victim's personal belongings. The psychic was open about the fact he did not get any readings from the belongings and could not help with the case. As we were leaving his home, he surprised me when he said, "You are a lot like your father."

I could see how he would make that assumption, considering my career. Thinking he had incorrectly assumed I was the daughter of some police officer or military officer, looking for "daddy's approval," I quietly rejected his assertion, saying, "Actually I am more like my mother."

"She may have supported some of your choices, but it's your dad you are most like." He said with an unshaken wisdom. I was sure he was wrong. My mother had spent her unmarried life seeking out adventure, while my father had remained on the family farm. The only exciting thing he ever did was chart the ice road to Kingston each winter. *That was a waste of time*, I thought as Rick and I drove back to the detachment with no more leads to the murder than when we left.

The case was growing cold quickly. The footprints had told us there were two suspects, and that made the likelihood of solving the case much higher. Seldom are two offenders both so devoid of humanity that they would both remain silent forever. Sooner or later, one would talk.

It was ten years almost to the day when, as MacKay had predicted, one of the two killers talked about it to the wrong person, and the case was solved. The victim was a native from Ontario; everyone seemed to have lost track of when she moved out West.

Even though the murder investigation never got past stage one while I was on GIS, I now had an appreciation for how detailed and demanding a crime of that magnitude could be. Certainly not the type of crime I needed to demonstrate I could be more than one-half of an interrogation team. But I didn't have long to wait for the right crime.

I awoke for day shift to find the radio was abuzz with a heinous assault by several belligerent young men on a young woman on crutches in a residential area of North Vancouver the previous evening. Now that the media had decided to make it their top story, there was no doubt it would be bumped up to the GIS member on call that night, and that would be me. I appreciated that the general duty members had done the preliminary investigation rather than call me out at one in the morning.

After reading the night shift report waiting on my desk of the vicious attack, I was a bit surprised to find that the hospital had already released the complainant. The emergency room nurses seemed uncharacteristically unsympathetic to the victim and at odds with the male doctor over his medical assessment. After a little prodding and a promise of confidentiality, I discovered why.

The complainant had a history of making unfounded medical complaints. Once she even claimed to be dying from cancer until she discovered there were verification tests and not-so-nice treatments. The nurses could have forgiven a hypochondriac, but she was a well-researched malingerer. The complainant's new claim of MS (multiple sclerosis) was the perfect disorder with no definitive test or treatment.

The doctor, who had never dealt with the complainant, choosing to disregard the nurses' warnings and to give her the benefit of the doubt, conceded possible cracked ribs, which often do not show on x-rays. He also accepted the woman's refusal to undergo the internal rape examination as understandable, considering her emotionally distraught state. The willingness of the male doctor to devalue the advice of the nurses and to believe the persuasive complainant reminded me of the dispatchers' and members' occasional communication problems.

Of course, that didn't mean she hadn't been attacked, and as an investigator I had to struggle to remain objective and open. My job wasn't to determine guilt; it was only to gather evidence and ask lots of questions. I had gone to the hospital to find answers and instead left with more questions.

I returned to the detachment file room, where I found corroboration of the cancer claim the complainant had successfully used several years earlier to play on an investigator's sympathies and avoid a minor charge.

"Haven't you talked to her yet?" Hill had tracked me down, hoping for an update. "Her friends are calling the local radio talk show and working up the public. It's becoming political, and a trust fund is starting to build. It's gone out on the national news wire, and we need an update to get the press off our backs."

"Can you stall?" My request surprised Hill--he had assigned me a straightforward assault investigation. "I don't feel comfortable with a press release yet." By his expression he understood that my real request was: *Trust me, I need more time.* I was asking a lot of him and I got it.

"All right, I'll brief the superintendent," he said; adding, "but he won't like it," to emphasize the limited nature of the time-out I had been granted.

Armed with a recruit who just happened to be in the constable's room when I passed by, we headed to the "victim's" place. En route, I confided to her that I might need a witness--a silent observer--if the interview went badly.

The landlord, who lived on the ground floor of the two-storey house, answered the door. He unlocked a second interior door at the bottom of a long, steep, flight of stairs. "She saw your car and called me to let you in. She's too shaky to come down the stairs."

"How does she normally manage these stairs on crutches?" I asked.

"It's very hard for her, but she can't work and has only social assistance. She can't afford to move," he said sympathetically.

She was either a very pathetic person or a very manipulative sociopath, I thought. I struggled to remain impartial, but it was becoming increasingly hard for me not to believe the latter.

The complainant was standing supported by crutches at the top of the stairs. I thought I read a fleeting, faint expression of surprise, or perhaps disappointment, as she realized the investigator was female, but it vanished so quickly behind her sad, pain-racked façade I couldn't be sure I'd accurately read anything. I had never encountered someone so difficult to read; or maybe I was looking for something that wasn't there.

It was hard for me not to feel sorry for her has she hobbled to a chair, softly sighing with each step. The recruit and I took a seat on the couch on the other side of the coffee table on which she had laid her crutches when she sat down. It was time for me to do what I did best.

I busied myself taking her statement. The complainant summed up the whole tragic event in a neat paragraph--not surprising, since she had told and retold the story so many times during the past twelve hours. She appeared fatigued by my questions that probed her for more details--a lot more details. I had stressed her as much as I dared when I finally finished the written statement and offered it to her to read and sign. She was convincing, but my police instincts were still on edge.

As she handed it back to me, I asked to see the injury she had received when she was knocked unconscious with her crutches.

"The doctors have already treated me. It's in their report," she protested weakly.

"I'd like to show my recruit evidence of the kind of blunt trauma that can cause unconsciousness."

Reluctantly she complied. Even when I asked her to separate her hair to allow a better look, there wasn't a lot to see; but then again, I was not a doctor.

"Can you tell me why you refused the rape examination?" I asked, devoid of any emotion except genuine curiosity.

My question hit an emotional nerve, and she snapped, "I never said I was raped!"

"No, but you did tell the attending officers and the ambulance attendants your panties had been removed and torn while you were unconscious and you couldn't be sure you weren't," I said as politely and as professionally as possible in an unsuccessful effort to de-escalate the building outrage in the complainant. "It's a question you may be asked on the stand when we catch the assailants."

"Get out!" she screamed. "Get out!"

It was time to leave before things got even uglier. I nodded to the recruit and we retreated down the stairs with dignified, but well-paced haste. As we closed the door, the unmistakable thud of a crutch thrown from the top of the stairs slammed against it.

It is quite an awkward thing to upset a physically challenged person enough for her to fling her crutch at you. It could have been more embarrassing had we been a touch slower, I thought, searching for anything in the situation to recover my professionalism. Unfortunately, we weren't the only ones on the other side of the door at the bottom of the stairs. I turned directly into the gaze of the complainant's disapproving landlord.

"She's a little upset right now; could you bring her crutch up to her?" I said as I quickly walked toward my police car, where I radioed the North Vancouver Dispatch day shift NCO to expect a complaint against me.

"She is already on the line," I was told.

I was beginning to feel like a suspect and I didn't like it. I broke the awkward silence in the police car by asking the recruit what she thought.

"I think she is pretty mad at you," stating the obvious.

"Yah, I'd have to agree with you on that. Was there anything else you noticed?" I don't know what I was expecting her to say. If she had sided with me, it would have been dismissed as peer support.

"I noticed an expensive medical book on her coffee table, a kind of encyclopaedia of disease, and I thought it was an odd thing for someone like her to have."

It was something I had missed, something that added to the balance of circumstantial evidence. Not a smoking gun, but a small indicator that my intuition could be right, and I hadn't just re-traumatized a victim.

"Well done!" I said.

Our neighbourhood enquiries were inconclusive. No one had seen or heard anything until the complainant started shouting for help. There were lots of concerned witnesses to the torn clothing, minor scrapes, and the crutch caught high in the tree where it had been thrown, but no one had seen or heard the suspects. Just like the complainant's MS, the assault would be difficult to disprove.

I dreaded my return to the office. There could be no more stalling on my part. I handed the press release to Hill for his approval. It was short and inoffensive, I hoped.

"North Vancouver RCMP are having difficulty substantiating the reported overnight assault. Anyone with information on the alleged crime should contact the police at 985–1311."

"It didn't happen!" Hill stated in surprise.

"I didn't say that," I protested, hoping to hide in the ambiguous construction of the statement.

"Yes, you did," he objected. "Do you or don't you think this is a real crime?" he asked with the precision of a defence lawyer on cross-examination.

It wasn't long before I was sitting in front of the superintendent airing my doubts about the complainant.

"The media has been relentless on this one. Are you sure?" he asked.

"No," I confessed. "I would prefer more time to investigate this before I can be certain." It wasn't difficult to see that answer would not do. The media attention had painted us into a corner. We had to say something, or we would become the story by appearing incompetent or uncaring. Either way, they would sell a lot of papers.

Time to make a stand, and I did. "I think it's a scam for money and sympathy."

In a tremendous gesture of support, the superintendent allowed my unedited press release to go out. The media continued to fan the flames of the firestorm that followed. It didn't take long for the minority group advocates to start calling.

In the GIS office, Corporal Rick Jones answered the phone but was only able to state the standard "GIS office, Corporal--" before the emotional tirade began. So passionate was the caller that Rick had to hold the phone away from his ear, and as a result everyone in the small office overheard the condemnation of the North Vancouver RCMP by the self-identified representative of Rape Relief. Certain accusations stood out amid the deluge of insults: allegations of "typical male stereotyping," "blatant bias," and "systematic, deliberate re-victimization."

Several times, the corporal tried to interrupt the rant only to be over-spoken by the outraged caller. Finally, as the caller paused, at a loss for either words or breath, Rick seized his chance to say, with a look of mixed amusement and satisfaction, "Perhaps you should speak to the investigator," and handed the phone across the desk to me.

"This is Constable Greenwood. Can I help you?"

There was shocked silence on the other end. So I filled the void, "I sympathize with many of your concerns, but I can assure you no one has prejudged this case and it remains active."

"Are you a peace officer?"

"Yes."

"And are you in charge of the case or assisting?"

"I am in charge."

The conversation ended shortly after.

The rape councillor was much less intimidating than the original general duty investigator who confronted me at my desk when he came on night shift.

"What in the hell are you doing?' he demanded. When I challenged the complainant's story I had inadvertently challenged him, an excellent and senior member.

"There is no doubt in my mind that this is a legitimate complaint. Someone with MS couldn't possibly throw her crutches that high--"

"I am not convinced she has MS," I interjected, hoping to sidetrack him.

"The ambulance attendant confirmed it!" he shot back.

"But there is no definitive test for the disorder. If doctors can't be certain, how could an ambulance attendant know?"

There was little I could do to settle the officer's ruffled feathers. I was willing to admit he might be right, but somehow he was not able to concede the same possibility to my position.

Later, in the solitude of my apartment, I nearly buckled under the stress created by a day in which I had: enraged a complainant, a rape relief organization, and now a senior member and most of his watch. Not only had I had risked my professional reputation on instincts and circumstantial evidence; my supervisors, the Detachment commander, and the Force itself could be embarrassed if I were wrong. And just when I thought it couldn't get any worse, it did.

The night shift station NCO phoned to say a witness to the assault had called to support the complainant's story. My heart sank as I realized I may have over-analyzed the complainant and arrived at an incorrect conclusion.

There was little sympathy in the NCO's voice, the same NCO from the night before, when he advised the witness would be at the office at nine the next morning to give me his statement. It wouldn't be the last sleepless night my career gave me but it was the longest.

The next morning, everyone in the office knew about the witness. My fall from grace was even harder to accept knowing that it was my own youthful arrogance that had caused it. I had chosen to walk a tightrope without a net by not doing what everyone wanted me to do in the investigation. My choice had damaged more than my reputation, probably irreconcilably; every female member would share my disgrace vicariously. I had let everyone down.

The seconds seemed like hours as I waited at the front counter, my eyes fixed on my statement pad, hoping to avoid the equally stinging gazes of sympathy and self-righteous satisfaction. I retreated into a self-imposed limbo, as I sadly contemplated the credibility blow I had dealt present and future female members and the broader negative implications it might have for the Women's Movement.

"How could I have been so blind, so reckless, so wrong?" I asked myself over and over again, but the answer came from an outside voice--the voice of someone who was still prepared to believe in miracles, even if I was not.

"I don't think anyone is coming," suggested the front desk civilian.

The voice awakened me from the depth of my despair as I realized the seconds had indeed become hours. The weight of the world, or at least the weight of the female population, began to lift from me as I discovered the so-called witness's telephone number and address were non-existent, as was the name given. My confidence and my focus were slowly returning when I requested the day shift NCO replay two taped phone calls, first the one with the "witness's" voice, then the other one with the complainant complaining against me. What a relief it was to be right.

In the end, rather than destroying my reputation, the case had the opposite effect. More than that, it had proven an effective way to ferret out false complaints without exposing the Force to unfair criticism.

As handy as a female investigator might be in that type of investigation, I had no desire to be limited to sex crimes. My success may have created nearly as much of a problem as my failure would have for future female members. I now had to guard against becoming the "go to" member for sex crimes.

It wasn't long before my fears of being stereotype were triggered when S/Sgt. Hill requested I assist a general-duty member in a routine rape case. I stormed into Hill's office in an insubordinate protest to point out the request did not meet GIS's normal criteria for assignment. Unless rapes were serial in nature or involved aggravated assaults, G.D. members were expected to handle the file. I ended by pointing out the same request for assistance would not have been made of a male GIS member.

S/Sgt. Hill seemed to have anticipated my objections and disarmed me by conceding the validity of my concerns. He did not need to accommodate my complaints or even acknowledge them, but he did. He even promised to guard against any such case screening in the future if I took the file. The professional courtesy he extended made his request much more palatable.

"It will only take an interview. Two teenage girls have made up a bizarre story, either as a joke, or they are looking for attention. The member was hoping you could get them to tell the truth before they get themselves charged with public mischief."

I was headed down to the interview room before I had a chance to wonder how Hill had gotten me to agree to an investigation I had sworn not to take only five minutes earlier. In the room, I found two fourteen-year-old girls nervously waiting. The heavier of the two was only there for moral support of her friend, the victim, a hesitant complainant.

The two girls had an unusually complicated story that spanned several days--a story that began when at a bus stop they met a good-looking, extraverted, psychology major from Simon Fraser University. The student enlisted their help as hypnotic subjects for one of his course assignments. In return, he even promised to help them lose weight, by leaving a post-hypnotic suggestion.

Armed with the fearless recklessness of youth, they followed the attractive stranger back to his apartment, where they found that his attempts at hypnosis were both unsuccessful and deceitful. The post-hypnotic suggestion he attempted to implant had nothing to do with weight loss and everything to do with making them sex slaves. The teens were quite happy to put an end to the adventure by quickly leaving his apartment.

The next day, the suspect returned to the bus stop where he had met the girls the day before. He waited in the bushes until one of them returned; then he raped the victim as he chanted the hypnotic command. Too shocked and ashamed to tell anyone but her friend, it took several days before she was convinced to report the crime to the police, but it was too late to collect physical evidence as corroboration.

I could see why the investigator had not believed their story. Hill was waiting for me when I returned to my desk from the interview, statement in hand.

"Did you get them to tell the truth?" he asked. It didn't appear any of the other members or secretaries were paying any attention to the conversation until I replied.

"I believe them," I said cautiously. Suddenly the office became very quiet until Rick, my new partner, spoke. "You're kidding, right?" he asked in a low, serious voice.

Handing him the statement to read, I tried to explain. "It's not *what* they said--it's *how* they said it." It was difficult to articulate what had influenced my decision when I wasn't quite sure myself.

The countless interviews and statements I had taken from rape victims in the past had provided a pattern of physical demeanour as a cross-reference for my subconscious mind. I am not referring to obvious and expected behaviours like tears and crying, but victim behaviours: the unconscious drawing in of their legs almost into a fetal position; the lowering of their voices so no one unintended would hear what unthinkable things had happened; avoidance of eye contact indicating shame, not lies. Only one rape complainant had lacked these unscripted behaviours, and that was the only false complaint of rape I had investigated.

Until that interview, I had not realized how important body language had become in helping me to form an opinion of the reliability of statements. It was only when I was forced to defend my opinion that I realized how much I was beginning to rely on it during investigations.

However, it would take a lot more than feelings and hunches to sway anyone else's mind, so I returned to my favourite research tool: the record room's Rolodex, a mechanical system capable of locating names of persons from previous files. I ran the suspect's name and found the corroborating evidence I needed to convince the others.

Triumphantly I returned to the GIS office with several previous files involving the suspect and young girls. The circumstances of each file seemed nearly as bizarre as the current one. In one file, he pretended to be a doctor, using stolen medical equipment; in another, he was a child photographer. Even more remarkable: in every file, the members had believed the suspect, not the victims, leading to no charges being laid in any of them. Only a small percentage of the population--sociopaths and psychopaths--possess the skill and lack of morality to lie so effectively that even the police believe them. This would be my second encounter with one.

Ironically, the only thing I had been wrong about that day was my objection to being assigned the file in the first place. The public mischief complaint had quickly turned into a serial sex offender file. Since little could be expected from an interrogation with this type of offender, Rick and I busied ourselves collecting background and evidence before the arrest.

With a little more digging, I found out the suspect was not a Canadian citizen but an immigrant from an iron curtain country.

"This is too easy; we can deport him!" I announced naïvely to Rick. At that time, non-Canadians who committed indictable offences could be deported.

"No, we can't. He has claimed refugee status," Rick replied in disgust. "Refugee status" was the first in a series of immigration loopholes criminals were quick to cash in on.

"Well, he lied to Immigration when he entered Canada; the Americans threw him out when he broke their laws."

"Doesn't matter; Canada has decided it's our duty to protect another country's criminals."

"Score one for American self-interest," I said, disappointed.

The arrest was uneventful, and although we knew it would probably be futile, Rick decided to attempt an interrogation. I was surprised to see Rick's stoic expression had been replaced by a faint smile when he returned to the GIS office.

"Did he admit to anything?" I asked optimistically.

"No," he said, as his face returned to its stern norm.

In search of the secret behind Rick's smile, I wandered down to cells to fingerprint and photograph the suspect. I found him in his cell crying like a little boy.

"He called me a DP," he lamented, referring to his exchange with Rick. "What does it mean to be a DP?" he asked.

I had seen grown men wet themselves when dealing with police, but this was the only time I heard one cry like a little boy before. I couldn't tell him what "DP" meant because I had never heard the term before. It was not based in police or legal jargon.

"What is a DP?" I asked Rick when I returned to the office. He smiled. "Displaced person," he said. No wonder Rick was smiling; he had managed to emotionally demolish a suspected sociopath with an obscure abbreviation. Canada may have been stuck with a sexual predator, but we didn't have to be nice to him.

Old files on Marcel were reopened, and new sexual assault charges were laid. In a bold move, Sgt. MacKay decided to use the newspaper to find out if there were more unreported cases. Marcel's picture and the charges were published and anyone with information was urged to contact the police.

"Advertising for victims," an unhappy defence counsel called this new type of partnering with the media. It was controversial but successful, resulting in several more charges.

How unlucky for Marcel we worked Monday to Friday. The result was a pattern beginning with his Monday morning release by the courts and ending with our Friday afternoon arrests for new charges, landing him in jail for several weekends.

It was on the occasion of the third Friday night arrest that even the defence lawyer seemed to understand that Marcel was someone we intended to inconvenience as much as was legally possible.

"Do I need to block off any more Friday evenings for arraignment with the 'Lunatic'?" he asked. "Lunatic" was a play on the suspect's last name. That was the only time I ever heard a defence lawyer hint that he may have been as disgusted with his client as the police.

The final tally of sex offence charges was both impressive and intimidating. After a successful preliminary trial, the case stalled in the justice process, apparently because neither the lawyers for the defence nor the Crown were clamouring to present the menagerie of charges before the Supreme Court of B.C. While this case was held in limbo, my GIS team had more to do than sit around waiting for the next trial.

A reported male body in a backyard in the affluent Capilano Zone sparked a murder investigation worthy of a TV "whodunit." Unlike the majority of murders outside of organized crime, the crime was the result of a chance meeting and an unknown motive. It was a fascinating case to work on, the type of case where "time" is the enemy. The entire section worked nineteen hours the first day, then after a three-hour rest we returned, knowing we could not sleep again until the suspect was in jail. I didn't know how long I could effectively function without sleep, but I was about to test my limit.

In a small section like ours, we all had lots of work to do and everyone had a job; mine was Exhibit Person. This was perhaps not a flashy job, but an important one in any case, particularly a murder. The chain of continuity had to be provable beyond question. I catalogued and bagged hundreds of pieces of evidence from the scene and the autopsy. I commandeered the conference room as an exhibit room where wet possessions were properly dried in preparation for the forensic lab analysis.

The twenty-eight-year-old victim's exemplary lifestyle had allowed him to live well past the expected lifespan of someone with cystic fibrosis. It nearly broke the members' hearts when they notified his mother that her only child would never return from his weekly racquetball game with his best friend.

The staff at the bar corroborated the friend's account of the evening, which ended with their usual single beer. While we were in the process of tracking down the bar staff, the victim's car was located in Pemberton, a small, isolated community in the Whistler area, an eight-hour drive from the scene. Constable Intense and Craig Gates, the two main investigators, left to pursue what turned out to be a dead end.

Only a few people were at the North Vancouver bar at closing time on the night of the offence. The young waitress recognized one of the people who left around the same time as the victim as a student from her old high school. With no way of knowing if the young man was a witness or a suspect, Sgt. MacKay and Cst. Wait began the interview, but it wasn't too long before Sgt. MacKay decided to handle the interview himself. It was a patient and long interview handled by a master. MacKay had an unexpected advantage working for him: the young man was native, and as such he was burdened with a spiritual consciousness in conflict with the white culture he was tempted to adopt. His inner turmoil provided the key to MacKay's strategy.

MacKay picked up on the guilt-ridden body language the murderer was exhibiting and turned it to his advantage.

"Have you read *Body Language*?"[17] he asked. The book had been in vogue recently, especially among young singles looking to improve their dating techniques by reading the potential partner's body language. MacKay could hardly believe his good fortune at the response.

"Yes, I have," replied the suspect.

"Well, look at what your body is telling me. It is telling me you did it."

The suspect became aware of his defensive posture and conceded his guilt. It was almost with relief that he was finally able to speak the words out loud to himself and for the record that he had killed a man he had met only an hour before. His native culture and morality was in conflict with his actions, and it was tearing him apart. His account sounded true, but it wasn't entirely so.

"My two friends and I got a ride from this guy at closing. We dropped off one of my friends, then the rest of us parked off Lonsdale to drink some beer. I went into the backyard of a house there to pee and the guy comes, too. He makes a pass at me and I lose it and kill him. I'm not like that." MacKay wasn't sure if he was referring to murder or homosexuality, but he wasn't prepared to interrupt a written, warned confession to clarify the point.

"My friends didn't know what happened; they were passed out in the back seat when I drove the car to Pemberton. On the train ride back to North Vancouver I asked, "You can smell the death on me, can't you?"

A couple of witness statements and a few more exhibits were all that seemed to stand between a good night's sleep and us.

I was surprised that the friend answered the door at three a.m. as if he had been expecting us. He also was young, nineteen, Caucasian in descent, and the product of a dysfunctional upbringing, a background he shared with his friend. Absent or inadequate parenting does not respect cultural, religious, or racial borders. The effects are remarkably standard. The young man was very quiet and co-operative.

"You know why we are here?" Rick said at the door.

The young man nodded in acknowledgment.

"We have a search warrant to seize the clothing you were wearing that night." Quietly and quickly he led us to a laundry hamper, from which I removed unwashed, blood-spattered jeans, socks, and shirt. His shoes were also seized.

[17] Julius Fast, *Body Language* (New York: Pocket Books, 1971) (originally published by M. Evans and Co., Inc.).

"We need to take a statement from you back at the office," Rick advised.

"Okay." It was the only word I recall his saying during the entire exchange.

It was pushing four a.m. when we returned to the second-floor GIS office. I continued down the hall to the conference room with the exhibits for drying and cataloguing on a flow chart. Rick led the witness into S/Sgt. Hill's office for a statement. It wasn't until Rick asked him to tell the story that any of us realized this young man was not simply a witness but an accomplice to a cold-blooded murder. The story he told did not diverge from the original suspect's until he said he heard sounds of fighting in the backyard and investigated, only to find his friend standing over the victim's badly beaten and unconscious body.

"'You know we will have to kill him now?' I said 'Okay,' and ran to the curb to break a beer bottle." The first suspect cut the victim's throat while our "witness" held his head back.

The confession took Rick completely by surprise. Rick masked his shock as he quickly read the police warning. Not one word changed in the subsequent written statement. Accused number two was booked into cells. The dawn was beautiful, but the light hurt our tired, red eyes as the team continued with the investigation, now close to forty-eight hours after it had begun.

We had twenty-four hours from the time of the first arrest to present the preliminary case to the judge. Everyone had lots of work to do before any of us could sleep. Even with two signed confessions, we could not assume they would stand. Every piece of evidence we could gather to support or disprove their story had to be investigated. We had been taken by surprise once in this investigation. We didn't want that to happen again.

Intense and Greg had arrived back with the vehicle from Pemberton disappointed to have missed all the twists and turns of the investigation. Identification Section was combing through the car. Youths from the local arcade on Lonsdale were asked to participate in a police lineup. I wasn't even aware we had the facility to do a physical lineup on Detachment, but we did, complete with one-way mirror.

I supervised the witnesses as two separate lineups were sequentially shown to the waitress and the bartender. The first group was comprised of similarly aged and built native youths and the second group were Caucasians for accused number two. My sense of relief when both witnesses made a positive ID for both accused was shattered when the waitress hesitated and picked out a second, unknown teen from the Caucasian lineup.

I was so tired my stomach felt sick. The impact of growing fatigue was blatantly recorded in my steadily eroding penmanship. There it was in black and white for anyone to see from the beginning of the case until this point--

now almost illegible. How could any of us push past the exhaustion if we had accidentally uncovered another unexpected twist in the investigation?

"Finished?" Rick's voice brought me back to reality.

"No. Please ask the subject to stand by. I need to talk to you. "

Fortunately, when we spoke to the third identified patron, it was clear he had been in the Coach House that evening but was completely unrelated to the crime. It was just strange coincidence that this young man had been part of the lineup. We couldn't have asked for a better credibility test for our waitress as a witness.

By this point in the investigation, we knew the third youth who had been in the two accused's company on the night of the murder was only a witness, but he didn't know that and he had gone into hiding. I knew the group of late teens he hung with and phoned one who owed me a favour. Within an hour, the final member of the trio appeared at the Detachment front counter looking for me. He was so scared during his statement, he tried to stop his hands from shaking by clasping them together--and still they shook. Mine were shaking, too, from exhaustion, as I finished the last document the Crown needed for the arraignment.

Finally, we were able to get some rest. We looked grey, ill, shaky, and wrinkled; but we were satisfied that our diligence and persistence had solved a very challenging crime.

The age-old belief that things come in threes rang true when the third murder occurred the following week. It was unusual to have one, let alone three, murders in any one year in North Vancouver. Fortunately, this murder was an open and shut domestic incident on the City South reserve. The husband was stabbed once through the heart by his wife. Nothing difficult--just very sad.

In the midst of my GIS rotation, the union representing the majority of municipal and city workers in North Vancouver went on strike. The unions in B.C. were much more powerful and politically active than in Ontario. The Detachment lost its civilian support staff who performed front desk, cells guard, typist, and records duties.

While inconvenient, the strike wasn't crippling to Detachment operations. Most RCMP detachments are small rural postings where members perform all of those duties. We may all have been capable because of our training and experience, but no one would willingly volunteer to fill the role of filing clerk, receptionist, or typist, so the superintendent decided to employ the Force's traditional selection process for undesirable jobs, a fair process that is blind to all but length of service.

For the duration of the strike, arriving recruits and those on Recruit Field Training were reassigned to fill the clerical void--a role they performed rather well, clearing filing backlogs quickly and running the office efficiently on a smaller workforce. As the strike ran on, even the recruits got their first taste of the privileges seniority earns in the Force when they were replaced by newer recruits fresh from Depot.

"Mrs. Mac" and "Jeanny," the long-standing clerical staff of the GIS office, were not so easily replaced. Their knowledge and wisdom were an integral part of the GIS team.

There were a couple of interesting moments during the strike, like the morning I was confronted by a picketing union leader as I walked through the parking lot toward the Detachment for day shift.

"You can't cross this picket line," he ordered as he planted himself directly in my path like a schoolyard bully. He had been rude to me, so I returned in kind. Borrowing a line from Trudeau, I said, "Just watch me," as I stepped around him and continued to the office, a move that caught him off-guard for a moment. I was almost at the door when he caught up to me.

"If you walk through that door, you can kiss your job goodbye. What's your name?" he demanded. He had obviously mistaken me for a civilian worker.

"Really?" I said. "My name is Constable Greenwood, and if you would like to try to stop me, I would love to arrest you for Obstruction."

I caught some smiles on the picket line, almost exclusively female, behind him. I knew very little about strikes or the significance of picket lines. Farmers don't have unions, at least back then they didn't.

Like the Masons, the more I learned about unions, the less I liked the way they treated women. It seemed to me, like bank managers and school principals, the men always got the positions of power and money in the union and the women did the work. It would be nice to think that the female-dominated inside workers, the majority of the union, would benefit from the financial hardship the strike created; but in the end, it was the outside workers, the garbage collectors and maintenance workers, almost exclusively male, who received the biggest pay concession.

The strike did provide a lighter moment. Herbie, the former "B team" leader from B&E Squad, called down from his new posting outside the Lower Mainland to check on a trial date. I just happened to answer the phone in the GIS office when he rang. Apparently he hadn't heard I was back on GIS and assumed I was filling in for Jeanny and Mrs. Mac.

"I heard about the strike and I am glad to see you have finally been given an appropriate job."

"That's right, Herbie, *they gave me your spot.*"

I surprised myself pleasantly at how quick I was with the comeback, which left him speechless. Thank goodness the OIC didn't think like that. Members will do anything asked or ordered as long as it is fair. The clock on "time in the rank" was gender blind, at least in North Vancouver.

When Rick left on holiday, Cst. Intense and I were teamed up as partners again. Just like in our old uniformed days, we slipped back into our bickering ways. We must have sounded like Hepburn and Bogy in *The African Queen*, with two important exceptions: neither of us was the other's type, and we had an unmarked police car, not a boat, although there were times when I would have preferred a leisurely cruise to Intense's aggressive driving habits. I was both embarrassed and amused at how he could work himself into such a state over real and imagined traffic infractions. It was then I understood why his wife, Suzy, never got her licence. She must have thought driving was some kind of war. Usually, I just closed my eyes to prevent being a witness and bit my tongue as passenger, a strategy that worked well until one evening on West Georgia when Intense asked me to assist him.

An expensive sports car was stopped at a red light in the through lane of West Georgia Street, when Intense pulled beside him in the turn lane that branched off to Stanley Park after the intersection. Intense revved the motor as we waited, intending to beat the other car off the mark and slip into the lane in front of him. He seemed oblivious to the side glances of disbelief both the driver and I cast in his direction. Unmarked GIS cars were assembly-line sedans, commonly referred to by our own traffic section as "gutless wonders." We were halfway through the park before Intense caught up to him. I would like to point out that we were speeding at this point, and the other driver never had to.

"Get the fire ball out," barked Intense, caught up in that old male, macho, competition reflex, which appears to be more ingrained in some males than others. I couldn't indulge Intense this time. "What ticket are you going to give him?" I asked, hoping to give him cause for rational reasoning.

My question gave him pause, but only for a moment before he replied, "I'll think of something."

"You'll have to," I conceded, "because the only thing I can think of is attempting to pass on the right--*but that was us.*"

Intense's foot lightened as he considered my point, and the matter was dropped without further action or discussion. I was beginning to admire Intense's passion even if I didn't share his reasons for it.

Intense was passionate about everything and absolutely unshakable in his belief that he was correct at all times. I saw his confidence shaken only once during all the time we knew each other. It happened on a routine enquiry in one of the most expensive neighbourhoods in Vancouver. After the well-dressed woman who had met us at the door provided the info we requested she mused, "So you two are peace officers. I never would have guessed . . . except for that tie."

Oh my God, it was all I could do not to explode with laughter. Intense was a very handsome man with very conservative taste in suits; however, his taste in ties was something else. My lips were nearly white from biting them when we got back into the car and I watched him pick up the end of his tie and study it in confusion for a minute. His face was flushed and the veins in his neck were protruding when he gave in and asked: "What is wrong with this tie?"

It was the only glimpse I ever had behind the wall of self-assured righteousness he had constructed. He wasn't entirely bulletproof after all. Like the rest of us mere mortals, he could be hurt by someone else's opinion.

"Maybe Suze should pick your ties," I suggested gingerly.

"Yah, I guess she might be better at it," he conceded. That was the only suggestion I ever made that was immediately and unquestionably accepted by him.

After the three murders, there was a quiet period for major crime. Making routine enquiries and analyzing crime reports was not what either Intense or I was hoping for.

"That is the most pathetic armed robbery attempt I have ever heard of!" Intense said as he tossed forward a report from the night shift.

I had to agree. A scruffy-looking male in his mid-twenties had pulled a butter knife on a cab driver, only to be disarmed and chased for several blocks. Nobody was going to waste a lot of time trying to solve that crime; but it turned out to be one that solved itself.

Several hours later, the suspect, who had been waiting to be arrested, came into the Detachment to confess. He turned out to be as pathetic as his attempted robbery. He had a long history of minor offences, foster homes, and incarcerations.

I can't recall his name, but I recall almost everything else about our exchanges. Let's call him "Joe" from this point on. The first thing Joe asked when he was arrested was what was for lunch. Meat pies were the meal du jour each and every day in North Van cells.

"Oh," he said disappointedly. "West Van P.D. serves Macdonald's." He didn't get to eat many meat pies before he was in court.

Even the judge took pity on him and sentenced him to probation for the armed robbery. No one was upset with the sentence--except the suspect. He liked being in custody. It was the only time he was sure of a warm bed and something to eat. "Institutionalized" was the term I remembered from my old psychology course. The reality is much more pathetic than the term sounds. Intense and I didn't have long to wonder if he had moved over to West Vancouver because the jail food was better.

It was approximately one-thirty a.m. when Intense and I were called out to an arson on West 3rd Street. Arsons are difficult crimes to investigate; by their nature, evidence of the crime is consumed by the fire. The abandoned house was fully engulfed in fire, requiring Traffic Section to block traffic at the surrounding intersections to all but emergency vehicles.

The career traffic member, on pointsman duty rerouting vehicles around the fire, recognized Intense and me as we approached the scene and suggested in a very casual manner, "You might want to talk to that guy over there. He's been a real nuisance."

There stood Joe on the sidewalk, where the traffic man had ordered him to stay, waving warmly at Intense and me.

"I am so glad you are here. I have been trying to tell this cop," indicating the traffic member, "that I did it. I set the fire. He didn't believe me. He told me to sit down over here before he arrested me for Obstruction."

Back at the office in the interview room, he was given the police warning; not that you could have stopped him from confessing. He had been living in the abandoned house for days when he hatched the plan. He set the fire then waited outside for someone to notice and report it before it got out of control. When no one did, he banged on the neighbour's door and raised the alarm himself, then waited for the firefighters and police. When the house cooled, the firefighters confirmed the point of origin of the fire with Joe's story.

"I get five years for this," he said cheerfully.

This arson was nearly as pathetic as his armed robbery, but he didn't want to hear it. He had looked it up in the *Criminal Code of Canada* before planning the crime.

"Arson is straight indictable, commanding a term of five years or greater incarceration."

Sentencing by 1980 had already started to lighten, and we didn't want him to be too disappointed at court a second time. I couldn't resist asking: "Why do you want to go to prison so badly?"

"I just can't make it out here yet. I finally got a job at an arcade at the PNE, then my probation officer called to confirm it and they fired me. I need federal time so I can get the job training I need to survive on the outside. The armed robbery should have been enough. Can you let the judge know?"

He was right. If he got "federal time," two years plus a day, he could access job training that didn't exist in provincial jails. He was so proud of his plan and how he believed it was unfolding, he was on a kind of adrenalin high. We, however, were bone tired and there was still the matter of prosecutor's sheets to do for court in the morning. It was rolling up to five a.m. when we were booking him into cells.

"You two look tired," Joe remarked sympathetically. Then it dawned on him that he was the reason and he apologized. "I am so sorry. If I knew it would be you and Intense they were calling out I would have set the fire earlier."

Joe was the only accused I have ever allowed to call me by my first name. I am quite sure the same could be said for Intense. Joe seemed more like a victim than a criminal, and we treated him accordingly. The last paragraph on the prosecutor's sheets was a "Note to Crown" explaining "Joe's" circumstances and reasons for wanting a lengthy sentence. The last thing we did before going home for some sleep was to drop off some Macdonald's for Joe.

The following day, the headlines in the *North Shore News* read, "Judge Makes Arsonist's Day." Joe was given the opportunity he wanted; I hope he made good use of it.

During the last month of my rotation, I received my last call out from my good friend Gary Proulx, who was working the midnight shift. The crime was an armed home invasion. This type of crime at the time shocked even the members by the brazenness of the offence and the potential for a lethal outcome during the crime.

Two young men wearing nylon stockings over their heads kicked in the front door of an upper-class home at midnight. After dragging the husband, wife and child from their beds and threatening them with handguns, they bound them with packing tape and left with $50,000 dollars in jewellery.

As luck would have it, the wife recognized the voice of one of the offenders as an acquaintance of her son. Her son and I had a long history that had begun when I was a recruit. He made his first pipe bomb at thirteen and had continued in his criminal career into his teenaged drug-trafficking years. Our relationship appeared to be an almost cordial game of cat and mouse, in which the mouse always seemed to be just one step ahead.

I knew his circle of friends and associates well. More important, I knew I had a decent chance to get the offenders and the guns off the street if I acted quickly and had more manpower. It was two-thirty a.m. when I called Sgt. Ron MacKay to brief him.

"I am really sorry to disturb you, but I know this group. I think I can get these guys, but I'm going to need some help," I said, hoping that the seriousness of the crime and the impact it would have on the perception of security in the North Vancouver community would entice Sgt. MacKay to come out himself rather than simply going to the next GIS member on call. A sergeant could authorize additional manpower and equipment without delay if the case progressed as I hoped.

"I'll be there in fifteen minutes," he said wearily.

So began one of the fastest-paced major investigations I had ever been on. Best of all, I was the lead investigator. All of Rinn's training on turning informants was put to the test.

"I don't know their names. They are from out of town; they are really bad. They killed someone in Alberta and they will kill me if they find out who talked," my reluctant confidential informant told me.

Finally I pried out of him the motel they were staying at in Burnaby. This type of situation today would be a mandatory ERT (Emergency Response Team) call out, but that would have slowed us down; and it was up to MacKay's discretion to call them or not. Sergeant MacKay, Gary Proulx, and I kicked in the door of the motel at four a.m., only to find the room was empty, apparently abandoned by the suspects after it had been searched in relation to a string of armed bank robberies by Vancouver City Police the day before. There was enough documentation to identify the suspects and support the reliability of my informant. There were even photos of the suspects in the room.

There were two possible courses of action after the motel, one favoured by Sgt. MacKay and a different one by me. Sergeant MacKay could easily have pulled rank. He had many more investigations behind his decision than I, but I had the informant. Again, a GIS NCO placed his trust in my abilities, and we prepared to head off to a downtown office building.

The day shift was arriving as we were preparing to leave. MacKay reassigned Cst. Sean Murphy of Fraud Section to assist with our stakeout. We arrived before nine a.m. to set up the surveillance of the multi-storey office building.

The directory inside the large lobby listed many possible fences--lawyers, geologists, jewellers--on a number of different floors. Without more precise information, we would have to take the suspects down in the lobby before they got to one of the many elevators.

In the lobby there was an empty desk and chair in front of the directory where a receptionist might sit, and Sean seated himself, opened the paper, and faded into the background in the lobby. The son of an Ontario judge, Sean could be depended on to adapt quietly and effectively into any situation. Gary Proulx and I took up an observation point across the street at the doorway to the department store. It afforded a view of people approaching in either direction on Pender Street. Sgt. MacKay took up a position in an unmarked police car in the parking lot behind the building with a view of the side street.

Surveillance is a waiting game, a game of patience in which the enemy is boredom. We waited, scanning the pedestrians as they passed and entered the building, searching for the faces we had seen in the photos at the motel. It would have been easy to call it off after two hours of fighting fatigue. We really were working on some wishful police guessing. When MacKay suggested shutting down, I successfully pleaded for one more hour.

It was only minutes later that Gary and I saw not two but three young men walking toward the building. We knew it was them, not because of the fuzzy photos, but by their demeanour.

"It's them!" I radioed as we raced across the four lanes of morning traffic. The three suspects, one of whom was on crutches, entered the office building lobby then paused as they spoke briefly inside the door, giving Gary and me time to catch up, just as the suspects split up. The man on crutches remained just inside the door of the lobby as the other two moved toward the elevators.

Sean casually moved from behind the desk toward the man on crutches while Gary and I positioned ourselves directly behind the other two. There were about ten to fifteen businessmen and women in the lobby waiting for or exiting elevators, and MacKay was missing, but we couldn't wait. The doors were opening to the upward bound elevator they were waiting for. It was like a well-practiced movie skit.

The three of us simultaneously pulled our guns, touching the barrels to the base of each suspect's skull, as Gary's baritone voice bellowed: "Freeze! Police."

It was almost surreal as the entire lobby immediately froze, mid-stride, mid-sentence, mid-breath. The lobby remained absolutely silent as we completed the arrest. The three suspects were searched, cuffed, and in the process of being escorted out the door within a minute, two at the most, when the silence was finally broken by a collective exhalation. As we exited the building, I heard one man, obviously a lawyer, say meekly, "I hope they're not my clients!"

An understandable statement, considering that less than twelve hours after the offence, two of the suspects had been apprehended armed with weapons, and the third, probably the wheel man, with all of the jewellery in his pocket.

MacKay was pleasantly surprised at the arrest but disappointed that he had not heard the call to action on the portable and missed an armed takedown. Still, he was quite pleased that North Vancouver had "maintained the right" and quickly apprehended out-of-town criminals, ending their trans-Canada crime spree.

They were professional criminals and admitted to nothing incriminating, but that didn't mean they didn't want to talk to me as I fingerprinted and photographed them at the Detachment. They didn't mind talking in general, matter-of-fact, terms about their chosen profession.

"In Quebec, everyone does armed robberies. Out here they all do B&E's. We just couldn't get out of the habit."

There they were, talking casually about different localized crime trends in Canada as if they were style trends in skirt lengths.

They had a question they wanted answered as well. "How did you know where we would be?"

The life of my informant depended on their never finding the answer to that question.

"Just a lucky guess," I replied. That wouldn't be the end of their attempt to find out, however.

I was involved in just one more stakeout before my rotation to GIS expired. Confidential information had been received by the Break and Enter detail concerning the bank inside the Capilano Mall.

A joint B&E/GIS project resulted in Len, who was on a B&E rotation at the time, and I being paired. We were tasked to remain in the mall until closing, while everyone else monitored our transmissions from the outside.

The shoppers thinned as closing time drew near. Len and I went into a jewellery store opposite the bank and pretended to be customers.

"Can we see some engagement rings?" Len asked. I smiled at the inside joke.

Even though we had been going out for nearly three years, few members knew. After I had tried on everything in the store, we left. It was apparent the robbery was not going to happen that night.

The night wasn't a complete waste of time for Len. Two weeks later, he surprised me with a proposal. I surprised myself when I said "yes." So much for being the modern, single career woman.

The route I had charted when I left the Island's shores had just taken a big turn I never anticipated. The shortest distance between two points may be a straight line, but navigating life, like navigating powerful rivers and lakes, requires much more than simple mathematical equations. I wasn't an ice road marker like my father, but I had learned from him that the right route can't be mapped standing on shore, where distance creates a mirage of uniformity over the water, lending an illusion of strength and safety. The only way to create the route was to walk it slowly, watching for any change in the surface texture that might warn of shoals, currents, and thin ice, listening for every crack echoing danger, knowing when and where to break the ice to test for thickness and strength.

Successful pathfinders were never arrogant enough to think of their task in terms of winning a battle against the water. All they hoped for was to strike a temporary truce with it for safe passage, always knowing a strong east wind might make even a well-mapped route unsafe within hours. The first crossings each season were left to those few adventurous souls who were brave enough to challenge the water but humble enough to fear it.

Chapter 8

Slack Tide

Everything was changing so quickly in both my personal and professional life. I had no more control of the route I was travelling than a salmon moult as it is carried out to the ocean by the spring's mountain runoff. It certainly wasn't the route I had planned as a child, or even as a young adult.

I returned to uniform, to a new watch, new NCOs, and a new role as a trainer of a female recruit. A female member training a female recruit may have been a first in North Vancouver, but it was not a Force first.

Joyce Graham, my friend and troop mate, had been trained by a female, Chris Mackie, in Burnaby. Their pairing had been a very successful teaming that led them both to better things. Joyce and another female were the first in Lower Mainland to be accepted on a drug section. Joyce achieved this milestone in typical Joycey fashion--by hard work and good humour.

Joyce's trainer had gone on to another first of her own on the Musical Ride, the most recognized symbol of not only the RCMP, but of Canada. It may have been politically correct for females to join the ride, but, it would not be easily accepted by traditionalists. Chris and my troop mate Joan Merk thought they were prepared when they became the first two female members on the Musical Ride. Vivienne Stewart had also been offered a spot on the ride at the same time, but declined the two year-posting. Several years later, Joan Merk confided in me she wished she had done the same.

I didn't have much to complain about back in female-friendly North Vancouver. How hard could it be to train a recruit? Neither she nor I was ready for it. Perhaps if she had been a little older and more mature and I a little more experienced in supervisory skills, the whole thing would have gone better.

I was disappointed to see she took for granted the atmosphere of respect that had been built between male and female members. My recruit was not the only junior, young, female member that seemed to share an attitude of entitlement, lacking by disposition the independent toughness that drove and defined the earlier female members. I was beginning to appreciate the *Vancouver*

Sun writer's apprehension about female gains sliding back because of the next generation of females.

"Be careful you don't reap what you sow. It may be fun to be everyone's little sister now, but in six months they will need a partner they can trust with their lives. Police work isn't the kind of career that has a middle ground. You will be labelled an asset or a liability. Whichever label you earn will follow you for the rest of your service," I warned.

Perhaps it wasn't her fault. It was like asking a teenager to hurry up and mature. The recruiter, in my opinion, should have deferred her for a couple of years, but the politicians were demanding more visible minorities, and so the floodgates began to open.

In 1981, the federal government was openly recruiting females, French, and other minority groups. It was politically motivated and badly thought out. All applicants had been treated uniformly until that point. It was a source of pride within our minority groups that we had risen to and met the challenges based on merit. The resentment created by the new preferred hiring categories was about to threaten that. Politicians didn't care what problems were created for minority groups then and in the future by the Canadian version of "affirmative action." A quick, superficial fix was all that was needed to fit the short-sighted four-year lifespan of the Canadian politician. Self-serving politicians did not understand that "maintaining the right" was a state of mind shared by the best persons of all cultures and religions and both genders--like a young First Nations man who arrived as a recruit.

Now *he* was a pioneer! Until that point, almost all other natives within the Force were "special constables" destined to police the reserves; their function was not much more than that of a liaison between the Force and the population on the treaty land. This young man had met all the educational and physical requirements and, in many ways, like a true pioneer, he exceeded expectations. He was young, athletic, and learned quickly. He didn't ask for any special treatment and he received none. He earned his spot in the family of North Vancouver Detachment. The members had great respect for his courage and empathy for his socially isolating situation, the burden that comes with being the first, and, for a while, the only one.

He was a young man with one foot in the past and one in the future when Staffing took the ground out from under his feet. Rather than leave him in North Vancouver after his recruit field training, where he could have developed as a member and a person, Staffing transferred him to a rural community with a larger First Nations population.

"Apples" was the derogatory term some natives would occasionally use as an insult--"Apples" because they were red on the outside but white inside. From his midnight phone calls to the Detachment, the North Van members knew he was unhappy and lonely, but no one realized the depth of his sadness until it was too late. During one of these calls, a single shot from his service revolver rang out--a tragic example of what could go wrong when social change is rushed, rather than allowed to evolve.

Unfortunately, suicide was not uncommon within the Force, especially in Lower Mainland. The instrument of choice was the service revolver. Every member has lost someone because of it. I am sad to say I have lost three friends and nearly a fourth to it. Burnaby Detachment, the largest RCMP Detachment at the time, had quite a rash of suicides. Perhaps it was our small-town policing ways in conflict with big-city demands . . . but none of the rank and file bought that. It was more likely a combination of the internal stresses within the Force itself and the extremely high performance expectations we placed on ourselves.

We had to be strong to uphold our spot in the red wall. We were the protectors, the reason the public could sleep well at night, the ones who would willingly risk our lives to save others.

Police run in where firemen fear to tread.

All operational members at one point or another in their service have been involved in situations that warrant the Commissioner's Accommodation Award, but, unless the NCO is articulate and motivated enough to fill out the necessary forms, such situations go unnoted. How fortunate it is for the public that members rise above their own instincts for survival for internal, not external, reasons.

One midnight shift at about four a.m., the Lions Gate Hospital fire alarm sounded in our NCO's office, causing him to walk out to the front steps of the Detachment and look across the road to the hospital. The firemen on the other side of the intersection did the same. Nothing looked wrong from the outside of the building, but then again you couldn't open the windows in the hospital. The first firefighters accompanied the NCO as they wandered, almost casually, up the stairs to the hospital floor in question--at which point the NCO used his portable to declare a "ten-thirty three," causing every member on shift to rush to the fire.

It wasn't until I exited the stairwell to the ninth floor and had the breath sucked from me by the thick black cloud that I appreciated the magnitude of the fire. I stepped back into the stairwell for a brief moment to taste the sweet flavour of fresh air. The most basic instinct of life is to breathe, and it takes a lot to override that instinct. I filled my lungs and joined my watch. Choosing to override that instinct for duty is the bravest thing I have ever witnessed.

The members assisted the nurses with the evacuation of the patients while the firefighters in full air-breathing protection fought the fire. The floor looked like a war zone: nurses collapsing across the stretchers onto the patients they were trying to evacuate; members tripping over the firefighters' hoses. One of the members challenged the firemen, asking why they were not assisting in the evacuation--after all, they could breathe, we could not. He was ignored. Later, we were surprised to find that the firefighters' protocol is to first put out the fire, then save the lives.

In the end, the fire was put out and no one was lost. The NCO didn't want to do the work necessary to request the Commissioner's Award for each member in attendance. He suggested the watch pick one person to recommend for it, but no one would break ranks to accept an honour everyone deserved; so no one's name was put forward.

All things considered, North Vancouver was a kind of Camelot of policing at the time. Empowered by the support of upper management, the public, the courts, and--most important--Canadian law, members were inspired to rise to the highest level of service and duty. Even lawyers were sometimes held to account by other lawyers.

Lonsdale streets were lined every Tuesday night with Alpha males hoping to "get lucky," awaiting their entrance into "lady's night" at one of the local bars. It was a brilliant stroke of marketing for a slow business night to allow only females into one of the local watering holes until a certain hour. Fuelled by cheap drinks, the mating ritual was repeated each week with only minor variations. Like a wildlife documentary, the Beta males, who left without mates, worked out their sexual frustration by brawling on the street.

This Tuesday night, the fight was a little early and much smaller than usual, involving only a bouncer and a patron. Of course, there was a large crowd of onlookers who flowed out of the bar to watch the fight. It wasn't really much of a fight because the patron was quite drunk.

Not much of a file, really; I had no trouble dispersing the crowd and identifying both participants. It would have been a simple matter of statements to sort out the details on a minor assault had the "victim" not been an articling student (lawyer-in-training).

Back at the office, the victim told me how he and his classmates had been at a drinking contest, which he had won prior to setting off (by transit, I hoped) to regroup at the Lonsdale bar. At the door, the bouncer (justifiably) refused him entrance because he was already intoxicated.

The victim was in the process of leaving the area when his friend, also an articling student, arrived, turned him around, and tried to plead his case to the bouncer. They were both in the process of being lawfully evicted when it became physical, resulting in a bloody nose for my victim.

I was just forming the opinion there wasn't much of a case, when S/Sgt. Monk knocked on the interview room door to say that several of these intoxicated aspiring law students were at the front desk of the Detachment demanding to represent the victim. The most obnoxious of them all was the friend who had escalated the event in the first place.

Well, as we all know, "a little knowledge is a dangerous thing." Not only did he feel he should represent the victim; he was demanding to return to the bar for a positive identification of the bouncer. The victim and his other friends agreed with our advice that the best thing they could do for the moment was catch a cab home. However, the loudest one continued to raise noisy complaints, even after S/Sgt Monk cautioned him to leave or be arrested for public intoxication.

"Go ahead!" he invited, drunk with legal indignation.

It was the wrong staff sergeant to try that with. There was nothing George Monk liked better than dragging drunk lawyers over the front counter of the Detachment, as he had demonstrated in the past on numerous, often legendary, occasions. When George was the station NCO, many a lawyer, filled with legal indignation and perhaps one too many gin and tonics, rushed to the Detachment intending to rescue their summoning client, only to find themselves second in line for the Breathalyzer.

As I booked the articling student into cells, still unrepentant and verbally aggressive, the young man demanded to call *his* lawyer, who just happened to be a partner at a well-respected agency of senior lawyers the RCMP sometimes contracted with for federal charges.

It was three a.m. by now, and I was quite sure the call would be unwelcome. After several minutes, the budding "lawyer" opened the door and sheepishly asked me to dial the number, which he was too drunk to do for himself. I was pleased to "help" and careful to leave the room as he began his slurred, privileged conversation.

I couldn't help but notice he was much quieter when the conversation was over and I finished booking him into cells. Not surprisingly, shortly after, S/Sgt. Monk said the senior partner of the law firm had phoned him to ask for details, then apologized for the incident.

The next day, I had a call from the lawyer who had apologized to Monk the night before. He was prepared to take the matter to the law society, an action that could be professionally devastating for the student. It was a tempting offer;

the man had been quite a jerk the night before, but to end a career seemed disproportionate to the offence. I chose to show compassion--something he may have been incapable of himself--and requested only a letter of apology. It was no doubt the most difficult letter he had ever drafted. The solution I requested and received was in keeping with the principles of justice as they had existed in Canadian law until the *Charter of Rights* was created.

It was hard for junior members like me to heed the warnings of the chiefs of police across the country as they sounded the alarm that a new Act of Parliament was about undermine the principles on which our justice system was balanced. How could anything that sounded as good as The Charter of Rights and Freedoms be something to fear?

Looking back, perhaps like most Canadians I was too naïve or too busy to understand the paradigm switch the poorly constructed new Act about to be created would have on the Canadian justice system, changing the Canadian criminal justice system from one based on justice to one based on law--a system in which the process would become more important than the outcome. Perhaps affection and trust in its architect, Trudeau, encouraged the dismissal of the fears of the more informed members of the RCMP and policing community as a whole. Or perhaps it was the inadequacy of language itself that destined the task to failure. Whatever the reason, I still prefer to believe Trudeau's intentions were simply to solidify the common law practices of the Canadian courts, which had evolved under the Canadian Bill of Rights, not to undermine them. Trudeau's background as a civil lawyer in Quebec appears to have blinded him to the impact the *Charter* would have on criminal law. Unfortunately, concepts like justice, wisdom, and moral leadership are too complex to be defined and constrained by written language. Justice, like music or art, cannot be reduced to a formula to be quantified and qualified. Only a fool or a lawyer would think otherwise.

The newly crafted *Charter*, cloaked as a tool to protect the average citizen, became a weapon for criminals and their lawyers--lawyers who rejoiced in the largest make-work project the federal government had ever created. Along with most members of the public, especially those in the West, I was only vaguely aware of the nasty, paranoid mood that had seized Canadian politicians, who seemed unaware of, and unconcerned with, the profound effects these changes would have on the very fabric of Canadian society.

The unbalancing of the justice system was a symptom of a much bigger trend in Canadian politics. No one had seemed to notice that the traditional, multi-professional mix of elected representatives in Ottawa had been eroded and replaced by lawyers and career bureaucrats who now held the reins of power and were quietly but skillfully transforming Canada into their vision of a perfect society-- a society that was controlled by the new powerbrokers in Ottawa, who patiently waited for political opportunities to increase their power and control. How easily they transformed a rather creative investigational misjudgment in which the only casualty was a barn, into a Royal Commission. The Commission paved the way for a new, more politically sensitive agency, CSIS, to replace the Secret Service arm of the RCMP.

The new civilian agency, CSIS (Canadian Security Intelligence Service), a political construct, wanted to distance itself from the RCMP and its members as quickly as possible. Members already working in the old Secret Service had the two-year transition period for the changeover to the new civilian agency to decide whether to resign from the Force and be absorbed or to transfer back to police work within the Force. Predictably, faced with a chilly professional climate, most members chose to leave, even though there was no guarantee they would retain their rank if they did not meet the regional service average for it. The purging of seasoned Mounties from the new agency's ranks also resulted in the loss of valuable investigational experience and skill that could not be easily or quickly replaced in the new agency.

The resulting discourteous expulsion resulted in my new partner-to-be's transfer to North Vancouver. Not surprisingly, he seemed to have some anger issues, and, as often happens, he looked for the easiest minority group to vent it on. Reports of his off-colour behaviours and innuendos soon spread among the female office staff and female members. I didn't think I would be a target, because I didn't feel much like an easy victim; until Adrienne warned me she'd had a run-in with him. If he was indiscriminate enough to take a run at Adrienne, why should I think he wouldn't try it on with me as well?

Even armed with advance warnings, I was still taken by surprise when, at morning briefing on my first shift back, he let out a loud "wolf whistle," the kind you might expect from a drunken construction worker. The other male members in the briefing room went silent in shock. The initial shock registered because this newcomer did not realize that kind of base behaviour had no place in "Camelot." The second shock was that he had picked me--the most outspoken advocate of women's rights in the Detachment--to try it on. The male members in attendance smiled in anticipation of my response.

Enraged, I stepped into his personal space and, pointing my finger like a weapon directly in his face at his nose, and struggling to control my rage, said: "This is your only warning. If you ever try something like that again, we will be having our next discussion in the superintendent's office."

"And what might we be discussing?" he asked, trying to regain the upper hand.

"Just off the top of my head, I think I would start with a charge of 'Conduct unbecoming.' I am sure I can think of a few others if I put my mind to it."

My aggressive reaction had stopped him dead in his tracks. He tried to laugh the exchange off, but he was the only one laughing. However, I may have won a battle but the war was a long way from over. My "partner" decided to change tactics.

It wasn't very long before Brent Barbor, a good friend on the watch, told me the member had a lot to say in the locker room. "Do you want the watch to tune him in?" he asked.

Brent was one of the last people I would ever have expected to offer such a physical resolution to a problem. Although he was six foot two and in perfect shape, his perpetual boyish features and irrepressible good-natured smile always reminded me of an Eagle Scout. I was grateful for the offer but too proud and naïve to accept it.

"Thanks, Brent, but I can handle it," I mistakenly said, in a decision I would soon regret.

My sheltered career to date had left me ill-prepared to handle the work stress that can be created when the supervisor doesn't step in. The new staff sergeant, who was my partner's constant coffee companion, turned a blind eye to the locker room attacks and the constant dumping of files on me. I was already dealing with the additional workload of training a recruit; now I had to do three members' work.

The lesson my partner learned from our first encounter kept him from providing me with anything substantive to complain about. As if it weren't bad enough that I had to handle all the investigations on our watch while trying to train a recruit, one day the senior constable burst in as I was in the process of obtaining a written, warned statement, in an attempt to slough off a new file on me. I was outraged that my partner, who had been completely absent when I arrested a machete-carrying drug addict one hour earlier, had now surfaced to try and dump his only file of the day onto me as well. That was the day I realized I could not handle the situation by ignoring it.

My day shift watch had gone home when I finally finished booking in my prisoner, and the station NCO was from a different watch when I marched in totally frustrated with my work environment. To my horror, I could not separate my feelings from my complaint. Until that moment, I thought I had finally mastered the male ability to turn anger outside. I had only just begun to make my case for being upset with my partner when I felt my eyes threatening to water. I knew my voice would be next to betray the depth of my emotion. It remained an intellectual quandary to me how I could have mastered my emotions when dealing with murderers, rapists, and lawyers, remaining professional, detached and unassailable, and yet I remained so vulnerable and could be so wounded if an attack came from within the Force, even by a member I neither liked nor respected. I still deserved a "D" for systemic-emotional self-defence.

The sergeant, sensing my distress, stepped in. "Let's pull the file log for the past several months."

The log revealed in black and white that well over ninety percent of the calls were mine--providing undisputable corroboration for my complaints.

"I can handle it from here," the sergeant offered; and this time I gratefully accepted the help. Within the week, I had a new partner and watch. My old "partner" paid a heavy professional price for his behaviour. His ranking on the superintendent's promotion list dropped, delaying his promotion for at least a year. Still, in a way I had grown from the unfortunate incident by learning a few painful but important lessons from my "partner": if you don't complain, nothing will change; men in the middle of divorces are the worst partners; when someone offers to help there is no shame in accepting it; and--the most important lesson--the disappointing revelation that I was still not able to stop the tears if I were really upset.

Fortunately, not all former members of the Security Service had confrontational dispositions. The exodus of members from the old Security Service included the new OIC for North Vancouver, Superintendent Burns. It wasn't long before the female members at North Vancouver realized he could be counted on to maintain the gender-neutral management the previous two OICs had established. With such a positive work environment, the North Vancouver Detachment's female member's night out had mushroomed to include female members from almost all of the detachments and some from the interior.

Superintendent Burns had heard about our gatherings and did us the unprecedented honour of asking to attend one. The request caused quite a stir among the male members. It was an accepted taboo within the Force at the time for an officer to socialize with non-commissioned ranks.

The superintendent wasn't the only male to ask for an invite to the dinner. Two junior male members from the watch asked if they could come in drag and under the guise of being my troop mates from outside detachments. It was perhaps not the wisest, but certainly the boldest practical joke I ever participated in. It took a lot of make-up and props to transform Rod and Doug into Rodberta and Di.

Truthfully, Doug was a lost cause. Even freshly shaved, he had a five o'clock shadow that make-up barely hid. Rod, on the other hand, made a stunning but rather tall woman.

Rodberta

At The Keg, no one was fooled by Doug, but Rod (Rod Booth) was unrecognizable. His handsome baby face had been transformed. He was so striking and statuesque that he could have been mistaken for a model and so convincing that no one but my recruit and I knew the answer to the question on everyone's mind when we entered The Keg:

"Is she a he?"

Rod, still under the influence of the warm-up party, stayed in character, but as the evening wore on he went a little far and began to openly flirt with the superintendent. After a sober second thought, he and "Di" excused themselves for the night before his identity was discovered. The men back on the watch couldn't believe we had the nerve to pull off so risky a stunt. It was easier for female members who had no military background to bend traditional protocols. Maybe we were given more latitude because we were so different; or maybe the female disposition was having more of an impact on the Force than we realized, beginning with progressive and efficient detachments like North Vancouver.

It wasn't the first time Rod had acted rashly but escaped unharmed. As a recruit, Rod had almost gotten himself killed trying to stop an impaired driver. Senior members on the midnight shift had been trying to pull over a full-sized Cadillac, but the driver ignored the police cars, continuing to drive up and down the streets of City South in a low-speed pursuit. Rod, who had dropped his trainer off at the office just minutes before, thought he could help by pulling his police car sideways across the two northbound lanes of Lonsdale in a symbolic blockade. (The other two lanes were completely open.) As he picked up his microphone to radio in his ill-advised plan, he saw the lights of the Cadillac as the driver floored it, aiming directly at Rod's car. The impact folded the police car like an accordion and sent it flying three-quarters of a block up the street. The members following were sure Rod had been killed. They couldn't believe their eyes or their ears when they opened the driver's door of Rod's car and found him dazed but apparently unharmed.

"I think I'm all right," Rod said, more concerned that he had broken Force policy by using his police car, now destroyed, as a barricade.

"No you're not--you're in shock!" shouted his trainer, who had beaten the pursuing members to the scene. They continued the dispute over Rod's condition all the way to the emergency department, where Rod's trainer had to restrain him from getting off the stretcher. He didn't believe Rod's claims *until* Rod said, after looking at the nurses, "Thank God I have clean underwear on!"

All of the members present stopped and smiled. We had all been given that piece of wisdom by our mothers. The only injury he sustained was a bruise on his hip where the driver's door had pushed his Sam Browne into his hip.

In the shelter of North Vancouver Detachment and its atmosphere of tolerance and discovery, I had enjoyed a level of social and professional success that became the foundation of my service, providing exceptional investigative and court experience few junior members are lucky enough to have.

The GIS cases I had worked on were going forward at the B.C. Supreme Court, located in downtown Vancouver. It was a new building reflecting the best of modern architecture, the centrepiece of which was a striking sloping glass roof that functioned as a huge, open skylight.

The courthouse had just opened when we attended the murder case we had all worked so long and hard on. The order of dress for this level of court was suit or red serge. We all wore suits. The lawyers and judges dressed in the traditional black dress robes with high, stiff, white collars. It was a formal affair.

Ironically, the atmosphere on the stand was much more relaxed than at magistrates' court. The Crown lawyers were senior and enjoyed the luxury of ample time to prepare their cases. This placed them on a slightly more equal legal footing with the defence. What a change from magistrates' court where Crowns suffering from a crushing caseload read many cases for the first time one hour before court.

Only indictable cases were held at the Supreme Court level. Sometimes the cases were presented in front of the judge alone, but most often it was in front of a judge and a jury of twelve. The judges, who were senior as well, were addressed as "My Lord." They were wise and firm and had no tolerance for the cheap grandstanding or slimy defence lawyer tactics too often seen in the lower courts. When a jury was watching, everyone was on his/her best behaviour.

I didn't appreciate how different the acceptable code of behaviour was between upper and lower courts until the second Supreme Court case in which I squared off against a lawyer I knew all too well from previous legal aid cases at the magistrate level. His trademark, an aggressive and abrasive demeanour, had been replaced by a quiet and polite façade. The enigma only intensified when none of the other members on the case noticed the change in his approach.

During one of the breaks, in a rare show of familiarity, he confided the reason for his atypical behaviour in the upper court: "I think it is highly unfair of the RCMP to employ female members. I can't try to push you around in front of a jury or they will think I am a bad guy."

Not only was the mystery solved, but his comments offered some interesting insights into how a defence lawyer plays to a jury.

"So--they will get it right," I joked back.

In true lawyer fashion, he had cleared one mystery while at the same time creating another.

"Why was he talking to you outside of court?" Sgt. MacKay asked. "Lawyers don't talk to members unless it's to gain some advantage."

"I can't imagine what he was hoping to gain--we didn't speak in specifics about the case," I reassured him.

It didn't take long to solve this new mystery. My testimony on the second murder case would have been limited to the remarkably boring entering of exhibits, except for my minor contact with the second accused prior to his confession. Perhaps the defence lawyer felt he couldn't attack me, but that didn't mean he wouldn't try to *trick* me. The cross-examination began innocently enough.

"You were not present when Constable Rick Wait took the statement from my client, were you?" he asked.

"No," I conceded. How fortunate for him I had not been the one taking the statement.

"And would you consider Constable Wait a *large* man?" he asked.

Lawyers have a way of setting up statements to best advantage their clients. Only politicians and writers are as good in a game of semantics. He was trying to lead my answer to assist him in trying to focus the jury's mind on an irrelevant issue in an attempt to gain their sympathy. Our little chat at the break may even have been part of his plan to lower my guard by "humanizing" himself. The jury would see Rick for themselves soon enough. I had no intention of playing into his hands.

"Constable Wait is the average size of RCMP members," I hedged.

"I don't know about that; but he is approximately six foot two and 220 pounds, isn't he?" he said, rejecting my verbal sidestep.

"About that," I was forced to concede.

There were no further questions, and the judge excused me from the stand. As I walked towards the door, the senior Crown, Sullivan, could not resist lightening the mood.

"Perhaps it should be noted that this constable is *not* the normal height and weight of most RCMP members."

The humour, at my expense, seemed to serve as a universal release valve from the weighty task of detailing a murder. Everyone--the jury, the judge, the audience, and even the lawyers--took the opportunity to laugh, loud and long. It seemed to propel me out of the soundproof courtroom doors towards the members waiting to give evidence. It could still be faintly heard after the doors closed. All the members wanted to know what the laughter was about, but I was hardly going to tell them.

"The Crown counsel tripped," I lied.

I was off the hook for the moment because nothing further could be asked for fear of witness contamination.

The murder case had been so strong that after the preliminary trial, both the defence counsels for each of the accused had offered a plea to second-degree murder--an offer we felt morally obliged to decline, because the act was premeditated, even if only for the moments it took to decide to break the beer bottle before cutting the victim's throat.

Although all points of law went in our favour, the defence lawyers were successful in highlighting the dysfunctional upbringing the two young accused had endured. Violence, drinking, and poverty painted the two in a very sympathetic light. They were pre-programmed to react with violence to the alleged homosexual advance of the victim--a defence that by today's societal standards would be considered, at best, a successful gay bashing.

I would like to point out that the members neither believed nor cared if the homosexual "defence" was true, because Canadian law would not accept it; but the jury did. Both accused were convicted of only manslaughter and sentenced to two years less a day. All of the legal professionals in the case were shocked. There was, however, nothing to appeal. Jury decisions, unless tampered with, are not challengeable.

I now knew why members preferred to have a case decided by a trained judge who understood both the law and the role of the courts in the balancing act of justice. For obvious reasons, defence counsels preferred a jury trial. But sometimes it was not an easy choice.

The defence for the armed robbery/home invasion trial was faced with a no-win scenario. No amount of "smoke blowing" would stop a jury from identifying with the helpless victims, wakened at gunpoint, shattering the sanctity and safety of their home; but, on the other hand, a judge understood the use of police informants. I am sure the Crown considered it a gift when he found out the case would be heard by a judge alone. It was such a neat package, the Crown had to double-check his good luck at the pre-trial interview by asking for clarification of the information contained in the prosecutor's sheets: "In the first paragraph, you describe the offence in North Vancouver, and in the second you are suddenly staking out a downtown office building, waiting for the accused. What is missing?"

"Confidential information," we replied.

His smile conveyed his satisfaction that he had received the answer he had anticipated and hoped for. "I understand; but more importantly, the judge will as well."

The effective use of an informant would have provided an opportunity for a clever defence lawyer to blow a lot of smoke to cloud the issue and confuse a jury; conversely, a professional servant of the court and the public like a judge would understand and appreciate a well-executed case.

The case was so strong it was remarkable that the accused had continued to contest the charges after the preliminary. They had been in custody since the initial arrest months ago, and prolonging the legal fight while they did "dead time" would only increase their final incarceration time. There had to be a reason, and MacKay was the first to figure it out.

As MacKay emerged from the courtroom after giving his evidence, he warned me, "They are fishing for the identity of your informant."

It was a well-chosen "heads-up" that did not break our duty concerning witness contamination--not that I had any time to ask for further details, because I was the next witness.

On the stand, the defence counsel was not quick to accept that that I, a relatively junior member, had been the lead investigator for so major an investigation. The only obvious reason a well-seasoned investigator who outranked me would play second would be if I was the informant's handler. He probably thought MacKay was trying to shield the informant's identity, when the truth was he didn't know it. It was the second time I had noticed an unscrupulous lawyer applying his own lack of morality to others.

A wise old saying I remembered from my childhood provided a valuable insight: "People judge others by their own standards."

Perhaps in dealing with this type of lawyer, the saying could be modified to "lack of standards."

I was unaware that, when MacKay was on the stand, the lawyer had asked to see his notebook. MacKay had very sketchy notes, further strengthening his suspicions. Senior members might be forgiven for brief notes, but the defence lawyer knew a junior member would never be allowed that kind of professional latitude. So it wasn't long into the questioning before the defence requested to see *my* notes on the case.

"Do you have any objections?" asked the judge.

"No, my lord, so long as I am present and the review is restricted to the pages dealing with the case," I replied.

In anticipation of the request, I had used two elastics to define the pages dedicated to the case at hand and to prevent any unrelated cases from being viewed. The defence could not mask his surprise at the number of pages I had written.

The court fell silent as the defence counsel began to read. After several minutes, the judge asked impatiently, "Is this going to take much longer?"

"I am sorry, my lord, I had no idea there would be so much." Unwilling to give up the possibility of finding some useful information, he asked: "Perhaps if I could have an adjournment to read through this?"

Once again, the judge bypassed the Crown, asking me directly, "Any objections or conditions?"

"No objections, my lord, but one condition: defence counsel has to read it in my presence."

"Very well, court is adjourned for one-half hour while Constable Greenwood supervises defence counsel's reading."

The lawyer didn't seem to mind the condition, probably because he thought he could trick me into answering the question he was really after even if he couldn't find it in my notebook.

"What my clients would really like to know is who told you where they would be?"

"I am sure they would. You won't find it in there," I said, indicating my notebook.

For a change, the lawyer took me at my word, closed the notebook, and handed it back to me. But he wasn't ready yet to toss in the towel. "Just between you and me, how did you know?"

How naïve did he really think I was? There is no such thing as "off the record" when dealing with legal aid lawyers or "yellow" journalists. "You really don't expect me to answer a question that could cost someone their life, do you?"

He seemed caught off-guard. Lawyers are comfortable asking questions, not answering them. Apparently from his reaction to my next statement, lawyers aren't comfortable being confronted, either.

"As an officer of the court I cannot believe you would be a party to a future offence," I said.

Like a slap in the face, my innuendo seemed to snap him back to morality, and he quickly said, "Of course not."

The morning the verdict was to be handed down, the judge ordered the sheriffs to search all spectators in the court for weapons, leaving little doubt as to what the verdict would be. I am sure the defence counsel was less than pleased that so many of the suspects' scruffy, tattooed street groupies had attended the proceedings. Still, the only weapons identified by the search were a couple of canes belonging to the seniors who made up the usual audience in the Supreme Court.

After my second or third day on my first jury trial, I had noticed a few white-haired men, unrelated to the case, in the audience and asked one of the senior GIS members about them.

"Oh, that's the crew."

"The crew?"

"They are always here. They check the court-posted docket and pick the most interesting trials to watch. Beats the heck out of soap operas or mall watching. They become quite knowledgeable about the law as well as the personalities and quirks of judges, lawyers, and police. If you ever want to know how a case is progressing, they are as informed a source as you can get."

Not surprisingly, the seniors who had figured out such a brilliant source of free real-life drama were themselves brilliant. They could be grouped into two categories: the ones who followed certain crimes, e.g. rapes or robberies, and those who followed judges or Crown lawyers--a little like judicial groupies.

It was the second group that I found most intriguing. They could read the body language of a judge as well as any peace officer. Armed with this information, I made a practice of seeking the independent insight they could give on the progress of cases I was involved in. They could predict everything except a jury discussion (that was more like predicting a lottery). I learned the painful truth of that analogy on the only rape case I ever lost--a case the Crown won on points of law but not in the eyes of the old-world jury the defence had picked.

I hesitated to call the victim, a young Australian girl working as a nanny on a work visa, because her employer and I had convinced her to pursue the charge. I worried that my overconfidence in the ability of the Canadian Justice system to always arrive at the correct verdict had been proven wrong at the victim's expense. I could have understood if she was disappointed in me or angry for enduring first the preliminary, then the jury trial, but she wasn't.

"I am sorry the jury didn't believe me," she began soulfully, her voice gaining strength as she continued, "but I am glad I went through with it. I know I told the truth, you know it, and the rapist knows it. I didn't let him get away with it. Now I can get on with the rest of my life knowing I fought back even if the system failed."

I felt maybe there was some hope for the next generation of females if they had half her tenacity, dignity, and strength of spirit.

The numerous Supreme Court cases my plainclothes duties had involved me in created a monetary boost for my wedding fund. The twelve-hour shifts on uniform duty that I now worked meant almost all my court appearances were on days off, which meant double time.

In the RCMP, the amount of the paycheque often does not reflect the amount of work done. For example, in the first murder case when everyone on GIS worked thirty-six hours in a row, our pay rate went from straight time to time-and-one-half for sixteen hours then back to straight time for eight hours as we worked back into our scheduled day shift. NCOs, who had not had the luxury of overtime when they were constables, and officers who received bonuses at the end of a fiscal year if they ran their detachments within budget, were remarkably stingy with members.

I must confess I rather enjoyed teasing Hill about my court windfall, since he had been one who enforced the strict interpretation of the overtime policy during the investigation.

"It's a sad day in the Force when a lowly PB (his nickname for me which stood for police broad) makes more than her old staff sergeant," he teased, knowing he was the only member of the Force I would ever have allowed to use such a nickname.

It seemed since I joined the Force different people had awarded me different names, from "midget" to "GI Jane." I didn't mind; they were all a little funny and spoke more of what the creator valued than myself. It didn't matter to me what people called me--I always knew who I was.

I was a little surprised to find that my somewhat traditional decision to change my name for marriage surprised so many people. I could understand why people who didn't know me very well might think I would embrace the new feminist trend and retain my maiden name. I didn't anticipate that my decision would be questioned by both my mother and S/Sgt. Hill, both of them voicing similar views on the topic: "You have established your career and your professional reputation for five years under one name; it would be better to retain that name."

I would have agreed with them five years ago, but at that time I only wanted a career. Now, I found myself wanting more. I wanted children--not right away, but someday--and I wanted us all to have the same last name. It was a matter of practicality to me. I didn't need to retain a name in order to retain my independence and identity.

Len never voiced an opinion one way or the other on the matter, but I think he was relieved at my decision. The media publicly and repeatedly eviscerated Joe Clark, leader of the Conservative Party, because his wife, Maureen McTeer, had not changed her name, creating an unflattering, weak-kneed stereotype for partners of strong women. Fortunately, strong women attract strong men.

The apparent lack of support in the media was all the more surprising, considering even the Catholic Church was trying its best to make some of its rituals more politically correct.

When we began our marriage preparations with the local priest, he proudly pointed out that the vows for the marriage ceremony had been modernized. "You can choose from a number of vows; or write your own if you wish."

After looking over the list, Len shook his head in disagreement and soberly said, "Just a minute, Father, I want the one that says, "love, honour, and *obey*."

The priest looked a little shocked and uncomfortable as he responded: "Well, I suppose if your fiancée doesn't have any objections, we can use the traditional wording."

"No, Father, I have no objections at all if *Len* wants to swear to love, honour, and obey *me*."

With some relief, the priest began to laugh at our quirky sense of humour.

My choice to wear the traditional white dress rather than the red serge seemed to cause even more controversy, only this time my mother understood it better. One of the most dramatic differences between men and women in the Force appeared to be rooted in how much of our own identities got intertwined with the mystique of the Force. I never confused what I *did* with who I *was*. As important as my career was, I had a life beyond the limits of that mandate and obligations to family, friends, and myself to develop that part of me as well.

"I can wear the serge at any regimental ball or dinner. I only get to wear the white dress once," I told Hill. As he shook his head in disagreement, I added,

"Besides, Len said if *I* wore the serge, *he'd* wear the dress." Now *that* Hill could understand.

Neither the name change nor the marriage was going to sit well with the Force. Mounties had never married Mounties before 1975, and it appeared Staffing would prefer it to stay that way. Adrienne had already warned me from personal experience that Staffing had been less than receptive to her own engagement.

Adrienne had become engaged to a member six months prior to me. She had requested a routine, five-year Staffing interview around the same time, seeking advice on how to gain a transfer to commercial crime. She was shocked and offended when the Staffing officer seemed only to want to talk her out of her pending marriage, citing the negative impact marriage would have on her career. He had picked the wrong female member to try that on. Adrienne walked out of the interview and down the hall to a supportive OIC. A new Staffing interview was arranged, and she got her transfer. However, neither of us was naïve enough to believe the general attitude of Staffing had been corrected by this exchange; it had only gone to ground.

The OIC told me he felt he could successfully retain both Len and me at the Detachment, because the Force's policy at the time did not prohibit married couples working together so long as one was not in a supervisory position over the other.

Although that was the Force's policy as stated in the administration manual, the Staffing rule differed. They clearly preferred separate detachments for married members. If Len and I were to stay at North Vancouver, it would only be under the restriction that neither of us would ever be on the same air frequency at the same time. It was a restriction that would have stymied one or both of our careers, had we accepted. It was a professional compromise I wasn't prepared to make. I was senior, so I asked for the Staffing interview.

Armed with the Force policy in my briefcase, I prepared for the interview with the Staffing Officer as I would for an interrogation. As it happened, I did not need to walk out as Adrienne had, but it was definitely not a relaxed interview. The Staffing member made it clear the marriage would restrict my career. He was less blunt, but basically made the same prediction that S/Sgt. Hill had made on the matter: marriage at this point in my career to another member would disrupt my career in a negative way. Staffing did not like the extra posting headaches that came when members married members.

"You can look forward to spending the rest of your service in Lower Mainland."

I knew promotions often entailed unrestricted mobility, but he didn't know he was speaking to someone whose ego wasn't wrapped up in rank.

"It's just too expensive to transfer two members," he added as a hedge against a complaint.

"What an idiot!" I thought. "They can't even figure out one set of moving expenses for the price of moving two members." I really didn't want to leave LMD at that time, so I kept that piece of fiscal logic to myself--a logic that seemed to escape Staffing for the next ten years. If he could push I could certainly push back.

"You mean I don't get to go up North and fight the Indians?"[18] I said sarcastically. "*If you want to put that on paper, I'm prepared to sign right now.*"

I am sure Headquarters' Staffing was wondering what kind of Amazons North Vancouver was supporting--first Adrienne, now me. The rest of the interview was like a hard-fought negotiation. I had no desire to be put into another lower mainland detachment to begin the task of re-establishing myself professionally when I was already being offered plainclothes section at North Vancouver.

Unlike Adrienne, however, I had no appreciation or understanding of the various federal positions at the RCMP. One plainclothes section sounded much like the rest over in the Vancouver Headquarters. I had been quite happy being a medium-sized fish in the little pond of North Vancouver. There was more than irony at work when Staffing assigned me to the Customs and Excise Unit, which focused on the Act that covered the only question I couldn't be bothered to answer in my recruit field training exam.

There was payback in Staffing's selection, but it would be months before I understood the crooked smile on the interviewer's face at the end of the interview. He didn't scare me; I knew I was stronger than he thought, even though I wasn't as strong as I would have liked. I didn't even care when Hill's reaction to my new section was, "The Force has written you off because you've gotten married." I didn't care, because I'd had such a wonderful orientation to all the interesting sections on Detachment during my five-year stay. I was ready for a new adventure, another windmill. It was time for me to leave the shelter of North Vancouver Detachment, just as it was time for new members to come.

One of the members who transferred in was a female who had a stellar reputation among members of every rank and both sexes, Cst. Bev Busson. She was not only from the first female troop; her regimental number was the most senior of all regular female members. One day, she was driving to the school where she taught when she heard that the RCMP was accepting women; she

[18] My apologies to the First Nations, but that was the jargon back then and it packed the semantic punch I wanted in the circumstances. It was also common knowledge within the Force that the descendants of the Northern warrior tribes could be quite a handful under the wrong circumstances.

immediately drove to the nearest detachment to enlist. She had demonstrated that decisiveness and courage consistently in her career, earning her the respect and admiration of her co-workers and supervisors.

Bev arrived in North Vancouver, from her previous posting in the B.C. interior, already a well-rounded, seasoned investigator. There was nothing pretentious or ambitious in her disposition. Now here was a trail-blazer, and what a trail she was blazing: single, hard-working, and well-liked by both male and female members. She was destined for greatness. She was living the dream I had thought I wanted until I found I wanted more. I could hardly believe I had changed so much in five short years. I didn't just want more--I wanted everything. I was going to be one of the new superwomen who could be equal to men in the workforce, in the bedroom, and on the playground.

Even though I knew in my heart that the ancient waters surrounding the Island were insulated from the ravages of time, I had to rush out to the dock in front of my parents' house and stare into the waters for confirmation. It was one of the fleeting times when the water's surface, stilled by the slack tide,[19] mirrored back my reflection. The bond I felt for the water had never been stronger as at that moment in time.

I spent the week before the wedding introducing Len to family, cousins, and my extended family of Islanders. Nearly everyone one on the Island seemed to lend a helping hand in the preparations for the wedding, from my bouquet, made up of local wild flowers and arranged by my parents' neighbour Laurel Connell, to the beautiful wedding cake made by my mother and decorated by Pauline Frasso.

Pauline's family had moved to the Island when she and her twin brother, Paul, were young. The twins, who were exceptionally good looking and friendly, were quickly accepted by the local islanders into the community. Paul was tragically taken by the ice along with Claire McAllister, a member of a long-standing Island family, in their senior high school year.

The double tragedy was sudden and senseless. The two teenage boys, late one night, in search of Kingston pizza on snowmobiles, disregarded one of the cardinal rules of the ice, and it cost them both their lives. You didn't have to be an expert on the ice, only an Islander, to know the rule: "Don't venture onto the ice if the wind is blowing."

It doesn't take much wind or much snow to make whiteout conditions on the

[19] A term that refers to the neutral time between two tides; a brief moment of aquatic détente, the twilight of large water masses, a brief time when the water stills before it reverses its previous direction.

Honour Guard

ice, and though the ice may be thick in the dead of winter, there is always an open boat track along the route.

Pauline's beautiful, smiling face could never mask the sadness in her eyes and in all Islanders' hearts, which did not diminish with time. What we Islanders didn't know was the unthinkable fact that the ice had not finished extracting its cruel, nonrefundable toll from Pauline. As unbearable as the senseless deaths of two teenage boys was, it would pale in comparison to Pauline's destiny. I will write more about Pauline in a later chapter, but for now I prefer to remember Pauline sitting proudly with my wedding cake in my parents' living room at the Island shower my family threw for us. Happy memories of a happy time.It was a typical Wolfe Island wedding except for the uniforms and honour guard, complete with nine-foot bamboo lances from the Musical Ride in Ottawa. The members at Kingston Detachment were delighted to attend in red serge to make up the guard. They hardly ever got a chance to wear their serge in the non-contract province of Ontario. They also knew the reception would be a great Island party. Shelly Baker, the only female member at Kingston Detachment at the time, was joined by Linda Butler in the rank at the top of the church steps in female red serge.

There were lots of parties, both at North Vancouver with members, and back on Wolfe Island with friends and mostly family. It was great--a colourful Catholic/military service. Quite a spectacle, actually, like a fairy tale, or perhaps a dream, full of military, religious, and even Island traditions.

On the Island, the bride and groom are taken from the church in a horse-drawn vehicle: a sleigh in the winter or a coach or buggy in the summer. When two members from the honour guard jumped on either side of Kenny White's black carriage, which was pulled by two matching white horses, Len and I joked we even outdid Princes Di's wedding the year before! As we drove onto the streets of the village, our procession encountered some American cars en route from Horn's ferry to the Wolfe Islander. They mistook us for a parade and stopped to take pictures. There was no mistaking it; this was a twist in the road less taken that would take me where I never thought I would go.

We were having such a good time at the reception, Len and I would have missed the last boat off the Island that evening if my first cousins, Joe and Gerald Nolan, hadn't persuaded the boat crew with a "forty pounder" of whisky to wait for us.

It was amazing how far both Len and I had travelled before our paths crossed. We may have begun our journeys from distant origins, but we were strikingly similar in disposition, education, and family backgrounds and aspirations, sharing the same dream for personal and professional success in the future.

Despite my women's liberation mantra, however, I was not so naïve as to believe our paths would be equal.

I watched from the deck as the ferry pulled away from the Island, knowing that nothing in my personal or professional life would ever be the same again. The impenetrable, black night waters surrounding the ferry mirrored back my gaze. It was no more than I expected. Great and powerful waters never give up their secrets to spectators. I knew that five years ago when I left the Island the first time, and that hadn't turned out so badly. Yet the waters that night, cloaked in darkness, seemed different, more mysterious . . . ominous . . . beautiful. Still, I knew my path once again was leading me away from the safe shores of Wolfe Island, and there was nothing that could have stopped me, once again, from diving headfirst into the unknown.

Chapter 9

Dancing with Dinosaurs

My new section, Customs and Excise, was located in the Division Headquarters (HQ) at 33rd Avenue and Heather Street in Vancouver. The two main buildings of HQ were functional but devoid of the character or ambience distinctive to the Force. They were buildings without a personality or soul, undeserving of any name other than the "Ops" (short for operational) building or the admin building.

In sharp contrast, on the northeastern corner of the property stood Fairmont, the original HQ. Fairmont was a turn-of-the century, stately, heritage Tudor building. Although it was barely adequate for its then current function as the centre for E Division training, it was capable of stirring emotions of pride and tradition in the members who worked next to this visible link to the past--a daily reminder of the continuous line of RCMP service to the Canadian public. Stepping into the NCOs' and officers' mess, located in the basement of Fairmont, was like stepping into history. The carefully preserved rich, dark woodwork from floor to ceiling displayed a level of craftsmanship and attention to detail that had somehow been lost in the cost-efficient modern world. Black and white framed photographs and plaques lined the wall, immortalizing past members. Members shared the unspoken belief that there was more than bricks and mortar at Fairmont. The same ESP that members trusted for their police instincts was also sensitive to the occasional close encounter with one of Fairmont's ghosts who watched and trusted that their traditions would be maintained.

Farther south on the lot was the Forensic Crime Laboratory, where members from all over B.C. sent physical evidence requiring expert examination for major crimes. Regular and civilian members worked side by side at the laboratory to provide members with ballistic and tool mark matches, chemical analyses, and even DNA testing. During my first five years, I had attended a couple of courses at the training branch, Fairmont Academy. I had also been to the lab many times to drop off and pick up exhibits. However, I had never ventured into either of the other two buildings on the site, the operations and the administrative offices.

The admin building housed Health Services, Financial Services, and Staffing, among other non-operational functions within the RCMP. There were a lot of female public servants assisting with the running of these sections, but male members were in charge. In the past, members in admin were those who had been injured in the line of duty and were no longer able to function in an operational capacity; but a more recent trend in staffing these positions had begun to emerge. Members less suited to the operational demands and perhaps lacking the interpersonal skills required for active policing had been dumped into or migrated to the sections. If they couldn't handle people, maybe they could handle paper.

They could handle paper--maybe a little too well. It was like letting lawyers or politicians write the rulebook. The promotion system began to change slowly but steadily to reward administrative Mounties. It soon became common knowledge within the Force that there were two tracks to the promotion system: the work/reward method, and--the fastest track--through non-operational sections within administration. If a member were really ambitious, he or she would transfer to Ottawa, where it was predominately administrative. But within the contract provinces of the Force, the non-operational side was looked upon as being lower in status even than Traffic Section. The operational members preferred to rise through the ranks the hard way. It may have been slower, but they had their pride. Ambitious members seeking a quick and easy route to rank and power didn't seem to care what operational members thought of the early stages of a system change away from job performance in promotion criteria within the Force.

The operations building had been adapted from an old Workman's Compensation building "sold" to the Force for one dollar after they outgrew the original Vancouver post. The Force was used to accepting hand-me-down workplaces. The "new" HQ fit the profile of many detachments with the Division, which utilized old farmhouses. Like the military, the members of the RCMP were grateful for what they got. Complaining wasn't in our nature or our work culture. The real estate values of the land of the surrounding neighbourhoods of Kersidale and Shaughnessy were well out of the price range of members, but the burden of commuting was eased by the use of unmarked police car pools.

My new staff sergeant was also my first car pool driver. He seemed pleasant and laid-back, comfortable with his position in charge of Customs & Excise--a position that was no doubt a retirement move, a reward of a quiet, undemanding section after years of service. On our first commute into HQ, he welcomed me to the section and was quick to tell me I wouldn't be isolated as a female member because another female member, Nancy Fehr, had also just been posted to the unit. I smiled to myself, thinking how overly sensitive the Force appeared to be, worrying about isolating female members. But then he gave me cause to question my assumption.

"A couple of years ago, we got a female member from the first troop. I had no idea she wasn't happy until she went to Staffing and requested an early transfer out. If you aren't happy, I would like to be the first to know," he said.

It was a reasonable request. After all, the chain of command would dictate that he should be the one to go to if there were a problem; still, there was an ambiguous tone to the conversation. I could not quite decide if his request was a warning or an order. He sounded like a good guy, but from that point on I could never be sure. Senior female members were a very tough, proud group. If one had breached military protocol to request an early transfer there must have been a very compelling reason. Still, I preferred denial; if there had been a problem on the section, it didn't mean it was still there or that I couldn't overcome it.

Customs and Excise was the cornerstone on which the Force based all of their federal sections. During the early nineteen hundreds, the Federal Customs Agency, now Canada Customs, was racked with corruption and incompetence charges, prompting the federal government, through an act of Parliament, to expand the mandate of the RCMP to handle criminal offences against the Customs Act. Through the years that followed, the success of the early section had paved the way for the RCMP to expand its powers into other Federal acts, such as Drug Section to enforce the Narcotic Control Act and Commercial Crime to enforce the Income Tax Act and the Securities Act.

The working relationship with Canada Customs was almost non-existent, and Canada Customs controlled the ports, intelligence, and paperwork that imports/exports generated. Over time, due to a combination of lack of interest in the section on the part of the RCMP and a strong desire within Canada Customs to reclaim its responsibilities, my new section had turned into a dumping ground for members. Without Canada Customs co-operation, we were left with enforcing the dregs of the Customs Act. It seemed to me that Staffing had transferred me to the traffic section of plainclothes.

The members on the section didn't seem to mind. There were no midnight or afternoon shifts, no stressful cases, court, heavy workload, or physical demands. Not only was it a much easier job than contract work, it paid better, because of perks like plainclothes allowance, meal claims, and an opportunity for easy overtime on security details. There was also the matter of a company car for the commute to and from work.

Like the rest of Headquarters, the section members were all senior with at least five years' service. Headquarters had more NCOs and commissioned officers per square foot than anyplace else in the division. All the dinosaurs of the Division seemed to be there. Female members were few and far between in these halls.

The Customs and Excise Section's organizational chart, like all "org." charts within the Force, looked like a pyramid. Members were grouped in fours: three constables and one corporal. Each group answered to one of three sergeants, who in turn answered to the staff sergeant in charge of the section. That was the chain of command, the structure of power. Chains of command are very important and very formal in the RCMP.

Again it appeared I had lucked out by being placed in the nicest pod. Corporal Paul, my new partner, was a tired but likable fifteen-year member. He was very knowledgeable on the Customs Act, but more important, he was honest, humble, and kind. The other two constables in my group were pleasant, and the mood on this squad was light and realistic. They didn't delude themselves into thinking the work was challenging or important. Others on the section might have gotten a little arrogant because they were in plainclothes, but not them. The work was easy and there were no shifts. Life was good.

I have often thought how ironic it was that the two questions I did not bother to answer on the final recruit open-book exam were on the Customs Act. Needless to say, this section had an up-to-date Customs Act, and it didn't take me long to appreciate that it was a simple but powerful Act, with a much lower legal threshold for members to meet.

In criminal offences, a peace officer was required to have reasonable and probable grounds to "believe" an offence had been committed; but the Customs Act required the officer to only "suspect" before taking action. The powers granted to the officers under the Act of search and seizure were almost draconian.

Writs of Assistance--blank search warrants--in the possession of some senior members actually ensured we never had to use them. The Force had exercised extreme discretion in their use in the past and by this time had chosen to discontinue their use. Although the members knew that, the offenders did not, and the knowledge that we had them was enough to open any doors. A member who suspected something had been illegally brought into the country could not only seize the item but any transport used in the offence or subsequent transportation of the item as well. From the moment of seizure, the item, and potentially the car, boat, or plane used to transport it, were immediately the property of the government of Canada.

A member's authority didn't stop at seizure. The member had the choice of proceeding criminally or civilly in the matter. Civil was always better, with no *Charter of Rights* to slow it down--a quick report on the matter into Adjudications in Ottawa, and on to the next file. In effect we were the investigator, Crown, and judge. There was an appeal procedure, but our recommendations were almost always backed up.

The fines were substantial. The previous owner had the option of paying the fine, which sometimes came to the purchase value of the item as well as double the duties and taxes; or it would be auctioned off to the public later. The reason the Act was so powerful was because it was a revenue source for the government. You can't mess with taxes in Canada.

The Excise Act, also a revenue Act, offered some variety. The Excise Act dealt with taxes for liquor. I am talking stills. Yes, some people still do that. The government makes a lot of money taxing liquor and it was not about to miss one penny of it. Most of these files involved small, backyard operations. No Al Capones here. Still, there was a rumour of the "Angels" using illegal liquor at one of their Surrey bars. It would be like the Holy Grail of the Excise Act to locate and prosecute that one. An investigation like that would require either a lucky break or an informant.

I was pretty sure not many on this section had actually handled informants. Not that Hell's Angel informants are easy to come by or live long enough to be of much use. But I had to have something to dream about as Cpl. Paul and I went about our routine border runner and personal smuggling cases Customs occasionally tossed us.

I wasn't on the section long before the annual shoot was scheduled, providing what I thought was a good opportunity to place another friendly wager. In keeping with the lower profile I was trying to achieve in this land of dinosaurs, I suggested a team approach to the competition. The highest combined score between our two partner groups would win--Paul's and mine versus the scores of the other two constables, Frick and Frack.

Paul wasn't keen, but Frick and Frack were quick to accept. The weapon of plainclothed peace officers was a snub-nosed .38 Smith and Wesson. The physics are simple: the shorter the nozzle, the less accurate the gun. The course of fire was modified slightly to reflect that. Paul and I were scheduled to shoot the day before Frick and Frack.

I found the shorter course easier and my score reflected that. Paul, on the other hand, barely qualified to carry the weapon. I then understood why he hadn't been keen on the bet. Our combined score wasn't intimidating. We would have to do some serious psychological warfare if we were to unsettle Frick and Frack.

En route back to the office, I convinced Paul to inflate his score. The deception would only last long enough to try and rattle Frick and Frack when they shot the next day, then we could come clean. The first question on their lips when we returned to the office was "what did you shoot?" Paul advised them of our combined, imagined, score but they smelled deception and wanted a breakdown. Paul told them my score and the fictitious number we had decided on for him.

Frick and Frack weren't buying it. I thought they had figured it out until they simultaneously looked across their desks and said accusingly, "That's not your score!"

The funny thing was they were speaking to me, not Paul. Relieved, I assured them it was, but they refused to believe me, inadvertently setting up the perfect sting.

The next day at the range, they checked my score, but not Paul's. The additional pressure of believing they had a very high combined score to beat helped lower their performance. When the dust settled, each of the combined scores were so close I can't even recall which group of partners bought the round of beer in payment of the loss. It didn't take long for the word to get out in the section that I could shoot. Can a gun really be that much of a phallic symbol?

Apparently so for some of the smaller minds who held their morning court in the coffee room of Customs and Excise each morning. It wasn't hard to notice the voices abruptly silence when I entered the coffee room, and the low whispers that commenced once I left. The ringleader at the constable level of the group was a cherub-faced man whose countenance belied his mean spirit. He was the kind of person who can feel superior only if he is tearing down someone else.

Although he didn't seem to want to speak directly to me, he had no problem being vocal around everyone else on the section, including the NCOs. Because no one challenged him or his views, he seemed to gain power by having the implied consent of the higher ranks in the section. He became bolder and bolder, until one day he broke the usual silence that accompanied my trip to get my morning coffee and began paraphrasing the news article he was reading to his audience before he dropped the paper in a feigned "aha" moment and addressed me directly. It wasn't just me he was aiming to insult; he was trying to drag my husband into it.

"It says here that the law governing name changes has changed and husbands can now change their names to the wife's. Does Leonard know this?" he asked with a mock sincerity in his voice. He spoke as though he knew Len, but he didn't even know me, and he was about to prove it. "Len can call himself Leonard *Hall* if he wants." He paused to flash a crocodile smile at the others in the room before he continued.

"Leonard *Hall*; it kind of has a nice ring, don't you think? What do you think Len would think of that?" he laughed, a nasty, hollow, condescending laugh. Small minds often make big assumptions.

"I guess he would think you were some kind of *idiot*. His mother has been calling him that since the day he was born." I took some satisfaction as I left the room hearing some of the others begin laughing at my antagonist. Just because I had chosen a high-profile, nontraditional field to work in didn't mean I was the poster child for many of the feminist emerging ideas of the time like retaining maiden names. The movement was about choice, not *which* choice. I wasn't nearly as adventuresome in my personal life as I was in my professional.

Contrary to the growing recent trend, Len and I had not lived together prior to marriage. One day over coffee with Paul, Frick and Frack, and Nancy Fehr it became obvious even Nancy assumed I was far less traditional than I was.

"I don't understand why you got married. Don't you realize over fifty percent of marriages end in divorce?" she asked.

I couldn't help but smile to myself, thinking how much she sounded like me only five years ago--until she added, "Why not stay common law until the inevitable happens? It's less hassle."

"I don't believe in common law. It's a bad deal for the woman. Len and I thought long and hard before we committed, because we both come from very traditional Catholic backgrounds. I will be married or I will be a widow. There is no other option," I said, hoping this comment would never get back to any of my troop mates whom I had lectured back at Depot on the pitfalls of marriage for women. Nancy was surprised into silence at my statement, but Frick and Frack couldn't resist jumping into the marriage debate.

"You can't say that!" Frick said. "What if Len falls head over heels in love with another woman, next week, next month, or next year?"

"You're not listening. I said I will be married or a widow," I said with a slightly menacing glint in my eye.

"But if he falls for someone else--" Frick continued, not quite grasping the inference in my words until Nancy broke in with a chuckle and a nod of approval, "--then she would be a widow."

Paul laughed and Frick and Frack looked a little shocked as they instinctively crossed their legs.

That night over dinner, I told Len about the encounter, and before I could tell him how it ended with Nancy's comment, he shook his head and said "Yah, you'd be a widow!" Then we laughed and raised our glasses to toast our marriage.

I don't wish to imply that the transition from single to married wasn't an adjustment for both of us. Len and I were used to our space and an apartment just wasn't going to cut it. Lucky for us, the real estate bubble of 1981 had burst, with mortgage interest rates hovering around eighteen percent--close to what the Criminal code of Canada considered "criminal interest rates." It was a buyer's market when we purchased a lovely back-split in the small bedroom community of Langley, a block from both an elementary and a secondary school. A nice place to raise a family. But not right away.

My car pool changed and the commute time increased slightly. The length of the drive was offset by the beautiful scenery and the quality of our home, complete with hot tub and swimming pool. It was rare back then for a wife to earn as much or more than her husband, and it didn't escape the attention of some NCOs that the wages of two constables surpassed their own. Perhaps it was a tinge of envy or simply idle chit-chat that caused one of the three sergeants at C & E to wander over to my desk one morning as my squad planned the day.

"How do you like the long commute in from farm country? I guess you could live without the smell of all the fresh cow droppings first thing in the morning," he said.

"It's not so bad. It kind of reminds me of Headquarters," I said with a very straight face. The sergeant was completely taken by surprise by the casually benign insolence in my tone. As he retreated back to his office, Frick and Frack exploded in laughter, and Paul shook his head in amusement as he repeated: "--reminds me of Headquarters." It seemed that even if I had landed on a poor section, I would be blessed with a good squad, at least in the beginning.

Len also had a change of duties around the time we got married. He had gone to plainclothes in North Vancouver on Fraud section. We were very fortunate to both have day shifts, which allowed us to establish a stable routine as we settled into our new life together. In Langley we expanded our social circle to include our new neighbours and members of community service clubs who knew nothing about our professional lives. Often on initial meetings, they would take one look at Len, his build, his demeanour, and his moustache, and ask, "Are you a Mountie?" They would look so pleased with themselves when he would confirm their suspicions.

"I can always tell a Mountie," they would say in a self-congratulatory manner.

Of course back then it never crossed their minds that I would be one, and I made it a point never to volunteer the information.

I worked eight-hour shifts Monday to Friday, and Len worked ten-hour days from Monday to Thursday. I had time to work out at aerobics and still have supper waiting when Len arrived. We would then retire out to the hot tub in the backyard and spend the next three hours talking about the day and the future. He was handling some interesting files and informants, which meant I could at least enjoy police work vicariously. We would go directly from the tub to bed. Friends accused us of not living there; no one ever answered the phone. We had to install a phone jack in the backyard. Life was good, at least off the job.

But it was amazing how much I slipped into the traditional role of "wife," even though I didn't think of it in those terms. I liked to cook and I was a better cook than Len anyway so I didn't mind; neither did I mind ironing his shirts for work, since I had to iron my own anyway. Until one morning it came to my attention that perhaps I had slipped too far into the traditional female role. I had been on course for two weeks, a course that didn't require ironed clothes, and consequently the iron had remained idle for that time. My course was almost finished when one morning in the usual rush to get ready for work, Len emerged from the closet and said in a tone that seemed more like an accusation than a statement of fact, "I don't have any ironed shirts!"

I hadn't stopped to realize that Len's upbringing, with a stay-at-home mother, had programmed him to expect things of me that I might do as a courtesy, but not as an obligation. It appeared to me Len had made some big assumptions that had led him to think I was somehow responsible for his dilemma. I said, "Oh. I didn't see that in my job description."

I think we both rethought our programming. I made a point doing only my own laundry after that. After about a year, I relaxed somewhat my boycott of the laundry, but I promised myself never to do his ironing again. After all, it wasn't as if he didn't know how; he had ironed the sheets on his bed back at Depot. If I was determined not to become my mother, why would I want to become his?

Six months after arriving at Customs and Excise, there was a shakeup in the office, and I was assigned a new partner, the only other female member, Nancy Fehr. The shakeup also meant I would be reporting to a different sergeant. I had enjoyed the laid-back, pleasant attitude of my old group and my old sergeant, who had shown himself to be an extremely kind, knowledgeable man.

I had observed that the other two sergeants had distinctly different personalities and styles. One was pleasant but forgetful, without a great depth of job knowledge. The other, our new supervisor, Sgt. Manly, was an intensely serious man. He had the ear of the staff sergeant and the allegiance of his men. It seemed the other male members on the section were very much like him, especially the cherub-faced constable.

It seemed surprising to everyone on the section, except for Nancy and me, that we were so dissimilar. It was more than a little ironic to me that while the male members joined out of a sense of conformity, tradition, and order, the women did not accept those values--or we would not be there. In a way, we were almost anarchists threatening the core values and assumptions of the organizational system itself. Females who joined the Force in the '70s were intensely individualistic and independent. All of the nuances of female personality seemed lost on some of the male members of our new section who functioned more comfortably with stereotypes.

My new section reminded me of the first few months in Depot and, being the eternal optimist, I believed we could win them over just as Troop 9 had done. I hadn't yet realized that the attitude change halfway through training was the result of the leadership of the new OIC of Depot. I was still young and arrogant enough to believe individuals had great power and could create their own destiny. I am glad I was so naïve. How else do windmills fall?

Nancy, a member of the second female troop in the Force, was a realist, old beyond her years. She had not been sheltered, as I had, for much of her professional life. She was already on her fourth posting.

Her first posting, Kelowna, was a beautiful city in a picturesque setting. However, being the first female member in town meant she had to live in a goldfish bowl where all her movements were scrutinized, not only by the citizens, who were very kind, but by the members of the Detachment as well. She enjoyed the work, but not the loneliness, prompting her to request and receive a transfer to the Lower Mainland, where she hoped to blend into the crowd.

Her next posting was Mission Detachment, which, although it was technically part of the Lower Mainland, was also a small town with similar restrictions on her private social life.

Eventually, Nancy was posted to a larger centre, first Coquitlam and then Customs and Excise. What a shock it was for her to learn that while she could now have a social life, her work life had become the problem.

Her perception of the atmosphere at Customs and Excise was a bit jaundiced, I thought. She quickly realized we were being assigned only the least promising files, and those assignments reflected the attitude of Sgt. Manly. I truly believed if we proved ourselves then we could win them over. Nancy never bought that for a minute. Time would prove one of us right.

We passed the time getting to know each other as we drove from file to file. The enforcement area we had was huge, spanning from Chilliwack in the East to the Sunshine Coast in the West. Nancy liked to drive, even though she had very little sense of direction. It is strange how some people can be so aware of their immediate surroundings, yet have difficulty figuring out how to get to a destination. Islanders knew that a good sense of direction could mean the difference between life and death. It was common local wisdom that "People with no sense of direction have no business on the water." That didn't mean Islanders never lost their bearings, but it happened infrequently, and when it did, it usually meant something was terribly wrong or distracting them.

It's too bad Nancy and I weren't on a surveillance unit because no one ever suspected two young women in a modest, mid-sized Ford were peace officers. Neither civilians--like the gas attendant who, when we produced our government credit card to pay, thought we had stolen the car--or the Burnaby traffic member who caught me in a radar trap one afternoon. Although we were quick to "tin" (flash our badges) the gas jockey, Nancy and I were divided on what to do in the radar trap.

Boundary Road Hill just off of Marine Drive had a zero tolerance for speeding because of a high accident rate on that stretch. It was one of those rare occasions when I was driving. We were the last in a string of three vehicles that were pulled over as a group when we topped the hill. We watched and debated as the traffic member "hung some paper" on the first and second driver.

"Just tin him," Nancy said. "You were barely speeding, and this is a hill, for God's sake."

"I was doing the same speed as the other two drivers. I have no operational excuse. If they deserve a ticket, so do I," I said, standing on principle; but secretly hoping the member would catch on as to who I was when I handed him my government registration with my driver's licence.

I watched in the side mirror as the member took no notice of my paperwork as he walked to the rear of the car, where he proceeded to write the ticket. It didn't take long for the experienced traffic member to bang off the ticket. The member walked back to my driver's window; but just before he arrived, he stopped in mid-stride and looked again at the registration, which read "Government of Canada." Then he checked the model of the Ford at the rear of the car before approaching my window. This time he crouched down as he returned my licence and registration and peered at the police radio mounted on the hump between the two front seats.

"Is this a police car?" he asked.

"Yes," I replied sheepishly.

"Are you both members?" he asked with a touch of irritation in his voice.

"Yes," I said with embarrassment in mine.

"Why didn't you tell me before I wrote the ticket?" he asked, now sounding a bit frustrated.

"Because I really have no more excuse than the other two cars you just wrote up," I said, trying to explain my moral dilemma.

"Do you want this ticket?" he asked.

"Not really, but I didn't want to place you in an awkward spot."

"Do you want this ticket?" he asked again.

"Sure, give me the ticket," I said, taking the moral high ground.

"Okay, here's the ticket," he said, ripping it out of his pad and handing it to me.

That was when I noticed he had given me not just the offender's copy but all the copies, even the one that needed to be mailed to Motor Vehicles Branch. "I leave it to your discretion as to how strongly you feel you deserve the ticket." He said with a smile, one I was quick to return.

Nancy and I were the real-life version of a popular 1980s TV show called *Cagny and Lacy.* The public was becoming aware there were female peace officers, and TV decided to cash in on the curiosity. Like Cagny, I was one of the first who believed I could have it all, career and family. I would go home to Len, and Nancy--like Lacy--would go home alone, to a hot bubble bath.

Our work was nothing as interesting or as serious as on the TV show--just border runners and routine follow-ups Canada Customs thought too small to bother with. Sometimes the follow-ups were to lend assistance to U.S. Customs or Border Patrol. It was interesting to see how the various federal departments in the States functioned.

U.S. Customs was nothing like our Canada Customs. These were rough and tough, armed, police officers. Drug enforcement and organized crime were their targets. If they wanted to make a ton of money in overtime and relocation pay, they would take a tour (tour as in military, not vacation) in Miami. *Miami Vice* was a very popular show at the time depicting open warfare with drug dealers and organized crime. I was shocked to hear it was not that great an exaggeration.

A couple of agents told me of their experience when their unmarked police car had a flat tire in a rough area of Miami. The agents quickly jacked up the rear of their car, only to realize that the front was also being jacked up. Guns in one hand, badges in the other they confronted the three men about to strip their car.

"Sorry, man, we jest thought you was doing the back," the thieves apologized as they backed away, hands raised.

"How could things have become so Third World in the U.S.?" I asked.

"You-all ever heard of the Miranda warning?" was the reply. "Man, you cops in Canada have it made. You just have to prove the guy did it. We have to prove we didn't."

That may have been the short answer, but there was more than the criminal rights issues making the job of U.S. law enforcement inefficient. The U.S. had too many competing agencies with overlapping enforcement responsibilities between local, state, and federal agencies. The resulting turf wars between departments created the fog of war that supported organized and unorganized crime. The RCMP did have it much easier in Canada, with only one outside competing agency, CSIS, to contend with.

The U.S. Customs agents were very nice to Nancy and me. Although they didn't have any female agents working with them, I don't think they would have had any issues there.

"Watch your backs" was a parting piece of brotherly advice we were given by a senior U.S. agent.

It was a bit embarrassing to think that the petty politics of some of our new section members at Customs and Excise had been noticed outside of the Force, smearing the Force as a whole with a reputation for intolerance it did not deserve. It's always unfair when a bad apple or two makes the barrel look bad.

The warning lent support for Nancy's gloomy assessment of our working environment--the one I wasn't ready to accept. One of my core beliefs was, *for every problem there is a solution*. The solution in this situation might be that we could wear them down with competence and good nature. If they knew us a little better, they might accept us. If we could change the cherub-faced member's mind, we could turn things around.

Within a week I had a chance to put my theory to the test. HQ's Serious Crime section needed assistance on a wiretap. I knew the main investigator from my North Vancouver GIS work, Fred Maile. He was one of the best and most determined "detectives" (the RCMP does not use that term, but the public understands it), and had been the lead investigator in almost every difficult murder case in the province for years. His most recent case was the Clifford Olsen serial murders. The investigator needed Customs and Excise assistance on a target, because in this case the only grounds for the wiretap were based on the Customs Act. It was the kind of "back-dooring" that the Americans used on Al Capone in the tax evasion charge. Serious Crime's sights were set much higher than a revenue offence, but for the time being, they needed the grounds for the tap.

The members of Customs and Excise were just window dressing, tasked with monitoring the taps--little more than exhibit custodians in the bigger scheme of the investigation. My partner in the task was the Cherub, providing me with an opportunity to influence his perception of female members. After all, we were going to be stuck together in a small room for entire boring shifts at a time.

The wire room seemed as frosty as the silent coffee room of Customs and Excise, as The Cherub buried his head in a newspaper for hours at a time. If I hadn't spoken, he would have sat there for eight hours in silence.

I found he was more than willing to talk about himself. Apart from an isolated posting, his experience was limited to highway patrol. In terms of policing skills, he was a big bluff--just a traffic cop in a suit. No wonder he was so happy being on Customs and Excise. During all our conversations, he never once asked about me. I could never decide if it was due to a complete lack of interest, or intentional rudeness. Mercifully, our time in the room was cut short.

The "Lunatics" serial rape case had finally made it to the B.C. Superior Court. I thought The Cherub would be happier with my male replacement, but he was confused as to why a court case would cause a reassignment.

"When I was transferred to Customs and Excise" he said, "I pulled all my tickets to eliminate my court." It must be true that some people judge others by their own standards. His standards were much too low. I decided to tell him so; time for a little of his own medicine.

"You can't pull a case at the Supreme Court level," I advised with a touch of his own condescension. "I have never been to traffic court. 'Better to have a sister in the whorehouse than a brother on traffic.'"

This was the first time I had ever intentionally meant to hurt someone's feelings. I had been raised to turn the other cheek. But I was tired of getting slapped. The only way to deal with someone like that, if the system won't, is to hit back.

It was a relief to give myself the licence to admit to the feelings of hurt and anger that had grown in this deteriorating environment. The charade was coming to an end. Time to take my hat off again.

When I returned to my normal C & E duties after the Lunatic's guilty plea, pornographic calendars started to appear, almost overnight, in the office. The snickers were like white noise to me as I ripped them down and tossed them in the garbage can each morning. A few days later, the situation would repeat itself so I began chucking the ashtrays off the closest desks, along with the calendars, into the trash as well.

The only supervisor intervention into the unofficial war that had erupted in the C & E office came from Sgt. Manly when he verbally reprimanded me for throwing out government equipment--the ashtrays. The game was afoot.

Ashtrays began disappearing as mysteriously as the calendars appeared. If the sergeant wanted to make an issue of one, the other would have to be brought into the discussion as well. Nancy and I were aware that not everyone in the section supported the offensive actions of a few, but no one rose to our defence. Nancy and I were on our own.

She had been right and I had been wrong. We were in survival mode, backs to the wall or to each other. I hadn't been there before, but she had. I was beginning to understand Nancy a lot better.

Customs and Excise was a small, unhappy section at Headquarters. Social change takes more time for some than for others. The most senior female members still had less than eight years' service. We were still an experiment without a proven conclusion.

The rest of HQ seemed to be at least trying to adjust its self-image to include females. One unfortunate incident in the Fraser Valley at that time demonstrated to me that Headquarters, as a whole, was capable of being unbiased.

A member had been forced to shoot and kill an extremely violent wanted man. The member had acted cautiously and prudently, but sometimes even the best actions lead to the worst results. Police shootings, particularly fatal ones, were rare events. A member has only seconds to act, followed by years of second-guessing by armchair police, the public, and themselves. This time it was the press that rushed to judgment.

Something like, "Female Peace Officer Shoots Unarmed Man," screamed the headlines.

The phrasing of the headline seemed to be part of an increasingly anti-police media voice--a voice I felt was now *implying* that female peace officers were more likely to shoot men, a chauvinist's worst nightmare; a voice with the potential to tarnish all female members in the public's and the policing community's eyes.

The sex of the peace officer had nothing to do with the action; yet it was very encouraging for female members to see male members of E Division form ranks around the female officer.

I can only imagine the pressure the female member was under as the story continued to dominate the headlines. Within the Division her reputation was untarnished. I am sure it sold a lot of papers and made the company a lot of money. In the end, she was legally exonerated. The growing adversarial attitude in the media toward the police was not just a local secret.

One day I was tasked with escorting an inspector on sabbatical from the Swiss police who was touring Canada while working on a Master's degree. In his thesis he wanted to examine the differences between the Canadian and Swiss legal system. He had already been at RCMP Headquarters in Ottawa, but that didn't really teach him much about day-to-day police work.

What he really wanted to see most was a court case. Court in his country sounded quite administrative by nature. The police prosecutor's sheets were read in as a matter of fact. Police officers were not required to testify. He needed to understand why police officers in North America not only had to testify at trial but were treated as *suspects* by the defence lawyers. There was no logic in undermining the legal guardians of society to his mind. What kind of a society doesn't trust its police--and why?

I defended Canadian common law, which had evolved to be much more co-operative and supportive historically than the U.S. style, but I did have to concede that the newly enacted *Charter of Rights* was creating a metamorphosis, altering the very nature of the administration of justice in Canada to resemble more closely the American system.

He was a very smart fellow and wanted to understand if this metamorphosis was a worldwide evolution of law, or a distinctly North American trend. Through our discussions, we suspected one of the root causes of the shift in justice delivery was probably the Americanization of North American TV and movies.

In Europe, television remained primarily an educational tool, while in North America it had been subverted into a marketing and entertainment medium. The '50s *Dragnet* had been replaced by *Perry Mason*. Police were quite often portrayed as incompetent or corrupt in shows like *The Dukes of Hazzard*.

It wasn't just TV that was creating and reinforcing the perception that the police and the justice system were off the rails. Blockbusters like *Serpico* and *Colours* added to the public's growing paranoia. This perception was distinctly American. All the stories, true or not, were about Americans and their system of justice, creating and inflaming irrational fears in the public, confusing fantasy with reality, where U.S. problems were accepted as Canadian as well.

The irony was, this perception accelerated the Americanization of our legal system, away from its English Common Law roots. The balance of power was tipping in favour of the accused and away from society. Fantasy was becoming reality. Policing powers were being limited to protecting citizens--not from criminals but from police, creating a dysfunctional cycle in which the more unsafe the public felt, the tighter the control of police, and then the less safe the public was. By trying to protect ourselves from the problems in the American system of justice, we were becoming them. This was a paradigm shift for Canada. One of the few positives of my posting to C & E was that we dealt with most offences administratively rather than through court. I was in a legal time warp, temporarily insulated from the *Charter of Rights*.

In addition to the Customs and Excise Act, the section was responsible for investigating a number of obscure federal acts such as the Cultural Properties Act, the Endangered Species Act, etc. While the other members on the section seemed to avoid these types of files, Nancy and I enjoyed the variety and learning entailed.

The Aeronautics Act and Air Carrier Regulations were two of the more complicated and interesting acts we began investigating in 1985. Infractions of these acts could result in airline disasters similar to some of the problems beginning to appear in the States. Nobody in the office seemed to take much notice of our investigations until we started filling in prosecutors' sheets and someone wondered out loud if the Aeronautics Act could form the basis for a repeat of the success our next-door neighbour at headquarters, Commercial Crime, had experienced.

Ten years earlier, Commercial Crime had expanded rapidly under the stewardship of Henry (Hank) Jensen, allowing members to develop expertise in complicated organized crime, drug trafficking, and high-level fraud. It was an aggressive, elite section that set its sights high on white-collar criminals in corporate and public positions. The resulting expansion rocketed members on the growing section through the rank structure. If this new section was a ticket to a promotion, everyone wanted in, especially because promotions were becoming far less frequent, and time in the rank was increasing as the demographics of the Force caught up with it. Customs & Excise quickly formed a new section to handle aircraft-related investigations, and neither Nancy nor I was on it.

The formation of the new section wasn't the only shakeup at that time. Belt tightening caused by the 1980s recession had resulted in a decreased overtime budget. An afternoon shift of one or two members was about to be introduced to address that.

The section had already lost the use of police cars for car pools to and from work. My new partner and I decided to be proactive in lessening the impact of the proposed rotational shift by devising a schedule that paired members on afternoon shifts to allow for car pooling.

We pitched it to the staff sergeant, who didn't see any problem with the proposal as long as we followed the chain of command by getting all three sergeants under him to agree. The first two sergeants were an easy sell, because the proposal impacted positively on the morale of the members without compromising the work. Since there was no love lost between Sgt. Manly and me, I asked my male partner to do the talking. He had just outlined the reasoning behind our schedule when Sgt. Manly interrupted.

"All right, I will look at it, but I tell you up front, I will not approve it if a junior member on the section, or a female member, will end up working by themselves."

This wasn't just a slap in the face for female members, it was the last straw; you know, the one that "broke the camel's back." I was enraged and, for the first time in my life, I was able to turn that rage outward without any tears. I rose to my feet and began to shout at Sgt. Manly, punctuating my sentences with a well-aimed finger pointed directly at his nose.

"How dare you make so blatant and biased a statement! After all, in six months the new member wouldn't be junior anymore; but Nancy and I would always be female."

He raged back his "justification." "I know all about female members. I had one working for me in my old detachment--"

My turn to cut him off. I wasn't prepared to listen to his excuse based on some nameless female member he had encountered years before. There we both stood, shouting at each other over his desk, while my poor partner cowered in his chair, wishing very much not to be there and hoping not to become a witness at some later service court offence.

If I had been a man, he would have hit me--and if I had been a man, I would have hit him back. Neither of us was backing down now. Finally I finished and out I stormed, knowing that I had committed a huge act of insubordination in a fight I was unlikely to win. Rank supports rank in a military organization because it has to, to maintain order. I understood this and I didn't care anymore. There was no doubt in my mind that everyone in the outer office of C & E and probably most of the people in the hall and neighbouring sections had heard our screaming match, but no one said a word to me about it.

That night at supper I told Len about the fight. We both knew I would have to do something drastic. Too many lines had been crossed.

"Are you going to quit?" he asked.

This was the first time I knew he had seen through my facade of "I can handle this" to how deeply wounded my inner self had been. On the street, where I knew who the bad guys were, I had no problem with stress; it was the internal stress that had made me snap. Office stress wasn't just one thing; it was the layered nature of the situation that gradually became unbearable. It was like being slowly buried alive by sandpaper. Minor irritation built on minor irritation until the combined weight was overwhelming. Harassment is an insidious trap. Individual offences taken in isolation seemed almost trivial, which was why I thought I would ignore or handle them myself. I didn't understand that the combined total would be much more than the sum of the individual offences. By the time I did understand, it was difficult to find the courage to act. It seemed as though any move would most certainly open even more wounds.

It's hard to fight back when your self-esteem has been eroded and your inner self has been worn down. I finally understood how some female members felt who had landed in similar and sometimes more difficult situations than I. It was humbling to now realize that as tough as I thought I was in North Vancouver, I owed my success there as much or more to the silent male guardians in the shadows backing me up. I was going to have to understand the workings of this organizational system much better if I were to recover. In a way, Sgt. Manly did me a favour by being so outrageously outspoken to my face. It gave me something solid to challenge. His tactical mistake became the catalyst for my maturing from a narcissistic adolescent into a survivor.

Office stress had made me snap, but it didn't make me cry. My feelings about the confrontation were actually ambivalent because even though it was likely I would pay a heavy price for taking on rank, I was pleased that I had finally mastered the "male" ability to turn anger outward into a weapon. I was pleasantly surprised to find that I felt good and powerful. I didn't care what professional price I would have to pay. Under similar circumstances I would gladly do it again.

"I'm not quitting. I am going to take Nancy to coffee and tell her I am going to Staffing to request an immediate transfer and encourage her to do the same."

It was a risky plan because Customs and Excise was a five-year posting. My staff sergeant could block the transfer if he wanted. When I walked into the office the next morning, the room quickly became even more silent than normal. There are no secrets among members--especially juicy ones like shouting matches between sergeants and female constables. Nancy and I were just picking up the car keys from the board to leave for coffee when Sgt. Manly emerged from the staff sergeant's office. There was little doubt in anyone's mind what the topic of conversation had been.

"Oh, heading for coffee?" the staff sergeant asked casually, noticing the keys and our jackets. "Can I see you when you get back?"

He disappeared into his office, closing the door behind him. It was time to face the music.

"Coffee can wait. Let's do it now," I said as I returned the keys to the board and went into his office. I braced myself in the chair opposite the staff sergeant for the consequences of the previous day's blow-up, but to my astonishment the topic never came up.

"Would you like a transfer to the Customs and Excise sub-office in Surrey?"

he asked in his usual deep, controlled voice.

It was as if the fight had never happened. I was taken completely by surprise by his offer. The sub-office, in Surrey detachment, was a plum location any member on the section would have taken. Clearly it was an attempt to make the incident go away. A bribe? No doubt about it.

"How soon can I go?" I asked cautiously.

"As soon as you would like," was the unexpectedly accommodating reply.

I packed my desk and was in Surrey that afternoon. I felt guilty abandoning Nancy to the Vancouver office, but clearly I was not as tough as she. I will never know if the staff sergeant had been indifferent or unaware of the harassment within his section. Recalling one of our initial conversations, he had volunteered the information about the first female member's leaving from Customs and Excise, and I had not done what he requested at the time--I had not asked him for help before deciding to take the "problem" outside the office. I am not saying I was wrong for not trusting him, only that I will never be certain I was right; but I had to follow my instincts.

The only thing I was certain of was, the last thing the staff sergeant wanted was a second female member--and possibly a third--banging on Staffing's door for a transfer. His leadership would be tarnished. For the second time in my career, I had accidentally placed an NCO in a professional choke hold, not unlike the one Cpl. Highbrowns had faced. The NCO had more to risk than me--not a promotion this time, but a professional blemish as a supervisor. By virtue of his rank, the staff/sergeant bore the responsibility for his subordinate's actions. Once again, the threat going on the record with the truth had protected me. Now that I had mastered my tears, my next task would be to learn how to use the truth as a strategy to resolve future conflicts before they became so overwhelming.

Compared to HQ, the C & E satellite section at Surrey Detachment was a cakewalk--ten minutes from home in a working detachment with real crime going on. A refreshing dose of reality after the politics of Headquarters. My old co-workers from the original Customs and Excise team, Frick and Frack, had been transferred as well to the sub-office. The old team was almost complete except for Paul, who had quit the Force and moved back to Saskatchewan to drive a bus.

The Surrey corporal, Cpl. Nervous, was a bit oversensitive to the stress of police work, but on C & E, where so little of it really went on, he was fine. It felt like a weight had physically been lifted off my shoulders. It was wonderful to work on a team again. Len, tired of the commute, had been transferred to Surrey

General Duty as well. Since I was in a sub-office reporting to Headquarters--not the Surrey OIC as organization charts go--Len and I weren't in the same office technically. Even so, on one file we did overlap.

Len was working the graveyard shift in Newton when he noticed some suspicious activity at an acreage in Surrey by the King George. The detachment sub-office overlooked a rundown house with a large outbuilding in the backyard, and Len had noticed the resident making several trips to the shed throughout the night, apparently to stoke the fire in the shed.

Could this be the still that was rumoured to be in the Newton area? It sure looked like it. Len called me at about two a.m., and I called the rest of the team to set up surveillance. Finally an interesting file again of which I was in charge! The rest of my team was equally excited. Our four-person section was already responsible for more customs seizures than the rest of our headquarters' section combined. If we managed to bust the Angels' still as well, it would be hard to wipe the smile off our faces when we dropped our paperwork off the next week.

It was all looking good for the next twenty-four hours as the fire was kept burning, but then the fire went out for several hours, after which it was relit. This didn't make any sense as a still, but it would make sense if it was a "grow operation." We were all disappointed. After thirty hours of work, we obtained search warrants under the Narcotic Control Act, then contacted Surrey Drug Section to hand over a neatly packaged bust. What a gift for the day shift Drug Section corporal to have waiting for him! Cultivation of marijuana was a major offence back then--an uncommon offence that was dealt with harshly by the courts.

Our Customs group maintained the surveillance until the Drug Section arrived to take over and do the kick-in. The Surrey corporal called for a meet on the road to be briefed and receive the file and warrants. If I hadn't been so tired, I probably would have taken offence when the first words out of his mouth after I pulled up were: "Where is your corporal?"

"Back at the OP [surveillance terminology for "observation post"], where he likes it," I said honestly.

"Why did he send you?" he continued, rudely.

Oh, so now I was getting it. Why should I have been surprised? After all, he was Drug Section; but I was too tired and too uninterested in doing verbal battle with a jerk who had the nerve to look a gift horse in the mouth.

"He sent me because it's my file, not his," I continued in a polite and professional tone as I handed him the paperwork he would need. "Here is the report, the warrant, and information to obtain the warrant." Then I paused as

I adopted just the slightest hint of the condescension that had riddled his terse conversation with me.

"I trust you are capable of handling it from here. Our section is going home to bed, but if you run into trouble, feel free to call me." And with that I handed him the file and drove off. I had developed a thick enough skin to brush off irrelevant NCOs at this point, but he still managed to irritate me one more time.

I would have remained unaware the corporal had taken the time and effort to write 1004s (performance reports) for Frick and Frack praising their involvement in the drug bust if they had not told me. My partners had even tried to defend my professional interests by asking for one for me. Their paraphrased response to their request shocked even them.

"I don't give female members good 1004s."

Technically, the slight wasn't really a big deal. He wasn't my boss. As a matter of fact, the old staff sergeant had just retired, and Customs and Excise had just gotten a new boss--a happy, positive man, one who I was sure was in love with his wife. What a change. It was actually pleasant to go to Headquarters once a week to drop off the paperwork. When my next A26 (annual performance document) came up, I gave him a copy to read of the file on the still that had turned into a cultivation file. I then told him what the Drug Section corporal had said.

"I can fix that. I'll write you a 1004 on it, or if you like you can write it and I'll sign it," he offered. I accepted. After all, a staff sergeant beats a corporal any day, in the game of the Force.

Just when things were looking up and comfortably predictable at Headquarters, all hell broke loose.

"All E Division vehicles please clear your location. Proceed to West Vancouver. Switch to tack one (a police radio channel used for specialized operations). VIP section will provide further details."

Frack and I were one of the first to switch, even though we felt our assistance would be declined because were a one-hour drive away. We were wrong.

"All E Division units attend to the rear of the Consul General of India residence immediately and assist the uniformed personnel with riot control."

That was my first and only riot, I am happy to say. Actually, it was mostly over by the time we arrived. Riots are a very uncommon occurrence in Canada, and should never occur by surprise as this one had. Fortunately, the majority of the rioters seemed as unprepared for the event as the RCMP.

Still, I am sure the government of India must have wondered why their representatives and families in Canada were assigned such a low VIP security rating, considering the conflict between the Sikh extremists in India. Clearly the Khalistan independence movement of the Sikhs half a world away was going to be a security problem in Canada. It was the first--but unfortunately not the last--time conflict in India would endanger civilian lives.

It was easy enough for members of the Force to realize how the breakdown in communication had happened now that CSIS had taken over security.

The Sikhs had arrived by busload to demonstrate against the Indian government's representative. They were surprised to find so little security. Instead of a wall, there was only a hedge around a very plain middle-class home. Only a couple of RCMP VIP escorts stood between the consul general and a large, angry mob.

A handful of VIP members and a handful of West Vancouver police, faced with overwhelming odds, fought and held the scene until North Vancouver RCMP, followed by every available Mountie in LMD, arrived as backup. As the numbers of police grew, a riot line was formed and the crowd was pushed out to the street.

By then the camera crews were also in place. One of the more memorable shots was taken directly behind a member as he reached through the hedge and punched a Sikh several times, knocking the turban from his head. In the end the crowd retreated, but the RCMP was left with a new security problem.

Vancouver's VIP section was fairly small. They coordinated security for visiting politicians both domestically and internationally while they were in Vancouver. They did not have the manpower to provide the increased level of security that was clearly necessary for the diplomats from India.

A new section composed of seconded members from federal sections had to be temporarily formed until special constables, similar to the ones on Parliament Hill, could be trained to take over the duties. Even Customs and Excise was exciting compared to this detail. The specials couldn't get trained fast enough. No regular member would be content for long being a night watchman. As much as I hated sitting in an unmarked police car watching a residence for twelve hours at a time for the next few months, it did provide an unexpected opportunity to improve the working conditions of female members.

Any distraction from the boredom of the duty was welcome even if it was a corporal running for Division representative doing some politicking. We listened politely to Cpl. Thurston as he told us why he thought he would make a good representative for the NCO ranks. He had obtained a law degree through Force sponsorship, which at least indicated he was smart and worked hard. At the end of the pitch he asked, "What are female members interested in seeing improved?"

I was surprised at his query and a little cynical. Surely he could do the math and realize that female members made up an extremely low percentage of the Force. No point in courting female support; as a matter of fact, it could backfire with some of the male members if he was too sympathetic.

"The same as the male members," I said; "better pay, better pensions, better compensation for overtime--the usual."

He seemed to understand my reluctance to ask for anything special, because, as usual, I was the only female in a sea of male faces; but before he left, he asked me the question again, this time in private. So I opened up.

"It vexes me to know there is no paid maternity leave for members. The secretary typing my reports has compensation but members do not."

He seemed pleased that I had surprised him with a very reasonable and achievable goal. Like the RCMP, he had never stopped to consider that now that Mounties could become pregnant, our pay and medical benefits should reflect that change.

Then he did the unexpected. He took the time to explain to me the organizational workings of not only the RCMP system but that of the Treasury Board as well in relation to member benefits. The Force would never set a precedent with a new benefit for the RCMP unless it had already allowed the benefit for the other federal employees. Then he made me an offer I could not refuse.

If I would do the legwork and find out what maternity benefits other federal employees were getting, he would support it at the next pay and benefit meeting. Then he said something that demonstrated he was someone worth voting for. He told me to submit my information package to whoever was elected if he was defeated. He was elected, and several months later I submitted my proposal.

Doing the research and drafting the proposal had helped fill the boring hours in West Vancouver so well that I decided to draft another proposal. This one was for a job share or sabbatical leave for members who required the leave for family or education purposes.

Maternity leave was rubber-stamped by the Treasury Board at the next pay raise. It was a non-issue with them. Truth was they probably forgot there were females in the Force. The job share/sabbatical was referred for further study.

The special constables finally started arriving to replace the regular members. Most of them were quite content with their new position, but two of the younger ones were overly optimistic that this was the first step to becoming a regular member.

Although promotions to regular from special constable status did occur, they were unusual. I discussed the possibility with one of the Staffing members also stuck on the detail. The Force's stand was clear in recruiting specials. They often did not meet the standards of the Force for regular functions, but they could be trained for limited functions such as Airport Security, site security for VIPs, or the Surveillance Unit Special "O."

I felt sorry for the two younger members who believed they could slip into the regular members easily, but it wasn't my problem. With the specials in place on embassy duty, I returned to Surrey Customs and Excise.

Apart from the still/cultivation file, the only other duty Len and I shared while we were both at Surrey Detachment was a regimental dinner. Len's watch was tasked with organizing the event. Regimental balls are grand, formal dinner parties with gowns, dress uniforms, and spouses. Regimental dinners on the other hand are just for members, peace officers, and the military.

For over one hundred years, regimental dinners, steeped in tradition, had been all-male affairs, some of which resulted in liquor-induced career suicide. I decided to attend to ensure Len kept his feet on the ground and his career intact. He really didn't need my help, but I felt better going, and I may have been just a touch curious about the pomp and chest-beating that was almost a legend in the Force.

Dinners were rich in traditions, from the toast to the queen given by the junior member, a female this time, to the rule that no one can leave the table until the ranking officer signalled the end of the ceremony after the meal by lighting up a cigar. Things can get very uncomfortable, especially for males, when one goes so long without a washroom break. If the guest speaker was merciful, he would be brief.

The speaker at this dinner, an ex-member, had a reputation for having a good sense of humour when he was sober and for being a big redneck if he had gotten a little too far into the bottle. I sat with a handful of junior female members. Several WWII veterans were at the table parallel to us. It wasn't hard to tell the speaker had overindulged.

The male members winced as he ranted on about the good old days before the females and French changed the Force. The best thing about him was he was so over the top, like Archie Bunker, that everyone distanced themselves from him. He compounded his alienation from the audience as he went on and on way too long.

I noticed a number of very uncomfortable members planning their route to be first in line at the washrooms when it was finally over. These members almost gasped when the CO diplomatically thanked the speaker, then asked the junior female member if she had a rebuttal. Her succinct response justified my faith in the ability of the new group of female members to hold their own. She stood up and said: "We don't care what people like you think." Then as she raised her glass in a toast she finished, "To hell with you."

The female members, retired military, and male members of like mind rose to join her.

She was a bigger hit than the speaker, not just because of how well she handled the comeback but because she had been mercifully brief. Now that the cigars could be lit, everyone was finally free to rush for the bathrooms.

There was no real rush for the female one because there were only four of us. We casually sauntered past the long line for the men's, smiling back at envious eyes. I was the last to arrive in the large room with lots of stalls and surprised to find the other female members whispering in hushed tones, planning an ambush--one involving a bucket of ice, as I recall.

They quickly briefed me, because as senior member I was automatically in charge of the project. They had arrived to find one of the stalls already occupied by someone wearing male congress boots and banana pants--things not included in female dress order. Their reckless mischievousness reminded me of myself, not so long ago; but the responsibility of my senior service made it necessary for me to exercise leadership with my superior experience to protect junior members from rushing into a good-natured, but poorly thought out, course of action.

"Whoever this is, he is either reckless or fearless. Either characteristic would make him a dangerous opponent." I paused to give emphasis to a little piece of wisdom I had picked up over my years of service, "You should never start an unnecessary battle with an unknown adversary; you may need them as a friend in the future."

I don't know if I was mellowing or getting wiser, but my decision, which took a little of the fun and excitement out of their mood, proved to be the right one.

"Thanks, ladies. I hoped you wouldn't mind," the commanding officer of E Division said as he washed his hands. It was that kind of out-of-the-box thinking and risk-taking that had helped him rise to the rank of deputy commissioner. He had always been a strong ally for female members.

On my next visit to Headquarters, I decided to thank another strategically placed ally. I dropped into the Division representatives' office to congratulate and thank Cpl. Thurston and acknowledge the heat he had taken over the maternity package. A widespread rumour erroneously blamed the maternity benefit for a half-percent lower annual raise that year. There were only about 550 female members coast to coast by the mid-1980s, most of whom were unmarried, which could hardly have any effect on a wage settlement for over sixteen thousand members. True or not, the backlash seemed to have had no impact on Cpl. Thurston--he liked championing minority rights.

It wasn't long before he asked me for help. He needed female input into some proposed policy changes within the RCMP. There weren't many female members at Headquarters then, but I asked Nancy and Adrienne, who had made it to Commercial Crime about six months before my posting, to listen to Cpl. Thurston. He told us over coffee about how a parliamentary subcommittee was looking into the possibility of implementing a particular proposal within the Force.

The Force had already changed its hiring practices in an open attempt to inflate the numbers within the Force of the two groups. The change that had tilted the scale in favour of females and French had already created a bone of contention within the rank and file of the Force over the recently implemented preferred hiring categories. If Ottawa adopted a policy that accelerated those groups through the rank structure, it could open a wound within the Force that might never heal for the minority groups. The proposal, which seemed wrong on so many levels, also failed to take into account the ever-increasing service levels needed to compete for fewer and fewer promotions and the stress lack of advancement was having on the senior constable rank.

The reluctance of members to retire into a recession caused the average service for promotion to increase, delaying promotions by years. In a Force full of very competitive members who never entertained the possibility they might retire a constable, the atmosphere surrounding promotions had soured.

In the past, a promotion was a cause of celebration for everyone. Huge promotion parties were almost mandatory. Everyone was happy for the host of the party because they trusted that one day in the not too distant future it would be their turn, their party. That trust was eroding quickly within the rank and file.

Any attempt to distort the promotion cycle would undo all of the goodwill females had worked so hard to achieve. Even more than that, it would devalue and disenfranchise all female members. There was no evidence to suggest that the rank structure the Force was using was biased against females, since none of us as yet had sufficient service to compete.

The Ottawa politicians were again out of touch, with the wrong answers to the wrong problems. Recruitment standards were there for a reason, and all members took great pride in meeting them. Lowering the standard might have the initial effect of inflating minority numbers, but the attrition rate would surely increase as well, as less-suited members quit. The female attrition rate was already quite high. Ottawa would have been wise to develop an understanding and strategies on how to retain its members--not simply to hire more.

Even if that course of action were a viable solution, the increased competition for the limited number of spots in the English male category meant that successful applicants in that group would be the cream of the crop, better suited and better educated, creating a performance imbalance for the minority groups, which was actually the reverse of the current trend.

"No matter what a male member says against this proposal it will sound bad. They might listen to female voices." Cpl. Thurston was making the request because he knew senior female members were no different than their male peers of the time, in that we valued our social responsibility greater than our individual career ambitions. But there was a problem with his request. Female members had no unified voice. Our opinions and experiences within the Force were as unique as we were.

Adrienne wisely decided to not commit to paper. Well, as they say, "Fools rush in . . ." and Nancy and I did just that. Nancy wrote a very poignant and personal account of what it was like to be a female member. She wrote of the loneliness, the social isolation, and the sometimes deliberate indifference and mean-spirited behaviour she had endured throughout her service. It was a remarkably brave anecdotal account of how cruel the Force could be.

I wrote an analytical, deliberately diplomatic report highlighting the attrition rate and the lack of understanding for it. The OIC of E Division, Deputy Commissioner Venner, even footnoted my report prior to submission, writing that it was a fair and balanced account; but he requested that the information on the attrition rate, which I had researched, be removed from the final draft. It wasn't an oversight by Cpl. Thurston that the two reports were sent off, uncensored, to that black hole in Ottawa. There they were filed away like a time bomb.

One positive result did occur a few months later that year. Deputy Commissioner Venner penned a memo to the officer in Charge of Admin and Personnel for E Division raising his concerns that the Force needed to do more to support female members.

"I think we should do something constructive, helpful, and forward-thinking . . ."[20] His request was the catalyst for the largest and most comprehensive survey of attitudes of female members and towards female members held by their peers and supervisors.

Nothing seemed to change for a while. The "preferred categories" for hiring remained biased in favour of French and female. The next generation was now

[20] T.S. Venner, D/CMMR, Commanding Officer E Div., "Female Members--'E' Division," memorandum to the E Div. Admin. and Personnel Officer, Nov. 12, 1984.

joining the Force, a generation far less tolerant of rules and discipline, one quick to use the *Charter* and the media to combat the Force.

The *Charter* had empowered individuals with tools to challenge the rules of government. Some of these challenges were helpful in rethinking some antiquated concepts. Whether the *Charter* was good or bad is still open to much debate from many different social political camps. What isn't open for debate is that it was profoundly changing the balance of Canadian society from the rights of society as a whole in favour of individual rights.

The pendulum of social change was swinging again. The rights of the individual were becoming more important than those of society, and the Force was scrambling to adjust. Practices such as the fat boy club, which had motivated members to stay in shape, and previously unchallenged entrance requirements, such as height and age, had to be abandoned.

Since the old size restrictions had been thrown out, an entrance physical had to be adopted to ensure that new members were physically capable of doing the job. For a short time, the Force flirted with the idea of an annual physical, similar to our annual shooting re-qualification, but first the fitness level of the Force had to be assessed for a determination of a valid fitness requirement for the job.

A random sampling of a small percentage of male members and nearly 100 percent of all female members coast to coast was selected for a pretest that I hoped could work in my favour.

For two years I had dealt with the stress of C&E through an intensive aerobics routine five times a week. The examiner seemed very impressed when at the end of the physical he advised me, "You're in the top two percent within the Force in terms of personal fitness."

"That's great. I wonder what I would have scored if I hadn't been pregnant."

No one but Len, my doctor, and I knew I was three months pregnant at the time. Force policy dictated that pregnant members must be assigned to non-operational roles. Police work is normally hazardous by nature, and if I had been assigned to any other operational section within the Force I would have agreed; but the only injury any member on Customs and Excise could remember occurring was when someone tripped during a ship search. I was willing to take my chances until I finished the commercial file I was working on.

He was quite upset with my response and threatened to blow my secret until I reminded him of his initial promise to keep all the results of the voluntary test confidential.

As it turned out in the end, I didn't need the ammunition, because I didn't look pregnant for several more months--more than enough time to finish the file. When the Air India mass murder occurred, I did have to admit to my pregnancy to eliminate the possibility of being assigned to the huge federal task force being assembled. I was transferred back to Headquarters, Customs and Excise, to push paper until the birth.

The working environment was very much improved under the new staff sergeant. New members were arriving who were much more agreeable to work with. Nancy had been transferred back to Burnaby Detachment prior to my return. My nasty old sergeant was still there but he was keeping a low profile under the new leadership.

Being a female member in the late seventies and early eighties was a very unpredictable and sometimes dysfunctional place to be, but fortunately there were still more allies than enemies, and things seemed to be changing slowly but positively for females within the Force.

There had been some bumps in the road the female members had chosen, but all in all, the path had been a little smoother than most of us had expected. The Force as well seemed to have begun to turn our way. If nothing major happened to block our paths, it looked as though everyone going forward would have a good shot at getting to where they wanted to be. Unfortunately, life is full of bumps in the road, and we all would need a four-by-four and nerves of steel not too far in the distance.

Chapter 10

Animal Farm

The last few months of my pregnancy were spent back in Headquarters on administrative duties. I was disappointed to learn that Ottawa's parliamentary committee recommendations had influenced the Force's policies, at least concerning the French. A number of NCO and officer positions began appearing with bilingual status restrictions. Even Depot had become a bilingual posting. Most members at the time who were truly bilingual were the francophones who had been transplanted outside of Quebec after Depot. Applicants to the Force who were French or members of a "minority group" were given preferential treatment on the recruitment list. The term "minority group" chafed women of my generation; demographically, females were fifty-one percent of the population--making us the majority who allowed itself to be treated as a minority.

English-speaking recruits were now given the option of nine months' French language training prior to Depot, in an expensive endeavour with questionable outcomes and motivations. Even if the strategy were successful, the French had a ten-year head start on "bilingual" promotions.

The NCO and commissioned ranks were undergoing a metamorphosis that dramatically altered the power structure of the Force during this tumultuous period. The stronghold the Masons had on power within the Force was an unexpected casualty of the new Federal policy as bilingual, Catholic, French Canadians had an opportunity to escape the 1980s bottleneck in the promotions system.

On the backdrop of all these new controversial promotions, only five corporal slots were designated for females. These positions were for Depot instructors and were exempt from the new bilingual requirements. I felt caught in a moral quagmire because I was opposed on principle to accepting any unfair advantage for promotion rooted in reverse stereotyping; but under the system it would be a long time before Depot would have a significant number of female corporals to provide role models for female recruits.

The Division representatives missed the perfect opportunity to make a compelling argument against the need for bilingual status at Depot based on the female exemption, but everyone seemed to be not thinking straight. The disproportionate collective outrage within the Force over five "female" promotions to corporal allowed the much larger number of "French" promotions at much higher rank levels to go unchallenged.

The Depot promotions would be "hot" positions even though the senior female members had between seven and nine years' service, well within the norm of past Depot promotions. As a matter of fact, it seemed to be a bit of a manufactured crisis; if it had not been for the new rule requiring Depot instructors to be bilingual, female members could and should have already been teaching at Depot under the old system. Now that five had been designated as female, anyone selected would be working with her back to the wall. It was a tough decision whether to apply.

Len and I discussed it; then, with reservations, I submitted my application.

I was surprised that I made the promotion board for firearms, not academic instructor, which I thought my teaching degree would have made me better suited for. I was a good shot and by now I had shot "Crowns"[21] during one of my yearly firearms qualifications. But Milly Norry was on the same board and she was clearly the better candidate. She had more service, was bilingual, and was a competition shooter. Not surprisingly, she won the board. All of the successful female candidates for the board were outstanding senior female members. The only member of Troop 9 to make the list was Judy Best, who won the board for physical training.

The promotions focused the building resentment of the members outside of the "minority groups" on female members. Apparently losing promotional opportunities to "minority group" males was easier to accept than losing to a female. The resentment wasn't restricted to the five selected for promotion but was aimed at all female members. Ottawa seemed oblivious to the erosion of female support their clumsy handling of the female Depot promotions had caused, negatively affecting the day-to-day working environment of nearly all female members in the field.

On a "slow news day," The *Vancouver Sun* broke a story of gender harassment in the RCMP based on six anonymous female members' complaints. The story immediately went national, sending the media into a feeding frenzy and the opposition politicians grandstanding for political points on the floor of the

[21] "Crowns" is the term members use if someone shoots a perfect score during a timed annual qualification shoot. "Crowns" refers to the embroidered badge the member is then allowed to display above the crossed revolvers badge on the red and brown serge.

House of Commons. The "six female members" "went to ground," forcing the media to search for fuel to keep adding to the fire. That was when Nancy was dragged into a tempest.

The only comments on the record from any female members were the two earlier reports Nancy and I had been asked to submit to the parliamentary subcommittee. Thankfully, my report was so deliberately diplomatic I was mostly overlooked. A couple of writers tried to contact me, but I did not return the calls. But then again, I wasn't the real prize.

Nancy's unguarded, painfully honest, personal account was what they all wanted more of. Her name was unfairly touted as one of the anonymous six by newspapers and magazines. Politicians, both in power and those wanting it, hounded her, looking to use her as political capital for their own purposes. Poor Nancy was the centre of a national storm not of her making.

She did her best to remain unavailable to all callers, but she couldn't refuse a call from a cabinet minister looking for a politically expedient fix. He asked her to provide a list of any male members who had been biased toward her so they could be dismissed from the Force. How typical of a politician to look for a one-dimensional solution to a three-dimensional problem. She declined the offer; vengeance wasn't in her nature. It's a shame Sgt. Manly didn't understand female members as well as he thought he did, or he would have known he didn't have to submit his retirement papers.

E Division hastily arranged a meeting at HQ to provide a forum for the female members on how to deal with the unwanted notoriety the story had created. The media swarmed the front steps of HQ hoping for one of the participants to break ranks and speak to them, either before or after the meeting, but no one did. Female members filled the theatre in HQ. It was like a "females only" Deer Lake.

The meeting became a venue to speak directly to management on some of the issues specific to females in the Force. The commissioner had sent out a member from HQ in Ottawa to report back on the meeting, providing a rare opportunity for operational members from the West to have the ear of the power brokers in the East. It was the first and only time that a representative assembly of front-line female peace officers had an opportunity to speak in one voice on sensitive topics. The Force was trying to understand how to improve the situation, but institutionalized attitude changes would be slow. Still, that night created an opportunity to dialogue directly with Ottawa on some simpler issues that could be implemented administratively, like unpaid leave for family reasons and job-share similar to the ones already in practice in other Federal Agencies. Complaints about the hat and lack of boots and breeches were aired as well. What was said that night concerning more sensitive topics stayed behind the red wall of the RCMP.

Although it was obvious the six female members were in the audience, no one spoke up. There was no point, really. We were all investigators and we had pieced together the accidental nature of the story. Off-the-record comments at a social gathering had been the seed of the crisis. Offering up the six names would only damage their careers and continue the fuss. As unfair as it was, Nancy's was the only name the media would ever have.

It was sadly ironic that Nancy's name was tarnished as a whistle-blower when the opposite was actually true. Through her silence, the story would fade away. Prior to the incident, she had decided to leave the Force, a decision she delayed, to spare the Force any further embarrassment, until the media spotlight had turned away from her. Nearly one year after the story broke, she quietly resigned. Neither the media nor the male members within the Force ever knew of her loyalty and self-sacrifice.

Nancy wasn't the only female member to suffer silently, unjustly judged within the Force. Candy Smith, my friend and troop mate, had transferred from Ottawa to the University of British Columbia's RCMP Detachment. I hadn't seen her since the hospital in Verdin after the shooting in 1978. She had written many letters after graduation and before the shooting, but nothing since.

When we met for coffee, I was shocked to find that Candy's years in the Force had been a brutal endurance test. Without the benefit of professional counselling to deal with the post-traumatic stress of the shooting, she had managed as best she could. She had finally been transferred from Manitoba to Ottawa, where she hoped she could finally escape the ghosts of the tragedy years ago--a place to begin to heal. But she hadn't been there long before she was transferred out back to General Duties at her current posting.

The psychological damage done after the shooting was far greater than what the .308 had inflicted. It didn't take a psychologist to see the dramatic toll it had taken on her health. Mired in a deep depression, she had started giving away all her personal possessions. That was when a piece of advice gifted me years earlier by a very respected drug NCO, Smoky Stovern, surfaced from my subconscious mind: "'Help' is the most powerful word you can use, because the same egos that inhibit us from asking for it benefit from giving it."

I asked for her permission to try to get her help, and she agreed.

I went looking for help in the division representative's office, only to find that Cpl. Thurston was out of town, leaving the *other* Div. Rep., Cpl. Sailer, in charge. Cpl. Sailer had appeared unmistakably cool in disposition to the past collaborations Cpl. Thurston and I had made over female issues. He was a man's man, with a background on Drug Section, who didn't appear to have much time or use for female members. I would not normally have approached him, but I felt I couldn't wait for Cpl. Thurston to return.

To my surprise, Cpl. Sailer turned out to be the perfect person. He knew of the shooting and had no difficulty seeing the situation with Candy as a non-gender issue. The Force had come a long way in the past few years towards recognizing that traumatic events such as shootouts should be dealt with by psychiatric professionals.

E Division was leading the way in de-stigmatizing members asking for counselling. As a result, the need for members requiring counselling was slowly coming out of the closet. Cpl. Sailer could understand that historic attitudes would have worked against Candy back in '78. As he requested, I brought Candy to meet with him directly a few days later. He just let her talk. She did so with the brave understatement so characteristic of her. She was so understated, so practiced at masking her pain, I was afraid that Cpl. Sailer might miss it; but I had underestimated him. After listening attentively, he asked if she would accept a transfer to administrative duties and counselling for the event, and she agreed.

Cpl. Sailer excused himself, then returned in twenty minutes with transfer papers in hand, signed by the deputy commissioner, effective immediately. I hadn't realized until that moment how powerful, respected, and intelligent Cpl. Sailer really was. He may have been a Dinosaur but he was one who could dance if he chose to. I returned the next day to thank him and asked him to relay thanks to D/CMMR Venner. It was typical of E Division to step up to the plate and lead the way. The wrong done to Candy could not be erased; but with support and time it might be lessened. E Division's treatment of Candy was indicative of the supportive leadership of its commanding officer, D/Comm. Venner.

It was unfortunate that the news story on female harassment in the RCMP had broken in E Division, because E Division, at D/Comm. Venner's earlier request, had been the most proactive division in trying to assist female members by conducting the most comprehensive and relevant survey ever done on attitudes within the Force concerning female members. For a refreshing change, the entire policing culture, including the male peers and supervisors, were being probed. It would be years before the study results could be analyzed, but it was a good first step.

The ten-year reunion for troop nine was held in the summer of 1987. Though it made little geographic sense to hold the reunion in Langley, half of the troop came. A few of the troop--Lague, MacDonald, Brown, Jones, Stewart, and

Oracheski--had quit the Force and could not be located, but of those members I could locate almost all came. Those who couldn't come sent letters with updates on themselves and a promise to be at the next one, in twenty years. The distance didn't seem to be a deterrent to friends like Brenda MacFarlane, who came from Newfoundland; or Carol Anne Rose, Cathy Long, and Thelma Spinney, who came from the East Coast; or any of the others who travelled across Canada. Where there was a will there was a way; but not everyone had the will. One of our troop mates in BC chose not to come. While we could understand that she may have been disappointed--even bitter--about the Force, we felt the troop had an identity over and above the RCMP and that we shouldn't be tinted with the same brush.

The reunion was the first time in ten years many of us had seen each other. There was excitement and joy at the opening dinner held at the Bedford House Restaurant as troop mate after troop mate arrived. We may have been older now, but as women in our early thirties, we were in the prime of our lives and we looked good. Life may not have been easy, but it appeared time had been kind, and we all felt confident and secure and we showed it. Then Katie walked into the room. Katie, my "little sister" pit partner, had blossomed from an awkward, chubby-faced twenty-year-old into someone with a perfect figure, perfect hair, makeup, and designer clothes; she even had the walk and talk of a sophisticated woman.

"Is that Katie?" I whispered in disbelief to Linda Butler, who had remained in contact with her through the years.

"Yes. She's all grown up now. She even works occasionally as an undercover operator."

"Pretending to be what? A model?" I smiled, amazed at the transformation.

Linda had finally made it to a LMD posting where she could blend into the community in her off-hours. It was a welcome treat socially after being the first female at her previous three small BC town detachments, but there were extra politics that come with larger detachments, which took her by surprise. She was a little disappointed at some of the cool receptions she received from male members at her detachment who seemed to have prejudged her harshly. It fit the pattern of a nasty rumour--the currency of the locker rooms. It didn't take her long to track it down and back to the source.

"Cpl. Highbrowns is at the detachment and he told everyone that I was a troublemaker quick to lay sexual harassment charges. He said I did it to him at Depot."

"We should have, but no one from troop nine complained," I said.

"No, but someone from the next female troop--troop twenty--did, and he thought it was me. I confronted him and he just shrugged it off and left me with the reputation of being a whistle blower," Linda complained.

"Typical--can't even keep his victims straight. Still, it's kind of a sad comment on the state of things when a jerk like that can twist things around to make him look like the victim. It's like a rapist crying 'foul' if a victim complains," I said sympathetically. But there was little anyone could do to right the situation.

At the reunion I got caught up on Judy Best, now a corporal at Depot, who couldn't attend. I was surprised to learn she had been moved over to teach academics rather than filling the position on the physical training section to which she had been promoted.

"How did that happen? Was her knee acting up again?" I asked.

"No, it was politics acting up again. Depot can be even more intense for a corporal," was the well-informed response.

That was all that needed to be said. Behind the female red wall, we all knew about the random, invisible walls that still existed to shut us out. Small wonder our numbers had dwindled!

It was a bit discouraging to think out of the thirty-one who had graduated from the troop, ten had left the Force already. Some were like Thelma, who felt she had been too young and naïve when she joined and would have been better prepared if she'd been a little closer to the troop's average age of twenty-four. While Thelma's assessment was probably correct for her situation, I was saddened to see that two of my four closest friends in the troop were among those who had left.

Carol Anne Rose and Vivienne Stewart were both well educated, mature, and considered among the top of our troop. Like Thelma, the fact Carol Anne had left the troop did not stop her from joining Cathy Long and Brenda MacFarlane for the reunion. The girls from the East could never pass up a party. Brenda hadn't quite made it to a posting in Labrador from Newfoundland yet, but she was getting closer with each transfer. After her original posting to Stephenville Crossing, she was sent to Cornerbrook, Roddington on the northern peninsula, Baracheis Brook, and a small island off the coast of Newfoundland called Twillingate. She went everywhere the Force asked her to and did more than they expected, and later they would reward her when she became the first female corporal in Newfoundland.

In the beginning, the Force had been hesitant to place females in northern, isolated postings. It took determination and several outstanding performance evaluations to earn the right to be the first. No one was surprised to see Brenda blazing a trail for other female members to follow. She wasn't the only one in our troop to do so.

Joyce Graham, the official troop nine video camcorder person, also had been part of a first and was still an active, happy member of Drug Section. But not all groundbreakers had fared as well. Joan Merk was one of the first two female members to participate in the Musical Ride and was very happy to have that experience over with. She seemed to have more bitter memories than good ones to show for it. The reunion provided insights into the varied work environments of female members across the country.

It was interesting and a little discouraging to learn how some of my troop mates had fared during the decade since Depot.

Carol Anne Rose left the Force after seven years of service when the Canadian Transport Commission (CTC) needed a leader to set up their Atlantic office for the new section, the Air Transport Committee. She was bilingual, well educated, and already familiar with enforcing the Aeronautics Act Part II through the Force. The CTC offered her enhanced authority and stability of residence that the Force would not. Later, Fisheries and Oceans had no qualms about luring her away from the CTC with yet a better offer. She was sorry to leave the Force, but the Force was characteristically indifferent to her resignation.

The Force was officially gender blind and took no more notice of a female leaving than it did a male. The Force had lots of bricks to shore up the wall; one brick looked a lot like the next to them, but if they had looked a little closer they might have worried that the female members were eroding away at a rate much faster than the males of equal service. The Force might not have felt the departure of an individual member, but the senior female members did. There were so few of us to begin with that each departure increased the burden on those of us who remained, as we struggled to maintain our portion of the wall.

I was surprised to see another troop mate, Doreen Smith, who had seemed well suited to police work, had also left the Force. Her marriage to a civilian restricted her mobility at a time when transfers were routine and mandatory in small postings. Attrition because of marriage commitments seemed predictable enough, considering the social expectations on the different genders at the time, but the reality was that single female members were still the majority in the troop and more unmarried than married members had quit. Even some of the married members who left--like Val MacLean, whose official reason was "career conflicts with her husband's"--later admitted that wasn't the real story. It was just the socially acceptable one.

In the end, it appeared to me, talent and intelligence were not accurate indicators of success in the Force for early female members. The ingrained attitude of the detachment--or in some cases, whole divisions--female members found themselves in seemed to be a more profound factor in whether they were to be part of the red wall or shut out by it.

Early female members who found themselves on the outside of the wall had thrown themselves at it and, in doing so, some had ended up broken; some were emotionally bruised, battered, even scarred; and some had walked away realizing they would break before it did. The red wall was powerful, strong, and in some cases impeccable.

I found it troubling that we had lost so soon some of the cream of troop nine's crop. At least we still had Brenda, Joyce, and Candy; but Candy was pretty bruised and battered, and as much as we all wanted to believe it, it didn't seem likely she would ever fully recover from the aftermath of the Virden shooting.

The ten-year reunion wasn't the only female celebration I organized. A U.S. warship dropped anchor in Vancouver for a weekend, creating an opportunity for festive events to celebrate the bonds of friendship and professional respect shared by members of the Canadian and U.S. military. That is not to say there isn't a lot of competition, even in friendly matches. There were a number of male tugs of war scheduled between sailors, firefighters and police, but for the first time, there were enough female sailors to challenge the female members of the RCMP to a traditional tug of war.

I was tasked to organize our team, and had no trouble putting together one that would not easily be moved. I couldn't help but think back fondly to my first experience with a tug of war at Depot. This time, female on female, we were confident we could more than hold our own--and we were right. But it would be foolish to dwell on who won, since both the American female sailors and female Mounties felt a swell of pride in knowing *just being there* that day was a victory --a victory made that much sweeter by cheers of support from our male peers on the sidelines.

Opportunities for women had changed so much since the seventies, it was exciting and a bit frightening. I realized I had overestimated the difficulty of performing "male" roles and I was about to find I had underestimated some of the more traditional "female" roles.

I had some pretty unrealistic expectations of my ability to be as successful a mother as I had been a Mountie. My first dose of reality weighed in at six pounds, six ounces: Morgan Hall.

Len and I had gone to the prenatal classes, but I hadn't really practised any breathing because I was overly confident of my physical toughness. After all, I had been through basic training, and I was in the top two percent of the Force in terms of conditioning. I could run ten miles without changing pace.

How hard could this be?

Labour was about what I expected, but I must have missed the class on delivery. The old depot training, not to complain or show weakness, kicked in and worked against me. I didn't even say "ow," so I didn't get any painkillers. I know Len was only trying to compliment me on a job well done when it was all over, but I will never forget his immediate assessment: "Gee, that wasn't as bad as the film they showed us in prenatal class."

"And what room were you in?" I asked, incensed by his detachment from reality. "Even dying has to feel better than that!"

The first diapers I ever changed were Morgan's, in the hospital. No one should know as little about babies as I did, and have one. I had read all the theories, but the reality was something quite different.

For three years, we had been the picture of the New-Age couple: husband and wife equally educated and employed. It was time to add the next layer in the evolution of the modern Canadian family--children.

I was surprised how much I liked being a mother. I was achieving a whole new level of individual growth that I would never have reached had I not become a parent. How lucky I was to have diverged from my original course; I might have missed one of my greatest achievements in life.

Unlike education, religion, nationality, or social standing, parenting is a universal common denominator that binds the human race and perhaps more profoundly women than men. We may not all *be* mothers but we all *had* one. This new appreciation of a traditional woman's role was a significant challenge to one of the fundamental "truths" of my youth. It wasn't the first time and it wouldn't be the last that I realized I was no longer young enough to know everything anymore. Change means progress--at least most of the time it does.

The maximum maternity leave at that time was six months, and I took every bit of it and as much annual leave as I had coming to me. The timing was about right. Just enough time to recover, get bonded, but not too settled. Morgan would be well cared for by my neighbours and their two teenaged girls when I was at work. Secretly I was relieved to return to work. Motherhood is a 24/7 job when there are no relatives in the province to help. Work provided a chance to take a break from the responsibility of motherhood for a few hours.

Motherhood was a much more complex and challenging role than I had given it credit for. It was going to be a challenge to find a balance that would satisfy both work and family. My personal life had just gotten a lot more demanding and a little trickier. When I returned to work, I found the same could be said for the RCMP as well.

Although there was a history of distrust between the Force and politicians, modern prime ministers like Trudeau felt strongly that it was important to leave the Force to do its work, particularly its criminal and commercial crime investigations, free from political interference or even the perception of it. Paul Palango related Trudeau's reaction to being informed by Rod Stamler, head of commercial crime at the time, of a controversial investigation that seemed to be leading back to a liberal cabinet minister and powerful Quebec politicians. According to Palango:

"During that meeting Trudeau told Stamler that, in a democracy, politicians must never know what the police are investigating. If the practice were otherwise then the rule of law might be usurped by the rule of politicians, and the democracy endangered."[22]

Though members may have occasionally questioned the direction of Trudeau's government policy changes, I never heard any member of the RCMP question his integrity or honesty. It was therefore not surprising to members that he would make such a statement articulating his belief that an individual politician--even the prime minister--should have direct operational knowledge of ongoing police investigations, because the Force was required to be independent and empowered to attack large crimes and frauds free of partisan politics. This was the status quo the Force had traditionally enjoyed prior to the MacDonald commission when it was answerable to Parliament, not the prime minister.

Ottawa began altering the organizational structure of the RCMP, bringing it into line to behave more like other federal government agencies in structure and policies. Commissioner Simmons, an experienced policeman who had ridden the political storm from 1977–87, was obviously out of favour with the new government, and no one in the Force was surprised that he was about to be replaced, but they were surprised by whom. When Norm Inkster, an administrative Mountie by Western standards, beat out operational giants Venner, Jensen, and Wilson, operational members in contract provinces were stunned. It didn't take long to see that the Force was losing its autonomy. Career civil servants began appearing in powerful positions within the RCMP, some on contracts, and some given the same power, at least on paper, as high-ranking officers within the RCMP. Depot and twenty years of policing were no longer prerequisites for the leadership of the Force. The Mulroney government placed Michael Shoemaker as Inkster's deputy tasked to "reform and modernize the Force."[23]

[22] Paul Palango, The *Last Guardians/The crisis in the RCMP . . . and in Canada* (Toronto: McClellan & Stewart Inc., 1998), p. 78.

[23] Ibid., p. 133.

It might have looked as if the Mounties were still in charge, but things are seldom what they seem in Ottawa. In later interviews, both Inkster and Murray indicated they had two options: agreeing with the government or resigning.[24] Reporting major ongoing investigations involving politicians or large corporations through the chain of command now meant investigations were, at least in perception, compromised, with the commissioner a deputy solicitor general, flanked by a government appointment and Shoemaker as his deputy commissioner reporting weekly to the prime minister. The Force was reconfigured to conform to a business model, yet the decisions coming out of Ottawa didn't make any economic sense.

Management decisions were implemented in Ottawa that seemed both fiscally and structurally flawed. The rank of special constables, who never wanted to be investigators (many of whom did not meet the qualifications), were absorbed into the constable rank. The standards of the average constable were lowered in the stroke of a pen, and that same stroke inflated the cost of the work specials had performed at a lower rank. It wasn't long before airports began to look for cheaper private security. Worse yet, the Force made no distinction between the previous service of members at the lower rank of special and regular service, effectively inflating the constable rank and magnifying the pressure on the bottleneck in the promotion system. It wasn't rocket science to anticipate that this move would further damage the morale of the rank and file.

Ironically, because the Force had not conformed to the typical government agency mentality in the past, it was already running a lean, effective, innovative delivery system for law enforcement. The reason eight of the ten provinces chose to contract with the RCMP for police services was because the Force could do a better job for less money. Unlike other government agencies, there was no fat to cut. Fiscal cuts from the beginning would be cutting muscle the Force needed to hold up the wall. Career civil servants and politicians seemed to have a complete lack of understanding as well as an attitude of disdain and condescension for the inner workings of the Force, and for the dedication and expertise of members as they implemented major policy changes based on outside "experts." Common sense did not apply in Ottawa, and the Force's budget was under attack. Crime was now supposed to be evaluated in economic terms.

The fiscal restraint was changing the Force from proactive guardians of society to reactive complaint takers. Members I spoke with in the West felt these changes would not have gone unchallenged by any of the operational front runners for the commissioner's position, Venner, Jensen, or Wilson. Through any of those

[24] Ibid., p. 111.

three men, the Force would have had a strong, experienced voice, but members don't select their commissioners, politicians do.

Western alienation, which within the Force had been a fact of life for over one hundred years, reached new highs under the Mulroney government as we members began to feel alienated from our own commissioner. Like the general population of the West, we were all too aware that Eastern power-brokers did not care what we thought, so long as they held the reins of power handed them by Ontario and Quebec; but, unlike the general population, members were keenly aware of how unbalanced things had become in the nation's capital. The only way in which the rank and file in the West could voice their disdain was by a symbolic gesture.

VIP security details were suit and tie events. On one of Mulroney's visits to Vancouver, nearly every tie worn by the E Division members was red, the colour of the official opposition at the time. The symbolic challenge didn't go unnoticed. Members were informed by Ottawa not to wear red at the next state visit.

It was hard to watch the hypocrisy of a government that had no problem spending money creating expensive bureaucratic boondoggles in Ottawa at the same time it was disembowelling the Canadian military. The trend of previous governments to underfund the military was accelerated in a heartless fashion. Old-guard institutions were out of vogue with the new "me" generation. The pendulum of societal change had swung a little too far for my liking.

"Do more with less" was the reply from Ottawa to objections by the RCMP rank and file. This at a time when the government's mantra regarding its agenda was "Spend, spend, spend!" The pigs were at the trough.

In spite of the tensions between Ottawa and the members, VIP details for state visits remained an interesting change of duties. Security personnel tend to become part of the backdrop, part of the white noise of public life, hardly registering on politicians and diplomats. Being practically invisible, it is easy to see the worth and honesty of people when the cameras are gone and no one of consequence is looking. As someone wiser than I once said: "You can tell the worth of a person by how they treat people that can't do something for them."[25]

It was clear the current politicians weren't worth very much. That was not true of all VIPs. Of all the foreign state visitors, the British were always the most polite. On one state visit by Margaret Thatcher, I witnessed the worth of the British high commissioner and his wife.

[25] Source unknown.

Female members weren't often "lucky" enough to get day shift on VIP details, so there I stood at three a.m. outside the Vancouver Hotel suite as the British high commissioner to Ottawa and his wife arrived after a delayed flight. A regal couple in their late sixties, they must have been exhausted between the late hour and the time change, yet they stopped and chatted with me, as I stood guard outside the door to their suite, about my duties and shift hours.

"My dear, you can't be expected to stand here all night without a chair. Albert, get a chair from the room for this young lady," his wife directed as her husband dutifully disappeared in the room to fetch a chair.

"Thank you so much, but it is not necessary," I said respectfully.

"No trouble at all. I've just got to move this end table," came the voice of the British high commissioner from within the suite.

"Please don't bother," I said moving to the door in an attempt to stop him before he strained something trying to muscle out one of the large, overstuffed wingback chairs from their room. Then lowering my voice to let them in on the inside story--my only hope to bring them on side--I whispered, "As soon as everything is quiet, I wouldn't be surprised if a chair appeared for me."

Only then did they graciously agree to retire for the night for a well-deserved, if brief, sleep.

I was on shift in the same location the next night when they emerged from their suite, dressed in a well-tailored tux and elegant, embroidered evening gown, to attend a state dinner.

"Good evening, young lady. I hope that chair you spoke of did appear last evening," said the high commissioner.

"Thank you for your concern; yes, it did," I replied, humbled by their humanity.

As I watched them walk gracefully down the long hall to the elevators, a maid with a tray and two glasses appeared travelling in the opposite direction and, between the three of them, the tray and glasses were upset. The maid quickly apologized as she squatted down to clear the floor.

"It was entirely our fault," the high commissioner said as he bent down and assisted her.

It was inspiring to know that there are still people of that moral stature within the realms of politics. Unfortunately, I hadn't seen any of that calibre in Canadian politics since Trudeau.

Most members can tell many stories about special encounters while on VIP details with the queen, but that is not what this book is about. However, I would like to mention the special status the Force holds with the Royal family.

It was the queen's grandfather who gave the designation of "Royal" to our title. As to the "Mounted" part, perhaps it's the role horses still play in the Force that continues the connection. The queen's favourite horse for some years was a gift from the Force. Members took great pride that it never faltered when the starter pistol was shot in the queen's direction during a public parade in London.

VIP details were also a good place to run into old friends from North Vancouver. Constable Intense was on one of the state visits. He and Suzie were now in Ottawa, and he was a corporal still on a fast track to officer. I couldn't resist teasing him about having to take the French language training in the interest of future promotions.

"I figured it would hurt less than a sex change," he shot back in one of his best comebacks.

On one of the details, I ran into the ex-Secret Service member who had caused me so much grief in North Vancouver. I had heard he was on the detail, down from an interior posting to which he had been promoted. I did my best to avoid encountering him, but he seemed to track me down and surprised me totally by greeting me warmly at one of the breaks. I was polite but on guard, very suspicious of his intentions. He didn't seem surprised by my reaction and cleared the air between us.

"I just wanted to apologize for the way I treated you in North Vancouver."

That was the last thing I ever expected an old enemy to say. I didn't know how to respond, and he continued filling in the awkward silence with an insight I would have thought him incapable of making.

"It was a bad time for me--the demotion, a messy divorce. I know I took it out on you and I just wanted to say I am sorry."

There was obviously more to this man than my two-dimensional recollection of him. The manner in which management had handled our conflict in North Vancouver had allowed him to become a better member. North Vancouver Detachment appeared to have cultivated an environment where everyone dared to dream of professional and personal perfection.

Adrienne continued to hope for a Force-sponsored Law degree; with her acceptance in hand from UBC's law program, she waited optimistically. I admired her persistence, but she needed a sponsor at the officer level to crack that door open. One came from the most unlikely place.

Ottawa began questioning why no female members had been identified as candidates for the Force-sponsored law degree program--a valid question, considering that the higher post-secondary education levels of senior female members should have made them logical candidates for the program. E Division decided to seize the opportunity for its members. Adrienne had placed herself in the right place at the right time.

True to the previous pattern of two's for female breakthroughs, Staffing provided a second candidate, Bev Busson. You may recall that Bev was that extremely capable female member from the first female troop who transferred into North Vancouver just as I transferred out.

With little time to prepare, Bev passed the LSAT and was accepted at UBC as well. Adrienne's and Bev's names may have surfaced through a convoluted process of the new political correctness, but I could think of no two better female members to be selected.

There was one more female member in the UBC Law class that year, my troop mate Vivienne Stewart. Viv, after leaving the Force (tired of being underemployed by it, I suspect, but she will never tell), went looking for a new challenge. The Force may not have realized the calibre of senior female members, but I understand the UBC law school was impressed.

Ottawa was also mulling over the uniform issue, which had been raised at the female members' forum, and was finally open to reviewing the lack of standard uniform issue for female members. Again, it was E Division that chose to help facilitate the process. Corporal Thurston asked me for a second favour.

I was a lot more cautious about agreeing to help, after the controversy the last request had landed Nancy in, but in the end it proved too tempting an opportunity to pass up: a chance to try to finally to end the uniform double standard for red serge.

This time I approached the task in a much more stealthy and defensive manner by writing to every female member of E Division and asking for her input on the pillbox hat and blazer, which passed for serge.

I anticipated a low response because so many female members were tired of filling out surveys only to have nothing come of them, but many took the time to respond. Finally the responses were coordinated and organized, summarized, and the main areas of complaint highlighted under a covering memo to Ottawa.

The experience a female member had while performing VIP duties at Expo '86 seemed to finally place the matter in terms a male member could relate to. She complained of being repeatedly asked to take the photo of the tourist and the "Mountie," her male partner!

The RCMP uniform, arguably the most recognized police uniform in the world, was meant to identify and empower, not embarrass, its members. RCMP Headquarters in Ottawa finally understood what female members wanted and why and finally began issuing them forage caps, Stetsons, boots, and breeches. I thought it was ironic that our final victory coincided with a decision by the Force to allow a Sikh to substitute a turban for a Stetson and forage cap. In just a few short months, a recruit had managed to get the Force to relax one of its uniform traditions--a tradition female members had fought for fourteen years to be included in.

Red Serge Photo

Work at C&E wasn't terribly challenging, but it did have some satisfying moments, like when some of us decided to use the Customs Act powers of seizure in the same way the U.S. Customs used their powerful Proceeds of Crime legislation.

Under the Customs Act, the police had the power to choose civil or criminal dispositions for seizures of vehicles that had been used to transport smuggled goods. Since cocaine, the popular drug of choice on the streets at the time, was not indigenous to Canada and could not be legally imported, logically if it was seized in the country it must have been smuggled. The Customs Act even provided a dollar scale based on grams for illegal drugs.

Our Surrey Customs and Excise section invested the time to travel around speaking to drug sections of the Lower Mainland detachments and local police departments, suggesting that any vehicles drug suspects had used while in possession of cocaine be seized under the Customs Act instead of the Narcotic Control Act. They could then be turned over to our section for disposition, after which there would be no more paperwork or court for them concerning the vehicle.

It was an offer they could not refuse, and barely a week after our road show to Vancouver Police, I got a call from Vancouver's drug section to tell me they had seized an expensive four by four from a drug dealer. The penalty, based on the cocaine seized, was very close to the value of the vehicle.

It wasn't long before I got a call from his lawyer. He was surprised to learn that his client would be charged in court by the Vancouver police with Possession for the Purpose of Trafficking, but it was the RCMP and the Customs Act that had custody of the vehicle. Our conversation reminded me of the old "who's on first" skit.

"My client would like his truck back," he politely told me.

"The penalty is $17,000 against the vehicle," I informed him.

"We intend to appeal," he said stiffly.

I proceeded to explain to him the administrative appeal procedures under the Customs Act. He thanked me for the information, then restated: "My client would like his truck back."

"That will cost $17,000 by certified cheque or money order made out to the Government of Canada."

"But my client intends to appeal."

"Then you need to follow the appeal procedure I just explained," I said.

"Just a minute; are you telling me that *you* have already set the fine and he has to pay it first if he wants his truck back, *then* appeal it?"

"That's right, now you understand," I replied patiently.

"But that is *draconian*! No other act works that way!" he protested.

I couldn't resist. "Yes, isn't that a shame," I teased.

Actually the Income Tax Act worked the same way, but I didn't think the lawyer wanted too much information at that time. Good old George Monk would have *loved* this Act.

I occasionally dealt with investigators from other provincial and federal Canadian agencies while on Customs and Excise. It was sad to see that the open communication the RCMP had with public and private companies in the pursuit of criminals was coming to an end. In the past, members of the Force could refer to their discreet calls or tips from other federal or provincial agencies as "a confidential source of known reliability." The phrase was a kind of code for a judge to know the information came from a non-criminal source working hand in hand with us for the protection of the public--another federal or provincial department, or even a public company like the telephone or hydro company.

The new Freedom of Information Act and the Privacy Act were used to strip away the old unofficial information sharing. Such well-intentioned leaks could now cost someone his or her job. The investigators with outside agency departments were increasingly frustrated. There was eroding support for aggressive criminal investigations within both provincial and federal ministries.

No politician wanted to admit how many non-Canadians were crossing the border to collect multiple welfare or unemployment insurance cheques. There was no political desire to detect the true number of fraudulent claims on the health care system, which were equally as draining on the public purse. The small investigational sections within these departments, staffed mostly by retired members, were ostracized from within and discouraged from sharing information on frauds and suspected criminal activity with the RCMP.

Perhaps the investigators were no longer comfortable calling us, but we occasionally took the initiative to conduct a joint interview with another agency. A brand-new Mercedes with Oregon plates had caught my eye in Richmond. Background work indicated the husband and wife had lived between Vancouver and California most of their lives. They had run successful businesses on both sides of the border, but when American IRS agents questioned them they were Canadian, and when Revenue Canada did, they were American. When the husband needed heart surgery, he was Canadian.

They had successfully straddled the two countries without paying income tax to either for decades. It was a slick trick, and they were slick. Unfortunately for them, a health-care investigator arrived in tandem with me for a "routine interview." The suspects didn't know I was coming as well for the interview, to make it impossible for them play their little residency shell game. If they claimed to be primarily American residents, I would not be able to take the car; but there was that matter of the fraudulent open-heart surgery. As we walked from our cars to the luxury apartment building, the health-care worker phoned to confirm our appointment. I was shocked to hear her agree to postpone it for a day on some flimsy excuse. Her lack of police background was apparent.

After she left, I waited outside the underground parking lot, and as I suspected, the Mercedes pulled out with the wife driving. I pulled it over, and the wife--assuming I was the "health police"--advised she was a Canadian citizen and resident. Too bad that meant she shouldn't be driving an American car.

"I'm afraid I will be seizing this car under the Customs Act," I said politely.

"Don't be silly! This is my car and I need to go someplace," she replied condescendingly.

"Actually, this car now belongs to the government of Canada; but there is a pay phone over there where you can call a taxi."

"I'll be calling my lawyer, not a cab," she threatened.

"Then you'll need my card. The file number is on the back," I said politely.

Within two hours, the well-dressed man and wife came to my Customs and Excise office with their lawyer. Fortunately, like most lawyers, he was not knowledgeable about the either the Customs Act or the Health Act and did not realize his client would more than likely never have to pay back his health care money. Even worse, within three months his health care would be reinstated if he applied. But I wasn't about to start educating a lawyer.

"My clients consider themselves 'Americanadians,'" he said. Now that was one I hadn't heard before.

"Really?" I said politely but firmly. "I consider them smugglers. If they want their car back it will cost them $40,000."

The lawyer shifted uneasily, then turned to his client and instructed him to "pay the lady."

That was it. Not even an appeal. As they left, they seemed somewhat reassured that the "Health Police" wouldn't be after them. Personally I would have been much more concerned with Revenue Canada. George would have been proud of me.

As a civilian, I had been unaware Canada had an efficient military airline that moved Canadian troops and supplies both nationally and internationally. Empty seats not required for operational personnel were available for the immediate family of military or off-duty RCMP members. A three-dollar ticket could purchase a seat to fly coast to coast or even internationally. Except for the military uniforms worn by the attendants and many of the passengers, the flight was almost indistinguishable from Canada's government airline, Air Canada--not surprisingly, since many of Air Canada's pilots were trained in the military.

It was a bit of an adventure taking one of the flights because members, who had the lowest priority on the standby list, wouldn't know if they were getting on the plane until they had actually boarded; we could be bumped anywhere along the flight path. Members didn't complain; they knew they were in a much better financial position to finish the flight commercially than the family of the military.

The flights provided me with the means to make more frequent visits back to Wolfe Island. I don't know what I was thinking when I snapped up a ticket for Morgan, now eighteen months old, and myself at the end of July in 1987. As I emerged from the plane at Trenton Military Airfield, I felt the hot, moist air of a southern Ontario summer wrap around me like a warm, wet, oppressing, blanket. During the ten years I had spent out of the Ontario's climate I had become accustomed to the West. I had noticed the changes in my political views, but this was the first time I physically felt alienated from my home province.

The eight days I spent on the Island were relaxing, but the intense humidity and stifling heat felt overwhelming even at night. I spent many hours in idle conversation with my parents, sitting on the front porch overlooking the lake hoping for even subtle relief from the heat through the occasional whips of wind off the water.

"It's hard to believe the lake can be so hot in the summer and so cold in the winter," I said.

"It's not as cold as you remember. Even the ice isn't the same anymore; too much mercury and other pollutants. It comes later, leaves earlier, and is crueler than it's ever been," my father said, lowering his eyes in respect. A wave of sadness washed over, as my parents and I continued looking at the lake that was neither friend nor enemy to Islanders.

"I still can't believe Pauline and her beautiful children are gone," I said, breaking the silence. It was a bitterly cold winter night that had claimed eight-year-old Jeff, five-year-old Kerri-Lynn, and Pauline. Although her husband, Jimmy, had survived, he was not spared--rather, the ice exacted its highest price for his insult to it. Pauline and the children died quickly, swallowed by the dark, frigid waters, frozen in time, forever young and innocent. Their mortal lives were cut short, but their immortal spirits are preserved in verbal history. As in the past when the Mohawks inhabited the Island, current Islanders continue the tradition of honouring those who paid the water's toll by sharing their stories and passing them on from one generation to the next.

Jimmy was left for the rest of his life to relive a moment frozen in time, one he could not change and could never escape; the memory of the last look he had before the ice took them. Dad believed Jimmy, as a native Islander, bore the greatest responsibility for the tragedy.

"No one needs to die on the ice anymore, now that the government has promised to operate the ferry for us all year round," I said.

"They didn't die for want of a ferry. Jimmy just wouldn't wait for it," my father said. He was right, but that only made it more tragic to think about. "No one respects the old ways, the old wisdom. Too many mainlanders--even Islanders--these days think they can drive wherever the hell they like, whenever they like, because it's their right. I watch them every weekend following old ice roads that aren't safe. They don't know the difference between being lucky and being right," my father said with a wisdom that was definitely out of step with the modern times and the new "me" generation. Then, revealing a disposition he inherited from his pioneering ancestors, he added: "I think I would still trust myself on the ice more than trust the government to show us a safer route."

"You don't have to lecture a Westerner about not trusting the government," I said, trying unsuccessfully to lighten the mood with a bit of ambiguous humour. But my mother didn't want to let it drop just yet without sharing some of her scientific wisdom.

"The government certainly turned a blind eye to the industries that polluted the lake. The old Islander fishermen are dying of cancer and mercury poisoning." She had forty years of nursing experience to back up her statement, and, like my father, no government job or pension to worry about endangering if she spoke the truth. She was the first truly "green" person I ever knew, making correct links between health problems and human toxins in the environment decades ahead of official acknowledgement. Neither my father nor I would or could disagree with her. She was the smartest person either of us knew.

"I don't remember it being this hot and humid for so long without a good, old-fashioned thunderstorm. There must be a big one brewing. I am sorry I will miss it," I said, again trying to change the topic to something less oppressive.

"You won't miss it by much," my father said as he studied the water and sky from the porch. "Your flight's at ten a.m. from the base in Trenton tomorrow, isn't it?"

He was right about the scheduled time, but as we all found out the next day, it was delayed several hours because of bad weather on the prairies.

Members flew in uniform, by choice, out of professional courtesy for the military--a choice that may have saved Morgan's and my life one summer afternoon on a return flight from Trenton.

We'd had no trouble getting to Ontario, but returning to Vancouver was proving difficult. Tired of the humidity and heat on Wolfe Island, I had broadened my request to include equipment transport flights. As luck would have it, a "buffalo" (a large prop aircraft designed to carry cargo) was heading to Edmonton. Len and I had travelled on that class of plane before, and although it was slower, bumpier, and not going as far as I wanted, I took it.

The flight over the Great Lakes was rough--really rough. So rough that many of the passengers on the far side of the plane in the seats lining the wall of the plane facing us had to use their airsickness bags. Everyone one on my side looked nervously at each other, hoping no one would start a similar chain reaction. Even I, who had never had travel sickness before, felt ill. A member exiting at Winnipeg offered a Gravol™ tablet and I took it. Never having taken Gravol before, I couldn't know that not only would it settle my stomach; it would knock me right out. They had to wake me when we landed at the military airport. Morgan in tow, I grabbed my bags and asked how I should get to the commercial airport.

"You don't have time to change, but if you hurry, the driver of the military bus outside is transporting personnel to the base in Calgary. He might take you if you ask nicely."

"Sure, I can take you both right to the airport. It isn't too far off the highway," he said graciously, and we climbed on board.

Looking through the bus windows at the flat prairie landscape reminded me of Regina: lots of blue, cloudless sky on a 360-degree horizon. It was so clear it surprised me, because the flight had been so rough. But we hadn't gone very far before the weather began to change, and a lid of dark green swirling clouds moved in to quickly fill the sky, leaving a thin border of blue sky just above the horizon line in all directions.

Once you have seen a tornado sky, you will never forget it.

But never having seen one until that day, I knew only that we were driving into the fiercest thunderstorm I had ever experienced. No one on the bus knew we were driving into one of the worst natural disasters in Canadian history.

Just as the bus diverted off the main highway to head toward Edmonton's commercial airport, the thundercloud broke, dumping torrential rains and hail the size of tennis balls. Streets flooded, cars were dented, and windows smashed as Mother Nature unloaded her fury. It was obvious the bus driver regretted his offer to drive to the airport, but he was bound by his word, and completed the task without complaint, a hallmark of military professionalism.

I quickly made my way into the airport with Morgan and my luggage, only to find all of the flights bound for Vancouver were booked because of the August holiday weekend. I was leafing through the phone book at a pay phone looking for bus or train stations, still feeling groggy from the Gravol and a little overwhelmed to be stranded in uniform with a toddler in a city without friends or family to call on, when a member of my extended family found me.

"Where are you from?"

I looked up to find an airport special constable. The yellow strip on my uniform pants had acted like a beacon in the crowded airport. It was so good to see a friendly, helpful face.

"Vancouver, and I am trying to get back. Could you please watch my daughter for a minute while I call the bus or train station? Which do you think would be better to try?"

"I don't think you will even be able to get a taxi from the airport. Sergeant Major T. O. Lewis and I were in the airport tower and we just watched the largest tornado we have ever seen plow through Edmonton."

As I tried to think of a plan B for the new reality of my situation, the Sergeant Major T. O. Lewis rushed by towards the exit, but the special called him over.

"She's from Vancouver trying to get to a bus or train; could you drive her?" he asked, unintentionally putting the man in an awkward position.

"I was just heading home to check on my wife." He was almost thinking out loud, something members rarely do in uniform.

"No problem, I am sure I can make my way," I said, letting him off the hook.

"No, it's okay. I'll bring the car around to the front and pick up you and your daughter in two minutes."

As I got into the car, the radio was already on emergency broadcast. Details were sketchy, but a Force four tornado had cut through a section of Edmonton, very close to the route I had just taken. The full extent of the damage was unknown but it was major. People and buildings were missing, and there was the possibility of a second or even a third tornado occurring.

"Just drop me at the first hotel or motel on your route," I said.

"If you don't mind, I will take you home. We can form a game plan from there when it is safe."

It was a generous and gracious offer, one any member would have extended to anyone under the circumstances, particularly another member. Members know that no matter where they are in Canada, if they are in trouble, help is only as far away as the closest detachment. The same is true for all Canadians outside the country--help is only as far away as a phone. Any RCMP detachment in Canada will accept a collect call from a citizen in need anywhere in the world.

By the time we arrived at the corps/sergeant major's house the skies were blue, cloudless, and windless again. His wife, who worked at a local mall, had come home safe, but she told a heart-wrenching story of someone who worked in her store who had been called by a neighbour to "come home quickly" because the tornado had hit his house and they weren't sure where his wife and children were at the time. I immediately called Len before the lines were overloaded to tell him that Morgan and I were safe and to ask him to call Wolfe Island to let my parents know we were fine. Not grasping the scope of the disaster, Len said, "Do you think that is necessary?"

"Trust me--we will be the lead story on the *National.*"

After my call, the lines went down and the corps/sergeant major, his wife, and I glued ourselves to the TV as the CBC scrabbled to report the devastation in Edmonton and to find any piece of pseudo-science (e.g. open or close your windows) they could find on what to do if a Tornado is headed your way. Everyone was paying particular attention, because the government meteorologists who had failed to predict the first event were now suggesting in less than two hours the conditions to form a second funnel cloud could reoccur. It was scary to see how accurate they could be. At six-twenty, Sergeant Major T. O. Lewis and I stood guard in his backyard as his wife secured Morgan and herself in the basement corner foundation of the house--the safest location, according to the information we had received from the TV experts.

Sergeant Major T. O. Lewis and I watched as the same strange sky we had seen earlier that day returned, but this time we understood the extreme danger it held. This time we knew what we were watching, and we were both experiencing a healthy but profound fear--a fear neither of us by training or disposition would have betrayed to anyone outside of the red wall. There was nothing either of us could do to fight against or stop the storm's approaching from the southeast; still, it was our duty to stand guard, to raise the alarm for others, and to bear witness to the event. Only a member would have understood the fleeting side glance of professional respect we exchanged as we braced for the funnel cloud, which never touched down.

The next day, Morgan and I were on a commercial plane to Vancouver.

Back at the Surrey Customs and Excise satellite station, the old corporal was transferred and a new one was scheduled to arrive. The other two constables worried about the replacement. We had a nicely working little group. Everyone got along. Work got done. The research they did on the new corporal led them to believe he could be difficult to work for. I was very laid-back on the matter, considering we would be partners. My experience of being female in the Force had taught me that reputations are always subjective and sometimes unfair.

Sadly, this wasn't the case, and when Cpl. NewGuy arrived, it didn't take long to see that our personalities irreconcilably placed us on a professional collision course. My police instincts told me to prepare for an attack. If I was going to use the truth as a weapon, it was time to get ready for battle. I began keeping notes on him, and soon he made his move.

I had just finished a large commercial seizure, the first of the year for the section, when he sat me down for a negative performance evaluation (Form 1004). Never having received a negative one, I was curious as to what he could find issue with. Certainly not my work; even he admitted that.

I couldn't believe he chose such a non-issue to make a stand on. He didn't like one of my dresses, and I had a run in my stocking one day. I was a very conservative, tasteful dresser and well within the guidelines set out by the admin manual for female plainclothed members. He, on the other hand, routinely broke the male dress code by his casual attire and lack of a tie. His issue around my "offence" was indefensible, and his motivation suspect as well.

In a controversial move, Ottawa, in recognition that one blue suit would not do for female members working out of uniform, had decided to raise the plainclothes allowance for female members substantially above that of our male peers. This significant increase of a non-taxable allowance chafed some male egos. Imagine women making more then men!

In the past, I might have allowed myself to be personally wounded or intimidated, but that was then and this was now. Unlike my previous angry shouting match with my old sergeant, I now knew I could now control my anger and focus it like a laser during the confrontation. The corporal hadn't yet realized how badly he had underestimated his victim or how precarious his own situation was if push came to shove. Corporal NewGuy may have been my direct supervisor, but he was only one in a chain of command that had turned female friendly. It was only out of a sense of fair play that I had learned along with my battle skills from the Force that I gave him an opportunity to retreat.

"Your 1004 is out of line. This is a personality conflict, one which we should be professional enough to overcome," I said calmly. "I am not like your wife or your daughter; you can't pick my clothes or influence my hair styles, but that doesn't mean that we can't work together."

He rejected my assessment, pushed forward the 1004, and snarled, "That's *your* opinion, not mine. Sign this."

"I will not."

He seemed stunned by my refusal. The incident triggered memories of my first interrogation with Rinn as I turned the tables, "But I do want a copy of this 1004." Now he looked puzzled, so I spelled it out.

"If you insist on putting this in writing, I will answer it in writing, and I am prepared to go to service court on the matter. Are you?" I asked.

I was so happy with myself that I was learning the institutional skill of harnessing anger for self-defence. I was learning the masculine art of war and I had a secret weapon, one that could turn the system on itself. The threat to go on the record with the truth by laying a formal complaint had the potential to be a system breaker. Formal complaints had to be investigated and dealt with. Of course, no one would win in service court. Oh, I would most likely win this issue and do some damage to his career, but making a claim of discrimination was a lot like crying rape. It would cast a permanent professional shadow of suspicion over my career that I was at least a little guilty of *something*. Even female members could sometimes be guilty of distancing themselves from other female members who raised harassment allegations. I knew the price of my threat and I was prepared to pay, willing to put my career on the table. But was he?

He grabbed back the paper, muttering under his breath, refusing to give me a copy because he was withdrawing it. Continuing my offensive, I again demanded a copy; but again he refused, then left for home that afternoon with a migraine. My two other workers were amused. They didn't like Cpl. NewGuy and they seemed to share my triumph vicariously. It's pretty emasculating to get "out-aggressed" by a female, even by today's standards. Great coffee gossip, but it wasn't time to gloat.

I knew enough to know this was only a battle. Cpl. NewGuy could still win the war if I didn't make the next move before he regrouped. I had to remove my career from the corporal's control. I drove to Custom and Excise Headquarters to see my new sergeant.

The sergeant was a wonderfully supportive man who I'm sure had very solid relationships with all the women in his life. I advised him that Cpl. NewGuy and I had a personality conflict and I was requesting a transfer off his section. I further requested the corporal not have any input on my next annual assessment.

"No problem, Jane," was the immediate response. "Is he one of those guys who can't work with women?" he asked intuitively. "If he is . . ."

It was clear I had huge support if the issue was to go further. The Headquarters environment felt almost bipolar at times. What a difference leadership makes. I thanked him for his support, but I reasoned that since I was the only female member on the section, in fairness I could not say with certainty that our differences were anything other than a personality conflict, even though secretly I thought it was. I was hoping he would have the same epiphany that my North Vancouver partner had had and become a better supervisor because of our conflict.

The transfer back to HQ coincided with one of the largest security duties E Division had ever been tasked with, the Commonwealth Conference scheduled for the fall of 1987. Small individual visits of heads of state to events like Vancouver's Expo '86 were one thing, but the scale of training and planning required to accomplish a safe environment for all the heads of Commonwealth Countries was unprecedented in the Force. It was a time when the number of IRA assassination attempts on the British prime minister, Margaret Thatcher, were almost in a dead heat with those on India's Prime Minister Gandhi. The fact that Vancouver was home to some of the most dangerous Sikh militants at the time made the preparations for the detail that much more intense.

The conference took a year to plan, and the manpower demands on the Force in the West were huge. The site security was parcelled out to uniformed members in B.C. and Alberta. Those of us on the federal sections were selected for more specialized training.

One of the largest subsections within this detail was Driver Escorts. The training was done out at Boundary Bay Airport, where I learned to be comfortable driving six inches away from the next car's bumper at high rates of speed. I even got used to changing tires every half-day, because the tires were worn out from the stress of being driven on their sides as we swerved in and out of lanes and around corners at excessive speeds.

The old basic driver training method taught at Depot was discarded in favour of a new, aggressive driving method that focused on the "push-pull" steering method. I felt like I was being trained to drive a race car. From the driver pool, hundreds of trained members were assigned different classes of vehicles to drive for the conference. Some members would drive the limousines for the heads of state and their entourage; others would drive security/ramming cars. The Force leased hundred and hundreds of vehicles of every shape and size for the detail. I confess I was a little disappointed to find I had been given a van--I imagined I would be guarding and transporting luggage. But nothing was further from the truth.

There weren't enough limos available for the detail so a fleet of leased Bonnevilles was used instead. These cars, although top of the line, do not have much leg room, particularly for the African politicians. It didn't take long for the word to get around the delegates that the vans provided much more room inside for the passengers. Vans were used to transport the low-security risks, the spouses. With the exception of Margaret Thatcher, that meant females. The first night of the detail entailed numerous trips to ferry delegates and their entourages from the airport back to the Pan Pacific Hotel. The designated driver for the Sultan of Brunai was an old friend of mine.

"Quite a war story to be able to tell your kids," I teased; "chauffeur to the richest man in the world."

My friend laughed, then teased me back with a piece of information he knew would get my old feminist fires burning.

"Yah, they had to be careful not to offend a Muslim head of state by putting a female member in front of him as a driver."

Having learned not to be easily baited, I probed for the truth: "You're kidding, right?"

He smiled as he shook his head and pointed to the female member in the Bonneville behind him. "They didn't completely cave, she is driving his brother-in-law."

"How much would it cost me for you to switch vehicles with me right now?" I asked, but he would have none of it at any price.

It irked me to think that an enlightened country like Canada was so quick to abandon its support for the women's movement, but I guess in the larger scheme of things this was a small concession. We soon realized even Muslims from the East weren't insensitive to the new roles women enjoyed in North America; they apparently had anticipated it might affect them while guests of Canada.

The entourage from Brunai, led by the Sultan himself, stopped halfway down the portable plane steps to point to the female driver designated for his brother-in-law, then they all laughed, continuing to do so almost all the way to the hotel.

All of the drivers were from a pool to be drawn on indiscriminately as the need for a driver arose. As RCMP drivers, we performed a dual role as chauffeur and bodyguard. Much to my surprise, on the second day, my van was reserved for the ten-day conference by the group of three delegate wives and two local hosts whom I had driven the first day.

The visiting dignitaries were beautiful, well-educated women from Africa who all seemed to know each other from other such state visits. I noticed there was an unofficial, but undeniable, hierarchy of status between the three wives. All three countries were similar in international status, but one of the women seemed to be older, wiser, more reserved; almost melancholy. The other two held her in the greatest respect.

Two local women--one from Bowen Island and the other from West Vancouver--were volunteer hostesses for the diplomats' wives. The ten-day conference would be one big shopping/sightseeing event for the five, activities they apparently felt much more comfortable doing with a female member. Despite our ethnic, racial, and status differences, we all became friends quickly.

The second day of the visit, the media were dominated by the story of a toddler Morgan's age who was trapped down a well in the U.S.A. As mothers, we all could empathize with the pain and terror of the situation. We spoke of it every day as the drama played out in the international media, until, miraculously, there was a happy resolution. We all rejoiced and spoke of our own children;

all but the older woman, who listened silently. Wishing to draw her into the conversation, one of the local women asked if she had any children. The other two women's smiling faces quickly became sober as a quiet tension grew until it was broken by the eloquent, painful answer.

"My two beautiful daughters and I were returning from shopping one day when the driver lost control on the mountain road. It was days before I woke to find only I survived. I awoke to find I had no future, only a past."

The silence that followed resonated with the wisdom she had the courage to share with us. I felt honoured that she chose to tell us of such an intimate and intensely painful moment that had destroyed her life. How wise, how sad, and how heroic she was to expose a wound that would never heal, to help those of us who listened to never lose sight of what really matters in life. On the surface, she was the perfect modern woman, a national and international role model, with power, beauty, wealth, and education; but none of that could replace what she had lost. The death of her children was a tragedy from which she would never recover. That poor toddler's mother had more than she did. She had a future again. It is too bad that the international power brokers at the conference were not as blessed with traditional female insight and values.

Her words caused me to re-examine my priorities. I had quite often felt stretched and torn between my duties as a mother and my profession. Perhaps I had been unrealistic thinking I could have it all, the perfect career and the perfect family. Life isn't perfect, and neither was I. It was time to make the choice.

The transfer back to Vancouver meant that a nasty one-hour commute each way was going to further erode my time with my daughter. I had noticed with envy that Len, who was now on twelve-hour shift in Surrey, had far more time with her, and I wanted that, too. My five years were almost finished on Customs and Excise, and there was a natural transition time in the immediate future that could work to my advantage: I was again pregnant.

I put in my transfer paper, which my new/old staff sergeant Tom Hill reluctantly signed.

"Are you sure, Jane? I was kind of looking forward to trying to keep you out of trouble."

"I don't think you would be any more successful with me than you were with Patty. She's stationed in Alberta now, isn't she?"

"God damn you, Greenwood, you're as insubordinate as ever," he said, pretending to be cross. I had just reminded him that I had been right: his youngest daughter Patty had joined the Force.

I would always be sheltered if I was under his "watch." I could continue on in a relatively stressless environment, confident of the support of both my sergeant and staff sergeant. As unpleasant as HQ had sometimes been, I had come up with some valuable insights into the Force and myself, and had learned some new skills, all of which made me stronger and humbler.

Even if the Force hadn't been headed into a firestorm in the not too distant future, my timing was off on the feminist front as well. As much as I wanted to believe in the new concept of the "superwoman" who could handle career and family with equal success, my observations on the job and my own inner voice told me that it was still a dream for women of my generation--a transitional generation. We could have one or the other but not both--not yet, and maybe not ever.

Chapter 11

The Charter of Wrongs[26]

On May 11, 1988, John Hall was born, and we now had the modern family ideal: a girl and a boy. The six-month maternity leave was perfectly timed for us to make maximum use out of the boat we had purchased with the overtime from the Commonwealth Conference. I am sure my friend from Africa would have approved.

That summer was the perfect break from both our professional lives. Len and I looked back on our own roots and started laying the foundation of our children's lives. It felt like old times to be back in touch with the water as we explored the San Juan Islands off the West Coast. There we found a whole new community of boaters who were different in backgrounds but similar in dispositions.

The border between Oregon, Washington, and British Columbia was of no importance on the water. We who lived in the West of both great countries shared more in common with each other than we felt with each of the Eastern national political power bases.

Time and experiences in the West had eroded the unshakable, nationalistic belief of my youth in how well Canada was representing its citizens and how happy everyone was. As a converted Westerner, I finally understood what my troop mates had been complaining about back at Depot.

The West wanted its fair share of political power in the House of Commons and the Senate[27] but the federal government was unwilling to meaningfully amend the balance of power in Ottawa, which had favoured the original provinces since 1867. The East clung to the structures of the past, refusing to recognize the reality

[26] The "Charter of Wrongs" was rumoured to have been coined by a brilliant legal mind within the operational justice system. Although no one dares own it, it spread throughout the community of lawyers, judges, and police officers. The phrase embodied the frustration and disillusionment felt by the Old Guard of the Canadian justice system.

[27] The political under-representation remains an injustice today that will take a constitutional amendment and the goodwill of the rest of Canada to correct. British Columbia and Alberta have just under one-quarter of the national population; and the lion's share of the raw material and energy wealth of Canada are currently represented by 12 of the 105 seats in the Senate.

of the present in the West. As frustrating as it was to be ignored or marginalized, feeling exploited was worse. The federal government used redistributed wealth from the raw material wealth of the West[28] to buy more votes in the East to retain its power and continue the political status quo.

The centralist government was behaving like some dysfunctional family headed by over-controlling parents unwilling to relinquish their control over the newer provinces. Ontario and Quebec seemed completely self-absorbed in their endless bickering, as they each struggled for political dominance, oblivious to the possibility that they risked a future family crisis by doing so. For the time being, in true apathetic Canadian form, the West chose to ignore the politically rigged games of Ottawa and to go about the day-to-day business of life.

Life seemed to be unfolding as it should, allowing new growth opportunities at every turn. From adolescence to adulthood, from lake to ocean, there seemed to be a pattern of evolution in my life.

The Pacific Ocean was nothing short of spectacular, much larger and more intense than I was used to. Although it never froze, it could be much more dangerous than the waters back home. Even the boats were different. The lake boats I was used to would be nothing less than death traps in these waters. It wasn't the size so much as the design that mattered; still, a following sea or a powerful eddy could swallow even crafts specifically designed for the northwestern waters. True boaters are humble because they understand what Wolfe Islanders have always known: we cannot triumph over the water; we can only hope for a truce, for some moments of splendour, a chance to test individual courage and resolve, a chance to glimpse heaven on earth.

Days of ocean boating were followed by nights at dock, meeting kindred spirits--the artists, writers, doctors, and peace officers--and sharing boating stories of adventure and danger. There were even some lawyers in the group, as we discovered one evening at Browning Harbour.

A brewing "blow" sent boaters looking for the closest safe harbour; ours was Browning. We were in the process of securing our boat, *Crime Pays*, in the last berth when a large sailboat entered the bay. Fortunately there was a spot at the end of the pier that was long and deep enough to accommodate the vessel, but the wind and current were against them. The two men on deck were grateful that Len and I were able to catch their lines and help them dock.

"Thank you," said the sailboat's captain as he stepped onto the dock; then,

[28] The National Energy Policy introduced by Trudeau in 1980 as reported by the CBS clearly stated its aim to redistribute the wealth created by Alberta's oil industry to the rest of the country.

looking at the name of our boat, he smiled and turned to Len and asked, "Mountie, right?"

Len regarded the very expensive, sleek, sailing yacht that had a name I can't quite recall. It was along the lines of "*Recess*" or "*Adjourned*" and as he nodded in agreement, he replied, "Both of us are. Lawyer, right?"

"Crown, actually," the man said.

"That's a pretty nice boat," Len said. Crown were normally very overworked and underpaid.

"It's my brother-in-law's boat. He's a judge," he said as the second man stepped from the yacht and into our conversation. "I was right! *Crime Pays* belongs to a Mountie--actually, two of them!"

The only thing boaters love more than thinking up clever names for their boats is guessing the reasons behind other boat's names. We all shook hands and exchanged names. I am sure they wouldn't be able to recall ours any more than I can theirs this many years later.

"What detachment?" asked the judge.

"I'm in Commercial Crime and Jane is in Langley. We were both in Surrey before that."

The judge looked long and hard at me and commented, "I occasionally fill in in those areas but I don't recall seeing you in my courtroom."

"That's because the people I charge either plead guilty or run away, your honour," I said with a cheeky smile.

"Really?" chuckled the judge.

"Almost always," I insisted, knowing that the first time I did appear before him it would be hard for both of us not to think back on our first meeting and smile.

It was a tight-knit community that never took the ocean for granted. We were all ready to respond at a moment's notice to a stranger's distress call, all the time knowing that the next day the roles could be reversed. The art of navigating dangerous waters was actively passed from generation to generation.

The Power Squadron course taught Len how to navigate in the Coastal Pacific. It was a course I intended to take later when I didn't have to sacrifice any of my personal time with the children. It didn't bother me that I was slipping into the traditional female role as Len handled the helm while I tended to the children. We both had our priorities: his was to keep the boat safe, mine was to keep the children safe. Rocks and dead heads can't move as quickly or be as unpredictable as toddlers near the water. My natural sense of direction and knowledge of the weather in combination with my Island water sense proved valuable several times during our outings; still, I regretted not being able to read the charts and plot a course, or confidently take the helm.

We all like to think we chart our own course, only now was I beginning to understand how little control I had over mine. Much of my path had been simply a matter of riding a rising tide of change. I may have chosen to leap in, rather than watch, but most of the journey from that point out was largely the result of opportunities created by previous generations and lucky timing on my part.

The arrogance of my youth was slowly being washed away as I realized I had also become two things I had never intended to be--a wife and a mother--and because of that I was able to learn secrets of life I would never have uncovered had I remained on the course I had originally planned. Even if placing the best interests of my children first meant I was voluntarily losing some of my independence, it was necessary and, I promised myself, temporary. The price was worth the rewards.

In my new role I was able to experience the simple joys of being able to see the world once again through a child's eyes--a gift of unparalleled value. Youth may be wasted on the young, but parents are given a second chance to learn the real lessons of it. Watching the innocence and trust of my children helped me to understand how simple and clear life could be without the personal baggage we take on as we grow up--baggage that often harbours negative feelings that hurt only ourselves.

So much of my generation's motivation for change had been founded in a quiet, hidden anger--anger with the status of women, minority groups, and the old feudal order of society, in which none but the privileged few held positions of power. Anger created the motivation and the energy required to topple some windmills and make some breakthroughs in society, but anger is not a sustainable emotion. I wonder if anger is an emotion at all. It might be better compared to a chemical reaction like fire; a catalyst for change that, like the ocean, remains itself unchanged. The danger of uncontrolled fire is its potential to consume the host. Still, there is something cleansing and rejuvenating about a controlled fire. My ancestors have used it for centuries to clear the fields of old crops in preparation for a new growing season.

In the fall I was pleased to return to work at Langley Detachment in General Duty, only five minutes from home, completely confident in my ability to handle myself not just on the street, but now in the office as well.

On my first night shift, a call of Break and Enter in progress came in as I was just sitting down to dinner in a restaurant with two members of my new watch. I was surprised they didn't think it was worth clearing to attend.

That wasn't the way I had been trained. I left, and they followed, heading for the last place the suspect's vehicle, a large, older, dark-coloured vehicle, had been seen. My old policing instincts kicked in as, en route to the scene, I passed a similar car heading West on 72nd Street, opposite to the last reported direction of the suspect's vehicle. I slowed and watched as the brake lights flashed briefly in my rear-view mirror, confirming my suspicions, and the chase was on. What a rush--just like old times!

Several minutes later, I found the vehicle abandoned on a dead-end street with the stolen property and bolt cutters still on the back seat. As I called for a dog and handler, the members of the watch radioed, asking how they could assist. They took up the perimeter locations I requested, and when the dog man arrived, we began tracking, in and out of ditches and over fences, until one of the criminals was found hiding in a bush in a farmer's field. Later, after I booked him into cells I submitted the prosecutor's sheets to Cpl. Halpennie, who smiled as he passed them to the sergeant, saying, "I told you we trained them well in North Vancouver."

I had been pleased to find Bush Halpennie, an old North Vancouver familiar face, occupying the corporal's position on the watch. Gladis, his wife, had left the Force as a regular member and now worked as a reader in Surrey Detachment. It saddened me each time I heard of capable senior female members leaving the Force--one less foundation brick in our wall--but I respected her choice. Still, I wished the attrition rate weren't so high.[29]

At the four a.m. coffee break, the junior members on the watch wanted to know all the details of the bust. Everyone loves to catch the bad guys in the act. They seemed surprised at my reasoning for initiating the chase. What would have been my reasonable and probable grounds for the stop if they hadn't run? After all, I had only a vague description and a vehicle heading the wrong way. What an odd, defensive question, I thought. The watch members also seemed concerned that I had held him in custody for court.

"Break and Enter is an indictable offence with a minimum five-year sentence. Under the Bail Reform act, a peace officer did not have the authority to release for so serious a charge. The shit rat is only one month into a probation for an old Break and Enter, so I am adding the 'breach' (Breach of Probation) as well. I would be negligent in my duty not to ask for a custody hearing," I explained.

The members of the watch looked at me like I was a dinosaur, then took the rest of the break to explain to me how things had changed during the five years I had been away from contract policing.

[29] An anecdotal observation supported by The Role of Female Constables in E Division Study, conducted by S/Sgt. S.E. Stark.

The Charter of Rights had been poorly drafted and had failed in its intended purpose to solidify the common law that had evolved in Canada under the old Bill of Rights. The Bill of Rights had provided judges with a guide to balance the rights of offender and society on the merits of each case, and then to produce a just verdict that would never "bring the administration of justice into disrepute."[30] Like King Solomon, judges were expected to use wisdom to interpret the law in each case and protect the interests of all parties. Under the pre-*Charter* system, if the rights of the accused and that of society conflicted, the tie was broken by the judge in favour of the good of society. Each case was custom-made to accomplish that goal. *The Charter of Rights* reversed that bias.

The Charter of Rights clearly stated French language rights and the rights of the individual in conflict with the government but neglected to include a balance to protect society. Initially, the judges continued to rule as they understood the spirit of the old act, but it wasn't long before the *Charter* was used as a weapon in the Supreme Court of Canada by clever defence lawyers to strike down lower court rulings. The Supreme Court used the *Charter* to aggressively defend the rights of the accused regardless of the public's expectation or perception of justice. The appointed judges on the Supreme Court were elevated above the elected politicians in Parliament. Canadian Law no longer answered to the people of Canada. The Canadian justice system had changed from a system based on justice to a system based on law.

The Canadian prison system was also modified during this same period. The number of prison spaces was limited, even though the Canadian population was growing, forcing the justice system to consider not only the costs to incarcerate a person but whether or not there would be a cell available. Administrative measures in the prisons and parole boards were implemented that resulted in reduction in the incarceration time the accused was originally sentenced to by the judge. Fewer and fewer criminals were serving time in custody, and the time in custody was shrinking as well.

The Canadian justice system and its servants, the RCMP and lower court judges, had been neutered. The "Quiet Revolution" was over, and "they" had won. The winners were not the people of Quebec. The winners were the lawyers and ambitious politicians. The RCMP in the West watched in shock, disbelief, and Parliamentary silence.[31]

[30] "Never to bring the administration of justice into disrepute" was the overriding responsibility of the justice system pre-*Charter*. The phrase referred to the duty of the courts and the police to act in a way that would always maintain the trust of the Canadian public in the law and its impartial and wise administration of justice.

[31] "Parliamentary silence" is a code of conduct in which criticisms and complaints about the government held by servants of the Crown are not aired in public.

Under these changes, Break and Enters had been categorized down to almost a victimless crime, one that no longer merited the expense of incarceration. It now rarely drew any time in jail for first and even second offences, creating a Catch-22. Lighter sentences meant more offences, causing even lighter sentences. The most senior member at the break left me with a piece of well-intentioned advice to assist me in my professional adjustment: "You'll never get in trouble in the courts for releasing an accused."

"And just why would I get in trouble for doing my job?" I asked.

"One of the local judges is a real stickler for members being heavy-handed on custody issues. A real champion if the accused's Charter Rights have been infringed."

Reluctant to believe the policing climate had changed so much in so little time, I returned to the office to look for corroboration, and sadly I found it in the computer printout I had attached to the prosecutor's sheets. Only a month earlier, the accused had received no jail time for the first offence, only probation with the order to "Keep the peace and be of good behaviour." Certainly continuing to do Break and Enters constituted a breach, but the next day the Crown did not agree and refused to lay the Break of Probation Charge because it wouldn't have impacted the sentence. The accused was released from custody the next day.

Langley Detachment's manpower and structure was a lot like North Vancouver's had been back in the seventies, but the magic that had cemented the detachment seemed missing. I couldn't put my finger on what exactly was wrong, but the fun, the aggressive risk-taking, and the trust seemed to be absent from the detachment as a whole. The climate for female members was positive, the direct result of the foundation established back in 1975 by two extremely competent and personally powerful members from the first female troop, Patti Lawrence and Donna Morris. Donna had transferred to another posting, and Patti was on my watch. In terms of seniority, I was the second most senior female member on detachment and third in seniority on my twelve-person watch.

The senior constable was a very low-key male, a good, steady member, but because he was apparently a little too laid back for the sergeant's taste, he was passed by for the "acting" NCO spot in favour of next in seniority--Patti.

It was a unique power structure on a watch back then to have a female in a leadership role on active duty, but Patti was up to the task. Seniority was one of the cornerstones of respect in the Force. She had "been there, done that." She also had a personal power that could be at times quite intimidating, keeping the junior members in line and the senior constable, the only one who could have challenged her for the leadership position, silent.

I knew my Sgt. Airwolf by reputation as a no-nonsense, colourful, passionate member. His nickname originated from his VIP duties riding in a helicopter during the pope's visit to Vancouver.

Initially, I was a little worried he might fit into my unofficial profiling of harassing bosses. Most of his service had been spent on Drug Squad and he had just undergone a divorce from a senior female member. But I soon realized I had nothing to fear. Several months later, I confessed to him that I had been worried about him but had changed my mind. Since I was being honest, he decided to reciprocate by telling why his personal experience had not soured his professional opinion of female members: "She was a much better member than a wife," he joked.

I don't know what kind of a wife she was, but she had an excellent reputation as a member, and if they had not both been in the Force, they might have remained married.

As marriages of members to other members were becoming more common, it became apparent that the divorce rate, already high for peace officers as a whole, seemed to actually be higher if both partners were members. I wondered why. Maybe marriages burdened by stress fail more often; or maybe women who had equal money and power had more options to leave, making it a little too easy.

The social stigma of single women and single mothers was slowly waning in Canadian society as well. Women were taking their place in the collective consciousness of North America, no longer just as daughters or wives, but as people in their own right. That change in social standing was beginning to be reflected in the laws as well.

I was pleased to see that British Columbia was in the process of leading the way to empower women by drafting a new policy on spousal abuse. This new policy required that arrests be made and charges be laid in all substantiated reports of domestic violence.

There was even an infrastructure in place to support the policy. A civilian victim's services group worked immediately with the wife and children to explain their options if they decided to end the relationship.

In the past, the best a member could offer a reluctant wife and her children was an overcrowded women's shelter. Now the husband would be immediately arrested and held in custody with the recommendation he be barred from the home and contact with the family until the matter was dealt with in court. While the husband was in custody, Victim Services encouraged the wife to secure the money in the family joint banking account before the husband was released.

Experience had demonstrated that would have been the first move an abusing husband would make to regain control of his wife. What a shock it must have been after being released to see his wife had beaten him to the punch.

Finally, some instant justice! This time it was the husband who had to leave his home because of this brilliant and brave policy that had the potential to finally deal a serious blow to generational cycles of spousal abuse. I was encouraged to note that the policy had taken into consideration not just the crime but the subsequent intimidation by the aggressor against the victim. No one could "drop the charges." It was a bold step forward, open to hot debate, even within the members' ranks on my first training day.

After the head of Victim Witness Services, a young civilian with a sociology degree, briefed us on the new policy, she was immediately challenged.

"How is the husband going to share the same bed as his wife after he has been thrown in jail because of her? I think we are breaking up families with this policy." I was surprised that the questioning member was Patti.

"The same way she chose to share the bed with him after he beat her. I think anything is better than the current policy," I suggested.

It was just another example of the strong opinions held by senior female members, but there was no guarantee they were common ones.

It didn't take long to see that the policy initially was a good thing, as men were forced to confront their own problems through "anger management" classes if they wanted to save their marriages and their homes. It didn't save all marriages, but the cycle of violence was broken for a substantial number of families.

Unfortunately, some repeat offenders adapted to the new law by finding a loophole. The law was gender blind, as it had to be under the *Charter*, which meant if the husband could get the wife to take the first swing, he had a legal argument that she, too, was guilty of spousal abuse and must be arrested if she complained about the much more severe beating her first swing invited. The law had been drafted to take away police discretion, and because of that the initial success of the law was eroded with time.

British Columbian judicial policy had taken a hard line on another long-standing social problem, impaired driving, by increasing the penalties to make them the harshest in the country. The public was beginning to understand that it was no longer socially acceptable to drink and drive; in fact, it was a crime.

Much of the groundwork for the new social awareness had been laid by the women who founded Mothers Against Drunk Driving, known more commonly by its acronym, M.A.D.D.

Canada was one of the best places in the world to be a woman. It was amazing to see how far we had come in such short time. We might not have achieved equality yet, but we were certainly much further along the road.

The government itself seemed to embrace working women by adjusting the tax structure to accommodate the increased revenues it gleaned from the second paycheque. As the income of the double-income family became the norm, taxation began to rise in parallel.

It was around this time that I noticed Census Canada no longer listed "homemaker" as an occupation. This benign delisting helped shape the social perception that the role of mother was no longer important enough to be counted. No one seemed to notice that women's choices were not expanding--just changing. Perhaps we chose not to notice because the seduction of power and money, which seemed finally within female reach, was too tempting.

We were the first generation of women to wield an absolute power science had given us--a power we had been asking for, the holy grail in the search for equality--the ability to control the timing and number of children we chose to have. For the first time, becoming a mother became a conscious choice, not a biological inevitability. Breaking the religious bonds that denounced the new science came quicker to some than to others, but as more and more women saw through the rhetoric the gatekeepers of the old social order and Church often used to attack and vilify the first few insubordinates, more and more women followed their lead, and the birth rate started to fall. No one seemed worried about population growth or the larger social/economic implications of such a dramatic change in the population demographics of a young, sparsely populated country like Canada.

The face of Canadian politics was an area which, though it had a promising start, remained fairly unchanged by the women's movement. I believe the "famous five"[32] who fought and won the legal status of women as "persons" back in 1929, cutting a path for the others to follow in politics, would have been surprised and disappointed when so few women followed their lead. A few stepped up to the political plate, like Judy LaMarsh and Flora MacDonald, but too few to make any real change in the traditional male flavour of the House of Commons.

Even more disappointing than the under-representation by women in politics was that the few new female political faces seemed to have sacrificed themselves in an effort to fit in. Perhaps to win in a man's game they had to mimic male behaviour and abandon or hide their female nature. There seemed

[32] Emily Murphy rallied Henrietta Muir Edwards, Louise McKinney, Irene Parlby, and Nellie McClung to mount a legal challenge to include women in the legal definition of "person," opening the door for women to serve in the Canadian Senate. It was a fight they had to appeal all the way to the Lords of the Judicial Committee before it was unanimously concluded that the exclusion of women from public office was a "relic of days more barbarous than ours."

to be something insecure and fundamentally flawed about that strategy--one that the senior female members of the Force had rejected. If pretending to think and behave like men was the price of political success, then the price was too high for the illusion of progress. But politics is all about illusions and trade-offs. Canadian politics seemed to de-evolve into a lawyer's game of "I win, you lose." No wonder most women avoided political life.

While female politicians seemed to be changed by Ottawa, the opposite appeared to be happening within the Force. The historic military disposition of the Force had been mellowed by the females as it adapted to the unique perspectives of the female cohort and slowly absorbed it into the new, softer, more flexible disposition of the Force.

The achievements of the female members of the RCMP had been felt in all areas of policing in North America. If NASA had been as fair and open, Geraldyn Cobb would have walked on the moon. This leadership role in women's equality is something not just the Force but all Canadians can be truly proud of; doors in many other traditional male areas of society were opening because of it. But the successes female members had achieved had not come easily.

The challenges along the path female members faced to date had been well documented in many psychological studies, such as Rick Linden's 1979 University of Manitoba study.[33] One of Linden's conclusions based on his and previous studies was: "One of the major problems faced by women peace officers is the attitude of their male co-workers." Linden also stated, "Most of the research which has been done on women police in Canada has also shown the prevalence of negative male attitudes." The attitudes centred around the male peace officer's belief that females were less capable of performing general duties. That belief flew in the face of conclusions of the same studies that found women to be as capable as men.

Still, we female members were encouraged to see so many scientific studies documenting the evolution of women in police because many of us assumed that concrete solutions would be developed, based on the data collected, to deal with some of the gender issues that continued to periodically plague the work environment for some of us.

Staff Sergeant Stark's study on "The Role of Female Constables in 'E' Division" had been designed to collect statistical as well as anecdotal data on attitudes from the three key groups in the policing community: female members, their male peers, and their supervisors.

[33] Rick Linden and Candice Minch, "Women in Policing: A Review"; "A Study of the Vancouver Police Department"; and "A Study of Lower Mainland RCMP Detachments" (Department of Sociology, University of Manitoba, under contract with the Solicitor General of Canada, 1982).

When this study was finally disseminated to all E Division detachments in 1988, I was disappointed and perplexed to see no real solutions being offered to the serving female members; even though the study not only demonstrated that supervisors were more likely to hold negative views, it contained outrageous quotes that some supervisors seemed to have had no qualms about articulating. My experience had taught me these types of supervisors were the exception, not the rule, but that did not lessen the havoc they could inflict on a female member's morale and career.

> "For those of us who have forgotten, women are different than men. The most important job the Force has to offer at the present is that of general-duty policeman. Female members, because of their unique makeup, are not able to physically, mentally, or emotionally do this job and do it well on a day-to-day basis. For these reasons, I have not rated them well in the more important functions, as my experience had been that they are not as capable as male members in these areas . . ."[34]

The study provided no tools for a female member unlucky enough to find herself facing a professional brick in the form of a supervisor to use for escape, defence, or offence. In the end, as with the other studies on the topic, the authors seemed to believe time would eventually correct negative male attitudes, and until then they were content to leave the female members to develop their own devices for professional survival. I didn't delude myself into believing I was professionally or personally invincible. The survival skills I had developed had worked only because I had been fortunate thus far in my career--the few supervisors with whom I'd had personality conflicts were not at or near the top of the chain of command.

As challenging as the work environment sometimes was, I was surprised to find it was not my greatest challenge. I had gone to test my limits in a man's world, only to find it in the last place I could have imagined--motherhood.

My small social conscience was starting to nag me that perhaps somewhere between the Women's Liberation and the Total Woman's movements, there might be common ground to which the majority of women could relate. I tried to balance the ideals of both groups, believing I could achieve the "win-win" scenario the new breed of "supermoms" had bought into, even if I had to compromise a little in my professional and private life to achieve it.

I had already compromised my career by leaving North Vancouver to go to Customs and Excise when I got married. Now I had chosen to return to uniform

[34] S/Sgt. S.E. Stark, "The Role of Female Constables in 'E' Division" (April 1986), p. 175.

to allow more time with the children because, in my "heart of hearts," I knew my children needed me more than the Force needed me or I needed the Force.

The Force itself seemed to be experiencing a duality of expectations among its members, a difference based not on gender but on generation. There seemed to be a growing cultural division based on length of service. Pre-*Charter* members felt successful if the bad guy was in jail, but post-*Charter* members felt they'd had a successful shift if they had not received any complaints against them.

Times had changed; now everyone was ready to complain. It was the flavour of the day in the media circus that focused the public attention on the new champion of citizens, the Complaint Commission. To launch a complaint, a person didn't even have to be involved in the incident. In some cases, they had only to read an article in the local paper or watch a newscast that led them to believe the police had done something wrong.

It was a culture that criminals loved. These days, the first words out of their mouths at the time of arrest weren't apologies but threats of how much trouble we, the police, would be in when their lawyer was through with us.

No one seemed to understand that the RCMP had always taken complaints against them seriously, investigating them and prosecuting offending members with an appropriate scale of punishment, sanctions ranging in severity from an administrative reprimand to service court or even criminal court. The Force had the best investigators and the harshest judges of police misconduct in North America.

The Complaints Commission had two corrosive effects on policing. First, it was quickly recognized as another tool for criminals to use to intimidate police. Organized crime groups even launched coordinated complaints if a member was getting a little too close in their investigations. The second was that the process treated the peace officer as a suspect. That was demoralizing and dysfunctional.

One day, Langley Detachment was abuzz because a member of the Complaints Commission had requested a ride-along. Management carefully selected a very senior, under-spoken, knowledgeable member as escort. The members on detachment viewed this as an unprecedented chance to give a member of the commission a view from the other side of a complaint. As it happened, it worked much better than members could dare hope for.

The odd couple were dispatched to a relatively benign complaint from a woman who had been "badgered" by the owner of a local corner store. No real crime had been committed, but the woman was angry that the shopkeeper, who spoke only Chinese, had confronted her on the street after she had paused to examine his fresh flower and fruit sidewalk display. He seemed angry with her and had tugged at the morning paper she had tucked under her arm and gestured for her to go into his store. She ignored the protagonist and returned home to call the police.

At the grocery store, the member, through the translation of the owner's school-aged child who was home for the lunch hour, sorted the misunderstanding out. There had been a recent rash of thefts from the sidewalk display; fruit and newspapers had gone missing on a regular basis. The owner mistakenly thought the lady had taken her paper from his display without paying for it. After explaining to the owner how to rearrange his sidewalk display to minimize theft and cautioning him that if he witnessed a theft he should call the police to handle it, the member and the lady from the Complaints Commission then returned to the complainant's home to advise her of the results of the investigation and the action taken by the member.

Everything had been sorted out and everyone seemed happy with the outcome--that is, until the NCO requested the member and his ride-along return to the office, where they were informed that a complainant had launched a complaint against not only the member, but the member of the Complaints Commission (whom she had mistaken for a plainclothed female member)! In the complainant's mind, the member let the shopkeeper off too lightly with only a verbal warning, and the "female member" who stood silently in the background seemed entirely unsympathetic to her distress, to the point of rudeness.

The members didn't know whether to laugh or stand up and cheer at the incident, which highlighted just how ridiculous and petty the public had become. The member of the Complaints Commission was horrified that she herself had become the subject of a complaint. (Who investigates complaints against the Complaints Commission?) She made several stressed phone calls to her superiors. Not surprisingly, I never again heard of another ride-along with any member of the commission.

The public as a whole seemed to want a neutered police presence--unless they themselves were victims, in which case they wanted the old Monty Mountie back to protect them.

A perfect example of the contradictory expectations around policing occurred one midnight shift on our watch. A drive-by shooting in the South of Langley had diverted all cars to the area in search of the suspects. At the same time, one of the local judges complained that his lawn had been intentionally driven on by a neighbour's son. The judge was less than civil with the dispatchers as they advised him that the matter would be dealt with in due course based on the priority of calls. When the judge called back, he demanded to speak to the station NCO.

"I am Judge Charter. I witnessed my neighbour's son do donuts in my lawn and I demand some action."

"Is it still happening?" asked Sgt. Airwolf politely.

"No, he is back at home. I can see the car in his driveway from here. I want a f--ing police car here right now to deal with this."

"The offence is not in progress, and the accused is known; when the zone car is clear of the shooting complaint, he will attend."

Sgt. Airwolf later told me he was surprised to hear profanity from a judge, but suspected by his tone, articulation, and enunciation that he was probably drinking at the time.

"I am not going to wait up all night for your junior constable. I want him to arrest that delinquent and hold him for my court tomorrow morning."

There was a little George Monk in all pre-*Charter* members, and Airwolf was no exception. Judges might have the right to question the police's use of discretion in arrest and custody matters in court, but no elected or politically appointed person had the right to dictate our actions during investigations. The irony that this particular judge was the one who passionately championed criminals' civil rights was not lost on Airwolf.

"Under the Bail Reform Act, a local accused who is not a flight risk or likely to reoffend and who is charged with a minor offence such as mischief should be released on an appearance notice by the investigating officer. It is my understanding you are one of the judges who routinely takes members to task if you feel they have acted in a heavy-handed manner."

"Don't try to quote the law to me, you f--ing horseman! I told you I want him in custody in my court tomorrow morning or I'll be down to discuss this matter with your inspector."

"I'll tell him to expect you when I drop off the tape of this call, but I respectfully suggest you may wish to review it before you press the matter further."

After a stunned silence, the call ended, and, not surprisingly, the judge chose not to contact the inspector on the matter.

The judge wasn't the only person in authority who found out members don't like to be pushed around or insulted. A local politician whose negative views on the RCMP were well known, publicly and privately, could not resist attending the RCMP ball at Langley. Even our biggest detractors can't pass up a "photo op" with members in red serge; it's good politics. He even brought his own camera for the propaganda, but perhaps he should have watched it a little more closely. He didn't notice when it disappeared or when it was returned to his table after an unofficial "photo op" in the men's washroom. He must have thought the smiles and chuckles cast in his direction indicated that, as usual, the members of the Force had "turned the other cheek" to his public attacks; and I guess in a way we had, just not the kind of cheek he expected . . .

The only picture better than the one planted in the politician's camera would have been the look on his face when his roll of film was developed, revealing what the members thought of him: the backsides of a line of senior constables, tunics raised, pants dropped. Naturally I wasn't in the washroom, but the cameraman tells me it was a great shot! NCOs like Sgt. Airwolf couldn't participate, but he did approve.

Sgt. Airwolf was a bit of an enigma. A large, aggressive, dinosaur of a policeman, he was very quick at analyzing and articulating the patterns of change that were occurring in Canadian society. It was his opinion that both the *Charter*, a federal government instrument, and the Complaints Commission, a provincial one, were telling the RCMP that they no longer wanted proactive policing. They weren't concerned with crime detection; they only wanted responses to identified crime, and that response was not expected to be aggressive.

Police were increasingly expected to help solve social problems created by absentee father figures in single-mother households. Indeed, it wasn't just single mothers who seemed to be having difficulty handling their teenagers. Teenagers occasionally called 911 trying to report their parents if they felt their rights had been infringed.

When the age of consent for sexual acts was lowered to fourteen years, the law that "protected" children to make adult decisions on sex even if their "partner" was an adult created a legal defence that shielded paedophiles and placed children at risk.

The public was confused by the changes in the system. They seemed outraged by the increasing inability of the justice system to protect them from criminals. They just didn't know why it had gotten so difficult. Crimes were getting less and less satisfying to investigate. Fortunately, the largest percentage of police calls are not criminal matters but assisting the public.

One evening shift, Sgt. Airwolf dispatched me to a theft complaint at Ms. Murray's house. It was unusual for the station NCO to say anything over the air concerning a routine call, much less dispatch it. I arrived at a turn-of-the-century wooden farmhouse on Glover Road just outside of Fort Langley. An elderly lady in her housecoat met me at the door and invited me in. I spent the next hour listening to her life's story, how she had been jilted as a young woman, returned home disgraced, and now, after outliving her parents, she was alone.

Ms. Murray had a mild form of dementia, but weekly visits from the social worker kept her functioning independently. She knew she had a slight social disorder and apologized in the end for taking so much of my time. But it wasn't a problem; the night was slow. When I cleared the call, the radio dispatchers apologized for the call. Ms. Murray apparently called a lot. Most of the time, Airwolf visited with her on the phone; occasionally he would send a member to check on her in person. Airwolf was certainly an enigma--a big, tough, sometimes outspoken peace officer with a surprisingly sensitive side. Once every other shift on a slow night, I would make my rounds to Ms. Murray. Airwolf spoke to her by phone almost every shift.

As I settled into my new detachment, I decided to continue policing the way I had been trained even if it was a little aggressive and out of step with the "new reality." In my spare time between calls, I was busy figuring out the active criminals in the area. I did so the old-fashioned North Van way, through vehicle and pedestrian checks and occasional confidential information. I looked to the Langley's Break and Enter section for some background on the accused I was planning to arrest. That was when I met Mike Draper.

Mike was pleased that I had identified and set my sights on one of the more active criminals living in a rundown townhouse complex in Langley. The only surprise I had arresting the suspect later that shift came at the end of the arrest. As I shut the rear police car door, I noticed Mike Draper leaning against his unmarked police car in the far end of the parking lot. It felt like déjà vu. A time warp back twelve years to Rick Winslow and my first impaired. Well, some things never change.

It was comforting to know personality types within the Crown Office had remained stable as well. The only noticeable change in Crowns was a positive one: there were more and more female lawyers. Langley's Crown counsel had two remarkable examples of these.

The senior Crown was an intelligent and strong female, from Dierdre Pothecary's era. You just had to look into her eyes to see she had been there and done that; but in those same wise eyes was a fatigue that comes only after years of battles, a fatigue that eats away at the conviction that caused her to enter the battle in the first place. There was no doubt that she was finally being groomed for a seat at the bench. It would be hers if she wanted it.

The question she was now asking herself was whether she really did want to begin the fight anew at the bottom rank of the next battlefield. She confided to me that she would be just as happy--perhaps happier--running a little Bed and Breakfast. At what point did she get to toss the torch to someone else and start to enjoy life? I sensed she was a person of remarkable social conscience as she struggled with the question of which path to take in her life's journey. Whatever she would decide, it was clear she owed no further debt to the next generation of female lawyers. It was comforting to know people like her and Dierdre had left such big footprints to follow.

It appeared the new generation of female Crowns would be more than up to continuing the task--females like the other Crown, Marnie Westbury, fresh and full of energy and idealism. She reminded me of Dierdre as she had been in the '70's. Langley was beginning to remind me more and more of my old North Vancouver days.

Two months after my arrival at Langley, I was pleased to see Mike Draper had been assigned as my partner after his rotation on Break and Enter squad was finished. He was "the typical size" of most members of his era, six feet one or two, 200–220 pounds, dark hair, and with that typical overgrown Boy Scout look about him. Mike decided to join first the military, then the RCMP, to continue the pledge of service to the country his father had begun a generation earlier.

Mike and I had lots of fun running Fort Langley zone for a couple of years. When things got quiet at around two a.m. on midnight shifts, we would set up a road block at the Albion Ferry to pass the time looking for impaired drivers. I teased him that he liked to set up the flares around our station because it reminded him of his Boy Scout days and campfires.

Mike was always relaxed but alert. He had learned the hard way how quickly even routine duties could go sour. As a junior constable, he had just finished his day shift at Richmond Detachment's front counter, replaced by his friend Tom Agar for the afternoon shift.

Mike was in the parking lot when he heard the first shot, probably the one that killed Tom. A man had walked into the detachment and opened fire. Ten minutes earlier, and it would have been Mike. Sadly, every few years someone would decide to kill a Mountie. We still don't have an effective defence against a random execution. Those unfortunate enough to be at the wrong place at the wrong time earned the right to have their names engraved on a bronze plaque on the Cenotaph at Depot. Mike spoke about it only once to me, then put it away behind that inner wall of buried memories we all have.

I have never enjoyed a partnership more than the one with Mike. Between us, we had over twenty years of Lower Mainland policing experience. There wasn't much that could faze us. We were equal in service, policing abilities, values, and optimistic dispositions. In the areas we were not equal, we complemented each other, like Mike's traffic enforcement knowledge and my sexual assault expertise; even our size--Mike was big and strong, and I was still small and diplomatic, the yang and yin of police work.

Our combined years of service and backgrounds allowed us to size up a call and communicate our opinions through a side glance or a raised eyebrow, a stealth code complainants and suspects never noticed. After calls, we would discuss them as we finished the paperwork at roadside "meets."

You may have passed such "meets" on your drives. Two police cars parked in opposite directions, drivers' windows aligned side by side. It was at one such "meet" at 2:30 a.m. that a call came in concerning a complaint of assault. The new boyfriend had been assaulted by the old boyfriend and he was waiting for us at a telephone booth on Glover Road.

"B 5 and 13 will attend," Mike advised.

A Domestic was, by Force policy, a two-person call. As we put our cars in drive, we exchanged one of our glances conveying our common assumption: "Oh joy, a teenage lovers' quarrel. One in which the new boy, probably a wimp, needs some backup to move off the old boyfriend."

We arrived in tandem at the phone booth, but the complainant was not what we had expected. He was a good-sized eighteen-year-old who had been badly beaten about the head. The swelling was only just beginning. His cheek and jaw were probably fractured. We were surprised to hear no weapon had been used, only fists. Another glance was exchanged, as we both reassessed our original assumption. "The suspect is a very dangerous man."

The complainant needed hospital care, but he refused because he had fled the house, leaving the suspect alone with the girlfriend. He didn't know the address in Fort Langley. It was the first time he had been to her house. The complainant directed our route from my passenger's seat. As I exited the vehicle, I could hear noises coming from the house. It sounded like a door had opened and shut. Mike was still in the car giving in our location to dispatch.

"Get out of the car, Mike," I warned, but he didn't hear me. The damage he had suffered in the military had made him all but deaf in one ear. The suspect apparently heard me. He emerged from the house still holding the girl by the arm.

"Let her go," I ordered.

He looked at the two police cars and let her go. She ran to my car as I snapped the cuffs on him. Mike searched him before placing him in the rear of his police car. There wasn't much of anywhere to hide a weapon even if he had one. He was wearing only jeans, no shirt, no socks, no shoes. He was a little smaller than the complainant but in very good shape. His only injuries were to his fists.

As Mike and I stood at the rear of Mike's police car, to coordinate our next steps in the investigation, the car began to rock, back and forth, back and forth. Each time, the car rocked a little further, gaining momentum as the suspect banged his head against the silent patrolman (the shield separating back and front seats in a police car), harder and harder. Another glance passed between Mike and me, as we both thought: "This guy is some kind of psycho."

"I am following you back," I told Mike. I said to the complainant and the girl, "Wait here for the ambulance, and I will meet you both at the hospital for statements within an hour."

"Stop that now, or we will hogtie you," snapped Mike to the accused. We were both hoping it wouldn't come to that. People like the suspect are like raging bulls when angry, pumped on adrenaline, which increases strength and blocks pain receptors. This is exactly the type of situation when someone, quite often the police, could get seriously hurt.

Fortunately the suspect stopped, and the drive back to the Detachment cells was uneventful. We locked up our guns in the prisoner bay and took him into the booking area. Once the form listing his effects and offences had been completed, we took his handcuffs off for him so he could sign it. This was a moment of truth. Even a pen can be a weapon. He signed, then stepped back and punched the cement wall, very hard, with his fist. We both instinctively flinched at the sound of flesh meeting concrete.

"Now stop that right now or we will put you in a straitjacket," Mike demanded.

The suspect turned and agreed to refrain from any more outbursts. It may sound strange to civilians that someone so violent and dangerous can be so compliant with the police. This type of behaviour pattern is a possible indicator to police of the disturbed mind of a cold predator--a psychopath--who picks his victims and only the fights he can win.

When I arrived at the hospital, the complainant was being X-rayed. Statement pad in hand, I took a seat next to the girlfriend and was in the process of recording the standard name, address, etc., when I noticed her posture. There she silently sat, knees tightly drawn up, elbows and arms the same, almost in a sitting foetal position, as she answered my questions in hushed tones with her eyes turned away unfocused on the floor pattern.

"Nurse, can we have a private room?" I requested.

Inside, I put the pen down and asked: "Have you been raped?"

"Not tonight. He would have, but you came."

Then the whole sordid story came out: how he had begun their relationship as an adoring older suitor, then slowly insinuated himself into her confidence and her sympathy. He shared secrets of a terrible childhood, painting himself as a victim who needed help; someone twisted enough to hang a crucifix upside down and mutilate his arms with razors. He needed her, first as a friend, then as a lover.

She was only seventeen and a virgin when she complied one night, only because he pulled out a razor and threatened to kill himself if she didn't. She broke it off the next day but he stalked her, threatening to tell her parents what they had done if she asked for help.

One night he showed up at her weekend workplace and talked her into his truck, "just for a drive and talk things out." He raped her that night, and again the blackmail worked; she didn't tell anyone. She was living a nightmare. Too afraid to be at home alone when her parents were away, she invited the complainant, a friend she worked with, back to her home to watch movies. The suspect broke in and attacked her friend, who escaped to call us. When Mike and I pulled up, she had been pinned on the floor and he was about to "do it again."

After I finished her written statement, I took only a brief one from the complainant. The effects of his painkillers were showing. A more detailed account of the assault would have to wait, but it didn't matter; the case had taken a much more sinister turn. It had become a sexual assault investigation with a dangerous, predatory male suspect.

Back at the office, Mike had completed the prosecutor's sheets for assault charges when I silently gave him the statements to read.

"Oh my God!" he said quietly as he finished. "We stopped a rape."

The accused was arraigned the next morning and released under strict conditions that he have no contact with either of the complainants and avoid all areas that they would frequent. Based on his interactions with us, we felt he would obey the court order.

Date rape remains one of the most under-reported, widespread problems facing teenage girls, but one of the most difficult charges to prove, since there were so many opportunities for "reasonable doubt"--opportunities for well-dressed and rehearsed suspects to play the "I thought no meant yes" card to the jurors. Without a doubt, the defence for the suspect would drag the victim's name and reputation through the mud based on the victim's first sexual encounter with the accused.

I researched the suspect's past three relationships and found a pattern of manipulation, stalking, and escalating violence. It was a dangerous pattern that I feared one day would not leave an accuser.

Marnie took over the preliminary trial preparations. She was so passionate, so thorough, so optimistic. She reminded me of Dierdre, and a little of myself years earlier. She interviewed and prepared the female complainant for the intense harassment she would receive from the defence lawyer. Nothing can really prepare a young victim to again be victimized, this time by the system. The *Charter* had been used to chip away at the "rape shield,"[35] and by now there was little Crown could offer by way of protection from aggressive defence lawyers.

The preliminary hearing was held in Surrey Courthouse. The male complainant's was short and sweet. The assault charge, the less serious of the three, was really a slam dunk. The defence wanted the sex charges dropped. The senior Crown handled the Crown's case with Marnie as her assistant. After his testimony, the male complainant wanted to stay in court to provide moral support for his friend.

I told him, "I'm sorry, but it is not allowed. Witnesses can't hear each other's testimony or discuss it until the case is finished, but if you would like to know how it is going, I can tell you. Just step over to the window in the door." We both peered through to see the defence in the process of cross-examination. I gave a blow-by-blow commentary.

"Do you see the very aggressive stance the defence is taking? He is very tall and he is standing in front of his desk as he talks, close enough to intimidate the victim but not so close as to allow the Crown to object. His gestures are deliberate and threatening as he peers down at her over his glasses, playing on her guilt over her first intimate encounter. Your friend is very upset. She knows she is under attack. She is answering the questions but feeling the strain intensely. Now look at the Crown. She sees it all and is objecting when she can, but she is worried. Look now at the judge, because he is the one who really matters. He is leaning over his notes in the direction of your friend, looking very sympathetically at her. If he were allowed, he would leave the bench and give her a fatherly hug of reassurance, but he can't. He is restricted to the occasional menacing look cast in the defence lawyer's direction, warning him not to overstep his legal role. They are now going to break for a few minutes, no doubt to allow your friend to stop crying and regain some control."

As I finished the narration, the victim burst through the courtroom door and ran to the washroom.

"Please go and talk to her," the Crown asked as she emerged. "She may not want to continue," she whispered.

In the washroom, I found the accused crying uncontrollably. She just wanted it over.

[35] Rape shield refers to restrictions placed on defence lawyers to focus on the crime in question. It prevents aggressive defence lawyers from turning a rape victim into an accused sexual harlot for any past sexual conduct with anyone at any time in her past.

"Why are future victims my responsibility? How could I be expected to stop such a monster? Haven't I suffered enough? How likely are we to win?" All valid questions I no longer had the answers to.

"Stay in here. I need to talk to Crown," I requested.

The court would comply with Crown's request for an adjournment until the next day because the victim needed time, and so did we. We did not want the defence to sniff out our reluctant and possibly withdrawing witness. As expected, the defence lawyer pitched a deal: a guilty plea to the assault in exchange for dropping the rape and attempted rape charges. We hated the thought of a deal, but we both knew that even if the victim agreed to continue we could lose. We both had lost stronger cases before. We put our poker faces on, intent on obtaining the best deal possible. The assault would be a conviction no matter what, so we would not accept any plea that did not include at least the attempted sexual assault conviction registered on his record. We stood firm on a crumbling hand and "won."

It was the only victory we could reasonably expect. A sexual assault conviction would help the future judge in the next rape apply a harsher penalty. Unfortunately, hollow victories were becoming a trend in the Canadian justice system. It was a good thing police work had so much variety, because a steady diet of frustrating court cases wasn't much to look forward to.

One evening shift, I was flagged down by a motorist in a pickup truck who begged me to follow him to help a deer he had hit on Glover Road. Mike had already received the call by phone from the sub-office but hadn't been able to find the deer, until the driver pointed out the exact spot. The deer had already died of shock. Apart from damage to the lower rear leg, the animal was in good shape.

"Do you want to take it home?" I asked the driver.

I can still recall the look on his face at my suggestion. In his mind, he had killed Bambi, and I was insensitive enough to suggest that he now eat it. He wouldn't even wait to have an accident report filled out to cover the damage to his vehicle.

Still, it seemed a waste to me. The deer would be good only for dog meat in the morning when the animal control people would pick it up. Like most male members, Mike was a hunter.

"It's a shame to waste it. Why don't you take it home?" I asked.

"No, it needs to be dressed tonight, I can't do it and I don't know if my hunting partner is available. I asked dispatch to call the animal removal people for a morning pickup." But after a few guarded phone calls from the sub-office, Mike asked dispatch to cancel the request and the deer discreetly disappeared.

From the stories of members transferring in from more rural postings, I understood this wasn't the first police cruiser's trunk to be filled with a freshly killed deer and I was sure it would not be the last. The only unusual thing about this one was it had not been shot by the member. Rural RCMP work was much different from the work in the Lower Mainland (LMD).

Members whose first postings were small, quiet, rural BC communities had to make a rather large adjustment in the pace of calls when they came to LMD. That was the situation Cst. Terry Kopan found himself in when he was transferred onto our Langley watch at the detachment with the highest caseload per member in the province.

Terry was very militaristic, even by RCMP standards; on his own time, he was an officer in the army cadets. His hair and moustache were always neatly and closely cut, his uniform crisp and sharp; but what stood out most about him was the amazing spit shine on his work boots. I couldn't help but notice that Terry made a discreet inspection of everyone else's boots at the beginning of each shift. I couldn't resist a little mischief.

"There is a new guy from up country on the watch. He has the best spit shine I have ever seen next to you, Len," I said over dinner.

"Must have a military background, then," said Len.

"Oh yes!" I said. Then with a smile I made my pitch: "I was wondering if you would consider a barter." Len looked up with a smile. He knew mischief was afoot. "I will iron your shirts if you polish my boots."

"Deal." He didn't even have to think about that one. Len's father had been a tank sergeant in the Second World War. Len himself had been a Scout and he, too, had been an officer in the cadets. The cultural knowledge he brought to his shine was as good as any drill corporal's and, I was willing to bet, better than Terry's.

And so began the unspoken competition for who had the shiniest black work boots. Every morning Terry's eyes would glance down to survey each watch member's boots, in a stealth inspection. His casual roving glance moved rhythmically from one pair to another without any change in facial expression, until my boots were in his gaze--gleaming boots that invited a longer look followed by the slight movement of his moustache, his top lip tensed as if being bitten from the inside. After several months of this, over coffee one midnight shift Terry complimented me on the boots and casually asked if my father had been in the military.

"No, he was a farmer and an Islander," I replied. Then I changed the subject.

I wasn't about to uncover the mystery; life is always more interesting if there is a little mystery, I think. I never told him I wasn't the polisher, I just slept with him. It was comforting to know that in the Force some traditions, at least, were being maintained.

The mosaic of Canadian society was in flux, causing a change in the nature of assist calls. The cuts to social programs for the mentally challenged had led to an abdication of the government's responsibility in the area of mental health. Riverview Hospital had been cut back and almost shut down, while the promised community support that was supposed to fill that void never met the demand. With no place specifically designed to deal with their long-term needs, we were forced to take the mentally challenged to the hospitals. The hospitals were fine diagnostic tools in such cases but were not designed for housing the number of people who needed it for more than a couple of days. If the measure of compassion in a society is reflected in how it treats its most vulnerable members--the children, the elderly, and the mentally challenged--this new Canada did not score well.

The medical system, which also helps define Canada as a nation, had not been spared Ottawa's restructuring. I listened to my mother, a nurse of some forty years, and her colleagues complaining that the doctors who had traditionally run the hospitals were being replaced by the same type of bean-counting, backward bureaucrats that were in the process of "modernizing" the RCMP. Career politicians and civil servants who followed the same warped economic theories looking to cut costs were in reality reconfiguring our guardian institutions not to "do more with less" but to "do less with more"--more money to provide less service to the public.

The first to suffer were the mental patients, who fell through the cracks designed into the system, back out to the streets, which many of them now called home. The cuts that eroded the general care of all patients were slower, less obvious, and less drastic, but in the end nearly as devastating for the social health care system. Still, the average Canadian chose to ignore the problems unless they were the ones on the waiting lists. Most Canadians, feeling helpless to impact the problems, turned a blind eye and concentrated only on their day-to-day existence. I was as guilty as the rest.

The twelve-hour shifts allowed for maximum time off--even more when I cheated myself out of sleep during the midnight shifts. Len and I had exchanged commutes when he accepted a posting to Headquarters in the commercial crime section. Morgan and John were happy. Family life was getting more and more interesting. We had a much more varied group of friends in Langley as a couple--pilots, teachers, and lawyers--than we'd had back in North Vancouver when we were single. The members' parties that had dominated our first five years had become far less common, reflecting a decrease in job satisfaction and morale.

Work life was beginning to get a little boring, but I didn't want to go back to GIS. It had been difficult enough to deal with sex crimes before I had children. Nor did I want a transfer and have to face a commute. I dropped by the Training NCO's office to see if there were some courses I could take. It was just at the right time, because he was looking to train a new detachment instructor. I took the next Effective Presentations Course and the St. John's Ambulance's First Aid Instructors Course, which qualified me to teach within the Force.

I had almost forgotten how much I enjoyed teaching. As an instructor, I was responsible for setting up the training in the subject at the Detachment. In theory, all members were expected to take a first-aid refresher course every three years, but the reality was that very few had more than the initial training as a recruit at Depot, because in the Lower Mainland there was immediate ambulance response. In truth, most members tried not to beat the ambulance to a call.

From a liability standpoint, that was indefensible, so E Division Training had pressured St. John's to develop a course specifically for police and firefighters called the First Responders. The course was extremely relevant; it dealt with infectious diseases and officer survival as well as practical first-aid intervention in the Lower Mainland, applicable on or off the job.

I spent the next year breaking up the monotony of general duties by training the detachment members. So many members at Langley were trained that St. John's gave me a couple of awards. Since sooner or later I would be out of members to train on detachment, Len and I decided it would be the perfect time to add to our family. Everyone was a little surprised that I would have a third child; after all, I already had the perfect modern family, one of each. It was easier to let some believe it was an unplanned event rather than explain why we wanted more (four, to be exact).

Six months in Readers Section[36] was not a bad career move. It wouldn't have been my first choice for a permanent position, but it did help round out my service with some administrative duties. During that period, on Christmas Eve,

[36] Readers Section was staffed by members who recorded statistics on all files on detachment and provided an extra review of investigations to ensure quality and thoroughness. Because the reader went through many files, sometimes cross-references to other files could be made by the member aware of a similar crime by the suspect.

the Detachment was broken into. It was an unprecedented crime and a huge embarrassment for the Detachment and to the Force. A large quantity of drugs and cash from a recent seizure were stolen from the exhibit room.

Langley Detachment was a pathetic old one-storey building with a flat roof that leaked so badly garbage cans were placed in strategic spots to collect the rain. It was through the roof that the entry appeared to have been made, which immediately cast suspicions on a roofing crew that had been working there, only a week before. It didn't take long to eliminate the roofers and conclude the crime was an inside job.

Everyone in the Detachment was under a cloud of suspicion. It was like being part of an Agatha Christie murder mystery or a dinner murder mystery. We all had our theories. There was never any doubt that the case would be solved. The major crime unit from Headquarters took over the investigation in early January, interviewing each and every civilian and regular member on the Detachment. I was the last person they interviewed and the interviewer started to apologize for almost overlooking me. I laughed and took him off the defensive.

"I just figured you knew I wouldn't have fit through the hole in the roof," I teased, showing off my very pregnant profile. The interrogator ran through his standard questions before he asked the key question: "Have you worked in plainclothes before?"

"Yes, I have; but I have never spent one day on Drug Squad. Isn't that what you are looking for?"

He smiled, as it became clear we were on the same page. Only someone with Drug Squad experience would know how to fence the stolen property. The interrogator spent the rest of the interview asking me what I wanted to do next with my career. He even gave me some advice on how to place myself in the running to be a Depot instructor.

The case was solved, and the Training NCO, an ex-Drug Squad member, was charged. Rogue peace officers were a very uncommon occurrence in the Force. Depot had trained us to know we would be judged by the weakest member. Perhaps that is why the members and the Force had so little tolerance for anyone who betrayed their oath of office.

The law might be changing, but the members of the Force were still happy to remain accountable to its higher standards; we were the bricks in the red wall that had protected Canadians for over a century.

Chapter 12

Be Careful What You Wish For

Matthew Hall arrived on May 19, 1990. The six months' maternity leave was occupied by the major renovations we did on our home to accommodate the live-in nanny. I had learned about live-in nannies from one of the female members on Detachment who already had one. It sounded too good to be true. They cooked and cleaned and looked after the children; as one of the wives observed, "You have hired yourself a wife."

It sounded odd at first, but in a way it was true. I had hired someone do the work that had traditionally been done by wives. Had the women's movement really intended to replace our roles with women from third-world countries? What did that say about how, even we as women, viewed child rearing? Oh, that's that old social conscience trying to click in.

I had thirteen years' service in at the time, too close to the twenty-year early retirement date to leave; besides, I had promised Janet Hill years earlier I would stay to earn my independence. I had never quit anything in my life and I wasn't going to start even if the load of working, shift work, and raising a family was starting to weigh heavily. Still, my mother, a nurse, had done the same thing. At what point do we become our mothers? Is it nature or nurture?

During my maternity leave, the Detachment had moved into a new, state-of-the art police building. My old corporal had been promoted out of the Detachment, and Mike Draper was also waiting for a transfer to the interior. When I returned from maternity leave, it seemed that many familiar faces had left.

I got a call from Ms. Murray on a slow day shift, and I told her I would drop by; but when I detailed myself to her house, the radio room advised, "Ms. Murray has been moved to a nursing home out of the area."

The statement resonated like a death sentence as I realized I could not keep my promise. I knew she would be lost in a nursing home, unvisited, and waiting to die. Not long after, I saw the "For Sale" sign appear on her property, and I knew she was gone.

I'd always had a soft spot for elderly people. It was the way my generation had been raised. One day, during a shoplifting complaint, I got a chance to right a wrong I had been party to as a recruit.

A young security guard at a large discount store had called for a member to pick up and process a shoplifter. I arrived to find a frail eighty-year-old woman crying in his office. The exhibit, a toaster, sat on the security man's desk. It reminded me of the first shoplifting complaint with the old couple so many years ago. This time I didn't have a trainer scrutinizing me.

"Can I speak to you outside?" I immediately asked the guard.

"I know what you are going to say, but it is store policy to charge everyone. We back onto a seniors' centre and we get hit a lot by old people," he said defensively. He could see I was not happy.

"Surely you must have some discretion?" I asked.

"No, I don't."

I had already decided not to recommend charges, but since the store security guard wasn't prepared to back down, I was unable to spare the woman the immediate humiliation of the situation. When I returned to the room, the woman continued crying softly as she answered my questions about her name and address. All the while she kept apologizing, asking our and God's forgiveness.

"I didn't mean to hurt the store. The box was damaged and there was a scratch on the toaster. I didn't think they could sell it that way. I know I shouldn't have done it. I think I have enough money to pay for it if you like."

She was breaking my heart. The guard tried to avoid eye contact with me as he completed his paperwork, pretending not to hear.

"Money must be tight," I commented, sympathizing with the woman and attempting to undermine the resolve of the guard.

"It's getting a little better now that Alfred is gone. His medicine was so expensive at the end."

That was it. Even the young guard couldn't bear it any longer. "All right. I'll drop the charges," he said.

The woman looked confused, continuing to sob.

"It's all right. You can go," I said.

"But I committed a crime," she said. At this point even the guard was having a hard time not crying.

"It's okay. The store detective forgives you, I forgive you; even God forgives you. It's fine, really."

Finally she understood and left to go about her meagre life, living below the poverty line like so many other seniors. After she left, I looked at the guard, who was still internally struggling with having contravened store policy.

"You will never look back and regret your decision today," I predicted.

Sgt. Airwolf was waiting anxiously for his appointment to inspector. He had been sitting high on the officer promotion list for some time as he watched junior bilingual members take a disproportionate number of promotions to officer allotted to them because of language reclassifications in Ottawa. He remained silent about his disappointment and suspicions until he lost a unilingual promotion he was clearly better suited for. He confided in me: "The French in Ottawa have taken over the officer list and they are bypassing the English guys, but they won't get away with it. I am launching a complaint and will do my own investigation."

I felt bad for Airwolf but couldn't help thinking to myself, if he was right, and he usually was, the French Canadians were now playing the same game the Masons had been rumoured to play in the past.[37] The shift in the balance of power hadn't changed anything, especially for female members; it just looked like it had. The power base of the RCMP in Ottawa, increasingly infiltrated with civil servants rather than members, was behaving more and more like the bureaucrats and politicians we disliked.

Before Airwolf got too far into his complaint, he was promoted to a plum position in Alberta. You know what they say about squeaky wheels.

My new sergeant had a different management style from Airwolf's. He was a little more serious and less flexible, and it took a bit of adjusting to for the watch. He liked to draw charts to help communicate his ideas, but in the end he was a nice man who would never intentionally go after a member or hurt his or her career.

Professional life is so much easier at work if you don't have to watch your back. He had been married a long time but had no children, which contributed to the only "hook" I ever had with him. It probably sounds strange, but we fought over Christmas--or more specifically, who should have Christmas Day off.

Our watch was scheduled to work day shift on the 25th, and the sergeant was reluctant to give me the day off because he remembered that one year ago the detachment break and enter had occurred on Christmas when a skeleton crew was working. Being new on detachment and a bit overcautious by nature, he didn't want to ruffle any feathers further up the chain of command.

It was an unrealistic fear, in my opinion, and not one I was prepared to sacrifice

[37] I found independent corroboration for Airwolf's claim in a book published in 1998 by McClelland and Stewart Inc. *The Last Guardians* by Paul Palango stated that seventy-five percent of members stationed in Ottawa were Quebecers or French Canadian by the early 1990s (page 115).

Christmas morning with my children for. The Langley B&E was unprecedented in the Force, which, considering how quickly and efficiently it had been solved, was not likely to be attempted again.

The truth was it should never have been an issue for a senior constable like me anyway. An unwritten but widely practised courtesy had always allowed senior members with young families to have first crack at Christmas holidays. The sergeant, on the other hand, seemed to identify with young single members who might want to fly home for the holidays.

I suggested a trade-off over the matter, since it was only Christmas morning that I wanted, and my house was only five minutes from the Detachment. I would be content with just the first four hours off and would be ready for a callout if anything major happened.

I guess I had some baggage around the holiday, because I was a second-generation working mother and had experienced the impact of an absent mother as a child first hand. I remembered every school performance missed, baseball game unwatched, and--worst of all--a Christmas morning my mother had missed because of nursing. I was determined my children would not have those empty memories if I could help it. As much as I loved my mother, I was determined not to become her.

The sergeant, being childless, did not understand how strongly I felt on the matter until I painted the picture for him: "I could never explain to you the importance to a child, on Christmas morning, to have Mother there, any more than I could explain the beauty of a rainbow to a man who has been colour-blind since birth; so I will put it in terms you can relate to: I will not be at work on Christmas morning unless there is an operational emergency. If you feel this is a matter for service court then I am prepared to go."

Now he knew how inflexible I could be in the matter of family. He acquiesced, but it was not the best foot to get off on with the new boss.

After Christmas, I tried to keep a low profile and bury myself in work when on shift. Mike's replacement was a young member from PEI, Brad Trainer, barely "off the book." The Albion Ferry two a.m. roadblocks were not as much fun without Mike, but they were good training for Brad.

One summer evening, the quiet of the countryside was broken by the unmistakable rumble of "choppers" heading for the ferry lineup. Finally they came into view. A "hog" followed by a pickup truck followed again by a "hog" proceeded to a stop in the ferry line beside our police cars.

Bikers are a predictable, uniformed group, almost always dressed in black leather, with skullcaps as helmets, all sporting lots of tattoos. Their behaviour as well was quite predictably standard when dealing with police.

Bikers comply only with what they are legally required to do, making roadside checks chilly, silent exchanges, but not dangerous. The victims of bikers are almost always other bikers. I approached the first bike, and Brad took the pickup. The biker silently handed me his driver's licence and registration in anticipation of my request.

"We are conducting a roadside check for impaired drivers. Have you had anything to drink tonight?" I asked; and was completely taken by surprise when a large smile broke out on his bearded face, in response to my question. "No, I haven't, officer, but I am very glad that you are checking." There was nothing sarcastic in the response, which sounded like it was straight from the heart.

What an odd response! I thought, as I ran him through the CPIC system. Nothing was outstanding, so I thanked him for his participation as I returned his papers, then proceeded to the second biker. The next exchange was a carbon copy of the first, including the remarkably agreeable change in attitude when I advised him of the reason for the check. "We so support you guys [the police?] in what you are doing. Keep up the good work."

The ferry line was moving, so I waved him on his way. I was feeling like I had entered a *Twilight Zone* episode when Brad excitedly motioned me over to his police car. "Do you know who they were?" he asked.

"The strangest bikers I have ever encountered," I mused, still trying to process the meetings.

"They are the MOTHERS!" he said, handing me one of the two posters the pickup driver had given him.

The MOTHERS! It now all made perfect sense. The MOTHERS were a small group of non-drinking bikers who had created a shadow group in support of Mothers Against Drunk Drivers (M.A.D.D.). It wasn't hard to figure out from the ominous group in the poster *these* "Mothers" were playing with a common profane insult.

"Why didn't you get them to autograph the posters?" I asked disappointedly.

The watch was getting younger and younger in service, and the new corporal seemed to be on one kind of leave or another quite often, creating the opportunity for some acting corporal experience. It didn't take long for me to realize that leading and doing are two different skills. NCOs walked a line of authority wide enough to take control not only of the situation but of the members. Being an acting NCO was similar to being a team captain. It was valuable on-the-job training to prepare a member for the next step up: to corporal. Corporals are more like coaches on a good day and bosses on a bad one.

To handle the next rank up and be accepted as corporals, we females were going to have to make different adaptations than we already had; and again

there was no clear role model to copy. Patti, now transferred, had her style, but I would need to develop one I would be comfortable with.

It looked like I would have a long time to practise being a corporal; the service level bottleneck had continued, making the average service at that time eighteen years for promotion to corporal.

This was also the time when Staffing finally figured out that it was half price to transfer married members. When a couple in the North wanted out, they looked to couples in the South. It resulted in a "B" letter from Staffing to me asking what I thought of a transfer to Prince George or Prince Rupert detachments.

There was an old wisdom at the constable level in E Division that warned: "You don't want to go to a posting if it has a 'Port,' 'Fort,' 'Bella' or 'Prince' in the name." The truth was I didn't want to go anywhere. I was five minutes from work in a community big enough to have excellent schooling choices and small enough to still be rural. The balancing act I had achieved between work and home was difficult, because I didn't have any family support in province. Why would I want to risk upsetting it for a pointless move?

I replied, by memo, that I was not interested in a lateral transfer, knowing full well if they chose to push the issue, it could get nasty. But Staffing dropped the matter, probably setting their sights on more junior couples who were easier to push around. That is how the world seems to work, even in parts of the Force, like Staffing--people who needed to push usually chose to push those who wouldn't push back. Human nature was becoming predictable.

Peace officers and everyone in the legal system seemed to enhance their natural emotional intelligence through years of practice, of learning to watch and listen to people. In terms of listening skills, judges seem to be on par with members and polygraph operators, having honed their natural aptitude through years of experience to sift through the often contradictory accounts of witnesses to get to the truth.

Good judges, like good peace officers, understand that if two or more witnesses recount identical versions of an incident, then there has been either collusion or condemnation. It is the nature of our individual personalities, which taints our perception of the world and memories of events witnessed. Slight contradictions that often drew the wrath of the defence were only a smoke screen for a jury. The variances actually suggest an unedited recollection of the witness, not deception. A story that Judge Leo Nymsic told me best illustrates the process.

Judge Nymsic and several other British Columbia Supreme Court judges were returning from lunch when a motor vehicle accident occurred right in front of them. They all returned to their chambers to record their witness statements and were amazed to find that even though they were professional observers, they all recounted the series of events slightly differently. These differences conveyed as much about them as the events they had witnessed. It was a human memory trait that police could use to their advantage in police investigations.

During a break and enter in the opening hours of the Willowbrook Mall, a suspect had boldly reached under the closed store's curtain partition to steal merchandise off the shelves. Several of the other shopkeepers had noticed the unfamiliar face in the common mall hall as they passed by to open their shops. The shoe store owner could describe perfectly the brand and type of shoes of the suspect, but little else. Similarly, the clothing retailer contributed the colour, size and cut of his jeans and shirt but little else. The pretty coffee clerk provided a physical description of the youth right down to the bounce in his step. The sum of the three witnesses' recollections painted a perfect picture of one of our most active criminals in Langley.

In another incident, a beer and wine outlet had been robbed at gunpoint and the suspect had fled on foot before the investigating member could get there. I was there as backup only and witnessed the member becoming more and more frustrated with the young female salesperson, who could provide no details on the type of gun that had been used. It could have been a shotgun, rifle, or handgun. It was black, had a barrel, and was pointed at her. Her physical description wasn't much more help because the suspect had distorted his facial features by wearing a nylon stocking over his head. That was when I jumped in.

"What shade of stocking was it?' I asked.

"It was an evening shade," she replied without hesitation.

The investigating officer looked slightly annoyed at my interruption, then continued taking the statement. I left to look in the empty lot into which the suspect had fled, and next to some running shoe impressions in the damp earth lay the evening shade stocking the girl had described. It seems people see only what is important to them. I was still learning more applied psychology outside of university than I ever learned at Queen's. Memories are by nature subjective.

For the second time in my career, I was given a recruit to train, Dave Williams. This time, I was more experienced and mature, and so was he. Dave's memory and observation skills were some of the best I had ever seen. He had a dry wit that helped lighten the mood. I could have used some black humour, as I had gotten a rash of suicides, a sudden infant death syndrome, and a few notifications of next of kin. How I longed for the days when as a junior member I could tell someone who answered the door with that panicked look, "It's okay. No one has died."

It also seemed I had become the favoured member to handle mental patients going amuck. One day, as dispatch detailed us to a schizophrenic man who had doused himself in gasoline and was marching around threatening to strike a match, my recruit asked, "Is it your intention to introduce me to every crazy in Langley before I get 'off the book'?"

As I chuckled, the dispatcher read out the suspect's lengthy record, which included arson.

"You may be learning something new; if we are not quick enough, you may be investigating the perfect arson." My mind wandered, and old memories were triggered.

"'Crispy Critters'[38] aren't nice to look at, so step it up a bit." In my peripheral vision I noticed my uncharacteristic use of callous police jargon shocked Dave, but he remained silent, intuitively sensing I was speaking from first-hand experience of the darkest part of the inner wall all operational veterans have; the part we wall off even from ourselves. I had earned the right to use the term.

I was not joking around when we arrived and had to talk the man out of his matches before taking him to the hospital for observation. At the hospital, the overworked duty nurse surprised me when she directed me to take a seat with the man in the waiting room because it could be some time before they could get to him.

"Perhaps you haven't noticed the aroma coming from our prisoner. It's GASOLINE, not aftershave. I suggest you get him immediately into the 'quiet room' (a room reserved for mental patents in the emergency ward) and hose him off before someone lights a cigarette and he goes up like a roman candle," I said discreetly but firmly.

The nurse looked up and over the professional wall she had built to insulate herself from the suffering patients she routinely had to tell to "take a number" and immediately called a "stat"--the nursing equivalent of 10-33 or "help me quick!"

The call and my reaction to it was an example of the black humour police use when dealing with nightmare scenarios, some of the darkest areas of the job--the type of politically incorrect humour we don't dare repeat in public . . . a form of denial . . . an indicator that years of police work were resulting in a numbing of the natural feelings. All feelings seemed muted after awhile.

The tone alert, which used to rouse my adrenalin, no longer elicited any response apart from annoyance at the interference with a scheduled coffee or interview. From speaking to other members with my service, I wasn't the only one in danger of falling victim to an attitude of complacency. Complacency in police work can get someone killed, and one night I fell into its trap.

The Otter Co-op in the centre of Aldergrove zone had been the site of a rash of nighttime break and enters. There was no real pattern as to which nights of the week or exact time of night. The MO (*modus operandi*) was the only constant in the crime. The front window would be smashed by a vehicle, and TVs, electronic equipment, and expensive running shoes would be taken. Even though members would arrive within five minutes of the alarm, the thieves were always long gone. There were few houses in the area, and no one was up in the middle of the night to provide any eyewitness help. Langley's B&E squad even

[38] "Crispy Critters" was police slang for bodies charred beyond recognition.

spent a few boring nights in the store, only to have it hit two days after they discontinued the stake-out, deeming it not good value for police manpower.

Since the insurance company for the store was threatening to pull its coverage, the store hired a night security guard, providing him with a cell phone and a video camera. My partner and I decided to remain close in between calls, especially between two and four a.m., when the majority of the crimes had occurred. We were only four blocks away exchanging paperwork for the office, when the dispatcher advised us that the security guard was watching two males who had just driven the back end of their pickup truck through the front window of the store and were loading it up.

My partner, who was facing the right direction and in a faster police car, had about a two-block jump on me by the time I got turned around. As I turned off Fraser Highway onto 248th Street, I saw my partner's police car pull into the Co-op's parking lot in a failed attempt to block the truck's exit. The driver of the four-by-four hit the gas and drove through the ditch, turning in my direction on 248th Street. He took his foot off the gas as I slid my police car sideways to a stop, blocking his way to Fraser Highway.

What was I thinking? There I was, a fifteen-year member, making a recruit's mistake (the same mistake Rod had made back in North Vancouver). There is a good reason why members don't use police cars to block exits, especially if we are still in them. I had made a potentially fatal mistake; not because I didn't know better but because I had grown complacent. The adrenalin didn't alert me to the danger until I heard the tires on the truck spinning for traction as he gunned it. I braced for impact, one which thankfully was avoided when at the last minute the truck veered off through the ditch to my right, between a tree and a building on the corner and onto Fraser Highway. (Later my partner and I returned and measured the space the driver had fit the truck through, and I still don't know how he did it.)

Once on Fraser Highway, it was the suspect's turn to make a poor decision. He should have turned East towards Abbotsford. It was his best chance at escape, because Abbotsford was policed by a much smaller municipal force on a separate air frequency, giving him miles of pursuit with only my partner and me in the chase. Instead, he turned west on Fraser, placing himself on a collision course with the remainder of our watch's night shift heading east. At the crest of the first hill, the parade of flashing dome lights led by the staff sergeant's car came into view; and with my partner and me on his bumper, he pulled over.

My partner arrested the driver while I arrested the passenger. The driver was quiet, but the passenger was quite mouthy, claiming to be an innocent passenger picked up as a hitchhiker by the driver. He continued his rant about his innocence, and how much trouble we would be in for the false arrest, right into the cellblock. After signing for his effects on the prison's form, he demanded to call his lawyer to start our prosecution. I took him to the secure phone room designed for such calls, but before I closed the door I suggested, "Make sure you tell your lawyer about the video."

"What video?" he snapped, still thinking he had a legal leg to stand on.

"Didn't you tell him he was on '*Candid Camera*'?" I asked my partner, who shook his head "no."

"What are you talking about?" asked the suspect, who was starting to show some concern that he may have something to worry about.

"Well, there was a security guard in the Co-op and he had one hand on the phone and the other on a video camera as he watched you drive through the window and load up the truck," I said nonchalantly.

Apparently he didn't tell his lawyer, because several months later, my partner and I were summoned to court for the case. The pretrial consisted of the playing of the video, which had recorded how quickly and efficiently they had "worked," taking only three minutes to complete the theft and drive away. No wonder they were always long gone by the time police arrived! The defence changed the plea to "guilty" before the trial began. The judge insisted on seeing the video before sentencing. Nothing like a reality check for a system based less and less in the real world and more and more in the technicalities of law--technicalities based on semantics that valued the letter of the law over the spirit of it.

And maybe it was a good time for me to remember my priorities. I was getting a little too cynical, and it seemed like the perfect time to round out the family with the nicely balanced number four. I had no doubt my inspector in charge would not be impressed with the idea of losing me to another six-month maternity leave. It is too bad that the administrative rigidity of the Force did not allow for temporary replacements of manpower during such leaves. It certainly would have helped smooth some of the resentment that female members sometimes faced. But I was far too weathered at this point in my career to give the inspector's feelings any weight in our decision on family size.

Perhaps from my point of view what was most discouraging was the new legal "morality" that seemed to be spreading from the courts into mainstream Canadian society. One snowy day shift, not long after the B&E, I was reminded it wasn't just lawyers and criminals who now were willing to accept what was legal over what was right if it meant avoiding personal responsibility for their actions.

It was the kind of winter blizzard the Fraser Valley rarely got. By noon the roads were so dangerous with packed snow on black ice, the detachment deferred any non-emergency calls to the next day. Unfortunately, the motor vehicle accident on a country side street in the middle of Aldergrove Zone that afternoon had injuries making my attendance mandatory.

The ambulance and fire truck were already on scene and tending to the teenaged female passenger. If the truck had hit the pole six inches further back, she would have suffered much more than cuts, bruises, and minor fractures. The eighteen-year-old male driver was shaken but unharmed.

"Driver's licence and registration, please," I asked as I had thousands of times before.

"I wasn't speeding. I was going the speed limit, sixty kilometers per hour," the driver said defensively as he handed over his documents.

I wasn't in the mood to debate his driving actions, nor did I need to. The snow bore silent witness to the route his truck had taken, beginning at the top of a long, steep hill, first sideways as he hit the brakes, losing control, sliding into one ditch, then across the road as he overcorrected, going into the other ditch, then back on the road backwards as the momentum and gravity hastened his descent. Fortunately, the gully before the next hill slowed his vehicle somewhat before the hydro pole ended the slide completely.

I took refuge from the snow in my police car as I ran the driving history of the young man and filled out the paperwork. In two short years, he had received several speeding tickets and now two accidents. At least he hadn't killed anyone yet. The ambulance had left with the girl, and the driver was busy supervising the tow truck to insure no further damage occurred to his truck when I returned with his accident report and his ticket to sign.

"I told you I wasn't speeding," he protested.

"I didn't give you a speeding ticket. I gave you a ticket because you were travelling too fast for the weather and road conditions," I said.

"I don't think that is fair. I wasn't speeding," he said, reluctantly signing the ticket.

"There's more than one kind of ticket. I don't give many, but there is no doubt in my mind you deserve this one. If you wish to dispute it, the instructions are on the back. "

If he was looking for a break he was looking at the wrong person. He didn't seem to know how lucky he had been, how close he had come to killing his girlfriend or that he had endangered the lives of all the first responders who had to rescue him because he didn't know enough to stay off the ice and snow.

After the accident, I went to the Aldergrove Customs sub-office to wait out the storm and the rest of my shift. I was in a bad mood, still annoyed at this driver for showing more concern for his truck and driving record than his girlfriend, when the radio room relayed a request to phone the mother of the passenger concerning the accident. I had no sooner introduced myself when she began an unexpected challenge.

"I don't think it is fair to give Bobby a ticket if he wasn't speeding?"

"Whose mother are you?" I asked, thinking I must have misunderstood and it was Bobby's mother I was speaking to.

"I'm Mary's mother," she said.

"How is she?" When I had called the hospital they were stitching up her face and waiting for the x-ray results of her jaw and wrist.

"I am told she will be all right. She is still at the hospital. I am calling from work."

The answer surprised me. I would have thought she would be at the hospital taking care of her daughter, not defending the person who put her there. It seemed to me the mother and the daughter's boyfriend would have made a good pair; they both seemed to have their priorities upside down.

"How can you charge someone for speeding if they weren't speeding?" she continued aggressively.

"Perhaps if it was a speeding ticket, you might have a point, but it was not. It was a ticket for travelling too fast for driving conditions," I said, showing more patience than she deserved.

"If he was going the speed posted on the sign, I don't think you can give him a ticket," she insisted.

"The posted speed is meant for ideal driving conditions. On bad driving days, you have to drive slower. Would you like to take a moment to look outside?" I said, exhausting what was left of my patience.

"Then the signs should say that!" she argued back.

Her single-minded--or should I say simple-minded--assumption that unless it was in writing, common sense and the law could be challenged broke through the façade of unconditional politeness Depot had helped me build so long ago. Her willingness to look for loopholes in the law to avoid personal responsibility was a growing trend in Canadian society, and that was perhaps what annoyed me the most.

"We don't have large enough signs for stupid people," I said as I slammed down the receiver. I am sure she was as surprised at my terse concluding statement as I was. It was my voice, but it was pure George Monk speaking. I probably should have had second thoughts about my rudeness, but I didn't. I actually smiled as I thought back to the woman with the cat up the tree and realized I had become a lot like George over the years.

I phoned the station NCO to give him the heads-up that I might be on the wrong end of a complaint against a member, but surprisingly she didn't call again. Perhaps all it took was some "Monk reality" to help reset her priorities.

During my "light duties" this time, I was often left on the watch in the NCO's office, freeing the new sergeant, who hated being stuck in the office. It worked out well. He was happy, and I was a lot less bored, as acting station NCO, than I had been as a reader. I continued to schedule first-aid classes during some of our day shifts.

My life's path had been quite comfortable and predictable until Depot called to ask me if I was still interested in a corporal's position. The promotion board would be held in the spring to staff positions the following fall, coinciding perfectly with my maternity leave. Was this Destiny knocking again?

When I heard my name had surfaced because Depot was again looking at replacing members from the four female blocked positions, I was more than a little disappointed. I didn't think the Force still needed a quota system for females at Depot and I told him so.

"Well, Depot is only slightly less competitive than E Division in terms of service. You need at least fifteen years' service, ninety percent or higher on the five-year average for annual assessments, and a teaching background."

"If you have my file, perhaps you could tell me what am I deficient in?" I asked.

"Just a minute--it's right here."

After several minutes, he said, with a bit of surprise, "Actually, nothing. As a matter of fact, I think you have a very strong chance of being selected if you let your name stand. There are only six people being considered for the four spots. You'd better be sure you are prepared to move to Regina before you say 'yes' to the board."

"That is kind of you to say. I would like to discuss this with my husband tonight and I will call you tomorrow with my answer."

I called the next day to say that I would let my name stand. Two weeks after the verbal offer was made, the official written one made its way through the proper chain of command.

The CO of Depot informed the CO of E Division, who informed E Div. Staffing, who called the OIC of Langley. The chain of notification is a matter of military etiquette, a formality respecting the chain of command; but when the Staffing staff sergeant, T. Rex, called me at home to inform me of the board, it was clear more had been discussed at officer levels than just my board.

"Constable Hall, your name has surfaced for a promotion board at Depot."

"Thank you for the call. Please advise Depot I would be pleased to let my name stand."

I was still half asleep when I answered, having been awakened between two night shifts. S/Sgt. Rex's attitude provided the adrenalin boost I needed to shake the cobwebs from my mind.

He paused, then asked, "Do you need some time to discuss this with your husband first?"

"I already have, and we are in agreement," I answered. It could have been an innocent question, but his tone and inflections told me he had something on his mind other than my promotion board. He paused as if he were trying to bait me into talking to give him an opening. As an accomplished interrogator, I was a little insulted that he was trying that tactic on me. Finally, he broke the silence.

"I understand you are pregnant."

I could feel his hand on the rug under my feet. Digging in my heels, I replied, "That has nothing to do with this board."

"I disagree," he said coolly. "Suppose the board was held next week and you won. You would not be able to perform the duties until after you had the baby."

"On the contrary, the position is for an academic instructor and next week I am instructing in first aid, which requires a higher level of fitness. My pregnancy is irrelevant to the position at Depot they are staffing for one year from now."

"I disagree. I will advise Depot of your anticipated dates for maternity leave along with your willingness to remain on the board."

"The only information Depot needs is my acceptance of the board. If you go further, so will I."

He didn't care. He was a staff sergeant, which is a fireproof rank, in the most powerful and feared section of the Force. I knew he wouldn't comply with my request, and the following week, my copy of his correspondence with Depot confirmed it. It was time to see how high up the rank structure I could count on the system to provide a fair forum for disputes.

I called the current division representative, who happened to be Adrienne's husband, Jim Bresowski, and he was outraged. Staffing's malicious meddling could taint the board against me, and he promised to do what he could to minimize the damage.

The results of the board came back just before I left for maternity leave. I had lost the board, but the support I had from the watch was comforting. All of the men were upset for me. My pregnancy was the only obvious reason for my failure. I was flattered by the support, but wasn't ready to jump to conclusions unless I could prove them. I began my own internal investigation.

I pulled my service file and read it from cover to cover for the first time. I had heard rumours of members who never knew a nasty memo had been placed on their file by an NCO or officer, tainting their reputation and impacting promotions in a cowardly form of silent career assassination. I had stepped on only a few toes in my career but at least one of them was still limping from it. The file was like reading a professional biography, from the first contact at Kingston Detachment, the score on my entrance exam, to every Depot assessment, every annual assessment, and a complete list of every course I had taken or taught while in the Force. I had no idea I had such a great service file. It would provide indisputable support for my candidacy as a Depot instructor.

Next I pulled the Depot board, which had been taped. Everything had been going smoothly during the board. Each board member read a candidate's service file, start to finish, then commented on the quality of his or her performance to date. The NCO who read mine was very supportive. At the point in my file when I received my first assessment after returning to contract work at Langley, he paused and said, "I really don't understand why this member hasn't been sponsored for the officer candidate program."

It was high praise I had not expected. After all, my old boss and friend Tom Hill had told me back when I decided to get married that the Force would "write you off."

Shortly after that statement, one of the board members asked for an adjournment, and there was a long, unrecorded break. When the tape resumed, the board voted, and I came in dead last.

Having completed my investigation, I felt confident that not only had I been the victim of sexual bias, but I could prove it; and for the first and only time in my career, I launched a grievance.

My old Break and Enter teammate Dave Zack was the division representative, and he assisted me in writing my grievance. When we got to the last portion of the form, he typed in under suggested resolution "a promotion at Depot." I objected to this.

There was no way under the sun that I would ever enter a position at Depot under the cloud of a grievance. He patiently explained to me that a member cannot launch a grievance without asking for a resolution, and it was standard on promotional grievances to ask for the original promotion. Even though it almost never happened, it still had to be requested.

He didn't quite understand why the position at Depot had been forever tainted, in my mind. I was too proud to accept a promotion because of a dispute; to have worked so hard for so long, only to come into a position under the cloud of a grievance. To my mind, a win by default was not a win.

"I'm not doing this for a promotion. I am doing this to prevent a future board from doing this again," I explained.

"You know they will anyway," Dave said. His honesty shocked me.

Although he was no doubt right, I didn't care. This was a matter of principle, a matter of fairness, and, like any member with my service, I was not going to let them away with it. Windmills still presented an irresistible challenge.

"Put in another resolution, one that I can live with," I asked.

"All right, how about a promotion within the list of indicated positions on your parade document," he suggested.

"Perfect. Now how do I remove Depot from the list quickly?" I replied.

The first level of grievance was launched within weeks of Katherine's birth, February 17, 1993. Our family was complete, and I was looking forward to a quiet, relaxed maternity leave. But Depot intruded once again.

A letter came from Depot asking me to take the Instructional Techniques course, which by inference meant they were prepared to take me as an instructor. The old squeaky wheel principle seemed to be working well within the Force. I phoned Dave at Headquarters to advise him, and he immediately responded: "Congratulations, Corporal!"

It was clear to Dave and me that Depot was probably trying to avoid the grievance by giving me what they thought I wanted; but I wouldn't be bought and I wouldn't be silenced. I refused the course and proceeded with the grievance. I returned to work in Langley in September 1993 as a senior constable on a new watch.

Aldergrove was the least popular of all the zones because it was a sleepy bedroom community that was quite a distance from most of the action in Langley. It was boring. Its only variations from farmland were a small town centre comprised of a few stores, a blue-collar pub, and a small mall.

"Dead" spots for reception and transition of our portable radios meant the zone member's safety was often compromised. Even if a radioed request for assistance got out, backup was at least twenty minutes away--and a lot can happen in twenty minutes.

Out of necessity, zone members operated as if we were policing a small, two-man detachment. Both members tended to get involved early in each other's files; it was safer that way. It was a precautionary measure that paid off in dividends one sleepy afternoon shift.

I can't recall who was assigned the "suspicious occurrence," but both Steve Giesenger and I attended. Experienced police officers know if a member of the public feels something is suspicious enough to call the police, nine times out of ten he/she is correct. Such calls are omens for much bigger problems and pending offences, like seagulls moving inland ahead of an ocean storm.

The complainant, who lived on one of the many five-acre parcels in the Poppy Estates area, had answered her door to find a large, disoriented man wearing only jeans and sneakers. His upper body, arms, and face were covered in scratches as though he had been running through the bushes for some time. He was out of breath, quite agitated and paranoid as he rambled on about Vietnam, being chased by the FBI and CIA. She asked him to remain on the porch as she made the call on his behalf for a taxi; but when she returned to the door, he had fled.

Steve and I recorded his description in our notebooks: thirty-eight, maybe forty years old, six feet three, 230 pounds, an unkempt red afro, no shirt and "a wild animal-like look" in his eyes. Not the kind of person to go unnoticed, even in a crowd. As we walked back to our police cars, Steve said, "Either we are going to get lucky and this guy has gone back into the bush, at least until our shift is over, or--"

I finished, "--or he is making his way to either the Alder pub or the mall."

Steve nodded and we both headed for the town centre, to our sub-office located on the second floor of the mall. The phone was ringing as we entered and Langley dispatch advised us of the next "suspicious occurrence."

A male matching our wild man's description had wandered into a dentist's office, just down the hall from our office, asking for drugs. On our arrival, we were told he had left the office five minutes ago.

"He is either stoned or psychotic; possibly both," the dentist suggested.

It was what we had already suspected, but it didn't hurt to have a professional doctor's opinion if we needed grounds later under the Mental Health Act.

"The mall," Steve suggested.

It was the most logical place for the suspect to go next and it was also the worst. On hot summer days, the air-conditioned mall was often crowded with young mothers and their children. It was much more of a social than a shopping event, with moms visiting on the mall benches as their children played. The buzz of their chatter fell quiet as Steve and I entered, and they all looked in the direction of the B.C. Telephone store. As we approached, a frantic voice cut through the silence from within: "You need to do this for me. I haven't any money but I need to get in touch with--"

"I think these people want to talk to you," said the young clerk, pointing with great relief at Steve and me standing at the door.

What a sight the man was! Often female witnesses overestimate the size of males, but unfortunately that was not the case this time. The blood from the scratches that covered his torso seemed to highlight his long, strong, and well-defined muscles in the way body wax is used by bodybuilders. He had that "look" Steve and I had both dealt with before. Even small, untrained "mentals" are dangerous, but a man this size, in this state, would take at least six large members to restrain. If we could not resolve the matter peacefully, the mall could easily be turned into a killing field.[39] Steve and I exchanged a brief look acknowledging that we both understood how high the stakes were.

I reached into my mental catalogue of police experience and again pulled out the one that Smokey Stovern, a wise old NCO, had gifted me years ago: "Help"--the most powerful word in the English language.

"Yes, come out here. I think I can help you," I said.

As I stepped forward, Steve, following my lead, stepped into the background. The suspect instinctively focused on him, assessing the threat. Steve smiled back and gestured open-handed, inviting him to step out into the hall with me.

"I'm sure I can help," I said, drawing his attention back to me. The suspect slowly joined me by the centre bench.

"We can help. What do you want?" I asked.

The question seemed to take him by surprise. "What do I want?" he mused quietly; then he began, slowly at first.

"I want to live in peace. I want to sleep in a bed. I want the police, the FBI and the CIA to stop following me." He was beginning to rant. "I want to kill the president. I want--"

He was working himself into a state--one that had to be defused quickly. He began rocking slightly back and forth, from his heels to his toes, and slapping his wrists together, harder, then harder again as he worked his body into the same chaotic state his soul was in.

"You don't care who I am. You don't know who I am, what I have done or what I am--"

I certainly didn't want to let him finish that line.

"But I do know. I know you were in Vietnam."

The comment froze him, snapping him out of his self-induced disconnect from the present.

"How do you know that?" he asked. That was a tricky question. He had already given me information that he distrusted the police. He thought he was

[39] Loose play on the title of a book on Vietnam, *The Killing Fields*.

being followed and targeted. How did I know about him if I wasn't part of the conspiracy in his mind?

"I could tell by your posture, by your actions, by your demeanour that you are a trained soldier. We know--we are Mounties--we are military, too. I can hear your American accent. You're in Canada now. Sit down and tell me how we can help you." And with that I sat, and to everyone's relief, he joined me.

As we spoke, Steve cleared as many shoppers as he could make eye contact with from the mall, and when the hall was close to empty, I asked the suspect to follow me and I would take him to a safe place where he would get a supper, a place to sleep, and a breakfast. It wasn't much, but it was better than he had in his immediate future. He agreed.

We walked side by side down the hall towards the exit, but when the police cars became visible through the glass mall doors, he almost had a change of heart. No doubt the sight of police cars was a familiar one to him--an image that awakened memories of unpleasant events.

"I am not getting into the back of one of those," he said as he stopped mid-stride and his eyes began to glaze again. If we weren't quick and smart enough, all of our efforts were about to be undone. This time it was Giesenger who had a stroke of brilliance. Steve, who had never been more than an arm's reach from us, stepped out of the background and whispered, "You don't want to scare the kids, do you?"

This snapped the suspect back to our reality as he looked at the few children still watching from behind their mothers.

"No, I don't."

As I shut the door to the back seat of my police car, finally containing him somewhat, Steve burst out--still in whispered tones-- "Thank God I was with a female member!"

I smiled. It was the first time a male member had articulated his appreciation for the de-escalating effect female members had on many police situations. Members would still rather avoid a fight than win one--or in this case, lose one very badly.

During the car ride back to the office, the suspect talked a little about his experience in Vietnam. He had been trained on a Special Forces unit in "Nam." I was surprised to hear him say he had completed three tours and couldn't help but ask why he would return twice by choice to a war he hated so much.

He hung is head as he answered coldly, "Because killing is the only thing I was ever really good at."

There was no bragging in the reply. The chilling thing about the statement was its absolute truth and his awareness of it. There was no place for him now in

American society and that was why he hated it and its politicians so much.

Before I left shift that day, I CPICed our federal sections and the American authorities about his threats against presidents and politicians. No one was particularly concerned. I guess Vietnam had created a lot of these types of disenfranchised men, who after twenty years had not been able to shake the ghosts of the war and in all probability never would. The American baby boomers had weathered a much harsher reality than my generation.

It wasn't just American Vietnam veterans that were disillusioned. The baby boom members of the RCMP felt as though they, too, had been on the losing end of a war--a war against politics and time itself. The midnight shifts were getting harder and harder, the older we got. Injuries shaken off at Depot were beginning to resurface. I was not immune, as my hearing, damaged by gunfire at Depot, diminished and the tinnitus increased. Senior members were getting tired, not just physically but mentally and perhaps even spiritually. Everyone had his or her war wounds, but the one we all shared was the painful loss of our idealism.

BC's tough penalties for impaired drivers in combination with legal aid lawyers and the Charter resulted in generating more case law on impaired driving than any other crime, including murder. Impaired charges increasingly meant years of adjournments and court appearances. Even if the charge ended in conviction, the legal aid lawyer, after launching a ten-thousand-dollar defence for which the public picked up the tab, routinely asked for, and received from the court, a reduced fine--and, to add insult to injury, time to pay it.

For the first time in my career, I began issuing "Twenty-four-hour Suspensions."[40] It was instant cheap "justice." The motor vehicle branch hit the offender with ten points, resulting in an often heftier fine for his/her licence than the courts gave, without any drain on the public purse. Unfortunately, it also meant no criminal record. It was a benign decriminalizing that I felt was a huge legal and social step backward in the war against drunk drivers. It chafed my moral standards to be part of the trend but, like other members, I was losing faith in both the legal system and in myself to maintain the right. This was the only time in my service that I felt I was no longer serving at the level I was capable of; and I wasn't the only one.

[40] A police officer has the discretion to proceed with an impaired driving investigation involving a breathalyzer and trial, and to issue an immediate roadside driving suspension for twenty-four hours with a hefty fine and negative driving points against the suspect's licence. Twenty-four-hour suspensions were meant for borderline impaired drivers, but discouraged members began issuing them for obviously impaired drivers because they no longer trusted the justice system to convict for a crime that had been burdened with years of poor case law and technical legal defences.

There was anger building within the policing system. Trials were becoming increasingly about legal technicalities and less about guilt or innocence. Members no longer stayed to hear the outcome after giving their evidence because their trust in the system was broken. The accountability to the public for the administration of justice had been replaced by the rights of the accused.

The business of justice seemed to divert funds from providing prison spaces to legal aid lawyers. It would be interesting to see a cost analysis of the changes to the justice system and if it was, as some of us suspected, possible that the taxpayer was actually paying more for less "justice." The very foundation of Canadian justice was being slowly eroded by a fiscal shell game.

The return radius for arrest warrants issued by local judges began to shrink. In many cases, arrest warrants appeared to be not a sentence to jail or prison time but rather a "get out of town" order by the local judge. Perhaps that might have been accepted as prudent fiscal offloading in the new economics of government, but it made no sense from a public safety or justice point of view.

Even the most disillusioned of old-school Mounties were shocked at the string of warrants transplanted criminals from the East had on the CPIC system by the time they reached the lower mainland. You could track every town they hit on their trans-Canada crime spree. Not surprisingly, the criminals did not try to run down to the U.S., where criminals still did serious time for serious crime. Why should they? British Columbia became the preferred province to be sentenced in.

British Columbia did not have the finances, the prison spaces, or the desire to foot the bill of incarceration attached to the growing migration of Eastern criminals. This resulted in sentences in B.C. becoming lighter and lighter, until they were the lightest in the country. It was a trend that served the criminals and the bean counters well, but not the public or the principle of justice the RCMP had guarded for over a century.

Even the judges' ranks seemed frustrated with their shrinking ability to dispense justice. Traditional judicial discretion had been almost crippled by the *Charter*. Everyone's expectations of the justice system were low and only getting lower.

The public no longer bothered reporting "victimless crimes" such as thefts from vehicles, hit and runs, wilful damage, and property crime, unless the insurance company required a police report. After all, it wasn't as if the police would even attend, let alone conduct an investigation, for such "trivial" offences. One senior member sarcastically joked: "Don't think of yourself as a crime investigator anymore--we are all just *crime recorders* now."

Soon the insurance companies actively discouraged theft reports by increasing premiums for repeat claims. Who knew crime could be "eliminated" by fiscal bullying?

Crime statistics recorded drops in crime rates that were in reality drops in reporting crime. The less crime reported, the more the new business model for the justice system was hailed as a success; at least that was the theory the politicians used to defend their methodology. You know what they say about statistics and politicians. It wasn't just the public who felt "the administration of justice" was now in disrepute.

Members were having a hard time dealing with their shrinking ability to maintain the right in Canadian society, and the senior members felt the greatest angst on the matter. After all, we were the ones who truly understood what we had lost. In good faith, we could no longer tell the victims of a crime that justice would be done. When as a peace officer you can't look the victim of a rape or a child molestation in the eye, it gets as difficult to look at yourself in the mirror. Members openly remarked that if their children were victims of a violent crime, it would be dealt with outside of the justice system.

It was into this growing professional disenfranchisement that Ottawa decided to add the last straw. The promotion system was going to be gutted and "modernized." Years of experience and job performance would have no value in the proposed system. Only an exam score, open to all members with seven years' service, followed by an interview, would determine who would be promoted. Members, who already felt betrayed by the justice system, were now faced with betrayal from within. The mood in the Force had grown dark.

The dangerous undertow in the Force was gaining strength. I, too, might have been sucked down into it, but suddenly the tide changed--at least for me.

My name surfaced for the last promotion board before the first exam cycle. It was an unusual double board to staff two corporal positions as training NCOs at Surrey. I could think of no job in the Force I would rather have than that of training NCO in the largest detachment in Canada, only a twenty-minute commute from my home.

It was too good to hope for, so I refused to allow myself to get excited. I had lost boards I should have won before. This time I would be the underdog, two years below the average service for promotions in E Division.

"Congratulations, Corporal!"

My new staff sergeant had tracked me down on days off to give me the news. It is widely known among the dinosaurs that the first promotion is always the hardest, and happiest, one to get. It took a day or two for it to sink in. It just didn't seem real until the following day when I got a call from an old friend, the other new corporal from the board, Cathy Robertson. Cathy had been the first female member to welcome me to North Vancouver, and now she was the first to welcome me to the new rank. Finally, I had everything I had been wishing for.

Chapter 13

Humpty Dumpty

The welcome Cathy and I received from the officers and administration NCOs at Surrey was reassuring but we knew not everyone at our new detachment would be as open and accepting of us, considering how elusive and rare promotional opportunities had become for most members.

Naturally, our senior years of service and assessment scores would not be part of the Detachment's rumours of affirmative action, "fixed" boards, and political interference. How else could bruised egos accept that the only two females on a board of six had won? The reality was that senior female members who had survived the years were faring well under the old promotion system. Although there were only a handful of female corporals in E Division at that time, the numbers were steadily growing.

As female NCOs, we knew we would have to prove ourselves worthy all over again, only this time we would be proving we were capable as supervisors, not just members. We also accepted that we would have to repeat this trial every time we were transferred or promoted, for the rest of our service. That was how it had been and would continue to be for the first females on each rung in the old male ladder--forging virgin territory each time.

At the end of the orientation tour of the Detachment, Cathy and I were finally left alone. Behind the closed door, we surveyed our new office for our very own section: Training Section. After checking out our new desks and filing cabinets, we both ended up at our window, which looked down onto the Constables' Room on the far side of the interior courtyard. Our eyes met several male constables looking up at us. We smiled and waved, but they did not acknowledge the gesture; they disengaged their glare and returned to their desks. It was nothing more than we had expected.

"Nothing has changed," said Cathy, unable to suppress her smile. The junior constables with the icy stares had no understanding or appreciation for how tough Cathy and I had had to be to have earned the right to our new positions.

"Only us," I suggested.

As Cathy and I had weathered our eighteen and sixteen years of service, we had changed. We were no longer "green" and had plenty of "wear," and a little baggage as well. Through the years of experience in adapting to the Force, we both had developed survival strategies suited to our personalities.

Cathy always managed to avoid confrontations, even if she had to bend a little. On the other hand, I had been unprepared to bend, a trait that had resulted in the confrontations I have written about. Though the confrontations had been relatively few in number, and so far I had won each of them, they had taken a toll. I hoped my grievance over the Depot promotion, slowly making its way through the system, would be my last.

Cathy and I made a nice team because our strengths lay in different areas. Cathy didn't mind the more administrative nature of the section and handled loading courses outside the Detachment and monitored the recruit field training. I handled in-service training and the auxiliary program.

Surrey had over 300 members, 120 civilian staff, and 40 auxiliaries. The office of the training NCO had been run by a corporal and a constable assistant prior to our promotions, both of whom had been promoted out a month before our board. The constable's position was upgraded to a second corporal, resulting in a double promotion board, a most unusual event in E Division.

I wondered if my grievance had had any impact on the circumstances that caused our board. If not for the double board in my specialized field of training, my name would not have surfaced for the promotion board.

The morning coffee flips outside the superintendent's office were a comforting echo of North Vancouver Detachment. Everyone was equal and felt comfortable contributing to the occasional war story as we chit-chatted. Although the further up the rank structure members went the more administrative their duties became, members with strong operational roots retained the common sense that career administrative Mounties seemed to lack. My staff sergeant recounted a story over morning coffee illustrating this point.

A section NCO was tasked with interviewing a member in a northern isolated posting. The trip required a flight north followed by a four-hour trip by snowmobile in sub-zero temperatures. The NCO dug out of his closet his winter dress, which would offer enough protection for everything except his feet. He purchased mukluks in the north and claimed them on his expense account upon his return to Vancouver. (It is perhaps timely to note that this old-school Mountie, unlike career civil servants and politicians, always claimed only the *actual costs* of meals and other travel expenses, rather than the per diem maximum rate offered by the federal government.)

The NCO at Financial Services Section (FSS) rejected the claim for the mukluks because there was no provision for extraordinary expenses in the Admin manual list of travel expenses. Common wisdom within the ranks of operational members held that both the Administration and Operational Manuals within the Force were guides for a wise man and bibles for a fool. Clearly the FSS NCO was the latter. A paper war followed over the mukluks. The cost in terms of lost productivity over what became a lengthy and nasty dispute quickly overtook the cost of the mukluks. But that didn't stop either the section NCO, who was fighting on principle, or the FSS member, who was fighting because he was a bean counter and didn't know any better. The section NCO lost the final appeal, but the FSS NCO's victory was short-lived, because the section NCO turned the system back on itself. On the next trip, the section NCO submitted his expense claim for the maximum amount of claims he was allowed. At the bottom of the sheet, he added a postscript addressed to his nemesis in FSS, which read: "The mukluks are in here--try to find them."

The war *didn't end there*, because from that point on, the section NCO claimed the maximum allowed travel amounts, making that pair of mukluks the most expensive boots the Force has ever purchased.

Administrative minds did not seem to realize how much money the goodwill of the average operational member saved the government by claiming actual expenses and only a portion of the overtime they worked.

The management at the top of Surrey Detachment was sound and positive, based on experience, not theories. One of the two inspectors was particularly outgoing. The first day I passed his office, he asked if I had a home life.

"I'm married to a member and have four children, aged seven, four, two, and nine months," I said, searching his face for his reaction.

"Wow!" He seemed both surprised and impressed. "You don't get a chance to sit down, do you," he said.

"Just when I come to work," I replied.

We both laughed, but there was more truth in the statement than humour. Some days I felt like I was being paid to take a break while my live-in nanny fed the children and cleaned my house.

Cathy had remained single and enjoyed a large group of friends. Her carefree, upbeat personality reminded me of Joyce Graham, with whom she had worked on Drug Squad. Training was only a step in her career for her, and after the mandatory two years in the position expected after promotion, she intended to return to Drug Squad as an operational NCO.

Cathy had noticed that so far none of the female promotions in the division had been to operational roles. She wanted to be one of the first. I was as sure she would succeed as I was that Bev Busson would be the first female commissioner.

I had placed a bet for lunch with now-retired Tom Hill concerning my prediction for Bev's final rank. I found it encouraging that such capable senior female members, the foundation layer for future females in the Force, had survived and were aiming high. It would be twelve years before I would win my bet.

I couldn't believe the luck I had had in my career to finally have the best of both worlds. Training Section allowed me to contribute meaningfully to the Force and enjoy a stable family life. This was what I had been wishing for. I really did have it all, at least for a few years.

I was just getting settled into my new role when Staffing called and asked for my help. They needed viable subjects who were not in the new promotion system to practise on, to train the NCOs who would be judging the interviews.

My promotion had exempted me from the first set of exams, and I would need at least one year in the rank if I wanted to write for sergeant. I agreed to help. I couldn't resist the chance to take a look at the system that was threatening to destroy the remainder of the *esprit de corps* of the Force.

It was only now beginning to register on the collective consciousness of members that the only way to be promoted was through the new system. It was my opinion that the underlying assumption of the new process demonstrated a huge lack of respect and understanding for the complexity of contract policing. No expertise or even experience was required to be placed in charge of specialized sections. Under the new system, a seven-year "corporal" could be placed in management positions over experienced veterans who'd had decades of expertise on specialized sections like commercial crime, drugs, or major crimes. A traffic cop could supervise a drug section under this system. Successful candidates who parroted the correct management clichés--clichés that had become the mantra of everyone in Ottawa--knew the new, hidden code words needed to attain rank and power within the Force. The civilian who had helped develop the process would be present for the "training interview" I had been invited to participate in, providing me with the opportunity to ask some questions.

It was mostly academic curiosity and a bit of anarchy that motivated my attendance. The interview would have no impact on my career, so I didn't bother to research and prepare for the task. I assumed they would be looking for a member with well-rounded service, both operationally and administratively, someone who'd had success in acting positions, and I framed my responses accordingly for the panel of NCOs asking questions. I could tell they were impressed by the variety and depth of my service, and the complexity of some of my investigations. In the old system, I would have been a shoo-in.

When it was over, one of the sergeants from Manitoba came over to chat; but it wasn't just a social visit. Halfway through his visit, he looked around discreetly, then in hushed tones he slipped me a piece of advice: "Use the word 'I' next time, and use it a lot."

I appreciated his hint, but unfortunately it supported my suspicions that this new system had been designed without any understanding or appreciation for the manner in which the Force operated outside of Ottawa. The Force military model functioned on the "plural" self, the one dedicated to the good of the larger society. Ottawa had rewritten the rules to reward those who thought in the "singular," where the individual was more important than the whole.[41] There would be no more "troop of one" under this model, only "one"--those who were "legends in their own minds." The new system, which would reward narcissistic tendencies without regard for a supervisor's assessment of work performance, appeared fundamentally opposite to the military culture of the RCMP and the promotion system that had operated within the RCMP for over 100 years. I couldn't resist an opportunity to speak to a representative from Ottawa.

"I am just curious," I began. "I am willing to suspend my disbelief and entertain that it is possible this new promotion system will identify the best leaders for the Force." Perhaps not the best foot to get started on, but I really didn't care. I continued.

"What strategies do you have in place to help the senior members who will soon realize they will probably never rise above their current rank in the new system?"

The condescension in her voice and the irritation at the insolence of my question answered my question better than her well-rehearsed response: "They will be upset at first but within three months they will return to their pre-exam performance, and it will have little or no effect on their morale in the long term."

I shook my head in disagreement as I said, "Those aren't the members I have been working with for the past sixteen years." And with that I left, wondering if it was ignorance or design that was about to shake the Force to its foundations.

The Force had been based on military tradition and a model of a co-operative team approach to serving the public. One of the strengths of the Force had always been that its officers had to rise through the ranks by working alongside

[41] Aristotle wrote about this competing concept of self, and I like to believe he would have seen the new model the Force was adopting as a regression, or, at the very least, inappropriate for a guardian institution.

everyone else--a "troop of one." The "I" attitude was the psychological opposite of that of the rank and file at the time.

Members had no respect for large egos who thought in terms of "I" rather than "we," because those people tended to be the ones who looked for shortcuts to feed those egos, often finding them in administrative positions. It was now clear that from those positions they had collaborated in Ottawa and changed the system, creating a new order of things, one better suited to the new business model of the Force. It didn't seem to matter to them that these system changes were being introduced at the worst time, with morale declining and Ottawa about to deliver a crushing financial blow to an already under-funded Force: a five-year pay and increment freeze.

It was a one-two punch from which the Force might never recover. How lucky I was to be where I was, in a position I had so long coveted, even if Len had been caught off-guard along with the rest of the operational senior constables in the West.

I was hurt to see that Len had to endure not just ambiguous teasing from the members of the Force concerning his wife's outranking him, but the almost malicious jokes from men outside the Force as well. He never complained. He knew I was senior, and had been at the right place at the right time; still it must have hurt, because I was breaking one of the three social taboos both Len and I had been brought up with.

At least for the short term, my career was more successful. I felt disappointed and uncomfortable that society still wasn't ready to accept non-traditional roles within a family.

I had never intended to become a role model for others, so I was surprised and unsettled when some junior members and even the female civilian staff told me I was an inspiration to them. I must have looked to them like living proof that success in professional and personal life was possible for the modern woman. The unsolicited social responsibility added extra weight I didn't need against my personal and professional walls.

Although I projected confidence and power in my professional life, I wasn't always sure I was on the right path. The competing and conflicting demands of two full-time responsibilities, work and home, were beginning to wear me down. However, I believed success was still possible if I could just strike the right balance between home and office, and if the work environment remained positive. I was careful not to complain aloud about my load when so many good members were facing much less attractive professional and personal paths.

Many of my peers and friends, too busy doing their jobs to take the time to study for the exam, had left themselves vulnerable to the new process.

Administration members who had the time or the nerve to spend hours of their workday studying the volumes of manuals in preparation for the exam out-scored the busy general duty and plainclothes general investigation section members.

The exam had been a closely guarded secret, *at least in E Division*, where operational members assumed it would be a form of competency measure; but they were mistaken. Theories of community policing and pseudo-management fads in Ottawa became the bonus marks required to make the cut for the interview board.

Everyone who fell short would have to mark time for two more years until the next exam was scheduled. After several months, the exam marks were finally available. A good example of how skewed the selection process was lay in the failure of the members of the Surrey GIS section to pass the exam. This busiest serious crime section within the RCMP, which recruited the most talented investigators and interviewers, with a work ethic to match, was renowned in the Division; and under the new system, they were not considered worthy of promotion. How did they feel to be so betrayed?

One of my friends from North Vancouver, who dropped by my office immediately after learning of his mark, answered that question.

"I just feel sick, Jane," he said. "It feels like someone hit me in the stomach and I just can't shake it. I will never put my red serge on again."

He was a seventeen-year member, a high performer who had taken every transfer and position the Force had asked of him, and was within six months of promotion under the old system. But now all of his past service and sacrifice meant nothing because he was one mark short.

I didn't have to look far to confirm that my friend's reaction was representative within the ranks of senior constables. Experience had taught me that in times of workplace strife, female members sometimes become a lightning rod for anger. It easier to dislike someone you don't know, and few knew me at Surrey. My new training duties would have kept me isolated on the second-floor administrative offices of Surrey if I had not decided to be proactive and to change that.

I scheduled 250 of the 325 members on Detachment for a one-day refresher course in first aid. I called in and re-qualified two lapsed first-aid instructors to assist me because it would take three months and a lot of work to get the training done. I was looking forward to getting to know who was who in the zoo.

It was an open secret that some members did not want the course, especially if it was going to be taught by a female at a rank they might never achieve for themselves. Others were happy to take the course, looking for an opportunity to vent their growing anger at the Force on anyone in authority. As an old chess player, I always began the course with a good offensive observation.

"Some of you don't want to be here because you think I am going to tell you to lock lips doing CPR on some shitrat you just choked out. You don't yet understand this is an officer survival course in which we will teach you how to avoid infectious diseases like hepatitis B and HIV. You also might not realize that you are more likely to use the skills I am teaching *off* the job than *on*.

"Some of you don't want to be here because you think you don't like me, even though you don't know me yet. At the end of the day, you still may not like me, but at least you will know who I am and what I am about."

For the first few hours of each day, I was kept on my toes, but by the end of the day, everyone understood and liked each other a whole lot better. It didn't matter to me if the individual members chose to continue disliking me; at least they now knew who I was.

My prediction that the members were more likely to use the first aid off the job than on became reality for one traffic member only weeks after he completed his training, when he was able to save his own three-month-old baby from choking. There were a lot fewer "no shows" for the course after that incident.

Just as the first-aid course was wrapping up, the second of Ottawa's one-two punches landed. It became official that the RCMP would be included in the federal government's five-year pay and increment freeze--a fate, it was widely rumoured, we would have avoided, had the head of one of the most powerful unions in Ottawa not threatened to strike if the Force was exempted. It still amazed me that members in the West were so in touch with the backroom deals of Ottawa, while Ottawa seemed so completely unaware of the West.

The members of the lower mainland, the most expensive place to live in Canada, were boiling with anger, and the division representatives scheduled road trips to detachments in an attempt to quell the collective outrage resulting from both the impending new promotion cycle and the new pay freeze.

At the Surrey meeting, the crowd spilled into the large foyer, which soon filled with members from many of the surrounding detachments who lived in the area. The meeting had to be adjourned to a more suitable venue, and two weeks later, a thousand angry Mounties congregated at Shannon Hall in Surrey.

Never before in the history of the Force had that many members ever been in one place at one time for such an event. The two division representatives took the stage to facilitate the meeting.

There were two microphones, one at the front of the seats and one at the back of the hall for members to use when addressing the speakers on stage. The media was there, but not allowed into the meeting itself. Rank did not matter that night. Thirty-five-year staff sergeants stood beside two-year constables. We were still a troop of one.

The audience was advised that the commanding officer of E Division and my boss, the OIC of Surrey, were standing by at Surrey Detachment, ready to attend if the membership wanted them to. We took a vote and they were invited.

While we waited, members grilled the division representatives over the pending new promotion cycle and the pay/increment freeze. Senior members spoke in defence of the junior constables who would suffer great financial hardship in the LMD postings under the increment freeze. Senior members also attacked the pending implementation of the promotion list under the new exam/interview system. It was clear that there was overwhelming opposition and distrust concerning the exam/promotion process.

After the officers arrived, the commanding officer spoke candidly regarding the pay issues.

The federal government was broke. The financial model Ottawa had embraced and implemented for over the past two decades had done more than undermine the service delivery system of services for Canadians; it had brought the country to the brink of bankruptcy. Canada was facing the very real possibility of currency devaluation similar to what New Zealand had been through recently.

For the good of the country, the members might have been prepared to fall on their swords and accept a pay freeze, but not a pay *increment* freeze, which would have had a devastating effect on the junior constables, particularly in Lower Mainland. No one wanted the clock turned back to where junior members were forced, once again, to rent out basement suites and count every penny. The membership expected the RCMP to at least try to champion the junior constables' cause.

The membership in the room also made it clear that they understood that even if the fiscal policy of the government might be beyond the Force's control, changes to the proposed new promotion system were not, because we in the West thought the process was solely the creation of the RCMP Headquarters in Ottawa.

Members were lined up waiting for their turn at the microphone at the front and at the rear of the hall. It's a scary thing to speak in front of your own peers; even scarier if there are a thousand of them.

Members who had handled life and death situations flawlessly stumbled for words and looked frustrated at their inability to articulate their complaints. I urged Len to speak on the points, because he was a trained media spokesperson; but he declined. "If you feel that strongly, then you do it."

He was right, so I reluctantly moved to the back of the room to await my turn in line--a wait I was grateful for, because it gave me time to get my breathing under control. I was a trained public speaker, fresh from teaching my first-aid course, but my audiences had never been more than forty people. The surge of adrenalin that quickened my heart and flushed my face, as I looked at the sea of members sitting shoulder to shoulder in the room, needed to be controlled. No other female member had spoken and none probably would. I needed to do a good job, to leave a good impression.

Finally, it was my turn, and I took one big, deep, relaxing breath. Just as I was about to begin, a male member at the front started to speak. The commanding officer, who had been watching the only female member foolish or brave enough to line up to speak out, interrupted him by politely saying, "The young lady at the back has been waiting, and I believe it is her turn."

The room fell silent as every eye in the place turned to see. It was intoxicatingly scary, but it didn't stop me. I spoke for five minutes, straight from the heart of every member in the room. I have never enjoyed speaking so much in my life. I could have spoken about either of the two compelling issues, the new promotion system or the pay increment freeze. I decided to speak on the pay issue since so many others had already articulated the key points of contention with the new promotion system. I was in The Zone. In the middle of my speech, I even injected some unexpected humour to emphasize the short-sightedness of cost-cutting changes, which now meant cadets at Depot paid for a portion of their training and were offered employment only after graduation.

"The RCMP is going to ask a young man or woman fresh out of Depot: 'How would you like to come and work for us in Lower Mainland, where we will pay you . . . just above the poverty line, where you will work long hard hours . . . because of chronic understaffing, and by the way . . . we won't give you a raise for the next five years . . .' and if they say 'yes,' . . . THEY ARE NOT SMART ENOUGH TO BE WORKING FOR US--" (I had to wait for a minute or two until the laughter died down to continue)-- "because they can go back to hometown Nova Scotia and afford a home and a life, or cross the pond to Vancouver and make a lot more money to do a lot less work."

The room thundered with laughter, then with applause as I followed it up with my concluding statement.

"Sir, when are we going to tell the media that this isn't about pay, it's a public safety issue, because we are going to breach our contracts in LMD?"

It was a strong finish that might have played well in the media and sparked my second standing ovation, even though everyone in the room knew members would continue to work in undermanned detachments regardless of safety issues because of their sense of duty to the general public.

The feeling of pride and camaraderie I experienced in that moment is still indescribable. In speaking out, I had been both reckless and brave, and that was something members could understand and respect.

If I needed corroboration that this time the tone was much more insubordinate than it was at the Deer Lake meeting in 1979[42] I had it when I was finished speaking and one of the first people to shake my hand was a sergeant from Internal. The next person was my old partner Mike Draper, unexpectedly in town for a course. There were many others I had worked with and respected; members of the extended family of the Force. It seemed everyone was there. I was as proud of myself as everyone else seemed to be.

Suddenly, in the midst of hugs and handshakes, I was tapped on the shoulder by another sergeant I knew, who led me to an outside room in the hope that I could be as articulate for the news cameras as I had been for the members.

I was not. I quickly found that speaking to a camera and a fuzzy microphone was a skill I did not have. Thankfully, I was so bad at it they didn't use the footage. If I hadn't been so shocked and intoxicated by the response of the members, I would not have agreed to an interview in the first place.

On the way back to my seat, I passed by the line of members standing at the rear microphone waiting to speak. The member whose turn it was to speak stepped back as I passed and beckoned me to speak again. I was flattered but signalled my decline. I had already said more than I had planned to . . . more than I should have . . . more than was wise.

For the second time in my career, E Division had flexed its collective muscles, but while we had numbers, Ottawa had the power. E Division still viewed the issue as an internal matter the Force could resolve. The commanding officer asked for time to bring the matters to Ottawa's attention and get a response to the members' concerns. There was no doubt we had the attention of the commissioner. A debriefing telex was immediately sent that night from Surrey Detachment to him, even though it was the middle of the night in Ontario.

After Shannon Hall, I found it hard to return to my preferred strategy of maintaining a low profile. Stories of Shannon Hall and a feisty female corporal seemed to be spreading through the rank and file. I wasn't aware of the buzz until I dropped by Langley Detachment the next week and one of my old partners and fellow Effective Presentations instructor, Gary Begg, immediately

[42] Deer Lake was the meeting described in the earlier chapter on North Vancouver, in which Ottawa was first made to realize the members in the West had a breaking point that, for the good of the Force, should not be tested.

greeted me with: "What the hell did you say? Everyone is talking about how you rallied the troops."

It was both flattering and frightening, because I had no aspirations of becoming the voice of an insurrection. Some people, even the current division representatives, thought I was going to run in the next election for division representative.

It might have been tempting to seize the moment and try to be the first female member elected division representative in the West, but for two factors. The Division Representative position would have doubled my daily commute, stealing an hour or more each day from my family. Of equal importance in my decision-making process was the systematic frustration built into the position, which lacked both the independence and the power of a union, making it nearly impossible to truly represent and defend members' interests. Still, I might have considered it if I had been single or even just childless; but I was not. I had four children at home who increasingly needed me there to champion their causes. I had fought for choices, and I didn't have any trouble seeing the right one for me. My personal wall was already carrying its maximum load. I returned to my duties and tried to lower my profile once again.

My office back at Surrey became a neutral zone where members felt safe to come in occasionally to complain or talk about their growing disenfranchisement with the Force. Rumours were rampant. There was talk that there would be some compromise on the pay increment freeze, but only for junior constables, and only to guard against recruitment from outside police forces. Ottawa thought senior members of the Force would remain loyal and resist recruitment. Although this was true for the majority of senior members within striking distance of a pension, LMD lost many highly motivated, experienced senior constables (the workhorses of any detachment) to city police forces in the Vancouver area.

As the LMD members awaited the next meeting, it became clear that the new promotion system was still moving forward, and even though the first successful candidates in this new system would not be promoted for several more months, the writing was on the wall. Some members seemed depressed, almost in shock that they could be so betrayed by the Force; others gave in to the bitterness and started to talk about doing only the work required and nothing more--no more voluntary overtime that the Force relied on no more self-generated files. Often heated debates over coffee began to arise between members. A vocal few argued that if job performance didn't matter to the Force, why should it matter to the members? The justice system had been turned upside down, and now the Force was following suit. A new, nasty acronym began to be whispered at the senior constable rank: "FIDO."

FIDO had taken root in some demoralized American police forces that had lost faith in the courts to administer meaningful justice. Frustrated peace officers who adopted the FIDO mentality began to turn a blind eye to anything other than the calls assigned. Crimes witnessed on patrols that in the past would have sparked a self-generated call (such as drug possession or street corner trafficking) were ignored. Investigations that in the past would have led to charges were written off. FIDO was knocking at the door, but the members of the Force were not ready to invite it in.

FIDO was a symptom of a systemic breakdown in the system of justice; but for it to take hold in the RCMP, more than the courts and the laws had to fail. For FIDO to take hold, the members themselves had to lose heart in both the Force and their individual ability to make a difference--to maintain the right. More than the Force was in danger if members' morale collapsed and FIDO became an acceptable option.

FIDO stands for "Fuck It. Drive On."

The Force, which had stood proud and strong for over one hundred years, maintaining the right against often overwhelming odds, had never had to endure a prolonged attack from within.

On June 9th, 1994, at the North Surrey Senior Secondary High School, the second meeting occurred, at which the commanding officer would respond, as he had promised, to the concerns raised by the membership at Shannon Hall. The stakes were very high that night. The air was full of tension, apprehension, and a sense of history in the making. Even the ghosts were watching anxiously!

The school was larger than Shannon Hall and this time it was filled by members from the whole division, not just LMD. The mood at this meeting was different. Shannon Hall had been an impromptu meeting filled with members who still hoped it would be possible to influence Ottawa's new policies. This meeting would show the members if they had been successful.

The new heir apparent to Inkster, Phil Murray, had chosen to attend with an entourage of department heads from Ottawa. It was an encouraging sign, because there was enough rank on the stage to un-set, or at least modify, the new promotion cycle if they so decided.

From the beginning of the meeting, the dynamics on the stage were not encouraging. There was a certain rigidity in the commanding officer's introduction of the commissioner-in-waiting, body language that members like myself interpreted as a sign of his dissatisfaction at being upstaged by Ottawa. Murray's rank made him the man in charge that night.

In retrospect, Murray's presence might not have indicated a lack of confidence in the commanding officer to handle the dissidents, but rather Ottawa's complete ignorance of the anger seething in the operational members of the Force in E division. His presence did provide an opportunity for members to size up the new commissioner in his first test of leadership--a test for which he appeared unprepared for.

The members listened in disbelief as Murray spoke completely off topic. He thought members were upset with commuting to Vancouver Headquarters and that a promise to move the Vancouver Headquarters closer to where the members lived, in the Fraser Valley, would be a solution to our discontent.

It was insulting to think how little the East understood the West. Member after member took to the microphone to restate the major issue of Shannon Hall. He heard how E Division members felt about the new promotion process, which they believed was gravely flawed and unsupported by the majority of the operational members.

Members spoke, but still the message did not get through. I watched the audience's growing frustration and dissatisfaction with the responses given by the Ottawa officers. The clichés and pseudo-management psychology that Ottawa had been parroting kept spilling out of their mouths. It was like throwing gasoline on a simmering fire.

The tension in the room was quickly rising. The officers at the table on the stage felt it, but seemed at a loss as to how to defuse it. The division between East and West had never been so great, so focused, or so fraught with anger as that night in Surrey. No one at the table appeared willing to break with the party line. Worse, they seemed to believe that the crowd could be charmed by the same nonsensical rhetoric that controlled Ottawa. One of the officers from Ottawa stood up and tried to appeal to the members' loyalty to the Force.

"Stand up and hold the hand of your brother next to you."

We could only guess from which senior management course he had borrowed that "warm and fuzzy" exercise. The assembly was insulted. It was the largest communications failure I have ever witnessed.

There was a pregnant silence in the room as the reality of the irreconcilable differences on both sides of the table sank in. Then, a very senior, very well-respected NCO stepped to the microphone; a quiet mountain of a man from a bygone era. His long career had personified "Monty Mountie."

"Sir, you have inherited a demoralized, fractured Force," he said, speaking directly to Murray.

Then he turned his back to the stage in a powerfully rude act of defiance as he addressed the audience of members.

"I am toast," he said. We all assumed he was referring to his imminent retirement--a wise move, considering his actions. "It is time for you young ones to decide what you want out of the Force."

Then turning to the stage, he said in a strong and respectful voice, "It is time for you to leave, Sirs."

It was a shockingly insubordinate statement, one that left the officers on stage motionless, unable to respond. Never in the history of the RCMP had there been such a large-scale breaking of ranks. The officers from Ottawa seemed completely lost as to how to deal with it. Only ten years earlier, it would have been unthinkable that this could happen within the RCMP. They sat, red-faced and silent, until the NCO spoke again, repeating his request.

"It's time for you to leave, Sirs."

All eyes were on Commissioner-elect Murray, waiting for him to react, to make the first move. But still he remained motionless, frozen in an apparent mixture of rage and disbelief, until suddenly someone stood up in the audience and began slowly clapping his hands and chanting, in an act of defiance that was immediately joined by every member in the audience, as we stood shoulder-to-shoulder, clapping and singing:

"Nan nan nana Nan nan nana hey hey goodbye!"

The auditorium thundered with our insubordination. And still those on the stage remained motionless. The longer the chant went on, the louder it got. It was a battle of wills, a battle between East and West, a battle that for once was being fought where the Force was strongest--the West. Finally, Murray rose, in an admission of defeat and, without a word, led the red-faced group of officers from the stage and out to the parking lot, where members having a smoke break reportedly overheard a heated outburst: "This division is out of control. It will be brought back under control!"

How typical of Ottawa to look to find scapegoats in the West for their mismanagement in the East. The meeting had left E Division without any reason to hope things would change in Ottawa under a new commissioner.

Perhaps only members can appreciate how truly sad was the turning point at which the Force had arrived. I was sure I could feel the ghosts standing with us that night and could hear them crying afterwards. Part of the Force died that night; a lance had pricked its heart.

Senior members struggled with conflicting emotions after the meeting. We were embarrassed at our participation in the breaking of tradition of military decorum and angry at the rigidity of Ottawa. Our collective show of power and solidarity would not go unanswered by the East, where the control of the Force was now in the hands of politicians, civil servants, and only the Mounties who adopted their ways. We could not win a fight within ourselves. Members left the meeting with the morbid fear that the wall was crumbling, marking the end of the Force as they had known it.

The division representatives regained order after the officers departed; and member after member offered job actions designed to alert the public to our complaints. Everyone had expected the division representatives to fall into the party line when the heat turned up after that night; and they did. For the second time, I heard talk of forming a union, but no one really wanted that. We had seen too many unions' leaderships turned into a venue for administrative bullies and quasi-politicians. In the end, nothing happened; no job action, no FIDO, no unionization, no change in the new promotion system. Or perhaps I should say nothing *quantifiable* happened.

Murray might have come to the meeting ill informed, but he left with eyes wide open. In a month he would be commissioner. Still, we didn't know how much power he really had, or how long it would take him to try to turn the Force around, even if he wanted to.

Like a freight train speeding down the track, it would take time to set a new course, too much time to derail the new promotion system that would be implemented in a month. Murray had borne the brunt of a rage that the Mulroney government and Inkster's compliance with it had created. As unfair as his reception at Surrey Secondary may have been, he now understood how close the Force was to imploding. In Ottawa he was surrounded by bureaucrats, high-ranking civil servants, politicians, and admin. Mounties. E Division had reminded him of his roots as an operational peace officer.

After the meeting, there seemed to be an eerie calm within E Division as we all waited for Ottawa's response. It reminded me of slack tide at active pass.[43]

Two high-ranking changes occurred in relatively short order: the commanding officer of E Division retired, and Surrey's superintendent was promoted to Headquarters and then retired. Because both meetings had happened in Surrey, Ottawa probably had the erroneous impression that the Detachment sparked the rebellion.

Surrey's top officer position was raised to the rank of chief superintendent and a new breed of officer won the board. Only the truest believers in the new Force order and management practices could successfully compete for promotions.

The Force had borrowed an old game from its political masters to accelerate the

[43] Active pass is a stretch of water in the BC Gulf islands that runs between Mayne and Galiano Islands. When the currentsand tides are slack, the water is like glass, but those times are brief. Three ocean currents colliding are the reason for the name "active," where large whirlpools and standing waves are the subject of many a boater's horror stories.

change in its traditional management style. Workforce adjustments, commonly referred to as "golden handshakes" in non-politically correct circles, were all the push the old guard needed to vacate their positions.

To no one's surprise in the West, the vast majority of these windfalls occurred in Ottawa; but what happened to the positions afterwards would have surprised the West. Many of the targeted positions were eliminated on paper, but non-members took over many of the operations. Rumour was that civilians were taking over positions in Ottawa and being given status equal to high officer ranks--some as high as deputy commissioner.

One of the strengths of the RCMP had been that the officer ranks were filled from members who had risen through the ranks. Even the commissioner had once been a recruit at Depot. For over one hundred years, no amount of wealth, "correct" politics, or family connections could circumvent that system. Rank was something earned, something respected, something to be proud of, the goal to which all recruits could aspire if they worked hard and learned their craft.

The working members of E Division had remained ignorant of the slow but steady infiltration of civil servants within the highest levels of the RCMP that seemed to have begun in the Mulroney era. Had we known, it might have helped us understand why this new breed of officers now wanted to be called by their names without reference to their ranks.

"To help break down the barriers between members"; "To help facilitate communication and camaraderie" was the official reasoning for the change, but it didn't ring true with operational members.

Rank was something to be proud of, something to be respected, and was a large part of our military tradition and our identity. Rank was only a problem for those who took the short cuts back in Ottawa. Perhaps in the interest of ambition the new breed of officers had to accept this, but in E Division, any NCO would hand you your head if you failed to show him or her respect for rank. No edict from Headquarters could make seasoned members abandon the old traditions that had been ingrained in our identity since Depot. Though I did not like the direction the Force was heading in, I did my best to ignore it as I busied myself with my training responsibility for the auxiliary program at Surrey Detachment.

The other major responsibility, Recruit Field Training, fell to Cathy. Surrey, the largest of all RCMP detachments, had a huge appetite for recruits. The low service level of the average member on detachment and the variety of the calls created an accelerated learning environment for policing--a lot like North Vancouver had been, back when I first arrived in the Division.

There was no denying Depot had been modified and "modernized" during the early nineties. I was happy that Cathy was the coordinator for the Recruit Field Training Program (RFT). I had some very strong operational views about clouding a recruit's first six months on the job with buzzwords of the latest pseudo-social fad rather than focusing on detecting and solving crime. It seemed the Force was being changed not just from the top down but from the bottom up. The senior constables and the NCO in the middle were out of step, as sure the changes were wrong as the others were they were right. One day, I had my chance to demonstrate my belief that there were more flaws in the new method of training than the old.

Surrey Detachment was one of the few detachments that held a review board at the end of the RFT program. It was an excellent idea, designed to ensure the recruit had received a good general foundation before he or she was cut loose as a fully operational member. The boards were made up of the operations officer, a shift NCO not connected with the recruit or the trainer, an experienced trainer from a different watch, a traffic NCO, and Cathy, representing Training Section.

Cathy was away on leave. This was the only time I was asked to participate. I watched and listened as the operations officer, followed by each of the others, took turns throwing out scenarios. The recruit seemed comfortable and prepared for the questions. The textbook answers filled with the buzzwords of the new "community policing" model brought smiles to the faces of the others, but not to mine. I couldn't help but notice the scenarios were administrative or non-confrontational in nature, not the entire reality of general duty policing in Whally or Newton (two of the roughest zones in Surrey, and possibly in Canada).

I had no issue with the recruit, but I did have some issues with changing Depot into some warm and fuzzy college campus with self-directed study to prepare recruits for policing. It was also my opinion that the overemphasis on "community policing"[44] had overshadowed times when other solutions were necessary. When it was my turn, not surprisingly, my scenario was purely practical.

"You have been called to a break and enter in progress. When you arrive, the neighbour hands over a twenty-five-year-old male he caught fleeing the scene.

[44] "Community policing" was in reality the manner in which the RCMP had historically gone about the day-to-day business of police work. It was born as much out of necessity--considering our historic undermining of posts and detachment--as by disposition. Some smart entrepreneurs gave it the catchy title and sold it back to the Force. It wasn't new to the RCMP operational members and it worked better with our own modifications in most--but not all--situations. One size does not fit all in police work.

What do you do?"

"I ask him for some identification and what he was doing," the recruit answered, but he was clearly unsettled. This was not the type of question he had prepared for.

"He says he has none, but he 'says' he is the resident's nephew from out of town, here for a surprise visit. When no one answered the door, he went around back to see if anyone was in the kitchen, and that was when the neighbour saw him. He ran because the neighbour was a big guy and he startled him. His name is Joe Smith from Saskatoon. Your backup has just arrived. What do you do next?

"Check to see if someone is home."

"Good. Your partner tells you no one is home but there are pry marks on the rear door and a crowbar on the doorstep. What do you do?"

"I arrest him for B&E and release him on a PTA (Promise to Appear)."

"But he has no identification, and you have never seen him before."

"He is my client, so I have to release him--"

"He is not your client. He is your suspect." My dinosaur tail was showing.

"He is my client. The witness is my client. They are all my clients," the recruit said, retrieving some well-studied phrase from his work memory; but suddenly he didn't seem so sure.

"The owner of the house is your client; the citizen who apprehended him is your client; this guy is your *suspect*. At the end of the day, the clients should be happy, but suspects aren't always." I didn't know if I was contradicting the "community policing" mantra, because I hadn't taken the course. I was just preaching a bit of George Monk wisdom from a bygone era--a pre-*Charter* era where the citizens who paid for the system were not confused with those who bled it. Continuing, I asked: "Can you release the suspect on a PTA?"

"Yes, I have the authority under--"

"How do you know whom you are releasing? He has no identification, no one knows him, he has just committed an indictable offence. Should you arrest him?" I was actually giving him a hint. I had no wish to embarrass the recruit, only to highlight some of the weaknesses I perceived in the new training model.

"He's my client--" the recruit was really shaken at this point and looking in the faces of the other board members for some hint to help him out. I stepped up.

"He is not your client; he is your suspect. Yes, you arrest him and transport him back to Surrey cells, where you find that none of the information he has provided about his name, age, or address checks out. He refuses to tell you his real name. The only way to be certain of his identity is to take his fingerprints, but he refuses to co-operate. Do you have the authority to force him to have his prints taken?"

In disbelief, the recruit asked the operations officer, "Does stuff like that really happen?" The officer nodded, and I answered.

"Yes, it does when the suspect is wanted for a much bigger offence already on our CPIC system. Under the Identification of Criminals Act you have the authority to use as much force as is necessary to take fingerprints *after* the charge has been laid for a dual procedure or indictable offence. So you have to get your paperwork done and brought before a judge first."

I left the board feeling a little bad that I had shaken up the recruit--I really had intended to shake up the system. The footsteps I heard follow me out of the room belonged to the operations officer.

"It's been a long time since those types of questions have been asked," he said.

"Sorry, I guess I'm not very politically correct and a little out of step with the new Force, but I don't think the criminals have bothered to study the new community policing model, either. I can't help but think we are confusing these young Mounties. They don't seem to know if they are a social worker or a peace officer anymore." Then I smiled and lightened my criticism with a bit of humour: "Careful not to step on my dinosaur tail, it sometimes gets in my way these days."

"I didn't say you were wrong--I said it had been a while," he said, returning my smile.

I guess I made my point, but rather than change the review boards, they discontinued them. I was glad I didn't have Cathy's job.

The tide of the Force was changing and slowly gaining momentum as I decided again to anchor myself in work. I took comfort in the auxiliary constables, of whom I was in charge. Correctly recruited, the auxiliaries could be quite useful to an over-stretched Force. The motivations for a good auxiliary included work experience for potential members of the Force, as well such as ex-military officers looking to recapture the comradeship and service to the public. Some were people who had chosen another profession but still wanted to contribute to the community. Auxiliaries such as Karen Summers helped lift my spirits by demonstrating that Canadians really hadn't changed--only the system had.

The Auxiliary Program had a large pool of trained professionals from which to draw on. There were teachers, bus drivers, and independent business people in the group, all of whom possessed a variety of skills and a strong sense of community. The only payment auxiliaries received was the spiritual kind: knowing they were doing a service to the public. It was refreshing to see so dedicated a group.

So many things had changed during the past twenty years; but the idealism and dedication of the new applicants and recruits had stayed constant. Outwardly they may have appeared much more varied in ethnic origins and gender, but in their hearts they were as we had always been: idealistic and ready to tilt at some windmills; prepared to risk everything in a life of service to Maintain the Right for Canada and Canadians. So much had changed and yet, so little.

One day, after hosting one of Surrey's recruiting information sessions, the father of a potential applicant called my office in search of some honest, tough answers. He was concerned about his son's interest in joining the RCMP, but not just for the normal personal safety issues; he wanted to know about our job satisfaction. He seemed keenly aware of the recent changes to the Canadian legal system and some of the resulting frustrations facing police. *A lawyer, or perhaps a judge?* I wondered as I spoke to his concerns; but he clearly wanted more candour than the politically correct rhetoric that I was offering. Cutting to the chase, he asked: "If you were in my son's shoes, would you join the Force again?"

"That is not a fair question," I objected. "You are looking for a linear answer in a world that experience has taught me is anything but straightforward. The Force and I were completely different in 1977 when I joined. I have had good times and bad times since then. The only answer I can give you is: I have never regretted the decision to join. I know I would have always regretted it if I had not."

"I understand what you are saying. Thank you for your honesty. I'll be driving my son to your office now to drop off his application."

The next promotion exam cycle was being planned. Already the cracks were appearing in it. Members had begun the slow process of challenging the system. Answers to questions marked "wrong" were proven right. Interview boards were overturned. The system's poor design was being systematically challenged by members, primarily from E Division. Members had even pressured the Force to publish the "right" answers to the first exams. I read through the answers Ottawa had accepted. It was obvious anyone who could parrot back the official version of "community policing," the new religion in the Force, could be successful on the exam.

"Forget the right answer," I advised the operational members preparing for the next process. "Give them the one they want to hear. When you have the rank, you can try to change things. You can't fight a system from the bottom up." It was what I would have done if I had decided to write.

The next exam was opening registration for the second round, and I was qualified to write for sergeant. It was a redundant matter in my staff sergeant's mind when he dropped by our office to pick up Cathy's and my memos declaring our intentions to participate. Cathy gave him hers, but when he looked at me, I said, "I'm not writing."

His expression became perplexed. It clearly had never occurred to him that someone who had written as many exams as I would not embrace the new system.

"Don't you want to improve yourself?" he asked in total bewilderment.

"Oh, I have never equated higher rank with improvement."

He struggled but could find no response and wandered out somewhat confused. As soon as he left, Cathy laughed out loud.

"Only you could get away with that!" she said.

I didn't mean to be rude. Our staff sergeant was a very good man and boss, but that was just the way it was. I had my perfect job in the Force, only twenty minutes from home. I was happy with the balance I had struck between work and family. My children were happier with the stability and predictability of my new section. They no longer raced into my bedroom in the middle of the night just to make sure I was there. It saddened me to think there were times when I had worked midnight shifts and had not been there for them. I had more to offer my children than a higher rank had to offer me. It was also a personal source of pride that I had succeeded to the first and acknowledged hardest rank under the old system of performance and service. Operational members who did not respect the new process also did not have the same respect for rank earned through it. Perhaps only other female members could understand that rank was not that great a motivator for me.[45]

As I expected, the inspector in charge of operations called me into his office to ask why I had chosen not to write. I liked him and he liked me. He had my interests at heart. I appreciated the concern but advised him I had at least five good reasons not to write, any one of which was sufficient on its own.

"I now have the perfect job, the one I have always wanted. I'm in charge of my own section. By everyone's assessment, including my supervisor's, I do a very good job, and my family life is easier with the stability the position offers. Why would I write?" He nodded, acknowledging my flawless logic.

I couldn't resist sliding in a parting shot. "Besides, if I were only looking for rank, I would write the officer's exam, not the sergeant's," I said with a cheeky

[45] One of the more pronounced differences in male and female member career expectations was identified by S/Sgt. S.E. Stark's 1986 survey, "The Role of Female Constables in 'E' Division." He found that forty-two percent of female members aspired to no higher rank than junior NCO. Only six percent of their male peers shared that modest goal (p. 44).

smile.

It hadn't escaped me that in the new order of promotions, corporals were now able to write for officer ranks, a change rumoured to have been motivated to allow the senior females to catch up to their French peers. He laughed and conceded my point even if he did not completely understand my motivations. He wasn't the only one who didn't understand what motivated me.

It was at this time that my grievance over the Depot promotion board hit the commissioner's desk, and he ruled: "If the decision on the board wasn't based in bias, it gave all the perception of bias."

His admission of the board's bias was all I had wanted, but Depot still did not understand that the commissioner's statement was sufficient. An NCO from Depot called the next week seeking a resolution. He knew there was no point in offering me a position at Depot, since I had a better one in Surrey. Still, the system demanded some form of redress, and to my surprise, he found an acceptable one.

"Would you accept a backdating of your promotion to the date of the Depot position?"

I was feeling pretty empowered, having won not just for myself but--at least in my own mind--a battle for future female members, so I didn't want to make it too easy for him.

"That depends on the date my promotion would be effective."

As soon as he told me the date, I quickly agreed because it took me out of the pay increment freeze I had been caught in by the Federal government. Imagine my surprise that I could take a moral stand and fight a system I felt to be unfair and unexpectedly get paid for it!

I continued on with the job of my choice in the best way I could, drawing on the many resources Surrey had to offer. There were a number of well-trained firearms, self-defence, and driving instructors on hand in so large a detachment. We members had so many tools now that we'd never had before. Force options such as pepper spray and batons bridged the gap between closed hand and lethal force.

The technology available was equally impressive. In an unprecedented coup, I arranged for Surrey detachment to be "loaned" a seconded FATTS machine, an interactive police situation simulator. The training was light years away from what my troop had had in the seventies. No more shooting at paper targets from a standing position. Now a member entered a room armed with a gun that fired laser light, a baton, pepper spray, and a radio. The wall they faced projected various unpredictable situations that might escalate or de-escalate, depending on the actions taken by the member or the mood of the instructor. If members were confronted by a shooting resolution, they were trained to seek cover first. This type of training not only improved officer survival it improved suspect survival as well.

Behavioural science based on police work had also been incorporated into the training to help members recognize when a suspect was exhibiting warning indicators. Body language cues, which previously members had had to learn on the job, were now identified, qualified, and categorized in a training setting. One of the extremely dangerous behavioural signs the instructor spoke of was the "thousand-yard stare," when a suspect ignores the police instructions and looks right through the officers. I immediately thought back to the American in North Vancouver whom I had pulled my gun on. That was exactly the look I had seen in his eyes. Had I had this training then, I would never have questioned the appropriateness of my behaviour. There was no doubt now in my mind that I was suitably employed in one of the few remaining safe havens in E Division.

Rumours of Vancouver Headquarters' deteriorating work environment were starting to spread as a new group of officers, and some old ones who had lurked in the shadows, began supervising with a heavy hand. I wondered if E Division was being "brought under control." The work environment was turning unhealthy. Candy's safe haven had become a pressure cooker; but this time, even E division was acting badly. Everyone was too busy looking after their own backs to look out for anyone else. Candy reluctantly resigned just short of the twenty years of service that would have given her the financial independence she deserved. As unfair as her situation was, it could have ended worse.

One of my old partners, now an investigator with the Coroners' Service, called as he left the scene of a member's suicide at Headquarters to tell me the victim was a member we both knew--a member who had been a young recruit at North Vancouver Detachment only fifteen years earlier. Our memories of him were frozen in that time, to a time when he had arrived full of life, humour, and, most important, idealism. A capable, dedicated member, he had been promoted and transferred to Vancouver. Could work stress really have caused him to do that?

His family may have thought so, because members attending the funeral were requested not to wear uniform. Funerals of members are colourful displays of respect. Yet this time, the birth family was rejecting the extended family of the Force. The turnout at the funeral was not diminished because of the unprecedented request, and the church was filled with suits and dresses. We were still a troop of one; at least at the grass roots level.

One day, I received a call from the daughter of a Surrey NCO. I had met her years before when, fresh out of high school, she started working for the Force doing filing. She was strikingly pretty and bright, much too smart to be filing forms; probably, I thought, looking to marry a guy just like "daddy." But I had been too quick to judge. Within a year of our meeting, she told me she had written the Force entrance exam,[46] but had not scored well enough to make the cut. It would be two years until she could reapply.

"Do you have any advice? How can I improve my chances next time?" she asked.

"Do you know what parts of the exam on which you did poorly? Was it the aptitude portion or the academics?" I inquired.

"I've always been weak in math and certainly could have done better on the English if I had brushed up on my grammar first."

"You've answered your own question. You have two years to take a few night courses in English and math before your next try."

Now, two years later, she called to say, "I did it! I made the first cut!" Her voice positively beamed over the phone.

"That is so awesome. Your dad must be proud," I said.

"I haven't told him yet," she said awkwardly. "I didn't want to tell him unless I was sure I was getting in."

She had applied and written at different detachments to help keep the secret, but now that she had made the first hurdle, it was definitely time to let him know.

"Better tell him now before he hears it through the grapevine," I advised.

"Yes, of course you are right. I will tonight."

The next day, I made a point of running into her dad, and he was beaming ear to ear. Pride radiated out of every pore as he told everyone he encountered about his "little girl" carrying on the tradition. It was a happy event in Force families when the next generation chose to continue the family tradition of service to queen and country. It had taken only twenty years for the NCOs of the Force to embrace the concept of their daughters' following in their footsteps. Quite a social evolutionary change to occur in such a brief time--the kind of change the early female members had been hoping for.

Just when everything was looking so positive, things took an ugly turn.

A few weeks later, I received a second phone call from the applicant. She was so distraught she could hardly speak. Once again she was looking to me for help, but this time for a much bigger problem.

[46] The entrance exam had been modernized since I had joined. It was no longer based on general knowledge. It was broken up into several sections that tested and identified defendable policing aptitudes such as memory and observation and analytical and critical thinking, in addition to the traditional writing and math skills.

"I was interviewed by a plainclothed member last night at work. Naturally I thought it was the Staffing officer, the next step in my application." Her crying worsened as she went deeper into the story.

"He was from Internal Affairs and he accused me of cheating. He said my score had improved too much. He kept asking me how I got a copy of the entrance exam to study from." She was shattered. How had the proudest moment in her young life become the darkest?

"He asked who I associated with in the Force. He asked about my dad! How can they think that? What can I do?"

"You have to call your dad right now and tell him what happened. He needs to know about this, and you need to remember you did nothing wrong. This mess has to be sorted out, but it might take a little time. Now call your dad. And please tell him I know about this."

I waited for an hour, then found some reason to knock on the NCO's door. He gestured for me to sit down.

"Can you believe this?" he said. A mixture of anger, disbelief, and embarrassment rang in his voice. Then the anger took over. "This is about me. Someone is using my daughter to get to me. I don't care how long it takes; I will find out who is doing this and have it out."

"I know for a fact and will testify that you were not aware of either the first or the second time she wrote," I offered.

"First time?" he was surprised.

It was all going to come out in the Internal review anyway. "She has done nothing wrong and neither have you. Anyone who knows either of you would know you are not capable of such behaviour. Cathy and I are the only ones who control the security of the recruitment exams at Surrey Detachment. Even if you wanted to, you would have no access to the exam. Do you want me to call Internal? I think I can help."

"Thanks, but I can handle this," he said. "I'll put an end to it right now!" He picked up the phone as I exited and closed the door behind me.

He was a large, gentle man who could be tough as nails when needed; a man of honour, intelligence, and integrity; a man who had over thirty years of unblemished, distinguished service to the Force. His service record was now threatened with a "rape" of sorts by an unfounded, dark, question threatening to smear his personal and professional character--a cloud that could leave a shadow even after it was disproved. I suspected it would take more than a direct phone call from him to end the unhappy affair, and I was right.

Two weeks later, the phone rang. It was a sergeant from Internal. He had an afternoon appointment he hoped I could attend at his office in Vancouver. He didn't know I was expecting his call. The matter involved a Surrey NCO, and I was told not to discuss our conversation or advise him of my appointment. Those instructions were repeated in the OIC's office at Surrey immediately after that conversation.

"I am disobeying a direct order," I said as I closed the door to the NCO's office. He looked up a little shocked at so honest and serious a confession.

"I am heading in to Internal in five minutes. I believe I can end this. I will let you know how I make out when I return."

As I was exiting, I heard him say in a disheartened voice, "Thank you for telling me."

He didn't owe me anything. I knew he had "had my back" on numerous occasions at higher levels than I was privy to; I was just pleased to be able to return a favour by doing the right thing.

The sergeant at Internal was a pleasant man, an excellent interviewer who had been enticed into the unpopular position of Internals through promotion. At least that was how the old system worked. I have no doubt that was how the sergeant had arrived.

"Just how did the accusation of cheating arise?' I asked.

"I am told by Ottawa the system flagged it up. The experts say the score on the second exam was too much higher than the first to be anything but cheating."

"No doubt these were the same experts who came up with the new promotion system," I said sarcastically.

"No doubt," agreed the sergeant. Apparently we held the same opinion on the new civilian experts back East.

"I wouldn't call myself an expert, but I have a post-graduate degree in Education and I would be curious to see if all parts of the exam or only portions were improved."

"Not a bad idea. Let's see," he said as he pulled out the scores from the first and second exams from his file. The aptitude portions had been high from the beginning. Only the English and particularly the math scores showed dramatic improvement.

"Well, as a teacher I can say that if a student could not improve either of those subjects through further study, why would we bother having schools?"

The sergeant nodded his head at the simple logic of the reasoning.

"There was no leak at Surrey Detatchment. Corporal Robertson and I control the security of the exams. I am sure you have already been satisfied of that, at the detachment where she wrote the exam. Furthermore, I have known both the girl and her father for a number of years and I know for a fact that he had no idea his daughter was even thinking of applying until after she passed the second exam. The girl has been taking math and English night classes between the two exams, and from the looks of things, she is a capable learner. She will no doubt be an excellent member if she still feels so inclined after this dog and pony show. A pretty sad way to treat a loyal member and a new recruit, eh?"

"Yah." The sergeant shook his head in agreement and disgust, then said, "Let's get this on paper so I can conclude this thing."

I continued my disobedience by reporting every word to the NCO upon my return to Surrey.

"I will not retire until I find out who went gunning for me," the NCO said.

What he was suspecting had happened in the past on rare occasions: an unseen hand, an abuse of power, used to settle an old grudge. With personalities as strong as members', conflicts inevitably occurred. But not this time. The investigation had been sparked by a mathematical formula in Ottawa, the kind of formula the bean counters love--a formula that placed no value on honour, service, or loyalty.

The unfortunate incident had been spawned not by an old enemy but by the new "system," a system created by the same type of experts who had modernized and standardized the justice system. The system, at least in theory, had no room for payback any more than it had room for any emotion--no more capable of malevolence than benevolence. What had happened to the NCO and his daughter wasn't personal. The system was above morality--or perhaps I should say *devoid* of it. The staff/sergeant found that hard to accept. We all should have.

Several weeks later, the NCO dropped into my office and sat in Cathy's empty chair opposite me. "I just had a call from Commissioner Murray." Calls of that nature were unheard of in the Force. "He called to apologize for the distress the unfounded investigation caused my daughter and me."

"I *am* impressed!" I said, and I was.

"So was I," he replied.

It was a powerful, signature ending with which to conclude the file. It was also an encouraging sign that the commissioner was reaching out to the working members. Someone in Ottawa seemed to be beginning to value our expertise and service more than the bean counters with alphabets behind their names. Perhaps there was still a place for humanity in the system, but it would take some time for the pendulum to swing back.

By now, all of the officers who had been present when I was promoted had been replaced by prime examples of Ottawa's new managers. The system was altering the Force starting at the top. The change in office management was evident at the morning coffee flips, which began to feel less like North Vancouver and more like Customs and Excise. Cathy and I soon dropped out of them. The new management began to monitor the practices and procedures first in the radio room, then in Records, with a seemingly critical, unblinking eye. The female-dominated support staff's stress level was already running high because the contract negotiations between the city and the union were strained over pay issues.

Even my supervisor seemed unsettled by the mounting office tensions. Instinctively I placed my chair a little closer to the wall and began closing my office door. The old wounds I had suffered in the past hadn't completely healed, leaving me much more vulnerable than I appeared--or would have admitted to. One day, my supervisor called Cathy and me into the office to caution, "Make sure you run everything you are doing through me. If you don't, I can't protect you."

It was an extremely odd statement to make. "Protect us" from whom? And why? The mood at Surrey began to sour as members, already demoralized by the promotion cycle, understaffing, and the pay/increment freeze, now faced a municipal strike that would eliminate our support staff.

When our administration section lost its two secretaries to the strike, I didn't anticipate it would be a big disruption. Cathy and I had preferred to type our own correspondence anyway. I assumed that, like the municipal strike in North Vancouver in the seventies, a recruit would be assigned to do any of the mandatory filing and typing required. It never occurred to me that Surrey's two female NCOs would be told to take their jobs.

Cathy chose the practical course of action and took her secretary's seat; but I refused. As much as I hated the thought of another confrontation, I resigned myself to one that seemed unavoidable. My old defence--of threatening to go on the record, which had worked so well on two corporals, a sergeant, and a staff sergeant--seemed inadequate for this situation, but I was determined to try. I was prepared to refuse a direct order and fight it in service court, where I planned to argue that such an order was rooted at best in complete gender insensitivity, and at worst in sexual discrimination. However, I was outmanoeuvred.

"If you don't take the secretary's spot, you will be transferred out."

In the long term, I might have won my case but the short-term price would be the loss of the perfect position I had worked so hard to achieve--a position that had allowed me to maintain the balancing act I had struck between profession and family. I was in a no-win position, and for the first time in my professional life I backed down.

I turned to the Division Reps for help, but they were not interested in participating in a professional suicide run. When I voiced my disappointment, the Rep tried to offload my request by directing me to a junior female member whom staffing had assigned to deal with a complaint of the nature I was suggesting. Senior female members like myself were much too weathered to trust the weak-kneed structure of the process designed to "handle" conflicts like this one. The administrators either didn't understand or didn't care that I didn't need a shoulder to cry on--I needed a weapon to defend myself. It was without satisfaction that a year later I learned the junior female member learned the hard way the flaws of the system when she brought her own complaint against an officer.

Herbie's old tease about "finally finding a job I was suited for" rang in my inner voice as I watched the muted smiles of some of the male members who found many reasons to walk by the civilian's desk I now occupied.

The changes in Ottawa's "modernized" RCMP that appeared to have undermined the old system's code of personal honour, collective responsibility, and accountability had also eroded the defences upon which I had relied in previous times of professional conflict. I couldn't see a way to fight back in the new system, no way to vent the rage I felt at the public undermining of my professional authority, no way to turn it to my advantage, so I hid it inside where the raging fire slowly ate away at not only my professional but my personal foundation. My sleep deteriorated to the point of insomnia.

The strike finally ended, and I returned to the piles of work I had watched grow as I intentionally messed up the office filing. Cathy and I would both have had our hands full for six months just to get caught up, but Cathy was offered a transfer out to Drug Section and she was gone in a flash. There I was left, spiritually wounded in a deteriorating work environment, now with a crippling workload, a setup for failure. The ice was cracking all around me, and I was unsure of my next step.

Exhausted mentally and emotionally, I wasn't in much condition to continue searching for paths. I felt so unsafe, I couldn't think my way out by myself, so I pulled out Smokey's old advice and called an old friend at Vancouver Training looking for help. He was happy to send me on a senior management course in Ottawa, where I would have three weeks to abandon my troubles at work and clear my head. On the weekends, I could spend some time at my home on Wolfe Island with my parents; perhaps in those surroundings I could try to find my way again.

Ottawa in mid-November is not a warm place, and neither were some of the course participants. The course was designed to teach NCOs management strategies. The member candidates--all except me, of course--were males ranging in rank from corporal to staff sergeant. The average rank and service seemed to be sergeant with twenty-eight years.

There were two other females, civilian members, who supervised civilian subordinates on the course. I chose my seat at the rear of the room, back to the wall, beside the sergeant I knew from Internal. At least there was one friendly face.

The course got off to a tumultuous start immediately after the Ottawa sergeant gave his opening welcome address. All the buzz words and management clichés that made up the coded language needed now for promotion sounded hollow to the audience of operational members. When he touched on some of the "exciting" new changes to the promotion cycle, his remarks created the perfect opening for an angry sergeant seated at the front.

"That may be all well and good for you people in Ottawa, but how am I supposed to motivate a twenty-two-year constable when a seven-year *female corporal* gets promoted overtop of him?" challenged a very seasoned East-coast thirty-three-year sergeant in a low, gravelly voice that bespoke his issues as much as his hostility.

The question was so charged, it stopped the Ottawa sergeant in his tracks. Admin Mounties in Ottawa are apparently not accustomed to, or comfortable dealing with, direct honest opposition. In one opening verbal volley, the question had attacked both the promotion cycle and me, sitting quietly at the rear of the class. An uneasy silence settled on the room as nervous glances were cast in my direction. I raised my hand. The course coordinator looked uncomfortably in my direction, then acknowledged my wish to speak.

"The sergeant from back East has raised a valid question that is being asked in the West as well. Has Ottawa developed strategies to maintain the morale and the motivation of senior members who will now sometimes be faced with NCOs of junior service? I am just not sure why the sex of the junior NCO has any relevance in the question."

I paused for a moment, then punctuated my question with a little of my old "in your face" attitude. "For the record, I was promoted under the old system and I am far from the most junior NCO here." And with that I sat down.

It would have been a long three weeks had I not chosen to meet the challenge head on. The ironic thing was, two of the other three corporals in the room were males of junior service, freshly promoted by the new system. I knew them and they knew me, and they were relieved that I chose to keep their secret.

The coordinator danced around the de-sexed question with the normal Ottawa doublespeak, and the matter faded away. At the break he came over to speak to me.

"Ottawa is looking for credible operational female members like you. You would do very well here," he said.

Even if I hadn't been in a precarious situation at Surrey, the years had worn me down. I had lost my idealism and my energy. I didn't want to drag my family across the country in pursuit of promotions; I simply wanted to return to my training position at Surrey and continue to do my job without feeling under siege.

"It is kind of you to think so, but you are too late. I am too tired to tilt at any more windmills," I replied cryptically. I didn't care that I left him looking puzzled. How could I explain in a sentence or two the toll the years on the front line had taken? There were a few credible female members still in fighting form already in Ottawa or on the path there: excellent members like Bev, Adrienne, and my troop mate Brenda MacFarland. The only rank and position in the Force I wanted was back at Surrey, a position that had turned from a dream to a nightmare.

After the morning coffee, the civilian co-coordinator for the course asked each of us to take turns stating for the class what we hoped to take away from the course.

"I am looking for tools or strategies to open the lines of communication between myself and the officer level at Surrey, to repair some damage created by a rocky start," I said, hoping others might see a route I could not.

All the operational members on the course understood what I was hinting at and how big my problem was. For the first time in my service, I had found myself on the outside of the Red Wall with no way of getting over it. I knew the paths before me: I could continue to throw myself at it and break completely, I could mark time and become bitter, or I could walk away. I was looking for a fourth path.

As our class dynamics moved from "storming" to "forming," the other NCOs did their best to suggest ways to achieve a truce to help easy my office tension. Although I didn't find any answers in class, it was nice to know so many members, even the bristly old East Coast sergeant from the first day, were trying so hard to help.

The course may not have helped, but the weekends did. Whoever said "you can't go home" has never been to Wolfe Island. The two weekends I spent back in my parents' home on the lake awakened the memories of less complicated times. It was so refreshing to walk through the village, where everyone still greeted me by name as if I had never left. Maybe in a fundamental way I never had. The quiet intimacy of the community I had fled in my youth now resonated with a simple honesty that had previously eluded me. I could now understand simple Island joys to which the passions of my youth had blinded me. I had come, full circle, back to my beginnings. So much had changed and yet so little.

For the first time in twenty years, I hated to leave the safe shores of Wolfe Island and return to the West. I was sure the path I was seeking was close; I just couldn't quite see it yet.

The first news I received when I got off the plane in Vancouver was that of the sudden death of my father. I was in no condition to deal with a personal tragedy on top of a professional one.

The early December morning after my father's burial was bitterly cold. "Good ice-making weather," he would have called it. Not that he had charted any paths recently. The mainlanders had made a law against it. Islanders like my father, experts of the ice, obeyed the law because that is what Canadians of his generation did.

Still, as I looked out at the ice in the bay in front of my parents' house that afternoon, I couldn't help but test it. I didn't venture too far from shore this time, though--it was too early; the ice was not safe. I wasn't as light as I once was; I had added the weight of my children every step I took. One of the reasons my father had been so successful on the ice was because his ego never stopped him from retreating when he found it too thin or the wind had turned. Sometimes the only way is to walk away.

I knew I was on thin ice in B.C. An Islander would have stopped, then retreated; but old-school Mounties never back down or back up. I struggled in vain over the following month as this final storm ate away at my wall's foundation--a foundation that years of erosion had already weakened--trying to find the same precarious balance between my Island nature and my Mountie disposition as I had between my family and profession; until finally, subconsciously, I "tapped out" one morning. I sat at my desk and began to cry.

I had spent so much of my professional life learning how not to cry, I had forgotten how good it felt, how cleansing it was, how natural, how feminine. Ironically, crying that day felt as liberating and as good as the shouting match I had with Sgt. Manly.

As I wiped away the tears from my cheeks, "The Cat" walked into my office. It was an awkward surprise. We had all but lost touch after my transfer out of North Vancouver fifteen years before, only bumping into each other on a handful of occasions since then: at first, at a regimental ball or two; more recently, at members' funerals.

Although he had been transferred to Surrey months earlier, he had never come into my office before and he didn't really seem to have any reason for being there now. He pretended not to see the state I was in, but it clearly concerned him.

"Are you all right?" he asked.

"I will be," I replied.

"Do you need help?" My apparent distress was clearly distressing him.

As I looked up from my desk, I remembered the first time I had noticed him, back at Depot--the day his troop mate had beaten me up, and he was being restrained to prevent him from coming to my rescue. He couldn't rescue me then, and only I could rescue myself now.

Matthew - The Next Generation

"No, thank you." I stood up. "It is time for me to leave." And I did.

Like the Depot mismatch, I would never have won if I had stayed; the new system wouldn't allow it. It had taken a lot to bring my walls down, but now there was no denying they had collapsed.

I wasn't ready to surrender completely and resign, so I chose my only safe course of action inside the Force. I accessed leave, a tactic that turned the system to my advantage, creating a temporary shelter that blocked my position, giving me the time to think, to heal, and to find my way again. It took a child's clarity of vision to make me realize it was time to find a new route.

Matthew, my six-year-old son, an "old soul," had always reminded me of my father, and he sounded like Dad the morning he asked, "If you have done everything you wanted to do in the Force, why are you still there?"

Perhaps I hadn't done everything I wanted, but I had done much more than I thought I could. He was right; I had been so busy searching for a path, I had failed to realize I had reached the end of it in the Force. At that moment, I finally understood what my father had always known was one of the most fundamental lessons the water had to offer: time was infinite for the river but not for Islanders. It was time for me to go; time for me to focus on my children; time to pull my hand out of the bucket of water. I had kept my promise to Janet Hill. I had my independence and it was now time to use it. Time for a new start.

At the beginning of my journey, I believed that the RCMP personified Canadian ideals and traditions of honour and service. It wasn't until the end of the path that I realized it is the members of the Force, not the Force itself, who now shoulder that responsibility. I am grateful and proud to have been given the opportunity to be counted among their ranks.

I now know I was on the right path the day I joined the Force and on the day I resigned, and I am still on the right path. I know it because I was taught by the best. What I didn't know was that the biggest and most important investigation of my life lay along my new path in the not too distant future--an investigation that would require all of the skills and contacts I had developed in the Force.

Afterword

I waited many years to write this book. I worried that, like the three judges, my perception would not be true enough or fair enough. In the end, everyone sees things a little differently. I have tried to provide a snapshot of what it was like in the past--the good and the bad. It truly was "the best of times and the worst of times."[47]

At the time I left the Force, I had done only four truly brave things in my life. The first was taking off my hat in church back on Wolfe Island; the second was walking onto the smoke-filled floor at the Lions Gate Hospital; the third was speaking out at Shannon Hall; and the fourth was writing this book.

If I write a sequel, I will be able to raise the tally to five.

[47] The beginning line from *A Tale of Two Cities* written by Charles Dickens, the father of one of the members of the original "March West" in 1874.

About the Author

Originally from Wolfe Island, Jane Hall now resides in Langley, B.C., but is still a frequent visitor to her family home. After receiving a B.A and B.Ed. from Queen's University, she joined the RCMP in June 1977. She retired in 1998.

Mrs. Hall's first love is Canada and its history. This book is an attempt to contribute to our knowledge and understanding of Canada and hopefully inspire others to do the same.

Mrs. Hall has a strong sense of social justice and social responsibility. She believes that for the first time in recorded history, women have not only the opportunity but the responsibility to stand together and provide a strong and clear female voice to governments and multinational companies--a voice to bring balance and humanity back into the world.

This is her first book.

To order more copies of

Contact:

General Store Publishing House

499 O'Brien Road, Box 415

Renfrew, ON Canada

K7V 4A6

1-800-465-6072

Fax: (613) 432-7184

www.gsph.com

VISA and MASTERCARD accepted